MW01491651

Japanese

A Linguistic Introduction

This comprehensive introduction to the Japanese language consists of six parts. Following the introductory section, it explores the Japanese lexicon, grammatical foundations, major clause types, clause linkage, and language usage. The discussions of formal and structural properties of Japanese such as sound structure, vocabulary, and grammar assist readers as they gain insight into historical and sociocultural aspects of Japanese; some are compared with those of English-speaking nations.

An ideal choice for instructors, the book includes twenty-eight chapters, sufficient for approximately ninety hours of hands-on instruction. Each topic has been rigorously selected based on the author's experience of more than two decades teaching Japanese linguistics.

The book's breadth and depth make it highly appropriate for learners of the Japanese language, for linguistics students interested in Japanese, and for researchers interested in Japanese linguistics.

Online resources include exercises and supplementary multimedia materials to enhance the reader's comprehension and enjoyment.

YOKO HASEGAWA is Professor of Japanese Linguistics at the University of California, Berkeley.

Japanese

A Linguistic Introduction

Yoko Hasegawa

CAMBRIDGE
UNIVERSITY PRESS

CAMBRIDGE
UNIVERSITY PRESS

University Printing House, Cambridge CB2 8BS, United Kingdom

Cambridge University Press is part of the University of Cambridge.

It furthers the University's mission by disseminating knowledge in the pursuit of education, learning and research at the highest international levels of excellence.

www.cambridge.org
Information on this title: www.cambridge.org/9781107611474

First published 2015

A catalogue record for this publication is available from the British Library

Library of Congress Cataloguing in Publication data
Hasegawa, Yoko, 1950–
Japanese : a linguistic introduction / Yoko Hasegawa.
pages cm
English and Japanese.
ISBN 978-1-107-03277-4 (Hardback) – ISBN 978-1-107-61147-4 (Paperback)
1. Japanese language–Textbooks for foreign speakers–English. 2. Japanese language–Grammar–Study and teaching. 3. Japanese language–Sound recordings for English speakers. I. Title.
PL539.5.E5H27 2014
495.65–dc23 2014023665

ISBN 978-1-107-03277-4 Hardback
ISBN 978-1-107-61147-4 Paperback

Additional resources for this publication at www.cambridge.org/hasegawa

To the memory of Charles J. Fillmore
(August 9, 1929–February 13, 2014)

Contents

Figures

Maps

Tables

Preface

Japanese: A Linguistic Introduction is intended to be a college-level reference book on the Japanese language that can also serve as the principal textbook in an introductory course in Japanese linguistics. It explains various linguistic phenomena organized by and in terms of analytical methods developed in the discipline of linguistics. I have endeavored to maintain breadth of scope and intellectual depth sufficient and appropriate for a college course, including discussion of why certain linguistic phenomena are interesting or important and thus continue to be investigated. The targeted readership includes undergraduate and graduate students who are interested in the Japanese language and linguistics, instructors of Japanese, and researchers who wish to survey the field of Japanese linguistics.

To reinforce the reader's comprehension, exercises and multimedia supplementary materials are available on the book's website: http://hasegawa.berkeley.edu/Cambridge/introduction.php. Many referenced works are also available online; their URLs are listed in the reference section of the book, although they might cease to exist at any time.

I am deeply indebted to many individuals. First and foremost, I wish to record my gratitude to my students at UC Berkeley, who for more than twenty years have provided inspiration and served as a sounding board. Without them, this book would not have materialized. I am also grateful to those who read earlier versions of the manuscript and offered critical commentary and editorial advice; they include Setsuko Arita, Dante Aurele, Kazue Hata, Yukio Hirose, Christine Jiang, Mika Kizu, Russell Lee-Goldman, Brendan Morley, Gabriel Pellikka, Dennis Ryan, Masaharu Shimada, Mitsuaki Shimojo, Eve Sweetser, Naoaki Wada, and Ikuko Yuasa. Special thanks go to Junko Habu for her expertise in Jomon anthropology, Minae Oda and Keiko Unedaya for helping me decipher the Kagoshima dialect, and Helen Rippier Wheeler for her continuing linguistic and moral support. Illustrations were created by Neil Cohn, Kosuke Kato, and Natsuko Shibata Perera. I also thank Helen Barton and Helena Dowson, editors at the Cambridge University Press, for their commitment to the publication of this book, and copy-editor Gwynneth Drabble.

This project was supported in part by grants from the University of California, Berkeley Academic Senate, the Center for Japanese Studies, and the Department of East Asian Languages and Cultures.

During the final phase of this book's production, I was deeply grieved by the death of my long-time mentor, Professor Charles J. Fillmore. Professor Fillmore began his Japanese Linguistics Seminar at UC Berkeley in 1987 when I was a graduate student, and continued offering it until the summer of 2012, when his health had deteriorated.

He acquired his fluency in the Japanese language while stationed in Kyoto after the Korean War. Following discharge from the military, he studied Japanese at Kyoto University. He proudly recited excerpts from classical Japanese literature. I fondly remember many discussions of the topics included in this book and his keen analyses in his low-keyed, warm voice.

YOKO HASEGAWA

February 2014

Abbreviations

#	unacceptable
?	questionable acceptability
*	ungrammatical
ACC	accusative particle
ADV	adverbial form
ATT	attributive form
CAUS	causative
CNT	contrastive use of *wa*
CNJ	conjectural form
COND	conditional particle
COP	copula
DAT	dative particle
EVID	evidential expression
GEN	genitive particle
HON	honorific form
HUM	humilific form
HYP	hypothetical form
IMP	imperative (command) form
INT	interrogative particle
INTJ	interjection
Lit.	literally
NEG	negative form
NEG-SCP	negative scope marking of *wa*
NMLZ	nominalizer
NOM	nominative particle
NP	noun phrase
NPST	nonpast tense form
PASS	passive form
PAST	past tense form
PLAIN	plain form
POL	polite form
PRES	presumptive form

QUOT	quotative particle
SFP	sentence-final particle
TE	conjunctive particle
TOP	topic particle
VOL	volitional form

Part I

Introduction

1 Typological and historical overview

This book attempts to describe and, in so far as is possible, explain various characteristics of the Japanese language. This introductory chapter provides a brief overview of its typological characteristics and historical development. Chapter 2 deals with regional dialectal variations. Although I strive to use minimal linguistic jargon, some technical terminology is inevitable, as ordinary language does not provide a sufficient vocabulary for describing its internal workings. Critical vocabulary terms are explained when they are introduced and are also listed in the index. Because this chapter and Chapter 2 employ a number of them, readers who are not yet familiar with general linguistics may prefer to read Chapters 1 and 2 after Chapter 7.

1.1 About the Japanese language

Japanese is the native language of virtually all Japanese nationals, approximately 128 million as of 2011,[1] the ninth largest native-speaker population among the world's languages.[2] Moreover, as of November 2011, approximately 128,000 non-native speakers in Japan were studying Japanese as a foreign language.[3] Overseas, approximately 3.65 million persons in 133 countries studied Japanese in 2009.[4]

Typologically, Japanese is classified as an **AGGLUTINATIVE LANGUAGE** because units of meaning are "glued" on one after another as exemplified in (1). (Abbreviations appearing in the annotations are listed before the beginning of this chapter.)

(1)	*tabe-*	*sase-*	*rare-*	*taku-*	*na-*	*katta-*	*ra*
	eat	CAUS	PASS	want.to	NEG	PAST	COND

'if (you) don't want to be made to eat'

1 The Statistics Bureau of Japan: www.stat.go.jp/data/nenkan/zuhyou/y0201b00.xls.
2 The SIL Ethnologue: www.ethnologue.com/statistics/size.
3 The Agency for Cultural Affairs: www.bunka.go.jp/kokugo_nihongo/jittaichousa/h23/gaikoku_1.html.
4 The Japan Foundation: www.jpf.go.jp/j/japanese/survey/result/dl/survey_2009/2009-01.pdf.

Tabe- is the invariant part of the verb *taberu* 'eat' (Chapter 5); *sase-* is the causative auxiliary (Chapter 11); *rare-* is the passive auxiliary (Chapter 12); *taku-* is the adverbial form of the auxiliary *-tai* 'want to do ~' (Section 7.6); *na-* is the invariant part of the negative auxiliary *nai* 'not' (Section 6.1); *-katta* can be considered as the past tense marker (Section 6.3); *ra* is a conditional connective particle (Chapter 18).

Many characteristics of the world's languages are predictable based upon the basic word order of subject, object, and verb in declarative sentences (Greenberg 1963). The vast majority of the world's languages are either subject-verb-object (SVO) or subject-object-verb (SOV) in orientation. Japanese falls into the latter group, and is characterized as an **SOV LANGUAGE**. As Greenberg's typology predicts, when an auxiliary element is attached to a main verb, it always follows the main verb as in (1); Japanese uses **POSTPOSITIONS** (e.g. *byōin ni*) instead of **PREPOSITIONS** (e.g. *to the hospital*) as in (2a); the interrogative (question) marker *ka* appears at the end of the sentence as in (2b); and the word order in questions involving an **INTERROGATIVE** word (e.g. *who*, *what*, *where*, *when*) does not differ from declarative-sentence counterparts as shown in (2c) (see Section 14.7 for further discussion).

(2) a. *Kinō* *byōin* *ni* *ikimashita.*
yesterday hospital to went
(I) went to the hospital yesterday.'

b. *Kinō* *byōin* *ni* *ikimashita* *ka.*
yesterday hospital to went INT
'Did (you) go to the hospital yesterday?'

c. *Kinō* *doko* *ni* *ikimashita* *ka.*
yesterday where to went INT
'Where did (you) go yesterday?'

Modifying elements – i.e. demonstratives (e.g. *this*, *that*; see Subsections 5.2.5 and 5.2.26), adjectives, and relative clauses (see Chapters 14 and 26) – always precede the modified noun, e.g. *kono* 'this' + *kuruma* 'car', *chiisai* 'small' + *kuruma*. When a proper noun and a common noun are combined, the former always precedes the latter (see Subsection 5.2.1), e.g. *Aoyama-dōri* 'Aoyama Street', *Sumida-gawa* 'Sumida River', *Shimogamo-jinja* 'Shimogamo Shrine', *Takao-san* 'Mount Takao'. In comparison constructions (see Chapter 10), the order of the constituent in English is adjective-marker-standard as in *heavier* [adjective] *than* [marker] *that chair* [standard], whereas that in Japanese is standard-marker-adjective as exemplified in (3):

(3) *Kono* *isu* *wa* *ano* *isu* [standard] *yori* [marker] *omoi* [adjective].
this chair TOP that chair than heavy
'This chair is heavier [adjective] than [marker] that chair [standard].'

In linguistics courses, Japanese is a stock language for illustrating pitch accent (see Section 3.5), sound-symbolic vocabulary (e.g. onomatopoeia; see Subsection 5.2.8), case marking (see Chapter 7), the topic–comment construction (Chapter 8), indirect passive constructions (Section 12.2), internally headed relative clauses (Section 14.3), honorifics (Chapters 20–21), and gendered language variation (Chapter 28).

1.2 Historical development

The various developmental stages of the Japanese language are commonly associated with the following historical periods.

Prehistoric	~ AD 600	Jōmon, Yayoi, and Kofun periods
Old Japanese	592–794	Asuka and Nara periods
Late Old Japanese	794–1192	Heian period
Middle Japanese	1192–1603	Kamakura, Muromachi, and Azuchi-Momoyama periods
Early Modern Japanese	1603–1868	Edo period
Modern Japanese	1868 ~	Meiji, Taishō, Shōwa, and Heisei periods[5]

1.2.1 Prehistoric age

The Japanese archipelago has been inhabited for at least 30,000 years (Ikawa-Smith 1978: 276). The first inhabitants are believed to have migrated from southeast Asia during the Paleolithic period (a.k.a. the Stone Age) (Hanihara 1991: 7). The next period, called Jōmon, began approximately 16,500 years ago, triggered by rapid climate change at the end of the Ice Age (Habu 2004: 3, 245). The Jōmon people, evolved from the Paleolithic population, were gatherers, fishers, and hunters who inhabited the length and breadth of Japan, from Hokkaidō in the north to Okinawa in the south (Hanihara 1991: 7).

Around the third century BC, metal tools and paddy-field rice cultivation were introduced as part of the massive-scale migration from the north Asian mainland primarily via the Korean Peninsula, which marks the beginning of the Yayoi period. Newcomers formed small states, probably in northern Kyūshū, that eventually gave rise to a larger power structure, and by the sixth century AD an Imperial Court was established in the Kinki (Nara-Kyōto) district (Hanihara 1991: 24). Today's Japanese people are, ethnologically, an

[5] In addition to the Gregorian calendar, Japan uses a year designation system based on the reigns of emperors: Meiji 1 = 1868, Taishō 1 = 1912, Shōwa 1 = 1926, Heisei 1 = 1989.

Map 1.1. The Japanese archipelago.

amalgamation of the populations of both southeast and northeast Asia, and the development of the Japanese language reflects this amalgamation.

Many researchers consider this racial mixing to continue to be in progress in modern times. For example, Hanihara (1991: 18–19) contends that examination of the skeletal morphology of modern Japanese men reveals that north Asian characteristics predominate in north Kyūshū and west Honshū (the largest island of Japan), whereas Jōmon characteristics have been maintained in Hokkaidō, northeast Honshū (i.e. Tōhoku), Shikoku, south Kyūshū, and Amami and Okinawa islands. This distribution indicates that the regions which were little affected by the Imperial Court in the early historic ages have retained their Jōmon heritage. This hypothesis has been supported by studies of modern Japanese people in molecular genetics

(Omoto 1978; Hammer and Horai 1995) and in measurements of bodily dimensions (Kouchi 1983).

The origins of the Japanese language have been disputed. For example, Miller (1971) and N. Osada (1974) argue that Japanese belongs to the **Altaic** language family, while Murayama (1974) and Kawamoto (1980) attribute its origins to the **Austronesian** family of languages spoken on the islands of southeast Asia and the Pacific. Ono (1981), on the other hand, claims that Japanese belongs to the **Dravidian** language family, particularly close to Tamil (a language spoken in southern India and northeastern Sri Lanka). This book will not engage in this issue further because linguistic techniques and methods used to determine language origins are limited to the last 5,000–6,000 years, whereas the Japanese language originated much earlier (Matsumoto 2003: 45). As a result, there has been a consistent decline in interest in this topic among historical linguists since the 1970s (T. Osada 2003).

The end of prehistory – i.e. the Kofun period, the third to the sixth centuries AD – saw the unification of small states that ultimately gave rise to the Imperial Court. (*Kofun* means 'burial mounds', such mounds being constructed for people of the ruling classes.) Two significant cultural events occurred at this time: the Chinese writing system was introduced in the late fourth and early fifth centuries (Section 4.1), and Buddhism was introduced in 538 (or 552).

1.2.2 Old Japanese (592–794 AD)

The years from 592 to 794 are referred to as the Asuka-Nara period, following the locations of the imperial palace. Until then, Japan was mentioned only sporadically in inscriptions and in Chinese historical documents. However, it was during this period that the recording of the Japanese language, referred to as **Old Japanese**, commenced. The earliest recorded documents are *Kojiki* ('Records of Ancient Matters') (712), *Fudoki* ('Regional Gazetteers') (713), *Nihonshoki* ('Chronicles of Japan') (720), and *Man'yōshū* ('Collection of Ten Thousand Leaves') (672–771).

The syllabic structure of Old Japanese is very simple, each syllable consisting of a lone vowel or a consonant followed by a vowel, as shown in Table 1.1.[6] The voiced consonants /b, d, z, r, g/ do not occur word initially, and syllables consisting solely of a vowel occur only word-initially; that is, a succession of vowels is prohibited within a word, with very few exceptions (Hashimoto 1938; Tsukishima 1988: 189–90). (Slashes surrounding letters indicate that the sound itself, rather than the letter, is being discussed.)

[6] As a means of pronouncing words loaned from Chinese, Old Japanese likely included such complex syllables as /kya, gya, kwa, gwa/; however, to simplify the exposition, they are not discussed in this chapter.

Table 1.1 *Modern and Old Japanese syllables.*[7]

Modern Japanese					Old Japanese				
a	i	u	e	o	a	i	u	e	o
ka	ki	ku	ke	ko	ka	ki_{α} ki_{β}	ku	ke_{α} ke_{β}	ko_{α} ko_{β}
ga	gi	gu	ge	go	ga	gi_{α} gi_{β}	gu	ge_{α} ge_{β}	go_{α} go_{β}
sa	shi	su	se	so	tsa	tsi	tsu	tse	tso_{α} tso_{β}
za	ji	zu/dzu	ze	zo	za	ʒi[8]	zu	ʒe	zo_{α} zo_{β}
ta	chi	tsu	te	to	ta	ti	tu	te	to_{α} to_{β}
da	ji	zu/dzu	de	do	da	di	du	de	do_{α} do_{β}
na	ni	nu	ne	no	na	ni	nu	ne	no_{α} no_{β}
ha	hi	fu[9]	he	ho	pa	pi_{α} pi_{β}	pu	pe_{α} pe_{β}	po
ba	bi	bu	be	bo	ba	bi_{α} bi_{β}	bu	be_{α} be_{β}	bo
ma	mi	mu	me	mo	ma	mi_{α} mi_{β}	mu	me_{α} me_{β}	mo_{α} mo_{β}
ya		yu		yo	ya		yu	ye	yo_{α} yo_{β}
ra	ri	ru	re	ro	ra	ri	ru	re	ro_{α} ro_{β}
wa					wa	wi		we	wo
n									

The most controversial issue regarding Old Japanese is that, unlike the **Modern Japanese** five-vowel system (Section 3.1), there appears to have been more vowels, with puzzling distributions: some vowels were consistently recorded with two distinct sets of Chinese characters, but only in combinations with certain consonants. These vowels are designated as α and β in Table 1.1.[10] (Syllables that differ from Modern Japanese are shaded.)

A possible explanation for this peculiar distribution postulates eight vowels (e.g. Ono 1957), as demonstrated in the /k/ line in Table 1.1. Such being the case, why did the eight vowels occur only with some consonants but not with others? Furthermore, what sound values did the α–β distinctions represent? Hattori (1976: 4) proposes a six-vowel hypothesis in which ki_{α} corresponds to /kyi/, ki_{β} to /ki/, ke_{α} to /kye/, ke_{β} to /ke/, ko_{α} to /ko/, and ko_{β} to the central rounded vowel /ɵ/, as shown in Figure 1.1. However, as yet there is no consensus among Old Japanese specialists.

7 The sound values of some symbols appearing in Table 1.1 in the International Phonetic Alphabet (IPA) are: /u/ [u], /shi/ [ɕi/ʃi], /ji/ [dʒi], /chi/ [tʃi], /hi/ [çi], /fu/ [ɸu], /y/ [j], and /r/ [ɾ]. See Section 3.1 for further explanation.

8 "ʒ" represents the second consonant in the word *vision*.

9 The symbol "f" represents the friction sound created when blowing out a candle, i.e. [ɸ] in the IPA. It is different from English /f/, which involves the upper teeth.

10 The α–β distinction of /mo/ disappeared very early, so it is recorded only in *Kojiki* and not in subsequent documents of this period.

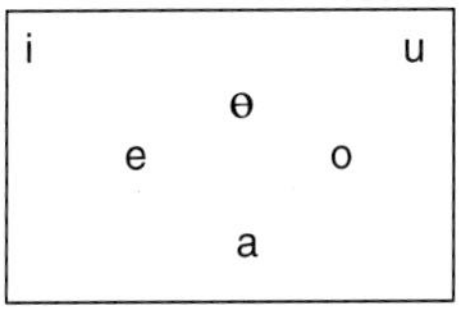

Figure 1.1. Hattori's analysis.

The Old Japanese consonant corresponding to the modern /s/ was likely /ts/ or /ch/ (Arisaka 1957), although only /ts/ is listed in Table 1.1.[11] The consonant corresponding to modern /h/ was /p/ (Ueda 1898), which changed during the Nara period to /f/ [ɸ] (Komatsu 1981: 249). The voiced consonants were likely to be preceded by a nasal sound (a phenomenon called **PRENASALIZATION**); that is, /b/ was pronounced as /^{m}b/, /d/ as /^{n}d/, and /g/ as /^{ŋ}g/ (Hashimoto 1980).

1.2.3 Late Old Japanese (794–1192)

In 794, the capital was relocated from Nara to Kyōto. The period until 1192 is referred to as Heian, and the language then spoken as **LATE OLD JAPANESE**. The α–β distinction of the vowels disappeared early in this period,[12] resulting in the modern five-vowel system. Late Old Japanese also witnessed the following sound changes (Tsukimoto 1988: 79–81):

(4) a. /e/ and /ye/ > /ye/: enoki 'Japanese hackberry' > yenoki; yeda 'tree branch' (unchanged) (The symbol ">" is read as "merged" or "changed to.")
  b. /o/ and /wo/ > /wo/: *oki* 'offing' > *woki*; *woka* 'hill' (unchanged)
  c. /i/ and /wi/ > /i/: e.g. *iru* 'to need' (unchanged); *wiru* 'to exist' > *iru*
  d. Influenced by the Chinese sound system, the voiced consonants /b, d, z, r, g/ began to appear word initially.
  e. /f/ [ɸ] in word medial position became /w/: /fa, fi, fu, fe, fo/ > /wa, wi, u, we, wo/, e.g. *fafa* (modern *haha*) 'mother' > *fawa*; *kafu* 'to buy' > *kawu* (= *kau*).

Today, the topic particle *wa* (see Chapter 8) is still written as は *ha*, reflecting this sound change. The consonant corresponding to today's /s/, which was /ts/ or /ch/ in Old Japanese, became /s/ or /sh/ by the end of the Late Old Japanese period (Arisaka 1957: 146).

In addition, a group of sound changes took place, referred to in Japanese linguistics as **ONBIN** 'euphony'. It can be explained with examples from the verb **TE-FORM** (Chapter 6). Originally, the conjunctive particle *te* was added

[11] This interpretation is still controversial. Murayama (1988: 18–19), for example, argues that both /ts/ and /s/ existed in the fifth century, and that /ts/ gradually merged into /s/ between the fifth and eighth centuries.

[12] The distinction between ko_{α}–ko_{β} and go_{α}–go_{β} was maintained until circa 900 (Tsukimoto 1988: 78).

to the verb adverbial form; however, when the adverbial form ended in /ki/ or /gi/, the /ki + te/ and /gi + te/ sequences respectively became /ite/ and /ide/ as in (5a).

(5) a. *aruki* 'walk' + *te* > *aruite*; *oyogi* 'swim' + *te* > *oyoide*

When the final syllable of the adverbial form was /bi/ (= /^{m}bi/), /ni/, or /mi/, the sequence with *te* became /nde/ as in (5b). By this process, the **MORAIC NASAL** (Section 3.3) was born. (The moraic nasal existed in Old Japanese only in words borrowed from Chinese.)

b. *tobi* 'fly' + *te* > *tonde*; *sini* 'die' + *te* > *sinde*; *yomi* 'read' + *te* > *yonde*

When the final syllable of the adverbial form was /ti/, /fi/, or /ri/, the sequence with *te* became /tte/ as in (5c).

c. *mati* 'wait' + *te* > *matte*; *ifi* 'say' + *te* > *itte*; *ari* 'exist' + *te* > *atte*

Also included in *onbin* is the change of some occurrences of /ku, gu, fi, bi, mi/ to /u/. This change created a long vowel, e.g. *nikuku* 'feeling disgusted' > *nikuu* (= *nikū*).

d. *kanasiku* 'being sad' > *kanasiu*; *waragutu* 'straw boots' > *waraudu*; *otofito* 'younger brother' > *otouto*; *yobi* 'call' + *te* > *youde*; *kamigamisii* 'divine' > *kaugausii*

Another noteworthy event in Late Old Japanese is the invention of **KANA SYLLABARIES**, which enabled Japanese people to record their language with their own script, rather than in the cumbersome manner necessary for using the Chinese writing system (Chapter 4). This invention facilitated the creation of great literature, e.g. *Kokin wakashū* ('Collected Japanese Poems of Ancient and Modern Times') (905), *Tosa nikki* ('Tosa Diary') (circa 935), *Ise monogatari* ('The Tales of Ise') (the late tenth century), *Makura no sōshi* ('The Pillow Book') (c. 1000), *Genji monogatari* ('The Tale of Genji') (c. 1000). The compilation of dictionaries also commenced in this period, e.g. *Tenrei banshō meigi* (a dictionary of Chinese characters) (c. 830), *Ruiju myōgishō* (a classified dictionary of Chinese characters) (the late eleventh century).

1.2.4 Middle Japanese (1192–1603)

In 1192, MINAMOTO no Yoritomo became the first *shōgun* 'a commander of a force' and established his government in Kamakura in Kanagawa prefecture, shifting political power from the Imperial Court to the warrior class and bringing about feudalism. In 1338, ASHIKAGA Takauji gained power and moved the capital to Muromachi in Kyōto prefecture. The Muromachi period ended in 1573 when the fifteenth shōgun was expelled by the warlord ODA Nobunaga. From 1573 to 1603 is known as the Azuchi-Momoyama period (a.k.a. the Sengoku 'Warring States' period) because Nobunaga built his castle in Azuchi in Shiga prefecture, and his successor TOYOTOMI Hideyoshi built his in Momoyama in Kyōto prefecture.

Table 1.2 *Modern and Middle Japanese syllables.*

Modern Japanese					Middle Japanese				
a	i	u	e	o	a	i	u		
ka	ki	ku	ke	ko	ka	ki	ku	ke	ko
ga	gi	gu	ge	go	ga	gi	gu	ge	go
sa	shi [ʃi]	Su	se	so	sa	shi [ʃi]	su	she [ʃe]	so
za	ji [dʒi]	zu/dzu	ze	zo	za	ʒi	zu	ʒe	zo
ta	chi [tʃi]	tsu	te	to	ta	chi [tʃi]	tsu	te	to
da	ji [dʒi]	zu/dzu	de	do	da	ji [dʒi]	dzu	de	do
na	ni	nu	ne	no	na	ni	nu	ne	no
ha	hi	fu [ɸu]	he	ho	fa [ɸu]	fi [ɸu]	fu [ɸu]	fe [ɸe]	fo [ɸo]
ba	bi	bu	be	bo	ba	bi	bu	be	bo
ma	mi	mu	me	mo	ma	mi	mu	me	mo
ya		yu		yo	ya		yu	ye	yo
ra	ri	ru	re	ro	ra	ri	ru	re	ro
wa					wa			we	wo
n					n				

Some of the most significant changes in the language occur in **Middle Japanese**, beginning with the disappearance of many Old Japanese characteristics and the development of Modern Japanese design features.[13] For example, as shown in Table 1.1, the /t/ and /d/ lines in Old Japanese were /ta, ti, tu, te, to/ and /da, di, du, de, do/, which evolved into the modern pronunciation of /ta, chi [tʃi], tsu, te, to/ and /da, ji [dʒi], dzu, de, do/ (Nakamoto 1981: 69). However, the /s/ line in this period was still /sa, shi [ʃi], su, she [ʃe], so/, differing from Modern Japanese (see Table 1.2).

As discussed earlier, vowel sequences were prohibited in Old Japanese, but as a result of sound changes in Late Old Japanese such sequences became widespread, and many evolved into long vowels.

(6) a. /au/ > /ɔ̄/:[14] *kyau* 'capital' > *kyɔ̄*; (*hayaku* 'early' >) *hayau* > *hayɔ̄*
b. /ou/ > /ō/: (*kinofu* 'yesterday' >) *kinou* > *kinō*; *sou* 'monk' > *sō*
c. /iu/ > /yū/: (*ifu* 'say' >) *iu* > *yū*; *tiu* 'middle' > *tyū* (= *chū*)
d. /eu/ > /yō/: (*kefu* 'today' >) *keu* > *kyō*; *teurou* 'ridicule' > *tyōrō* (= *chōrō*)
e. /ei/ > /ē/[15]

[13] An important historical change not included in this chapter is the disappearance of the literary phenomenon of *kakari–musubi* 'opening–ending', a rhetorical convention. See Shibatani (1990: 334–35).

[14] "ɔ̄" represents the long "open-o" as in English *all.*

[15] *Ruiju myōgishō*, written in Late Old Japanese, lists two pronunciations for 弟 'brother', *tei* and *tē*, so the inception of the long /e/ is likely in the eleventh century.

In the verb conjugation paradigm, the conclusive form (used today for listing dictionary entries) and the attributive form (used to modify nouns) have merged. (See Chapter 6 for explanations of these verb forms.) The pre-merge state is illustrated in (7a) and (7b). In (7a), the verb is in the conclusive form, and in (7b), in the attributive form, modifying the noun *namida* 'tear'.

(7) a. *Namida* *otsu.* [conclusive form]
tear drop
'Tear drops.'
b. *otsuru* *namida* [attributive form]
drop tear
'dropping tears'

However, after the merger, this distinction was lost, and the old attributive form began to function as the new conclusive form, as in (7c).

c. *Namida* *otsuru* [old attributive form; new conclusive form]
tear drop
'Tear drops.'

Another significant change in Middle Japanese involves the emergence of case particles (see Chapter 7), especially *ga* for designating the subject of a main clause.[16] The main-clause subject in Old Japanese was not explicitly marked as shown in (8a), the opening sentence of *Ise monogatari* ('The Tales of Ise') (the late tenth century). The subject, by contrast, is marked by *ga* in (8b), a sentence from *Heike monogatari* ('The Tale of the Heike') (c. 1200), although occurrences of *ga* as the subject marker were still scarce at the time.[17]

(8) a. *Mukashi,* *otoko* *ari keri.*
long.ago man there.was
'Once upon a time, there was a man.'
b. *Kyau* *yori* *Nobutoshi* *ga* *maitte saburafu.*
capital from NOM came
'Nobutoshi has come from the Capital.'

The emergence of *ga* is a strong indicator that Japanese people had begun to highlight sentence structure elements, and in particular to develop the notion of subject (Yamaguchi 1988: 90).

The Japanese first encountered Europeans in 1543 when Portuguese traders were shipwrecked off the Tanegashima island in Kagoshima prefecture in Kyūshū. In 1549, Jesuits settled in Kyūshū and began missionary work that

[16] Notwithstanding the establishment of case particles, case marking is not obligatory in Japanese main clauses.
[17] Most occurrences of *ga* in Middle Japanese functioned as a marker of possession, e.g. *Suefusa ga ko* 'Suefusa's child', which corresponds to *Suefusa no ko* in Modern Japanese.

included descriptions of the Japanese language in the Roman alphabet, which constitutes valuable data for reconstructing Middle Japanese. For example, *Vocabvlario da Lingoa de Iapam* ('Japanese–Portuguese dictionary'), compiled in 1603–04, lists approximately 32,800 Japanese words and explains in Portuguese their pronunciation, meanings, and usage illustrated by examples (Kokugogakkai 1980: 673).

1.2.5 Early Modern Japanese (1603–1867)

In 1603, TOKUGAWA Ieyasu relocated the capital to Edo, present-day Tōkyō. Thus commenced an era that lasted until 1867, known as the Edo period, which saw the emergence of **EARLY MODERN JAPANESE**. People came to Edo from all over Japan, and through contact they contributed to significant language change, assimilating and amalgamating traits from eastern and western dialects.[18]

During this period, the following sound changes took place (Nomura 1988), and the resulting sound system became virtually identical to that of Modern Japanese.

(9) a. /ye/ > /e/; /wo/ > /o/
b. /ɔ̄/ > /ō/
c. /she/ [ʃe] > /se/; /ʒe/ > /ze/
d. /f/ [ɸ] > /h/,[19] except before /u/
e. The distinction between /ʒi/ and /ji/ [dʒi] was lost (> /ji/), as well as between /zu/ and /dzu/[20]
f. Prenasalization, /^{m}b, ^{n}d, ^{ŋ}g/, gradually disappeared.

Until the Edo period, writing and reading had been associated almost exclusively with the ruling aristocrat and warrior (*samurai*) classes and Buddhist priests, but they became widespread among commoners mainly because of the launching of *terakoya* (privately run elementary schools) and the invention of wood-block printing. This rising literacy rate was instrumental in developing stories for commoners' entertainment. The **NARRATIVE** parts (i.e. retelling normally in chronological order of what happened) of these stories were written in Middle Japanese while conversation was recorded faithfully in Early Modern Japanese, which is virtually identical to Modern Japanese. For example, the utterances in (10) are indistinguishable from today's speech. (10a) is from *Kinkin-sensei eiga no yume* ('Master Flashgold's Splendiferous

[18] In 1843, Edo's population was approximately one million (Kamei *et al.* 2007: 13).
[19] Although it is written as /hi/, the consonant before /i/ is more fronted in the mouth, [çi] (see Section 3.1).
[20] As a native Tōkyō dialect speaker, I tend to pronounce /ji/ [dʒi] and /dzu/ phrase initially, and /zu/ phrase medially. I rarely use /ʒi/.

Dream') (1775) spoken by a waitress at an eatery establishment; (10b) is from *Ukiyoburo* ('Floating-World Bathhouse') (1809–13) spoken by a woman in her thirties.[21]

(10) a. *Moshi moshi, mochi ga dekimashita.*
hello rice.cake NOM has.been.ready
'Excuse me, (your) rice cake (dish) is ready.'

b. *Hai, mō setake bakari nobimashite, otonashiku gozaimasen.*
yes now height only grow.and obedient is.not
'Yes, (she [her daughter]) is now tall and no longer obedient.'

In the 1630s, the Tokugawa government prohibited all contact with foreign nations other than China, Korea, the Netherlands, and Ryukyus (present day Okinawa) because foreign influences were considered a source of political instability. This seclusion policy lasted until 1854, when the Treaty of Peace and Amity with the United States was ratified. The increasing foreign pressure that followed terminated the already languishing Tokugawa regime in 1867, and political power was restored to the emperor in 1868 – the inception of the Meiji period (the Meiji Restoration).

1.2.6 Modern Japanese (1867 to present)

Japan opened its doors in the midst of the predatory European colonial period and witnessed many Asian countries having been colonized. In order to preserve independence, the most pressing matters for the Meiji government were industrialization of the country and strengthening the military as rapidly as possible. People from all over Japan were recruited to work for factories, the military, and the government, which brought about communication problems because many, possibly most, of those recruits spoke mutually unintelligible dialects. Intellectuals, therefore, frequently had to communicate verbally via the written form of Japanese, which had been standardized since early periods but diverged significantly from their vernaculars (Okamoto 2009).

A movement to establish the *hyōjungo* 'standard Japanese' commenced not only to foster communication but also to awaken nationalism.[22] However, due to the presence of a large number of regional dialects, it was difficult to achieve a consensus that would serve as the basis of standardization. Eventually, following the proposal by Ueda (1895), it was decided that *hyōjungo* would be a refined variation of the dialect spoken by intellectual Tokyoites.

[21] Utterances of the warrior class depicted in fictions sound more like Middle Japanese and differ significantly from those of commoners.

[22] The term *hyōjungo* was coined by OKAKURA Yoshisaburo (a younger brother of OKAKURA Tenshin, the author of *The Book of Tea*) in 1890 as a translational equivalent of *standard language*.

The Meiji government aggressively enforced use of the standard as part of the newly established compulsory education, whereby dialects were viewed as a social evil. This biased view made many dialect speakers feel inferior (Shibata 1958: 90–139). Nevertheless, most people did not actually have opportunities to hear how intellectual Tokyoites spoke, so *hyōjungo* was considered by them as a kind of written language detached from daily life, its use enforced only in schools. However, 1925 brought the beginning of national radio broadcasting, and announcers were trained to speak only in *hyōjungo*, thus accelerating the spread of *hyōjungo* as a spoken language.

After World War II, the term *kyōtsūgo*, 'common Japanese', gained popularity in order to remedy the negative impact of the authoritarian enforcement of *hyōjungo* by the government. One way to differentiate the two is to remember that while *hyōjungo* is an idealized language, *kyōtsūgo* is a real language for use in communication across dialectal boundaries. Today, the term *hyōjungo* is rarely used in mass communication when the speaker's intent is to be politically correct.

Another significant linguistic event in the Meiji period is the **GENBUN-ITCHI MOVEMENT** (the UNIFICATION OF SPEECH AND WRITING) to vernacularize the written language. Reformers were convinced that the written language hindered literacy, education, and modernization due to enormous discrepancies between writing and common speech. From the mid-1880s, novelists who wanted to write in the vernacular joined this campaign. FUTABATEI Shimei's novel *Ukigumo* ['The Drifting Clouds'] (1887) is generally credited as the first successful use of a vernacular style in written Japanese. It opens as follows:

(11)

Chihayaburu	*kaminazuki*	*mo*	*mohaya*	*futsuka*	*no*	*nagori to natta*
[epithet]	October	also	already	two.days	GEN	left

28-nichi	*no*	*gogo*	*3-ji*	*goro*	*ni,*	*Kandamitsuke*	*no*	*uchi*
28th.day	GEN	P.M.	3-o'clock	about	at		GEN	inside

yori,	*towataru*	*ari,*	*chiru*	*kumo*	*no*	*ko*	*to*	*uyouyo,*
from	march	ant	disperse	spider	GEN	child	QUOT	crawling

zoyozoyo	*wakiidete kuru*	*no*	*wa,*	*izuremo*	*otogai*	*o*
streaming	spring.out	NMLZ[23]	TOP	all	beard	ACC

ki ni shitamau	*katagata.*
be.concerned	people

'(It was) about 3 o'clock on October 28th, when only two days remained until the end of the month. What sprang out, like marching ants or dispersing baby spiders from Kandamitsuke [a central district in Tokyo], were all gentlemen who were obsessed by the appearance of their beards.'[24]

23 NMLZ = nominalizer, see Section 15.1.

24 In the solar calendar, October has thirty-one days, but in a lunar calendar, days vary. In this case, October apparently had only thirty days.

Although this passage partially manifests genuine colloquialism, the epithet cliché *chihayaburu* to decorate the word *kami* 'god' as in *kaminazuki* (literally, 'the month when gods are absent; the tenth month of the lunar calendar', an archetypically old-fashioned rhetorical technique called *makura-kotoba* 'pillow word') reveals Futabatei's dilemma in choosing between a conventional style that is elegant yet stale and a vivid but still unconventional style which might sound frivolous.

The *genbun-itchi* movement advanced rapidly. Compare (11) with (12), a passage from KUNIKIDA Doppo's *Musashino* published in 1898, which exemplifies no archaic features:

(12)

Ganrai	*nihonjin*	*wa*	*kore*	*made*	*nara*	*no*	*tagui*	*no*
originally	Japanese	TOP	this	until	oak	GEN	kind	GEN

rakuyō-rin	*no*	*bi*	*o*	*amari*	*shiranakatta*	*yō de aru.*
deciduous-forest	GEN	beauty	ACC	not.much	did.not.know	it.is.likely

Hayashi	*to ie ba*	*omo ni*	*matsu-bayashi*	*nomi*	*ga*	*nihon*	*no*
forest	speaking.of	mainly	pine-forest	only	NOM	Japan	GEN

bungaku-bijutsu	*no*	*ue ni*	*mitomerarete ite,*	*uta*	*ni*	*mo*
literature-art	GEN	on	is.recognized	poetry	in	also

nara-bayashi	*no*	*oku*	*de*	*shigure*	*o*	*kiku*	*to iu*	*yō na*
oak-forest	GEN	interior	in	gentle.rain	ACC	listen.to	QUOT	like

koto	*wa*	*miataranai.*
event	NEG-SCP	can.not.be.found

'It seems that the Japanese, historically and even today, are unable to appreciate the beauty of deciduous forests like those with oak trees. When forests are mentioned in Japanese art and literature, pine trees are almost always the sole focus of attention. We cannot find in poetry any passages like listening to the gentle rain deep in an oak forest.'

2 Dialects

2.1 Introduction

The Japanese language is composed of numerous regional dialects, many of which are mutually unintelligible. It is not surprising, then, that **DIALECTOLOGY** (the study of dialects) has long been very popular in Japanese linguistics.[1] Regional dialects are, however, rapidly fading away, due mainly to the influence of mass communication, which routinely utilizes *kyōtsūgo* 'common Japanese' (Subsection 1.2.6). As of the mid-twentieth century, unique dialectal forms and traits were most conspicuous only in the Okinawa, Kyūshū, and Tōhoku regions (Sanada 2002: 15).

Dialects are valuable not only to appreciate the diversity of the contemporary Japanese language, but also to probe its historical development (see Section 1.2). Many specialists agree that peripheral (outlying/remote) areas tend to retain older forms. That is, dialectal variations – especially those heard in Okinawa, Kyūshū, and Tōhoku – are likely to be remnants of older forms once spoken in culturally central regions as well.

A methodological tradition in Japanese dialectology is to compare the various dialects in which the folktale *Momotarō* 'A Peach Boy' is recited.[2] The opening passage in common Japanese is provided in (1). This passage, spoken in the Fukushima, Tōkyō, Ōsaka, and Kagoshima dialects, is available at the book's website (http://hasegawa.berkeley.edu/Cambridge/introduction.php).

[1] Hino (1986: 10–38) provides a summary of major works in Japanese dialectology.

[2] Momotarō was born from a giant peach that was found floating down a river by an old woman who went there to wash clothes. The woman and her husband named this baby boy *Momotarō* and decided to raise him. When grown up, Momotarō left his foster parents and went to a distant island where he fought demons who tormented villagers. En route, he met a dog, a monkey, and a pheasant, who vowed to help him in his quest if he gave them some of the millet dumplings he was carrying.

(1)

Mukashi mukashi		*aru*	*tokoro*	*ni*	*ojīsan*	*to*	*obāsan*	*ga*
long.ago		certain	place	in	old.man	and	old.woman	NOM
arimashita.[3]	*Aru*	*hi*	*ojīsan*	*wa*	*yama*	*e*	*shibakari*	*ni,*
there.were	certain	day	old.man	TOP	mountain	to	firewood	for cutting
obāsan	*wa*	*kawa*	*e*	*sentaku*	*ni*	*ikimashita.*		
old.woman	TOP	river	to	washing	for	went		

'Once upon a time there lived [in a certain place] an old man and an old woman. One day, the old man went into the mountains to cut firewood, while the old woman went to the river to wash clothes.'

2.2 Okinawan dialects

The primary division among Japanese dialects is drawn between the islands of Okinawa and mainland Japan. In (2), *Momotarō* appears in the dialect of Naha, the capital city of Okinawa prefecture (Map 2.1).

(2)

Mukashi mukashi		*aru*	*tukurun*	*kai yō*	*tanmē*	*tu*	*hanshī*	*ga*
long.ago		certain	place	in	old.man	and	old.woman	NOM
mensēbītan.	*Aru*	*fi*	*tanmē*	*ya*	*yaman*	*kai*	*tamun*	*tui*
there.were	certain	day	old.man	TOP	mountain	to	firewood	gathering
ga,	*hanshī*	*ya*	*kāran*	*kai*	*arēmon shī*	*ga*	*ichabītan.*	
for	old.woman	TOP	river	to	washing	for	went	

This dialect, like most Okinawan dialects, has only three short vowels /a, i, u/, as compared to five in Tōkyō. However, it has five long vowels: /ā, ī, ū, ē, ō/, just as the Tōkyō dialect does. The short /e/ and /o/ in Tōkyō correspond respectively to /i/ and /u/ heard in Naha as shown in (3a–3b).

(3)

	Tōkyō	Naha	
a.	*akegata*	*akigata*	'dawn'
	kane	*kani*	'bell'
b.	*kotoba*	*kutuba*	'language'
	momo	*mumu*	'peach'

The vowel sequence /ao/ in Tōkyō is pronounced as /ō/ in Naha as in (4a), and /ai, ae/ correspond to /ē/ as in (4b–4c).

[3] *Aru* and *iru* 'exit/be/stay/locate' are **EXISTENTIAL VERBS**, and Japanese language textbooks uniformly explain that *aru* is used with an inanimate subject (something that is not alive and/or is unable to move by itself) and *iru* with an animate one. This distinction is a recent phenomenon. While *aru* has been a genuine existential verb throughout history, *iru* originally meant 'become motionless', and contrasted with *tatsu* 'start moving' (Kinsui 1984). As the unique existential verb, *aru* was used for both animate and inanimate subjects until late Middle Japanese. In the early twentieth century, *aru* could still be used with an animate subject, as shown in (1), but *iru* had become dominant in such cases.

Map 2.1. Okinawa.

(4)	Tōkyō	Naha	
a.	*aoba*	*ōba*	'green leaves'
	sao	*sō*	'a pole'
b.	*bai*	*bē*	'twice as much'
	mainichi	*mēnichi*	'everyday'
c.	*kaeru*	*kēru*	'go home'
	kangae	*kangē*	'a thought'

The /t/ and /d/ lines of the syllable inventory of the Naha dialect retain older pronunciations /ta, ti, tu, te, to, da, di, du, de, do/ (see Table 1.1), whereas those in the modern Tōkyō dialect are /ta, chi, tsu, te, to, da, ji, zu, de, do/ due to historical sound changes.

(5) Tōkyō Naha
a. *tegami* *tigami* 'letter'
asatte *asati* 'day after tomorrow'
b. *dengon* *dingun* 'message'
ude *udi* 'arm'
c. *tokoro* *tukuru* 'place'
oto *utu* 'sound'
d. *kado* *kadu* 'corner'
midori *miduri* 'green'

Nevertheless, /chi/ also exists in the Naha dialect as shown in (6).

(6) Tōkyō Naha
a. *chi* *chī* 'blood'
b. *chijimu* *chijimun* 'to shrink'

This phenomenon can be accounted for by positing that the rule /ti/ > /chi/ applied first, followed by /te/ > /ti/ (Shibatani 1990: 192). That is, applying each rule only once, /ti/ first changes to /chi/, and then /te/ changes to /ti/, which is no longer susceptible to the first rule.

The syllables /ki, gi, kya, kyu, kyō/ in the Tōkyō dialect correspond respectively to /chi, ji, cha, chu, chō/ in many, but not necessarily all, words in Naha.

(7) Tōkyō Naha
a. *kinō* *chinū* 'yesterday'
b. *Okinawa* *Uchinā*

but

c. *kizu* *kiji* 'a cut'
d. *sekiyu* *shikiyu* 'petroleum'

(8) a. *ginmi* *jinmi* 'examination'
b. *chigiri* *chijiri* 'vow'

but

c. *geta* *gita* 'wooden clogs'
d. *kage* *kagi* 'shadow'

(9) a. *okyaku* *uchaku* 'guest'

but

b. *Kyan* a traditional Okinawan family name

(10) a. *kyūbyō* *chūbyō* 'sudden illness'
b. *kyūji* *chūji* 'a waiter'

(11) a. *kyō* *chō* 'today'
b. *Kyōto* *Chōtu*

but

c. *Amamikyo* the name of a goddess

The Naha dialect also exhibits the old pronunciation of /f/ [ɸ] for the present-day /h/ (Subsection 1.2.5) as shown in *aru fi* 'a certain day' in (2). Other examples include the following:

(12)	Tōkyō	Naha	
a.	*haha*	*fafa*	'mother'
b.	*higashi*	*figashi*	'east'
c.	*fuku*	*fuku*	'good fortune'
d.	*haibun*	*fēbun*	'allotment'
e.	*hae*	*fē*	'a fly'

When surrounded by vowels, /w/ drops from words:

(13)	Tōkyō	Naha	
a.	*kawakami*	*kākan*	'upper parts of a river'
b.	*Okinawa*	*Uchinā*	

Furthermore, to confirm the claim that peripheral regions tend to retain older forms, the dialect of Nakijin (a village located in a northern part of the Okinawa main island) retains the old /p/, which changed in other dialects to /f/ [ɸ] during the Old Japanese period and eventually to /h/ as explained in Chapter 1.

(14)	Tōkyō	Nakijin	
a.	*hana*	*pana*	'flower'
b.	*hi*	*pī*	'day'
c.	*fune*	*puni*	'boat'
d.	*hae*	*pē*	'fly (insect)'
e.	*hoshi*	*pushī*	'star'

2.3 Mainland dialects

Numerous dialect divisions (groupings) have been proposed, among which four major geographical regions are widely recognized (adapted from Tojo 1953: 27):

(15) a. Eastern (Hokkaidō, Tōhoku, Kantō)
b. Central (Chūbu, Hokuriku)[4]

[4] When regional divisions are made for general purposes (vis-à-vis dialect studies), Hokuriku is usually included in the Chūbu region.

Map 2.2. The regions of Japan.

c. Western (Kinki, Chūgoku, Unpaku, Shikoku)[5]
d. Kyūshū

Dialect divisions are customarily determined according to the (i) sound system; (ii) vocabulary; (iii) verb/adjective conjugation; and (iv) pitch accent patterns. Different methods routinely lead to different dialect partitioning. In Map 2.2, regions are labeled in roman; and subregions, prefectures, and cities in italics.

2.3.1 *Divisions by sound system*

Regarding variations in sound systems, speakers residing in most areas of Tōhoku and Unpaku in Chūgoku as well as some areas of Hokkaidō and Hokuriku do not distinguish /i/ and /u/, pronouncing both as /ï/ (the

[5] Other than in dialect studies, the Unpaku area is rarely separated from the Chūgoku region.

NEAR-HIGH CENTRAL UNROUNDED VOWEL) (Kato 2009: 79).[6] The /t/ line in the syllable chart (Tables 1.1 and 1.2), whose consonants vary according to the following vowel in the Tōkyō dialect (/ta, chi, tsu, te, to/) is pronounced as /ta, tsï, tsï, te, to/. Consequently, the words *chichi* 'father', *chitsu(jo)* 'order', *tsuchi* 'soil', and *tsutsu* 'a cylinder' are all pronounced identically as [tsïtsï].[7]

Furthermore, in these regions, voiceless consonants tend to be voiced when occurring phrase-medially (i.e. flanked by voiced sounds), and voiced stops tend to be prenasalized, i.e. /^{m}b, ^{n}d, ^{ŋ}g/.[8] Until several decades ago, these dialects were pejoratively called *zūzūben* 'zū-zū dialect'. Eventually, Japanese people gained insight into the fact that regional dialects are indeed rich, vital parts of the Japanese language. *Momotarō* in (16) is in the dialect spoken in Goshogawara City in Aomori prefecture (derived from Sugito 1998).

(16)

Mugasï mugasï		*aru*	*dogo*	*nï*	*zïsama*	*do*	*basama*	*ga*
long.ago		certain	place	in	old.man	and	old.woman	NOM
atte ïda	*do.*	*Zïsama*	*wa*	*yama*	*sa*	*tagïmono*	*o*	*torï*
there.were	QUOT	old.man	TOP	mountain	to	firewood	ACC	gathering
nï	*basama*	*wa*	*kawa*	*sa*	*araimono*	*nï*	*ïtta*	*do.*
for	old.woman	TOP	river	to	washing	for	went	QUOT

Another dialect that exhibits a unique sound system is spoken in Nagoya in Aichi prefecture. There, /ai/ and /ae/ are pronounced as [ǣ] or [æə], /oi/ as [ø̄], and /ui/ as [ȳ],[9,10] The following examples are derived from Takeuchi (1982: 86–89) and Keshikawa (1983: 216–18).

(17)

	Tōkyō	Nagoya	
a.	*Akai*	[akǣ]	'red'
b.	*Hairu*	[hǣru]	'to enter'
c.	*kaeru*	[kǣru]	'to go home'
d.	*Omae*	[omǣ]	'you'
e.	*Koi*	[kø̄]	'love'
f.	*Omoi*	[omø̄]	'heavy'
g.	*Sui*	[sȳ]	'stylishness'
h.	*samui*	[samȳ]	'cold'

[6] A video clip to demonstrate the pronunciation of /ï/ is available at the book's website (http://hasegawa.berkeley.edu/Cambridge/introduction.php).

[7] A video clip of the Kesen dialect to demonstrate the pronunciation of these four words is available at the book's website.

[8] In Unpaku dialects, /t, k/ do not become /d, g/, and /g/ is not nasalized (Onishi 1993: 28).

[9] [æ] is the vowel occurring in *cat*; [ə] is the initial vowel in *ago*; [ø] is the vowel in the French word *bleu* 'blue', which is similar to [e] but the lips are rounded; [y] is the vowel in French *tu* 'you', similar to [i] also accompanied by lip rounding.

[10] A TV commercial from the 1970s that utilizes the Nagoya dialect is available at the book's website. The name of the window screen cleaner in this commercial is *Amilight* [amiɾaito], which is pronounced as [amiɾǣto].

In the Kōchi dialect of Shikoku island, distinctions are retained between /ʒi/ and /ji/ [dʒi] as well as between /zu/ and /dzu/ (Onishi 1993: 29). Both of these disappeared in most dialects during the Early Modern Japanese period (see Subsection 1.2.5).

	Tōkyō	Kōchi	
(18)			
	a. *fuji* [ɸudʒi]	[ɸuʒi]	'Mt. Fuji'
	b. *fuji* [ɸudʒi]	[ɸudʒi]	'wisteria'
	c. *suzu* [suzu]	[suzu]	'bell'
	d. *mizu* [mizu]	[midzu]	'water'

The Kagoshima dialect in southern Kyūshū exhibits another interesting sound characteristic. In the word-final position, the syllables /ki, gi, ku, gu, chi, ji, tsu, bi, bu, ru/ are all realized as a **GLOTTAL STOP** (Onishi 1993: 32), represented as a [ʔ] in the IPA, an abrupt termination of voicing by closing the glottis (i.e. vocal cords). (English uses a glottal stop in an interjection of dismay or alarm, *uh-oh* [ʔəʔoʊ].) Consequently, all of the following words are pronounced as [kaʔ] in Kagoshima:[11]

(19) a. *kaki* 'persimmon'
b. *kagi* 'key'
c. *kaku* 'to write'
d. *kagu* 'to sniff'
e. *kachi* 'win'
f. *kaji* 'a fire'
g. *katsu* 'to win'
h. *kabi* 'mold'
i. *kabu* 'a stock'
j. *karu* 'to cut'

The older form of /she, je/, corresponding to the present-day /se, ze/ (Subsection 1.2.4), are retained in most dialects in Tōhoku and Kyūshū and many dialects in Hokuriku, Kinki, Chūgoku, and Shikoku (Tokugawa 1979: 174).

(20) a. *sensei* *shenshei* 'teacher'
b. *zenzen* *jenjen* '(not) at all'

Most of those dialects also retain /kwa, gwa/, syllables originally borrowed from Chinese in ancient times (Tokugawa 1979: 178).

(21) a. *kaji* *kwaji* 'a fire'
b. *gaikoku* *gwaikoku* 'foreign country'

[11] An excerpt from a radio talk show in the Kagoshima dialect broadcast in 1978 is available at the book's website (http://hasegawa.berkeley.edu/Cambridge/introduction.php).

Another older pronunciation /wo/ for /o/ is found in many areas of Kyūshū and is also interspersed throughout Japan (Kibe 1999: 37).

(22) a. *ao* *awo* 'blue'
b. *shio* *shiwo* 'salt'

2.3.2 *Divisions by vocabulary*

Some dialects show amazing richness in vocabulary in certain conceptual fields. For example, the Izumo dialect of the Unpaku region divides a day into many periods as shown in (23) (Shibata 1958: 13–14). These fine divisions are possible and meaningful in agricultural villages where everyone follows a virtually identical daily schedule.[12]

(23)
a.	*yoake mae*	before dawn
b.	*yoake*	dawn
c.	*asama*	about the time when breakfast is over
d.	*asama no ochi*	until about 8 A.M.
e.	*hiru mae*	approximately 11 A.M. to 12 noon
f.	*chīhan jibon*	lunch time (noon)
g.	*chīhan shigi*	noon to 1 P.M.
h.	*kobashima jibon*	snack time (about 4 P.M.)
i.	*akeochi*	before sundown
j.	*fūkara*	noon to sundown
k.	*akakura*	just before sundown
l.	*hi no kure*	around sundown
m.	*bange*	sundown to dinner
n.	*yoi no kuchi*	right before dinner
o.	*yōhan jibon*	dinner time
p.	*ban*	after dinner
q.	*yabun*	before sleep
r.	*yonaka*	after falling asleep

For another example of vocabulary variation, a snail is called variously as in (24) (derived from Yanagita 1930: appendix).

(24)
a.	*namekuji*	northeastern Tōhoku, Hokuriku, many areas of Kyūshū
b.	*tuburi*	southeastern Tōhoku, Hokuriku, northern Kyūshū
c.	*katatsumuri*	western Tōhoku, western Kantō, southeastern Chūbu, southern Kinki, southwestern Shikoku
d.	*maimai*	eastern Kantō, Hokuriku, western Chūbu, Chūgoku
e.	*dendenmushi*	Kinki

[12] In many English-speaking nations, especially in farming and rural communities, the mid-day meal is 'dinner', the evening meal is 'supper', and there is no 'lunch'.

From this distribution pattern, Yanagita has concluded that *dendenmushi* is the newest form, found around the old cultural center of Kyōto, while the oldest form, *namekuji*, is found in the areas farthest from this center. Concerning this distribution, he hypothesizes that new forms are dispersed gradually and in succession from the culturally central region into outlying areas, so that the outmost regions preserve the oldest form while the middle regions evidence, by succession, a word's historical development, an effect much like rippling.[13] To investigate dialectal variations in vocabulary, an enormous amount of data for many concepts (mostly nouns) has been collected by Kokuritsu Kokugo Kenkyūjo (The National Institute for Japanese Language and Linguistics).[14]

The selection of an existential verb for an animate subject (see Section 2.1) also varies from dialect to dialect with a dividing line loosely matching the Itoigawa–Shizuoka Tectonic Line (ISTL), Japan's major tectonic fault, which runs from the city of Itoigawa in Nīgata prefecture to Shizuoka city in Shizuoka prefecture (see Map 2.3). Most dialects east of the ISTL use *iru*, whereas those located west of the line use *oru* with the exception of Wakayama prefecture, which utilizes *aru* (Sato 1979: 10). In the Tōkyō dialect, *iru* is the norm, although in polite speech (see Chapter 20), *oru* (*orimasu*) is also used. This variation came about because, as spoken in the cultural center, the Edo (an old name for Tōkyō) dialect incorporated many traits from the Kinki dialects.

Other examples to illustrate an east–west opposition around the ISTL are provided below (Kobayashi 1999: 68–69):

(25)	East	West	
a.	*kusuriyubi*	*benisashiyubi/ benitsukeyubi*	'the third finger'
b.	*hiko*	*himago*	'great-grandchild'
c.	*shoppai*	*karai*	'salty'
d.	*kariru*	*karu*	'to borrow'
e.	*koke/kokera*	*uroko*	'(fish's) scale'
f.	*nyūbai*	*tsuyu/tsuiri*	'(the beginning of) the rainy season'

For some vocabulary, the east retained older forms, e.g. (25a–25b); in others, the west retained older forms, e.g. (25c–25d); and in some cases both forms emerged during the same period, e.g. (25e–f) (Kobayashi 1999: 69–70).

[13] Fujiwara (1983) provides other vocabulary items shared by northern Tōhoku and southwestern Kyūshū to support Yanagita's analysis.

[14] www.ninjal.ac.jp/publication/catalogue/laj_map/

Map 2.3. The Itoigawa–Shizuoka Tectonic Line.

2.3.3 Divisions by verb/adjective conjugation

Negation is another parameter for dividing dialects: eastern dialects use *nai* or *nē* (e.g. *ikanai/ikanē* 'not go'); western dialects use *n* (e.g. *ikan*). However, in central Kinki (falling to the west of the ISTL), the default form of negation is *hen* or *yahen* (e.g. *ikahen* 'not go', *tabeyahen* 'not eat') whereas *n* is also used but only for emphasis (Tsuzuku 1986: 121). Negation of adjectives in Kinki is different from that in Tōkyō: *takaku-nai* (Tōkyō) vs. *takō-nai/takai koto nai/taka-nai* (Kinki) (Onishi 1993: 27, 117).

The ISTL is also relevant to the division of the forms of the copula, which is equivalent to the English verb *be* (see Subsection 5.2.2). In general, eastern dialects use *da* (e.g. *ame da* 'it's raining'), whereas western dialects use *ja* (e.g. *ame ja*). However, Aichi prefecture, located just west of the ISTL, belongs to the eastern group in this respect. Furthermore, Kinki and some parts of Hokuriku, Chūbu, Shikoku, and Kyūshū employ *ya* (e.g. *ame ya*) rather than *ja* (Tsuzuku 1986: 142–43).

The imperative (command) form of *ru*-verbs (see Section 5.2.2) in the east is *mi-ro* 'look!' while that in the west is *mi-yo* or *mi-i*.

The *te*-form of some verbs (see Subsection 1.2.3) developed differently in east and west (Shibuya 1999: 88–89).

(26) *kafu* [kaɸu] (*kau* in Modern Japanese) 'to buy'
East *kafi-te* > *kaf-te* > *kat-te*
West *kafi-te* > *kawi-te* > *kau-te* > *kɔ̄-te* > *kō-te*

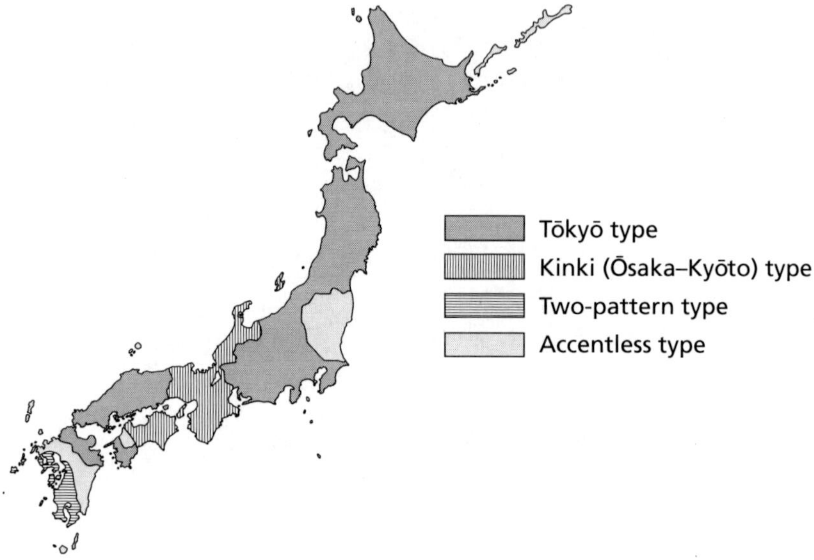

Map 2.4. Pitch–accent patterns.

2.3.4 *Divisions by pitch accent patterns*

In terms of pitch accent, Japanese dialects are commonly divided into four groups, as shown in Map 2.4 (Hayata 1999: 29, 36–41). The concept of pitch accent will be discussed in Section 3.5. Rudimentarily speaking, most dialects of Japanese differentiate certain (but not all) word meanings by modulation of vocal pitch from high to low or vice versa. For example, (27) provides contrasts of the words *ame* 'candy' or 'rain' in the Tōkyō and Ōsaka dialects.[15]

(27)

	Tōkyō	Ōsaka
HL	rain	
HH		candy
LF (fall tone from H to L)		rain
LH	candy	

The HL pattern exists in Ōsaka (e.g. *hashi* 'bridge', *yama* 'mountain'),[16] but not with *ame*. On the other hand, the HH pattern does not exist in the Tōkyō dialect. The LH pattern does exist in Ōsaka (e.g. *sora* 'sky', *haru* 'spring'),[17]

[15] A video clip is available at the book's website (http://hasegawa.berkeley.edu/Cambridge/introduction.php).

[16] Both *hashi* 'bridge' and *yama* 'mountain' are pronounced as LH in Tōkyō.

[17] Both *sora* 'sky' and *haru* 'spring' are pronounced as HL in Tōkyō.

Table 2.1 *Variations in pitch accent.*

Noun	Gloss	PJ	LOJ	MJ	Takamatsu	Kyōto	Tōkyō	Morioka
ushi (wa)	cow	HH(H)	HH(H)	HH(H)	HH(H)	HH(H)	LH(H)	LL(L)
ushi (mo)	cow	HH(L)	HH(L)	HH(L)	HH(L)	HH(L)		
ishi (wa)	stone	HF(L)	HL(L)	HL(L)	HL(L)	HL(L)	LH(L)	
ashi (wa)	leg	LH(L)	ML(H)		HH(H)			LH(L)
aki (wa)	autumn	HL(L)	LH(L)	LH(L)	LF(L)	LH(L)	HL(L)	HL(L)
iki (mo)	breath	LH(L)			LL(F)			
iki (wa)	breath	LH(H)	LH(H)	LH(H)	LL(H)	LL(H)		

but again, not with *ame*. The LF pattern is totally foreign to Tōkyō dialect speakers.

The two-pattern type of accent is represented by the Kagoshima dialect, in which the high-pitched accent falls either on the final syllable or the syllable next to the final syllable (**PENULTIMATE SYLLABLE**) of phrases, which is demonstrated in the book's website (http://hasegawa.berkeley.edu/Cambridge/introduction.php). Finally, in accentless dialects, all accentual contrasts have been lost; that is, no two words are differentiated solely by accent.

Retaining older accentual contrasts, Kinki dialects have more variations than the Tōkyō type. Table 2.1, derived from Hattori (1951), illustrates correspondences of pitch–accent patterns of two-syllable word groups among Proto Japanese (PJ, a hypothetical, reconstructed language from which attested variations of languages are believed to have evolved), Late Old Japanese (LOJ), Middle Japanese (MJ),[18] and the dialects of modern Takamatsu in Kagawa Prefecture in Shikoku (Kyōto type), Kyōto, Tōkyō, and Morioka in Iwate prefecture in Tōhoku (Tōkyō type). The first column lists nouns that represent each word group, *wa* being the topic marker (see Section 8.1), and *mo* being a particle to indicate 'also'.

The LH(L) pattern in LOJ has two reflexes in the Takamatsu dialect: LF(L) and LL(F). However, this split is unpredictable by mere examination of the sound qualities of words. Therefore, Hattori claims, PJ must have had two distinctive patterns for this group, but they were lost by the time of LOJ.

This distribution pattern of pitch accent challenges the widely accepted view that peripheral areas retain older forms (discussed earlier in this chapter) because, in this instance, older traits are retained in culturally central areas of Kinki.

[18] The accentual patterns of Late Old Japanese are based on *Ruiju myōgishō* (the late eleventh century); those of Middle Japanese are based on *Bumōki* of 1687.

3 Sound system

3.1 The syllable inventory

The Japanese language has a fairly simple sound system compared to English. If we ignore the short vs. long vowel distinction (see Section 3.2), Japanese consists of twenty-six distinct consonants and five vowels. There are, however, dialectal variations; for example, the Yonaguni dialect in Okinawa has only three vowels, while the Nagoya dialect has eight vowels (Nakamoto 1981: 63). English has a much more complex sound system, consisting of twenty-four consonants and twenty vowels, with some dialectal variations (Ladefoged 1982: 24, 28). Consonants and vowels combine to form syllables. Due to the large number of consonant–vowel combinations, English speech sounds are usually not counted in syllabic terms. By contrast, the number of combinatory possibilities in Japanese is limited, and it is common practice to consider Japanese speech sounds as an inventory of syllables.

Of the twenty-six Japanese consonants, fifteen are plain and eleven **PALATALIZED**. A palatalized consonant is articulated together with the tongue in high central position, like that in /i/. Consequently, the distinction between plain and palatalized consonants does not exist before /i/, e.g. /ki/ vs. /kyi/. The palatalized consonants occur with all other vowels. However, combination with /e/ is restricted, appearing only in borrowed foreign words (e.g. *jetto* 'jet plane') and **EXPRESSIVE VOCABULARY**, e.g. *che!* 'shoot!' (interjection).

In Table 3.1, representations of the International Phonetic Alphabet (IPA) are provided within square brackets.[1] The syllables with limited distribution are shaded. Each line in Table 3.1 is explained in the list below.

Line 1: e.g. *aki* 'autumn', *iki* 'breath', *uki* 'rainy season', *eki* 'train station', *oki* 'offshore'. The dialects in the Kansai (Kyōto–Ōsaka) area exhibit lip-rounding with /u/ (as in English), but the Tōkyō dialect does not do so in normal speech. The lips are relaxed,

[1] The International Phonetic Alphabet (IPA) is a standardized representation of the sounds of the world's languages.

Table 3.1 *Japanese syllables.*

1	a [ɑ]	i [i]	u [ɯ]	e [e]	o [o]				
2	pa [pɑ]	pi [pi]	pu [pɯ]	pe [pe]	po [po]	pya [pʲɑ]	pyu [pʲɯ]		pyo [pʲo]
3	ba [bɑ]	bi [bi]	bu [bɯ]	be [be]	bo [bo]	bya [bʲɑ]	byu [bʲɯ]		byo [bʲo]
4	ta [tɑ]	chi [tʃi]	tsu [tsɯ]	te [te]	to [to]	cha [tʃɑ]	chu [tʃɯ]	che [tʃe]	cho [tʃo]
5	da [dɑ]	ji [dʒi]	zu [dzɯ]	de [de]	do [do]				
6	ka [kɑ]	ki [ki]	ku [kɯ]	ke [ke]	ko [ko]	kya [kʲɑ]	kyu [kʲɯ]		kyo [kʲo]
7	ga [gɑ]	gi [gi]	gu [gɯ]	ge [ge]	go [go]	gya [gʲɑ]	gyu [gʲɯ]		gyo [gʲo]
8	ma [mɑ]	mi [mi]	mu [mɯ]	me [me]	mo [mo]	mya [mʲɑ]	myu [mʲɯ]		myo [mʲo]
9	na [nɑ]	ni [ni]	nu [nɯ]	ne [ne]	no [no]	nya [nʲɑ]	nyu [nʲɯ]		nyo [nʲo]
10	fa [ɸɑ]	fi [ɸi]		fe [ɸe]	fo [ɸo]				
11	sa [sɑ]	shi [ʃi]	su [sɯ]	se [se]	so [so]	sha [ʃɑ]	shu [ʃɯ]	she [ʃe]	sho [ʃo]
12	za [zɑ]	ji [dʒi]	zu [dzɯ]	ze [ze]	zo [zo]	ja [dʒɑ]	ju [dʒɯ]	je [dʒe]	jo [dʒo]
13	ha [hɑ]	hi [çi]	fu [ɸɯ]	he [he]	ho [ho]	hya [çɑ]	hyu [çɯ]		hyo [ço]
14	ra [ɾɑ]	ri [ɾi]	ru [ɾɯ]	re [ɾe]	ro [ɾo]	rya [ɾʲɑ]	ryu [ɾʲɯ]		ryo [ɾʲo]
15	wa [wɑ]	wi [wi]		we [we]	wo [wo]				
16	ya [jɑ]		yu [jɯ]	ye [je]	yo [jo]				

neither rounded nor split as with /i/. This unrounded /u/ is represented as [ɯ] in the IPA.

Line 2: The distribution of /p/ is unique in Japanese today: it occurs word-initially only in expressive vocabulary or foreign loan words, e.g. *pai* 'pie', *piripiri* 'a description of a tingling sensation', *punpun* 'a description of odor', *pen* 'pen', *pon* 'a popping sound'. Word-medially, /p/ occurs in regular vocabulary, e.g. *sanpo* 'a stroll', *ippiki* 'one animal', *ippun* 'one minute', *ippei* 'one soldier', *ippo* 'one step'. This irregular distribution is due to historical change. In Old Japanese (Subsection 1.2.2), /p/ existed word-initially (Ueda 1898). By the eighth century, it had changed to the consonant that occurs in today's /fu/, [ɸ]. Later, in the seventeenth century, this consonant further changed to /h/ (Komatsu 1981: 249). Most instances of word-initial /h/ today were originally pronounced as /p/. For example, *paru* 'spring' first changed to *faru*, and then to today's *haru* pronunciation. Examples of the palatalized /p/ are: *roppyaku* 'six hundred', *pyū* 'the sound of wind (onomatopoeia)', *ippyō* 'one vote'.

Lines 2, 4, 6: Say the English words *pin* [pʰɪn], *tin* [tʰɪn] and *kin* [kʰɪn]. You hear a puffing sound when the consonants are released into the following vowel. This puffing sound is called **ASPIRATION**, and it is represented as [ʰ] in the IPA. The Japanese /p/, /t/, and /k/ in word-initial position are accompanied by aspiration, but it is much less noticeable than that heard in English.

Line 3: While /p/ underwent changes over time, its voiced counterpart /b/ remained intact. Examples are: *bai* 'twice as many', *bi* 'beauty', *bun* 'a sentence', *benri* 'convenient', *bō* 'a stick', *byakuya* 'a night under the midnight sun', *byūsetsu* 'fallacy', *byōki* 'disease'.

Line 4: e.g. *taki* 'waterfall', *chiki* 'acquaintance', *tsuki* 'moon', *teki* 'enemy', *toki* 'time', *cha* 'tea', *chū* 'middle', *chesu* 'chess', *chō* 'super'. The combination /t/ + /i/ does not sound like *tea* [ti], but, rather, like the first part of *cheese* [tʃiz]. However, [ti] occurs in foreign loan words, e.g. *pātī* 'party'. The combination /t/ + /u/ does not sound like *two* [tu], but like the final sound of *cats* [kæts] followed by /u/.

Line 5: e.g. *dashi* 'broth', *deshi* 'disciple', *dōshi* 'verb'. The palatalized counterparts are identical to those in the /z/ line (line 12).

Lines 5, 12: Around the sixteenth century, /d/ + /i/ and /z/ + /i/ merged and came to be pronounced as the first syllable of *genius* [dʒiniəs]. Likewise, /d/ + /u/ and /z/ + /u/ merged and became *zoo* [zu] or, as a variation, like the end of *kids* [$\mathrm{k^h}$ɪdz] followed by /u/. The difference between [dz] and [z] is very subtle, influenced only by how abrupt ([dz]) or gradual ([z]) the onset of the consonant is. To the Japanese ear, the distinction between *AIDS* [eɪdz] (Acquired Immune Deficiency Syndrome) and *A's* [eɪz] (the Oakland Athletics professional baseball team) is very difficult to make.

Line 6: e.g. *kari* 'debt', *kiri* 'fog', *kuri* 'chestnut', *keri* 'settlement', *kori* 'stiffness in a body', *kyaku* 'guest', *kyū* 'nine', *kyō* 'today'.

Line 7: e.g. *gan* 'wild goose', *gin* 'silver', *gun* 'county', *gen* 'string', *gonge* 'incarnation', *gyaku* 'opposite', *gyū* 'beef', *gyō* 'line'. In the Tōkyō dialect, /g/ is **NASALIZED** when it is flanked by vowels or when it occurs after /n/. Nasalization means that the sound is released from the nostrils, rather than through the lips. A nasalized /g/ is like the final consonant in English *sing*. This sound is represented as [ŋ] in the IPA, e.g. *chigai* [tʃiŋɑi] 'difference', *ongaku* [oŋŋɑkɯ] 'music'. Nasalization of /g/ is less common among members of the younger generation.

Line 8: e.g. *mai* 'a dance', *miki* 'a stem', *mune* 'chest', *men* 'a mask', *mori* 'a grove', *myaku* 'the pulse', *myūzu* 'the Muses', *myōgonichi* 'day after tomorrow'.

Line 9: e.g. *nashi* 'pear', *nishi* 'west', *nushi* 'owner', *neko* 'cat', *nomi* 'lice', *rōnyaku* 'young and old', *nyūyoku* 'bathing', *nyōbō* 'wife'.

Line 10: The syllable /fu/ [ɸɯ] occurs in native Japanese vocabulary (see line 13), but the /f/ with other vowels occurs only in foreign names and loan words: e.g. *fairu* 'a file', *firumu* 'film', *fensu* 'fence', *fōkasu* 'a focus'.

Line 11: e.g. *san* 'three', *shi* 'four', *su* 'vinegar', *sen* 'one thousand', *son* 'loss', *shakai* 'society', *shu* 'species', *shea* 'a share', *shō* 'small'. The /s/ is palatalized before /i/. That is, /s/ + /i/ does not sound like English *sea* [si], but like the third person singular pronoun *she* [ʃi, ʃɪ]. The palatalized /s/ in Japanese is more fronted, creating a "higher" hiss sound than that in the English *she*.[2]

Line 12: e.g. *zai* 'wealth', *jiko* 'accident', *zure* 'gap', *zei* 'tax', *zoku* 'tribe', *ja* 'snake', *jū* 'ten', *jetto* 'a jet', *jo* 'preface'.

Line 13: e.g. *hari* 'needle', *hiritsu* 'ratio', *furi* 'disadvantage', *heri* 'edge', *hori* 'ditch', *hyaku* 'hundred', *Hyūga* 'the name of a city in Kyūshū', *hyō* 'panther'. The /h/ is a voiceless counterpart of whatever vowel follows it. Say /a/ and then stop voicing while maintaining exhalation. You hear a spirant sound, which is [h]. Next, say /i/ and cease voicing. The spirant sound this time is quite different from the one with /a/. This sound is represented as [ç] in the IPA. The third spirant sound to recognize is [ɸ]. This occurs when you stop voicing after saying /u/; it is the sound created when blowing out a candle. (This sound is represented in this book as /f/ although, unlike in English, upper front teeth are not involved in its enunciation.) These spirant sounds are made by the air moving through the narrowest point in an air passage, i.e. the vocal tract. With /a/, /e/, or /o/, it is your throat, but with /i/, it is at the central tongue area, and with /u/, the lips form the narrowest part of the passage.

Line 14: e.g. *ran* 'orchid', *risu* 'squirrel', *rui* 'a kind', *rei* 'example', *ron* 'theory', *ryaku* 'abbreviation', *ryū* 'dragon', *ryokō* 'travel'. Word-initially, the Japanese /r/ sounds like the second consonant of *rider* and *writer* [ɹaɪɾɚ] in fluent running speech in most dialects of American English. Acoustically, it is a short /d/, called a **TAP**.[3] When you record /da/ and make the initial consonant shorter, you will obtain /ra/. Word-medially, Japanese /r/ is frequently more like English /r/, e.g. *karada* 'body'. The /r/ is unique among the Japanese consonants in that it uses the tip of the tongue. For the other consonants, the tongue tip rests behind the lower teeth, even with /t/, /d/ and /n/.

[2] "A higher hiss sound" means that the sound is more concentrated in regions of higher frequency. Therefore, a more accurate representation in the IPA is [ɕ], rather than [ʃ].

[3] In some dialects (e.g. Kinki, Shikoku, Kyūshū), /r/ is pronounced as /d/, e.g. *rōsoku* 'candle' > *dōsoku* (Kindaichi 1953: 138).

Line 15: The syllable /wa/ occurs in native Japanese vocabulary, e.g. *wakare* 'separation', but the /w/ with other vowels occurs only in foreign names and loan words: e.g. *wīku* 'week', *webu* 'the Web', *wōtā* 'water'. The distinction between /wu/ and /u/ is virtually imperceptible so there is no /wu/.

Line 16: e.g. *yari* 'a spear', *yuri* 'lily', *yoru* 'night'. The distinction between /yi/ and /i/ is also imperceptible, so there is no /yi/.[4] The syllable /ye/ existed until the mid-tenth century, but it merged into /e/ (Komatsu 1981: 51); today it occurs only in foreign names and loan words, e.g. *Yerusaremu* 'Jerusalem', *yerō* 'yellow'.

3.2 Long vowels and consonants

Vowel length is not distinctive in spoken English. One can elongate a vowel without changing the basic meaning of the word, e.g. *slow* and *sloooow*. In Japanese, by contrast, elongating a vowel can change the meaning: e.g. *obasan* 'aunt', *obāsan* 'grandmother'; *ojisan* 'uncle', *ojīsan* 'grandfather'; *suri* 'pick-pocket', *sūri* 'mathematical principle'; *teki* 'enemy', *tēki* 'commuter ticket'; *ho* 'sail', *hō* 'law'.

Like the vowels, short and long consonants are distinctive in Japanese. Long consonants occur only word-medially. The long versions of /p/, /t/, and /k/ have a longer silence before they are released, e.g. *maki* [mɑki] 'firewood' vs. *makki* [mɑkːi] 'the final period'; *kate* [kɑte] 'food' vs. *katte* [kɑtːe] 'selfish'; (no word-medial short /p/ except for foreign loan words, e.g. *sūpā* 'supermar-ket') vs. *rippa* [ɾipːɑ] 'marvelous'. Long /g/ and /d/ occur in loan words, e.g. *beddo* [bedːo] 'bed', *badji* [bɑdːʒi] 'badge', *baggu* [bɑgːɯ] 'bag'. Some people pronounce *Web* as /webbu/. Long /s/ and /sh/ have a longer spirant sound, e.g. *isō* [isoː] 'transfer' vs. *issō* [isːoː] 'even more'; *ishiki* [iʃiki] 'consciousness' vs. *isshiki* [iʃːiki] 'a complete set of items'.

3.3 Syllables and moras

In English, some syllables are very complex. For example, the single-syllable word *strike* [stɹaɪk] begins with three consonants, /s/+/t/+/r/, followed by the gliding vowel /ai/, and concludes with another consonant /k/. In contrast, Japanese syllables are much simpler. Originally, they consisted almost exclu-sively of the combination of a single consonant and a vowel, and only /p/, /t/,

[4] In English, the distinction between 'year' [jɪə(ɹ)] and 'ear' [ɪə(ɹ)] is possible because [ɪ] is lower than Japanese [i]. In fact, Japanese [i] is very high and there is no room for gliding, which makes /i/ [i] and /yi/ [ji] indistinguishable.

/k/, /s/, /m/, /n/, /w/, and /y/ could appear word-initially. Vowels alone could form a syllable, but only in word-initial position; i.e. a succession of vowels, e.g. *baai* 'occasion', did not occur in native vocabulary (Watanabe 1997: 80). Complex syllables in earlier stages were all loan words from Chinese until some time in the tenth to twelfth centuries, when Japanese developed its own complex syllables (Watanabe 1997: 78).

The word *syllable* is commonly used in English, but it is difficult to define. Some contend that, for example, the word *communism* consists of three syllables, while others perceive four. This discrepancy is due to whether or not the final /zm/ forms a separate syllable by itself.

For the Japanese, syllable is an unfamiliar concept. When counting speech sounds, they use a unit called the **MORA** instead. The short syllables listed below each consist of one mora, the long syllables consist of two moras, and the super-long syllables consist of three moras. Unlike consonants and vowels, a mora is a pure counting unit, not a syllable component. The syllable structures possible in Modern Japanese are as follows:

Short syllables (one mora)

1. A short vowel	*i* 'stomach', *u* 'cormorant (a kind of bird)', *e* 'a handle', *o* 'a tail'
2. A consonant + a short vowel	*ma* 'interval', *ki* 'tree', *su* 'vinegar', *te* 'a hand', *to* 'door', *cha* 'tea', *shu* 'species', *sho* 'calligraphy'

Long syllables (two moras, or morae)

3. A long vowel	*āmondo* 'almond', *īsuto* 'yeast', *ūru* 'wool', *ēga* 'movie', *ō* 'king'
4. A consonant + a long vowel	*okāsan* 'mother', *onīsan* 'older brother', *sū* 'a number', *tēka* 'the list price', *gōka* 'gorgeous', *chāhan* 'fried rice', *jū* 'ten', *hyō* 'graph'
5. A short vowel + a nasal consonant	*an* 'idea', *in* 'a seal', *un* 'luck', *en* 'fate'
6. A consonant + a short vowel + a nasal consonant	*man* 'ten thousand', *kin* 'gold', *fun* 'minute', *hen* 'strange', *hon* 'book', *akachan* 'baby', *jun* 'pure', *hyonna* 'unexpected'
7. A short vowel + a consonant	*akka* 'deterioration', *ippa* 'sect', *ukkari* 'carelessly', *ekken* 'exceeding one's authority', *otto* 'husband'
8. A consonant + a short vowel + a consonant	*sakka* 'novelist', *jikken* 'experiment', *shuppatsu* 'departure', *zesshoku* 'fasting', *kokkyō* 'border'

Super-long syllables (three moras)

9. A long vowel + a nasal consonant	*ān* 'crying (onomatopoeia)', *īn da* 'It's OK', *ūn* '(interjection)', *ēn* 'crying (onomatopoeia)', *ōn* 'crying (onomatopoeia)'

10. A consonant + a long vowel + a nasal consonant	*gān* 'a boom (onomatopoeia)', *jīn* 'gene', *rēn* 'a lane', *rōn* 'a loan', *jān* '(interjection)', *chūnnappu* 'tune up', *jōn* 'Joan'
11. A long vowel + a consonant	*ātto odoroita* 'got surprised', *ītte itta* 'said OK', *ūtto unatta* 'groaned', *ētto odoroita* 'got surprised', *ōtto me o mihatta* 'became entranced'
12. A consonant + a long vowel + a consonant	*kātto natta* 'got angry', *jūtto shiteiru* 'is staying still', *zūtto mae* 'a long time ago', *kōtta* 'frozen'

The nasal consonant in syllable-final position, e.g. *hon* 'book' (lines 5, 6, 9, 10 above), counts as one mora and is referred to as a **MORAIC NASAL**.[5] It is pronounced as /m/ when followed by a /p/, /b/, or /m/; however, in this book, the moraic nasal is invariably represented as "n". For example, *sanpo* /sampo/ 'a stroll', *shinbun* /shimbun/ 'newspaper', *jinmyaku* /jimmyaku/ 'personal connection'. The moraic nasal is pronounced as /n/ when followed by /t/, /d/, or /n/, e.g. *juntaku* /juntaku/ 'abundant', *gendai* /gendai/ 'modern times', *konnan* /konnan/ 'suffering'. In all other positions, it is pronounced as the final consonant of English *sing*, [ŋ].[6] Before a vowel or /y/, an apostrophe is inserted after the moraic nasal to indicate a syllable boundary, e.g. *shin'ai* 'dear' vs. *shinai* 'inside a city'; *shin'yō* 'trust' vs. *shinyō* 'human waste'.

It seems reasonable to say that (i) a short vowel occupies one mora, (ii) a long vowel occupies two, and (iii) the mora count of the syllable-final nasal is identical with that of a short vowel. Lines 7, 8, 11, and 12, in which the first half of a long consonant counts as an independent mora, are worth further thought. For example, *akka* 'deterioration' has three moras, *a.k.ka*. As explained above, the realization of a long voiceless consonant is an elongated silence before it is released. Thus, the first half of the long /k/ is simply silence, and yet, it has the same moraic status as /a/ and /ka/.

Haiku poetry illustrates the significance of the mora in Japanese. Three verses consist of five, seven, and five moras. The following *haiku* are all by MATSUO Basho (1644–94), translated by William Cohen (1972).

> *Hi no michi ya* (5), *aoi katamuku* (7), *satsukiame* (5)
> 'In the rainy dusk, the flamboyant hibiscus, makes its own sunset'.
> (p. 48)

5 The syllable-final nasal consonant is sometimes called a *syllabic nasal*; however, it does not form a separate syllable.

6 The moraic nasal has more variations. For example, it is commonly a palatal (the roof of the mouth) nasal before a palatal sound, e.g. *kon'yaku* [koɲjɑkɯ] 'engagement'. It is sometimes realized as merely a nasalized vowel, e.g. *on'inron* [õiŋɾoŋ] 'phonology'.

This haiku consists solely of one-mora syllables. The next two *haiku* demonstrate that the moraic nasal and the first half of a long consonant are counted as separate moras.

> *Kono aki wa* (5), *nande toshiyoru* (7), *kumo ni tori* (5) (written two weeks before his death)
> 'In the autumn sky, its birds and its clouds, I feel my old age.'
> (p. 49)
>
> *Ume ga ka ni* (5), *notto hi no deru* (7), *yamaji kana* (5)
> 'Mountain road –, sun rising warm, into the plum scent.'
> (p. 44)

3.4 Vowel devoicing

Consider the phrase *ikimasu* 'I'll go'. It is not pronounced as /ikimasu/, but, rather, as /ikimasu̥/ (the small circle indicates that the vowel is devoiced). If the /u/ is not devoiced, the speech does not sound like Tōkyō Japanese. The so-called high vowels, /i/ and /u/, are normally devoiced in fluent running speech when flanked by voiceless consonants or when occurring in word-final position, e.g. *ki̥ken* 'danger', *ku̥suri* 'medicine', *aki̥* 'autumn', *aku̥* 'evil'. Devoicing of two or more consecutive syllables is possible (Hasegawa 1999a: 523–24), e.g. *ki̥fu̥kin* 'donation money', *hi̥ki̥tsu̥tsuaru* 'in the process of receding'. When all of the vowels in a word satisfy the devoicing condition, the final vowel is voiced, e.g. *ki̥ki* 'crisis', *tsu̥ki* 'moon', *ki̥ki̥tsu̥tsu* 'while listening'. Vowel devoicing is very common in Tōkyō Japanese.[7] In casual speech, I devoice even the low vowel, /a/, e.g. *Asḁku̥sa* '(a district in Tōkyō)'. A succession of voiceless consonants resulting from vowel devoicing gives a harsh impression to speakers of other dialects.

Voicing is a defining characteristic of vowels. The term **DEVOICED VOWEL** would therefore sound oxymoronic. Why not consider the vowel to be deleted, instead of devoiced? There are several reasons to prefer vowel devoicing to vowel deletion. Most prominently, vowel deletion would create a very complex sound system. That is, we would have to add a large number of complex syllables to the inventory, e.g. *ak*, as in *aki̥* 'autumn', which is not desirable. Secondly, although they are devoiced in normal running speech, vowels can be present in careful or emphatic speech. Thirdly, a devoiced vowel forms one mora in poetry.

> (1) *Ki̥ku no ka ya* (5), *Nara ni wa furuki̥* (7), *hotoke-tachi̥* (5)
> 'Chrysanthemums' scent – In the old town of Nara, Many ancient Buddhas.'
> (MATSUO Basho, translation by Makoto Ueda 1970/1982: 66)

[7] In Kansai dialects, vowels are fully voiced. The vowels in one-mora words are even frequently elongated and pronounced as two-mora words, e.g. *ki* 'tree' > *kī*; *ha* 'tooth' > *hā*.

And, finally, as discussed in the next section, syllables with a devoiced vowel can still carry a pitch accent.

3.5 Pitch accent

Accent is a prominence given to a certain syllable over other syllables in a word, independently of the mode in which this prominence is achieved. Languages are often characterized as **tonal** or **non-tonal**. Tonal languages utilize voice pitch to distinguish words, whereas non-tonal languages do not utilize pitch in this way. Tonal languages are further divided into **tone languages** (e.g. Chinese) and **pitch-accent languages** (e.g. most dialects of Japanese). In tone languages, no syllable is considered more prominent (i.e. accented) than any other(s). In pitch-accent languages, by contrast, the specification of one or more accent location(s) is sufficient to predict the tonal configuration, or melody, of the entire word.

Tōkyō Japanese has traditionally been described in terms of each syllable carrying either a high (H) tone or low (L) tone. For example, *yamazakura* 'wild cherry' is associated with the LHHLL pattern. Note that no syllable carries special prominence in this type of description. However, in recent decades, Tōkyō Japanese has been characterized as an archetypical pitch-accent language. That is, at most, one syllable is necessarily marked as accented. (Note that Japanese also has **accentless words**, without any marked accent.) In the case of *yamazákura*, marking the third syllable as accented correctly generates the LHHLL pattern by application of these rules (Miyata 1927).

		ya	*ma*	*zá*	*ku*	*ra*
(i)	Assign H to all syllables up to the accented syllable, if any, or to the final syllable if no syllable is marked accented.	H	H	H		
(ii)	Assign L to all syllables following the accented syllable.	H	H	H	L	L
(iii)	Reassign L to the initial mora unless the syllable is accented.	L	H	H	L	L

When the initial syllable is short, Rule (iii) applies straightforwardly as in *yamazákura*. When it is long, however, this initial lowering is optional. That is, *senséi* 'teacher' can be pronounced as *se* (L) *n* (H) *sé* (H) *i* (L) or *se* (H) *n* (H) *sé* (H) *i* (L).[8]

In this pitch-accent description, although only one syllable is marked as accented, every syllable is associated with either a H or L tone for pronunciation. However, acoustical analyses of Japanese utterances provide little evidence for such a claim. That is, tones appear to be more sparsely distributed

[8] A more natural pronunciation of the vowel sequence /ei/ is /ē/, e.g. *sensē*. However, this book consistently represents it as /ei/.

(Pierrehumbert and Beckman 1988). So in recent years it has been argued that Tōkyō Japanese is similar to **STRESS-ACCENT LANGUAGES** (e.g. English). In English declarative intonation, the most significant cue of accent is pitch, followed by length, and then loudness (Fry 1958). Accented syllables are typically pronounced with a high pitch that is longer and louder. In Japanese, on the other hand, accent is manifested solely by pitch; the accented syllable is neither longer nor louder than any others (Fujisaki and Sugito 1977).

One-syllable words have two accent patterns, two-syllable words have three patterns, three-syllable words have four patterns, and so forth. The addition of a *grammatical particle* (Chapter 7), e.g. *o*, after the word makes this clearer. For example:

(2) [One syllable word + particle]

kí o kiru	'cut a tree'	HL
ki o tsukeru	'pay attention'	LH [accentless]

(3) [Two syllable word + particle]

háshi o tsukau	'use chopsticks'	HLL
hashí o wataru	'cross a bridge'	LHL
hashi o aruku	'walk on the side of a road'	LHH [accentless]

(4) [Three syllable word + particle]

táyori o morau	'receive a letter'	HLLL
nakámi o shiraberu	'check the content'	LHLL
ikarí o osaeru	'restrain one's fury'	LHHL
mikata o tsukuru	'make an ally'	LHHH [accentless]

Two-syllable words have either the first syllable accented, e.g. *háshi* 'chopsticks', or the second syllable accented, e.g. *hashí* 'bridge', or are accentless, e.g. *hashi* 'side/edge'. As mentioned above, Japanese accent manifests as the H tone that is immediately followed by a L tone. (When the word is accentless, there is no fall from H to L.)

What happens when the accented syllable is devoiced is an interesting question. When no voicing is involved, neither H nor L tones can exist. Some researchers claim that accented syllables are not devoiced, but this claim is inaccurate, as demonstrated by *chí̥ka* 'underground', *kí̥kai* 'machine' and *akí̥kaze* 'autumn wind'. While it is possible to conceptualize such words as containing a sequence of H-L, in actuality, this tonal sequence is manifested as a single pitch fall. Therefore, if there is a noticeable drop in pitch, e.g. on *ka* in *chí̥ka*, the preceding segment *chí̥* is considered to be accented, i.e. apparently carrying a H tone (Sugito 1969/1982: 49–75; Hasegawa and Hata 1992; Hasegawa 1995). This ability to carry a pitch accent is one of the reasons that the vowels should be considered devoiced, rather than deleted.

3.6 Successions of vowels

Whenever I teach Japanese linguistics, one of the most controversial issues is whether or not Japanese has gliding (vis-à-vis steady-state) vowels as in English *I* [aɪ], *how* [aʊ], *bay* [eɪ], *boy* [oɪ] and *boat* [oʊ]. Many researchers claim that, unless each segment belongs to a different meaning unit, some sequences of non-identical vowels in Japanese should be considered gliding vowels (e.g. Poser 1985; Vance 1987; Kubozono 2001). That is, /ei/ in *neiki* 'breathing during sleep' consists of two syllables because they belong to different meaning units: *ne* 'sleep' + *iki* 'breath'. By contrast, vowels in such words as *ai* 'love' and *ao* 'blue' belong to a single meaning unit and, therefore, form only one syllable.

To me, this analysis sounds biased by native speakers' intuition or assumptions about the English sound system. Whereas vowel combinations in English are very limited (normally five, as listed above), all five Japanese vowels can appear in succession. Therefore, if we include all sequences of distinct vowels as single gliding vowels, we must recognize twenty vowels (/ai/, /au/, /ae/, /ao/, /ia/, /iu/, /ie/, /io/, etc.), in addition to five short vowels and five long vowels. All this adds unnecessary complexity to the Japanese sound system.

The second reason I argue against the gliding-vowel analysis is that each vowel in a sequence has the potential to carry an accent. In English, a gliding vowel behaves as a single unit in terms of accentual (stress) patterns.[9] That is, if the vowel in question has an accent, it is nonsensical to ask whether the first half or the second half is accented. In Japanese, by contrast, either vowel in a sequence can in principle carry an accent.

máiru	'go'	*maíru*	'be beaten'
háu	'to crawl'	*haúru*	'make acoustic feedback'
kíui	'kiwi'	*iú*	'to say'
kíe	'becoming a believer of a religion'	*ié*	'a house'
íon	'ion'	*shió*	'salt'
káeru	'go home'	*kotaéru*	'to answer'
áo	'blue'	*aóru*	'instigate'
kúi	'a stake'	*suímu*	'to swim'
tsúe	'a stick'	*ué*	'starvation'
Súō	(place name)	*uó*	'a fish'
óiru	'oil'	*oíru*	'grow old'
tóu	'ask'	*koúru*	'to love'
kóe	'a voice'	*hoéru*	'to bark'

I therefore consider each vowel in non-identical vowel sequences to count as one syllable.

9 The gliding vowel analysis of English is also justified historically. The gliding vowels in today's English were single vowels in Middle English. For example, as its spelling indicates, [eɪ] in *make* used to be a long /a/.

3.7 Sequential voicing (*rendaku*)

Words are frequently combined to express a new concept. Consider *iki* 'going' and *kaeri* 'coming back'. These words can be combined to express the concept *round trip*. In this case, the components are of equal status; neither is modifying the other. A word formed in this way is referred to as a **COORDINATE COMPOUND**.[10] By contrast, *kaeri* can be combined with a noun that specifies a location from which one returns, e.g. *Furansu* 'France', *kangoku* 'jail'. In this case, the combined word modifies or supplements the concept of *kaeri*; that is, the relationship between the components is stronger. In the former case, *kaeri* does not undergo any change in pronunciation, i.e. *iki-kaeri* 'round trip', but in the latter, the initial voiceless consonant of *kaeri* changes to its voiced counterpart, /g/, as in *Furansu-gaeri* 'returning from France', *kangoku-gaeri* 'returning from a jail'. This phenomenon is called **SEQUENTIAL VOICING**, or **RENDAKU** in Japanese. For example:

(5) /t/ → /d/ *tana* 'shelf' + *ta* 'rice field' → *tanada* 'terraced rice field'
/k/ → /g/ *waka* 'young' + *ki* 'tree' → *wakagi* 'young tree'
/s/ → /z/ *inu* 'dog' + *sori* 'sleigh' → *inuzori* 'dog sleigh'
/h/ → /b/ *mushi* 'insect' + *ha* 'tooth' → *mushiba* 'decayed tooth'

Note that when the /h/ undergoes *rendaku*, it becomes /b/. This irregularity is due to the fact that /h/ was originally /p/ (see Section 3.1).

Rendaku might have occurred regularly in ancient times (Miller 1967: 194–95), but in Modern Japanese it is impossible to predict whether or not the compound word in question will exhibit *rendaku*. Nevertheless, some generalizations have been proposed by researchers.

1. As mentioned above, with very few exceptions, *rendaku* does not occur in coordinate compounds.
2. Loan words from Chinese tend to resist *rendaku* (Okumura 1980), e.g. *kan* 'view' + *ten* 'point' → *kan-ten* 'viewpoint'; *hoken* 'insurance' + *kin* 'money' → *hoken-kin* 'insurance benefit'; *dai* 'big' + *shinsai* 'disaster' → *dai-shinsai* 'catastrophe'. There are numerous exceptions, e.g. *denryoku* 'electric power' + *kaisha* 'company' → *denryoku-gaisha*; *san* 'mountain' + *ka* 'river' → *san-ga* 'mountains and rivers'; *kin* 'gold' + *san* 'mountain' → *kin-zan* 'gold mine'; *bunko* 'library' + *hon* 'book' → *bunko-bon* 'paperback'.
3. Loan words from languages other than Chinese rarely undergo *rendaku*, e.g. *binīru* 'vinyl' + *tairu* 'tile' → *binīru-tairu* 'vinyl flooring'; *keshō* 'makeup' + *kēsu* 'case' → *keshō-kēsu* 'makeup pouch'; *kōn* 'corn' + *sūpu*

[10] A coordinate compound is also referred to as a **DVANDVA** compound, borrowed from Sanskrit, meaning *dva* 'two' + *n* 'and' + *dva* 'two'.

'soup' → *kōn-sūpu* 'corn soup'. The rare exceptions are: *ama* 'rain' (< *ame*) + *kappa* 'coat' (< Portuguese *capa*) → *ama-gappa* 'raincoat'; *uta* 'poetry' + *karuta* 'card' (< Portuguese *carta*) → *uta-garuta* 'poetry cards used for a game'; *mizu* 'water' + *kiseru* 'pipe' (from Cambodian *khsier*) → *mizu-giseru* 'hookah' (Vance 1987: 140–41).

4. Onomatopoeia and other sound-symbolic words (see Subsection 5.2.8) resist *rendaku*.
5. When the second component contains a voiced stop (/b/, /d/, /g/) or a voiced fricative (/z/), *rendaku* does not occur. For example, *kotsu* 'bone' + *tsubo* 'urn' → *kotsu-tsubo* 'cremation urn'; *hi* 'sun' + *kage* 'shade' → *hi-kage* 'shade'; *chichi* 'milk' + *shibori* 'squeeze' → *chichi-shibori* 'milking'; *aka* 'red' + *hige* 'beard' → *aka-hige* 'red beard'. This constraint is frequently referred to as **LYMAN'S LAW**, after Benjamin Smith Lyman (1835–1920), although he was not the first person to recognize this phenomenon (Shibatani 1990: 174).

4 Writing system

In striking contrast to its simple sound system, the Japanese language employs what is arguably the most convoluted writing system ever devised in human history. Sampson (1985: 173) declares,

> One reason why Japanese script deserves its place in this [Sampson's] book is as an illustration of just how cumbersome a script can be and still serve in practice.

This notoriety is ultimately due to the fact that Japanese writing evolved from that of Chinese, a language with substantially different sound and word formation systems.

4.1 Writing Japanese with kanji

In the late fourth and early fifth centuries AD, Chinese script was introduced to Japan under the tutelage of Korean scholars.[1] In Chinese (as spoken and written then), each meaning unit consisted of one syllable, and was represented by a single character called a **KANJI**, literally 'a character of the Han dynasty of ancient China' (206 BC–220 AD).

Recording a language with kanji is fundamentally different from doing it with, say, the Roman alphabet, which is designed to represent speech sounds. The method of recording speech sounds is termed a **PHONOGRAPHIC WRITING SYSTEM** (*phono* = sound). In kanji writing, by contrast, ideas, rather than sounds, are represented, so it is called an **IDEOGRAPHIC WRITING SYSTEM** (*ideo* = idea).[2] Each kanji is associated with one or more

[1] Ancient Japanese people were aware of the existence of kanji as early as the second and first centuries BC. However, they considered kanji merely decorative patterns, not understanding their genuine significance (Atsuji 1994: 210–13).

[2] Kanji is often characterized as **LOGOGRAPHIC** (*logo* = word); that is, each kanji represents a word, rather than an idea. When used for Chinese, kanji can be logographic. However, for recording Japanese, considering them as ideographs is deemed more appropriate. That is, the same kanji frequently appears in different, but conceptually related, words, e.g. 食堂 *shokudō* 'eating place', 食べる *taberu* 'to eat'.

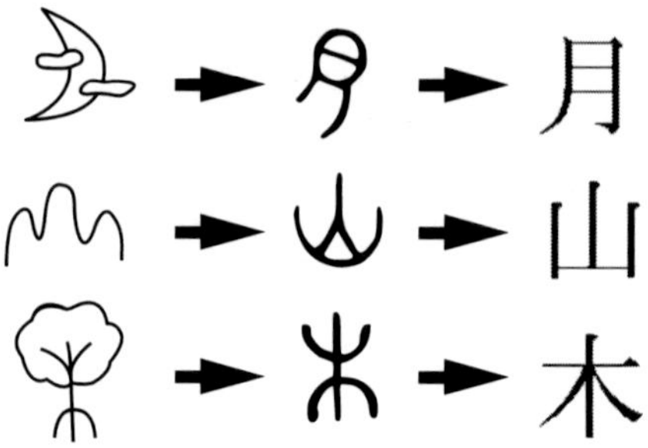

Figure 4.1. Pictographs.

strings of sounds in a particular language in which it serves, but, unlike phonographic systems, this graph–sound association is secondary to the representation of ideas.

Some kanji are **PICTOGRAPHS** (*picto* = picture), originally pictorial representations of what they designate. For example, in Figure 4.1, from top to bottom, the characters represent *moon*, *mountain*, and *tree*. However, most kanji are more abstract than pictorial.

Modern languages make limited use of ideographic writing: namely Arabic numerals. Symbols like *1*, *2*, *3*, etc. are pronounced differently from language to language, but they are nonetheless decipherable, regardless of actual pronunciation. Even within English, the character *2* is pronounced differently in *2* and *2nd*, but the idea/meaning remains constant – a quintessential characteristic of ideographs.

Ideographic writing can be considered less efficient than phonographic writing because it requires a huge inventory of symbols. A phonographic writing system, on the one hand, needs only to represent speech sounds – and each language uses a fairly small number out of all possible sounds that humans can intentionally produce. Therefore, if selected sounds are to be recorded in writing, a small set of symbols will suffice. By contrast, the ideas that humans can think of are limitless, so if they are to be recorded straightforwardly, an infinite number of symbols is mandatory – which is, of course, impossible. Kanji writing, therefore, is a compromise: each kanji character represents a group of ideas or an abstract concept, rather than a specific idea.

Ideographs do have an advantage over phonographs, however, as exemplified by Arabic numerals, wherein symbols are language independent. For example, in phonographic writing, a string of symbols such as *two* is meaningless unless one knows the language, whereas the symbol *2* conveys its meaning independent of knowledge of the language.

Japanese recorders borrowed from Chinese scribes not only kanji characters but also many words that they represented, e.g. *gakusei* 学生 'student' and *sensei* 先生 'teacher'. The loan words from Chinese are called **SINO-JAPANESE WORDS** (discussed further in Section 5.1). In kanji writing, ideas are frequently decomposed and represented by a combination of characters. The notion of student is written as 学 'to learn/study' + 生 'life' (= learning/studying person), and the notion of teacher as 先 'preceding' + 生 'life' (= preceding person). In Sino-Japanese words, the pronunciation of each kanji is highly consistent: 生 is read as /sei/ in both *gakusei* 学生 and *sensei* 先生.

The notion of 'tomorrow' was represented in Chinese as 明 'shining' + 日 'day', which was pronounced approximately as /myōnichi/ when it was borrowed. Because kanji are language independent, we can read 明日 as *tomorrow*. When we do so, it is not meaningful to specify that 明 is read as /to/ and 日 as /morrow/. Rather, 明日 as a whole is assigned the sound value /tomorrow/. This is an illustration of how ancient Japanese people adapted kanji to represent their language. The Japanese word for 'tomorrow' was *ashita*, so it was recorded as 明日 and read as /ashita/. Like the English example of 'tomorrow', it is not the case that the reading of 明 is /a/, and the reading of 日 is /shita/; rather, 明日 as a whole is read as /ashita/. The Japanese translation equivalent assigned to a kanji or a sequence of kanji is called a **KUN READING** 'the instructional reading', whereas the original Chinese pronunciation is called an **ON READING** 'the phonetic reading'.[3]

The granularity of Japanese concepts, as encoded in words, was coarse with respect to Chinese. That is, a single concept in Japanese was dissected into separate concepts, each represented by different kanji in Chinese. The Japanese verb *toru* 'take', for example, covered a range of meanings – and thus kanji – in Chinese. Therefore, when written in Japanese, these different meanings were, and still are, expressed with different kanji as shown in (1) below.

(1) 取る take (general)
 採る get/gather/pick fruits, nuts, flowers, etc.
 捕る catch fish, animals, etc.
 摂る intake
 執る take a pen in hand, manage, perform the duties of an office
 盗る steal
 撮る take a picture[4]

[3] Kanji were introduced to Japan during three separate periods – the fifth to sixth centuries, the seventh to eighth centuries and the twelfth to seventeenth centuries. Their *on* readings differed each time, reflecting different dialects of the reigning dynasties of the time, referred to as **GO-ON** (the fifth to sixth centuries), **KAN-ON** (the seventh to eighth centuries) and **TŌSŌ-ON** (the twelfth to seventeenth centuries). Consequently, some kanji have more than one *on* reading. For example, 行 is read as /gyō/ as in *gyōretsu* 行列 'a line/procession' (*go-on*), as /kō/ as in *kōdō* 行動 'action' (*kan-on*), and as /an/ as in *angya* 行脚 'pilgrimage' (*tōsō-on*).

[4] Before the invention of the camera, 撮 was used for picking up something with one's fingers.

With some ingenuity, it is possible to record English sentences with kanji. For example, *I bought a house* can be written as 私 (= I) 買 (= buy) 家 (= house). Although the *a* in *a house* is not represented, it is easily inferable from the context. But what about *bought*? 私買家 could mean 'I'll buy a house', so it is necessary to indicate that the event has taken place in the past. One solution is to write 私買-x家, where "-x" marks the past tense. The question then is what symbol should be used for "-x"? There are two possibilities: one is to use a kanji that represents the meaning *past*; the other is to use a kanji that is pronounced with a sound similar to the English past-tense marker *-ed*. The latter is preferable because what should be recorded here is not an independent word *past*, but, rather, a meaning that "modifies" the word *buy*.

To use a kanji for its sound value, rather than for its meaning, was revolutionary – an amalgamation of ideographic and phonographic writing systems. This is the inception of "a quite astonishingly complicated method of making language visible" (Sampson 1985: 172).[5] Although Chinese writing might appear daunting to the uninitiated, it is much simpler than Japanese, which involves unparalleled complexity (p. 172). This mixed writing system invented by the ancient Japanese is known as **MAN'YŌGANA** because it was used extensively in *Man'yōshū* ['Collection of Ten Thousand Leaves'], a literary anthology consisting of over 4,500 poems that was compiled circa 672–771 AD (Miller 1971: 4).[6]

The representation of Japanese speech sounds with kanji required many adjustments because of the drastic discrepancy between the two languages' sound systems. The Chinese pronunciation of many kanji utilizes a final consonant, but the syllabic structure of Japanese strictly dictates vowels at the end of all syllables, with or without an initial consonant, e.g. /a/ or /ta/. *Man'yōgana* resolved this problem in two ways. The most common method was to ignore the final consonant, e.g. *ten* 天 for recording the Japanese sound /te/. The less common way was to make a kanji represent two syllables by adding a vowel at the end, e.g. *kem* 険 became /kemu/ (Seeley 2000: 50; the sounds in these examples are slightly simplified for expository purposes).

Man'yōshū is written exclusively with kanji, but it actually involves three distinct writing systems. In the first, a kanji stands for its *kun* reading. This is an instance of ideographic writing. The second makes use of the Chinese sound (*on* reading) and ignores the meaning of the Chinese word that the kanji designates. This is phonographic writing. The third uses only the sound of the

[5] The use of kanji for their sound values was also practiced in ancient China, e.g. in the translation of Sanskrit documents. However, such usage was highly limited, mostly to recording of proper nouns (Kokugogakkai 1980: 846).

[6] *Gana* in *Man'yōgana* was derived from *kana* by sequential voicing (see Section 3.7). *Kana* 仮名 originally meant a 'tentative character'.

kun reading, ignoring the meaning of the corresponding Japanese word. This is another phonographic writing method. These three encoding systems mixed freely in the text without indication of how each kanji should be interpreted. For example, in (2).

(2) 此川乃絶事奈久
kono kafa no tayuru koto naku
'This river never ceases flowing'

此 *kono* 'this', 川 *kafa* 'river', 絶 *tayuru* 'to cease' and 事 *koto* 'an event' are *kun* readings, i.e. in ideographic writing. By contrast, 乃 *no*, 奈 *na*, and 久 *ku* are *on* readings, i.e. in phonographic writing. An example of the third type is 夏樫 for *natukashi* 'longed for', where /natu/ is the *kun* reading of 夏 'summer' and /kashi/ is the *kun* reading of 樫 'oak tree',[7] their meanings being totally ignored (Yasuda 1988: 66). Miller (1967: 98) describes this state of affairs as follows:

> The method of writing a given word in any particular instance would depend on scribal preference, the amount of empty space available for inscribing a given text (because *man'yōgana* used more graphs per Japanese word than *kun* writing), or other esthetic factors, and there is ample evidence that the early Japanese scribes took considerable pleasure in the possibilities for elegant graphic variation which the script afforded them.

4.2 Development of kana syllabaries

While *man'yōgana* continued to be used until the twelfth century (Tsukimoto 1988: 76), two syllabaries were invented during the ninth century, each originating as an aid for reading Chinese texts (Seeley 2000: 62). One of these is **HIRAGANA** 'plain kana', highly simplified cursive forms of kanji; the other is **KATAKANA** 'partial kana', consisting of distinctive features of kanji. Table 4.1 shows these syllabaries together with the kanji from which each kana character was derived (Shōgaku Tosho 1981: 2610–11).[8]

The sounds corresponding to ゐ, ヰ /wi/ and ゑ, ヱ /we/ became obsolete, and these characters are no longer used in Modern Japanese. The sound を, ヲ /wo/ is identical to お, オ /o/ in most dialects of Modern Japanese; however, the characters を and ヲ are still in use for representing the **ACCUSATIVE CASE PARTICLE** (see Section 7.2). The original kanji from which the katakana ン was derived is unknown.

In *man'yōgana*, voiceless and voiced consonants were distinguished, e.g. 加 for /ka/ vs. 我 for /ga/, but in hiragana and katakana writing, this distinction

7 The sound value of 樫 could have been /katsi/ or /kachi/. See Subsection 1.2.2.
8 The earliest sound chart of this kind appeared in 1079; the organization of sounds was derived from the sound chart of Sanskrit (Komatsu 1981: 36, 52–53).

Table 4.1 *Japanese syllabaries.*

Hiragana										Katakana									
a		i		u		e		o		a		i		u		e		o	
安	あ	以	い	宇	う	衣	え	於	お	阿	ア	伊	イ	宇	ウ	江	エ	於	オ
ka		ki		ku		ke		ko		ka		ki		ku		ke		ko	
加	か	幾	き	久	く	計	け	己	こ	加	カ	幾	キ	久	ク	介	ケ	己	コ
sa		shi		su		se		so		sa		shi		su		se		so	
左	さ	之	し	寸	す	世	せ	曽	そ	散	サ	之	シ	須	ス	世	セ	曽	ソ
ta		chi		tsu		te		to		ta		chi		tsu		te		to	
太	た	知	ち	州	つ	天	て	止	と	多	タ	千	チ	川	ツ	天	テ	止	ト
na		ni		nu		ne		no		na		ni		nu		ne		no	
奈	な	仁	に	奴	ぬ	禰	ね	乃	の	奈	ナ	二	ニ	奴	ヌ	禰	ネ	乃	ノ
ha		hi		fu		he		ho		ha		hi		fu		he		ho	
波	は	比	ひ	不	ふ	部	へ	保	ほ	八	ハ	比	ヒ	不	フ	部	ヘ	保	ホ
ma		mi		mu		me		mo		ma		mi		mu		me		mo	
末	ま	美	み	武	む	女	め	毛	も	万	マ	三	ミ	牟	ム	女	メ	毛	モ
ya				yu				yo		ya				yu				yo	
也	や			由	ゆ			与	よ	也	ヤ			由	ユ			与	ヨ
ra		ri		ru		re		ro		ra		ri		ru		re		ro	
良	ら	利	り	留	る	礼	れ	呂	ろ	良	ラ	利	リ	流	ル	礼	レ	呂	ロ
wa		wi				we		wo		wa		wi				we		wo	
和	わ	為	ゐ			恵	ゑ	遠	を	和	ワ	井	ヰ			恵	ヱ	乎	ヲ
n														n					
无	ん													?	ン				

was lost until the Kamakura period (1185–1333), when various diacritic markers became popular. The present system of using a set of "dots" (which appear more like tiny, diagonal slashes) for voicing, e.g. ぐ and グ for /gu/, and a small circle for /p/, e.g. ぱ and パ for /pa/, was developed during the Edo period (1603–1868) (Kokugogakkai 1980: 585–56).[9]

The invention of hiragana and katakana enabled Japanese people to record their language with their own script, rather than in a roundabout fashion with the Chinese writing system. Why they maintained the use of kanji is puzzling. Another enigma is that they kept two functionally identical sets of phonographic script, in regard to which Sampson (1985: 172–73) remarks:

Japanese society, during much of the period in which the script was developed, was characterized by the existence of an aristocratic class many members of which lacked

9 The set of two dots for voicing is called a **DAKUTEN** (*daku* 'voicing' + *ten* 'dot'); the small circle is called a **HAN-DAKUTEN** (*han* 'half' + *dakuten*). The latter does not make sense unless one is taking historical changes into consideration (see Section 3.1). A *han-dakuten* derives the consonant /p/ from the consonant /h/, both of which are voiceless.

political power or indeed any serious employment, so that their only role in life was as definers and producers of cultural norms, ways of civilized living . . . As a natural result, many aspects of Japanese culture, including its writing, were greatly elaborated, made exquisite and intellectually rich rather than straightforwardly functional. (This contrasts with the case of China, which at most periods of its history was a rather down-to-earth, workaday civilization and where the script, for instance, was shaped in the historical period largely by civil servants who had plenty to keep them busy.)

Kabashima (1977: 139–43) offers a different view. He notes that it took about 500 years to develop the kana script. Considering the simple sound structure of Japanese, this is excessively long; recording Japanese speech sounds required a mere ninety or so characters. He concludes that the purpose of continuing to import kanji was not to record the Japanese language, but to learn advanced Chinese culture and political systems. Abandoning kanji meant severance of precious resources. Until the end of the Edo period, all governmental documents were written in modified Chinese (Tsukishima 1988: 63),[10] and the ruling class was not concerned with establishing orthography for recording the Japanese language.

Regarding the existence of two kana syllabaries, Kabashima explains that they carried distinctly different functions. Katakana was developed as a supplement to the kanji writing system and used where kanji could not function well, e.g. as grammatical markers unique to the Japanese language. It was also used as an aid for reading Chinese texts. The shapes of katakana matching those of kanji esthetically, these two kinds of scripts formed a single writing system. For this reason, katakana was freely used in official documents. Hiragana, on the other hand, was detached from the kanji writing system and used in private spheres, e.g. in diaries, and was never used in government documents until the end of World War II (Tsukishima 1988: 63).

Kabashima (1977: 143) points out two additional reasons why kanji were not replaced entirely by kana. One is kanji's faster processing time, an advantage of ideographic writing over phonographic writing. Compare, for example, *fifty-three thousand six hundred and ninety one* with *53,691*. Likewise, 五万三千六百九十一 '53,691' is faster to comprehend than ごまんさんぜんろっぴゃくきゅうじゅういち or *goman-sanzen-roppyaku-kyūjū-ichi*.

Productivity was the second reason kanji was retained. For over 200 years, since 1633 during the Edo period, Japan secluded itself from foreign countries other than China, Korea, the Netherlands, and Ryukyus (present day Okinawa). When it opened its doors in the middle of the nineteenth century, enormous influences from the West swept across Japan. Literary works and

[10] This style of writing is called **KANBUN** 'Sinico-Japanese'. In *kanbun* prose, kanji are arranged according to the conventions of literary Chinese grammar.

treatises from Britain, France, Germany, Italy, Russia, and the United States were translated into Japanese at such an astonishing speed that it became necessary to coin new words to express western concepts. Such pivotal terms as *shakai* 社会 'society',[11] *kojin* 個人 'individual', *kenri* 権利 'a right', and *jiyū* 自由 'freedom' were all created during this period (Yanabu 1982). Without kanji's productive power, this momentous enterprise could not have been accomplished.

In Modern Japanese texts, kanji, hiragana, and katakana are freely mixed as illustrated in (3), the opening sentence of KAWABATA Yasunari's *Yukiguni* ['Snow Country'].

(3) 国境の長いトンネルを抜けると雪国であった。

'The train came out of the long tunnel into the snow country.' (Translation by Edward Seidensticker)

[Lit.] When (the train) went through a long tunnel at the border, it was snow country.

4.3 Orthography reforms

Even after the practice of writing became widespread among commoners during the Edo period (1603–1868), the highly complicated, mixed writing system of kanji and kana was retained. The first person who called for reform was MAEJIMA Hisoka, a translator at Kaiseijo (Institute for Western Learning). Because learning kanji was so time consuming, in 1867 (a year before the Meiji Restoration), Maejima presented to the shogun TOKUGAWA Yoshinobu a petition for the abolition of kanji. If the Japanese language were written only with kana, he argued, young people would be able to spend time learning other, more practical, and beneficial subjects.[12] However, because it was submitted in the middle of the political turmoil that ended the 265-year Tokugawa shogunate, the petition understandably failed to receive attention.

In the early Meiji period (1868–1912), the idea of abolishing kanji gained some popularity. The *Kana no kai* (Kana Club), leader of the Kana Only Movement, was formed in 1883, and the *Rōmaji kai* (Romanization Club), advocating the exclusive use of the Roman alphabet, was founded in 1885. (The *Romaji kai* became disunited due to different Romanization systems, which will be explained in Section 4.6.) Despite these movements, the reform

[11] FUKUZAWA Yukichi (1834–1901), the founder of Keio University, translated "society" as *ningen kōsai* 人間交際 'human association' (Yanabu 1982: 6–7).

[12] Maejima founded in 1873 *Mainichi Hiragana Shinbun*, a newspaper written exclusively in hiragana.

strategy adopted by the Meiji government, as first proposed by FUKUZAWA Yukichi, did not abolish kanji, instead restricting the number of kanji in use (Amanuma 1988: 1234).

All attempts to reform the Japanese writing system failed until the end of World War II in 1945. For example, in 1900, the Ministry of Education issued a new regulation that restricted the number of kanji taught in elementary schools to about 1,200, and in 1923, the Interim Committee on the National Language announced the *Jōyō kanjihyō* 常用漢字表 (List of Kanji for General Use), which consisted of 1,962 characters. The number of kanji on this list was reduced in 1931 to 1,858. In 1942, the Deliberative Council of the National Language compiled the *Hyōjun kanjihyō* 標準漢字表 (List of Standard Kanji), which enlarged the list to 2,528 characters.

In 1946, the Allied High Command, which occupied post-war Japan, sent an American delegation to Japan to study its education system. The delegation recommended the adoption of the Roman alphabet as the orthography of the Japanese language, because, it claimed, kanji use was not only inefficient, but also functioned as an underpinning of Japan's isolationism and exclusivism (Watabe 1995: 336–38). Nevertheless, the Japanese were able to reject the delegation's order.

In 1946, effective language reform began when two regulations were promulgated. One was the *Tōyō kanjihyō* 当用漢字表 ('List of Kanji for Current Use'), consisting of 1,850 characters; the other was the *Gendai kanazukai* 現代かなづかい ('Modern Kana Usage'). The latter contrasted with **REKISHITEKI KANAZUKAI** ('Historical Kana Usage'), which diverged significantly from actual pronunciation due to (i) reflection of original Chinese pronunciation rather than contemporary pronunciation of Sino-Japanese words, and (ii) sound change of native Japanese words. As an example of (i), the kanji pronounced as /gō/ in Modern Japanese were written as がう *gau* (拷), がふ *gafu* (合) and ごふ *gofu* (業). Examples of (ii) include the sound sequence しお /shio/, which was also written as しほ *shiho* 'salt' and しをり *shiwori* 'a bookmark'.

In 1948, the Ministry of Education selected 881 kanji from the *Tōyō kanjihyō* and designated them as *Kyōiku kanji* 教育漢字 (Education Kanji), compulsory learning during the first six years of schooling.[13] The *Tōyō kanji onkunhyō* 当用漢字音訓表 ('List of *On* and *Kun* for the Kanji for Current Use') was also issued in 1948, which limited the *on* and *kun* readings of the 1,850 *tōyō kanji*. For example, out of the four common ways of writing *tasukeru* 'to help' (助ける, 援ける, 扶ける, 介ける), only 助ける was selected in the orthography. In 1949, the *Tōyō kanji jitaihyō* 当用漢字字体

[13] Today, compulsory education in Japan is nine years at primary and middle schools.

表 (List of Forms for the Kanji for Current Use) was announced, and different forms of the same kanji identical in meaning (e.g. 宝, 寶 *takara* 'treasure') began to be regulated.

In 1959, twenty-six **OKURIGANA** rules were promulgated. Recall the example of 私買家 in Section 4.1, where a special character was needed to express the past tense. Such "additional" kana characters are called *okurigana*: the kana characters that, in the case of verbs, are appended after the kanji to indicate tenses and other grammatical categories. Japanese verbs are of three types, referred to as **U-VERBS**, **RU-VERBS** and **IRREGULAR VERBS** (see Subsection 5.2.2). The *okurigana* rules stated that with *u*-verbs, kanji represents the invariant parts, whereas the variant syllables are written as *okurigana*, as in the examples in (4), where the invariant part /ka/ is represented by the kanji 買:

(4)	買う	*ka-u*	[conclusive form]
	買わない	*ka-wanai*	[negative form]
	買います	*ka-imasu*	[polite, non-past tense]
	買った	*ka-tta*	[plain, past tense]
	買えば	*ka-eba*	[hypothetical form]

For *ru*-verbs, *okurigana* normally begins with the last syllable of the invariant part.

(5)	食べる	*ta-beru*	[conclusive form]
	食べない	*ta-benai*	[negative form]
	食べます	*ta-bemasu*	[polite, non-past tense]
	食べた	*ta-beta*	[plain, past tense]
	食べれば	*ta-bereba*	[hypothetical form]

When the invariant part of a *ru*-verb consists of one syllable, *okurigana* begins with the second syllable of the word.

(6)	見る	*mi-ru*	[conclusive form]
	見ない	*mi-nai*	[negative form]
	見ます	*mi-masu*	[polite, non-past tense]
	見た	*mi-ta*	[plain, past tense]
	見れば	*mi-reba*	[hypothetical form]

In 1973, the Japanese government took a more liberal stance by considering the preceding orthographic reforms as guidelines rather than restrictions. The *Tōyō kanji onkunhyō* of 1948 was revised, adding more readings as well as irregular *kun* readings, e.g. *heya* 部屋, *inaka* 田舎, *kyō* 今日, *musuko* 息子, *tsuyu* 梅雨. The *okurigana* rule of 1959 was also amended to permit more flexibility in usage.

In 1981, the *Jōyō kanjihyō* 常用漢字表 ('List of Kanji for General Use') – a revision of the 1946 *Tōyō kanjihyō* – was promulgated. This guide for kanji use contained 1,945 characters that pertain to Japanese social life, while not encroaching upon usage in such specialized domains as science, technology, and the arts. However, in order to facilitate smooth communication, this list was expected to be respected as much as possible in documents associated with laws, official announcements, newspapers, magazines, etc. (Nomura 1988: 333). In 2010, the *Jōyō kanjihyō* was revised, expanding a total of 2,136 characters, 820 of which have only *on* readings, and 77 only *kun* readings.

The *Jōyō kanjihyō* encourages the use of **FURIGANA**, also called **RUBI**, when the reading of a kanji or kanji word is anticipated to be difficult. *Furigana* are reduced-size kana added to the right side (when the text is written vertically) or top (when written horizontally) of a kanji or kanji word as in example (7).[14]

まんよう が な
(7) 万葉仮名 *man'yōgana*

This convention of *furigana* use can be exploited to add phonetically meaningful elements to the reading. For example, in the translation of a foreign text into Japanese, an original word in another language can be expressed as *furigana* in Japanese. In the following sentences, the Japanese reading of 雷 is *kaminari*, and that of 閃光 is *senkō*. Nevertheless, in the translation, their *furigana* read サンダー /sandā/ and フラッシュ /furasshu/, respectively, which represent the original English sounds adjusted to the Japanese sound system.

(8) "Thunder!" Miller yelled.

A moment later came the response: "Flash! Come on across!" (Max Collins, Saving Private Ryan)

サンダー
「 雷 ！」ミラーがどなった。
フラッシュ
ほどなく合言葉が返ってきた。「閃光 ！ こっちへ来い！」(translation by FUSHIMI Iwan)

4.4 The frequencies of kanji in Japanese texts

Naturally, some kanji are used more frequently than others. As shown in Table 4.2, the top 500 most-frequently used kanji account for about 75 percent of all occurrences in Japanese texts. If the top 1,000 are considered, the rate of recognition rises to approximately 90 percent (Nomura 1988: 342–43).[15]

[14] Traditionally, following Chinese, Japanese has been written vertically from right to left. Most texts were written in this way until the end of World War II. Since then, an increasing numbers have been written horizontally, excepting newspapers, magazines, and Japanese language textbooks (Satake 1988: 318).

[15] The newspaper data are derived from three newspapers issued in January–December 1966; those of magazines are from ninety magazines published in January–December 1956.

Table 4.2 *Kanji frequency of use.*

Kanji	Newspapers (%)	Magazines (%)
Top 10	10.6	8.8
50	27.7	25.5
100	40.2	37.1
200	56.1	52.0
500	79.4	74.5
1,000	93.9	90.0
1,500	98.4	96.0
2,000	99.6	98.6
2,500	99.9	99.5
3,000	99.9	99.9

4.5 Hiragana and katakana conventions

In both kana orthographies, palatalized syllables and long consonants (see Chapter 3) are represented by smaller characters, e.g. きゃ, キャ /kya/, きゅ, キュ /kyu/, きょ, キョ /kyo/, いっぱ, イッパ /ippa/, いった, イッタ /itta/, いっか, イッカ /ikka/.

Long vowels in hiragana are generally represented by the repetition of the vowel, e.g. おかあさん *okaasan* 'mother', おにいさん *oniisan* 'brother', すうがく *suugaku* 'mathematics', おねえさん *oneesan* 'sister', とおり *toori* 'street'. In Sino-Japanese words, however, long /e/ is represented as the sequence of /ei/, e.g. えいが *eiga* 'movie', and long /o/ as /ou/, e.g. そう *sou* 'a monk'. In the katakana orthography, long vowels are written with a bar, e.g. マーク *māku* 'a mark', チーズ *chīzu* 'cheese', ウール *ūru* 'wool', メール *mēru* 'mail', コース *kōsu* 'a course'.

Today, hiragana is an integral component of the Japanese writing system, but the use of katakana remains rather limited, used mainly for representing scientific terms, expressive vocabulary (see Subsection 5.2.8), names and loan words from languages other than Chinese, and for emphasis, similar to the function of italics in English writing.

To write a foreign word in katakana, some adjustment must be made to conform to Japanese syllable-structure constraints. Because, with few exceptions, Japanese does not permit a sequence of consonants, a vowel must be inserted between adjacent consonants. The default vowel is /u/ except after /t/ or /d/ when the vowel /o/ is inserted.[16] Figure 4.2 illustrates the word *strike*,

[16] In some older loan words, /i/, rather than /u/, was added after a /k/, e.g. ケーキ *kēki* 'cake', ジャッキ *jakki* 'jack (to jack up)', ステーキ *sutēki* 'steak', デッキ *dekki* 'deck of a ship/train'.

s		t		ri	ke	
	↑		↑			↑
	u		o			u
ス		ト		ライ	ク	

Figure 4.2. Vowel insertion.

which according to Japanese sound structure is pronounced /sutoraiku/.[17] (For the general rules of the katakana orthography, see Hasegawa *et al.* 2005.)

4.6 Romanization

While the writing conventions of hiragana, katakana, and kanji are taught in Japanese schools, those of *rōmaji* normally are not. Therefore, deviant **ROMANIZATION** is commonly observed in writings of both native and non-native speakers of Japanese. As shown in Table 4.3, two Romanization systems are in general use: the **HEPBURN SYSTEM** (**HEBON-SHIKI**) and the **CABINET ORDINANCE SYSTEM** (**KUNREI-SHIKI**). The Hepburn System, commonly used in general writing, was invented by the American missionary James Curtis Hepburn (1815–1911) and is based on English writing conventions. The Cabinet Ordinance System, which evolved from the Japanese syllabaries proposed in 1885, was established by the Japanese government in 1937 and has been used less frequently, mainly for scholastic writing because of its internal systematicity.

Long consonants are written by repeating the consonant – as in *ippo* 'one step', *itten* 'one point', *ikkai* 'one time' – or the first letter of the consonant as in *isshun* (Hepburn) or *issyun* (Cabinet Ordinance) 'one moment'. For the long /t/ when palatalized before /i/, the Hepburn system allows an exception, representing it as *tch*: *gatchi* 'agreement', not **gacchi*. (* indicates that the expression is conventionally unacceptable.) The Cabinet Ordinance System does not make such an exception, writing *tti*, as in *gatti*.

Because the English language does not distinguish between short and long vowels, neither did Hepburn when he made his transcriptions in Japanese: e.g. both *yoko* 横 'side' and *yōkō* 陽光 'sunlight' are written as *yoko*. Most Japanese–English dictionaries use the Hepburn system with vowel length marking.

The hiragana writing convention should not be followed in Romanization: **koko ha* (ここは), **koko wo* (ここを), **koko he* (ここへ). Instead, these

[17] *Strike* is written in two ways: one with /u/, ストライク, meaning a 'strike in a baseball game', and the other with /i/, ストライキ, meaning a 'labor strike'.

Table 4.3 *Romanization systems.*

Hepburn system						Cabinet ordinance system				
あ	a	i	u	e	o	a	i	u	e	o
か	ka	ki	ku	ke	ko	ka	ki	ku	ke	ko
が	ga	gi	gu	ge	go	ga	gi	gu	ge	go
さ	sa	shi	su	se	so	sa	si	su	se	so
ざ	za	ji	zu	ze	zo	za	zi	zu	ze	zo
た	ta	chi	tsu	te	to	ta	ti	tu	te	to
だ	da	ji	zu	de	do	da	di	du	de	do
な	na	ni	nu	ne	no	na	ni	nu	ne	no
は	ha	hi	fu	he	ho	ha	hi	hu	he	ho
ば	ba	bi	bu	be	bo	ba	bi	bu	be	bo
ま	ma	mi	mu	me	mo	ma	mi	mu	me	mo
や	ya		yu		yo	ya		yu		yo
ら	ra	ri	ru	re	ro	ra	ri	ru	re	ro
わ	wa					wa				
ん	n/m					n				
きゃ	kya		kyu		kyo	kya		kyu		kyo
ぎゃ	gya		gyu		gyo	gya		gyu		gyo
しゃ	sha		shu		sho	sya		syu		syo
じゃ	ja		ju		jo	zya		zyu		zyo
ちゃ	cha		chu		cho	tya		tyu		tyo
にゃ	nya		nyu		nyo	nya		nyu		nyo
ひゃ	hya		hyu		hyo	hya		hyu		hyo
びゃ	bya		byu		byo	bya		byu		byo
みゃ	mya		myu		myo	mya		myu		myo
りゃ	rya		ryu		ryo	rya		ryu		ryo

examples should be written as *koko wa*, *koko o*, *koko e*. Romanization is basically for those who do not read hiragana; therefore, the use of a hiragana convention that deviates from the actual pronunciation does not make sense.

In hiragana, *ō* is frequently written as おう (e.g. 東京 とうきょう, *Tōkyō*), and *ē* as えい (e.g. 英語 えいご, *ēgo* 'English'). This discrepancy between written and spoken language is the result of historical changes. While *ēgo* can still be carefully pronounced today as *eigo*, no one calls the city **Toukyou*, however carefully it is articulated. Therefore, the long *o* must be transcribed as *ō*, not as *ou*. An exception to this rule occurs when *o* and *u* belong to different parts of a word: e.g. in *omo-u*, the *u* is a marker of the non-past tense (see Section 9.2). In such a case, the word should be transcribed with *ou*. The おう sequence in a proper name is sometimes written as *oh*: e.g. *Ohta* (太田). As for *ei*, some people write it more faithfully to the pronunciation as *ē*, but this book employs the slightly more conservative spelling of *ei*.

The moraic nasal (see Section 3.3) is invariably written as *n* in the Cabinet Ordinance System, but in the original Hepburn System it is written as *m* when followed by a *p*, *b*, or *m*: e.g. *sampo* 'taking a walk', *shimbun* 'newspaper', *jimmyaku* 'personal connections'. However, this book employs a modified version of the Hepburn System in which the moraic nasal is always written as *n*.

Part II

Lexicon

5 Vocabulary

5.1 Word categories

The Japanese vocabulary consists of **NATIVE JAPANESE** words, **SINO-JAPANESE** words (borrowings from Chinese), **FOREIGN LOAN WORDS** (borrowings from languages other than Chinese), and combinations of them (i.e. **HYBRID** words). Chinese loan words that were incorporated into Japanese prior to Japan's regular contact with China are so deeply integrated that they are likely categorized today as native words, e.g. *kiku* 'chrysanthemum', *uma* 'horse', *ume* 'Japanese apricot' (Komatsu 2001: 34–35). The vocabulary of *Man'yōshū* ('A Collection of Ten Thousand Leaves'), written circa 670–770 AD, consists of 99.6 percent native Japanese words. Massive waves of borrowings from Chinese then commenced. *Genji monogatari* ('The Tale of Genji') (c. 1000) contains up to 8.8 percent Sino-Japanese words, and *Tsurezuregusa* ('Essays in Idleness') (c. 1330) 28.1 percent (Miyajima 1971).

Native words form the basic stratum of Japanese vocabulary, e.g. *yama* 'mountain', *hana* 'flower', *tori* 'bird', *aruku* 'to walk', *ugoku* 'to move', *akai* 'red', *samui* 'cold'. Sino-Japanese words are conceived of as more sophisticated, like Latinate words in English (compare *get* and *acquire*). Texts with high concentrations of Sino-Japanese words impress native speakers as being more formal, decorous, and dignified in tone, while those full of native words are considered more informal and amiable. Although Sino-Japanese words were borrowed in ancient times, most native speakers today can still distinguish them from native Japanese words because of their clearly differing sound patterns. For example, the second mora (see Section 3.3) of a two-mora *on* reading of a kanji is restricted to /i/, /u/, /ki/, /ku/, /chi/, /tsu/, and /n/ (Nomura 1988: 334).

(1) /i/ 開 *kai* 'open', 明 *mei* 'bright', 生 *sei* 'life'
/u/ 同 *dou* /dō/ 'same',[1] 幸 *kou* /kō/ 'happiness', 有 *yuu* /yū/ 'exist'

[1] This vowel sequence is pronounced as a long /o/, but the old pronunciation /ou/ is maintained in hiragana orthography.

/ki/	域 *iki* 'limits', 敵 *teki* 'enemy', 力 *riki* 'power'
/ku/	学 *gaku* 'study', 白 *haku* 'white', 格 *kaku* 'rank'
/chi/	罰 *bachi* 'punishment', 吉 *kichi* 'fortune', 七 *shichi* 'seven'
/tsu/	物 *butsu* 'thing', 月 *getsu* 'moon', 発 *hatsu* 'depart'
/n/	金 *kin* 'gold', 新 *shin* 'new', 天 *ten* 'heaven'

Foreign words convey a nuance of refinement and modernity, particularly favored in the fashion and technology fields. There are many doublets and even triplets that express essentially identical meanings, differing only in stylistic flavor, as in (2).

(2)

	Native	S-J	Foreign
'cancellation'	*torikeshi*	*kaiyaku*	*kyanseru*
'happy'	*shiawase*	*kōfuku*	*happī*
'home'	*uchi*	*katei*	*hōmu*
'hotel'	*yado(ya)*	*ryokan*	*hoteru*
'lunch'	*hirugohan*	*chūshoku*	*ranchi*

Examples of hybrid words are listed in (3).

(3)

Native + S-J	*natsu* 'summer' + *fuku* 'clothes'	→ 'summer apparel'
S-J + native	*kan* 'can' + *kiri* 'cut'	→ 'can opener'
Native + foreign	*nama* 'raw' + *hamu* 'ham'	→ 'uncured ham'
Foreign + native	*kōhī* 'coffee' + *mame* 'bean'	→ 'coffee beans'
S-J + foreign	*yasai* 'vegetable' + *sarada* 'salad'	→ 'vegetable salad'
Foreign + S-J	*supīdo* 'speed' + *ihan* 'violation'	→ 'speed violation'

Until the Meiji Restoration (1867–68), Sino-Japanese words had never dominated Japanese vocabulary (Morita 1989: 73). However, as discussed in Section 4.2, during the Meiji period a huge inventory of words became necessary in order to translate Western concepts. Compared with native Japanese, Sino-Japanese word formation rules are more adaptive and productive; therefore, an enormous Sino-Japanese vocabulary was coined. When counting distinct words that appeared in magazines published in 1994, Sino-Japanese words surpassed native Japanese words (Ito 2007: 12), a subject that will be discussed in detail below.

The term *foreign loan words* normally refers to borrowings from Western languages, although they sometimes include Korean and other Asian languages; these borrowings are typically written in *katakana*. Japan's contact with the West started with the shipwreck of Portuguese merchants in 1543, which was followed by a Dutch ship in 1600. Early borrowings from these languages are exemplified in (4).

(4) a. From Portuguese

kappa	'coat'	*karuta*	'playing cards'
pan	'bread'	*tabako*	'tobacco'

b. From Dutch

buriki	'tin'	*garasu*	'glass'
kaban	'bag'	*randoseru*	'backpack for school'

In the early nineteenth century, contacts with Great Britain, France, and Russia were established. Then, in 1853, Commodore Matthew Perry of the United States arrived and forced Japan to commence diplomatic and commercial relationships. In 1867, increasing pressure from Western powers ended more than 200 years of the Tokugawa shogunate government, leading to the restoration of the emperor to power. During the years that followed, an unprecedented number of translations from English, French, German, and Russian into Japanese enriched and changed the Japanese language, not only in vocabulary but also in sentence structure (see, for example, Sections 11.3 and 12.6).

Ito (2007: 11) analyzes two survey reports by Kokuritsu Kokugo Kenkyūjo (The National Institute for Japanese Language and Linguistics) on the vocabularies of 90 magazines published during 1956 (438,135 total word count; 39,930 distinct words) and those of 70 magazines published during 1994 (word count of 738,377; 59,222 distinct words). The percentages in (5) and (6) are adjusted slightly from the original because Ito employs a different categorization system.

(5) Total word occurrences (%)

	Native	S-J	Foreign	Hybrid
1956	53.7	41.3	4.7	0.3
1994	41.6	45.9	10.5	2.0

(6) Distinct words (%)

	Native	S-J	Foreign	Hybrid
1956	36.7	47.3	9.8	6.2
1994	27.0	35.2	31.5	6.3

Significant changes in vocabulary composition occurred during these four decades. In 1956, although distinct native words were fewer in number than Sino-Japanese words, they surpassed Sino-Japanese words in total word count. That is, native words formed a more basic vocabulary stratum, making it necessary to use them repeatedly in Japanese writing. In 1994, however, Sino-Japanese words exceeded native Japanese words not only in the distinct word count, but also in total frequency of use.

The growth of foreign vocabulary has been astonishing. In 1994, almost one third of distinct words were of foreign origin, surpassing native Japanese words and approaching the Sino-Japanese stratum. However, that high volume of distinct words constitutes only 10.5 percent of the entire word count. That is, although significant, foreign words are not fundamental, and are thus not used as repeatedly as native or Sino-Japanese words.

As with Sino-Japanese words, the structure of English loan vocabulary is considered by native speakers of Japanese to be highly versatile, encouraging them to derive many English-like words such as in (7).

(7)	*abauto*	(< about)	= perfunctory, e.g. *abauto na hito* ‘perfunctory person’
	afutā sābisu	(< after service)	= after-sales service, product support
	furī daiaru	(< free dial)	= toll-free telephone number
	furītā	(< freeter)	= part-time worker
	ōdā sutoppu	(< order stop)	= final order at a restaurant or bar (closing time)
	sābisu	(< service)	= complimentary service (without charge), free gift
	sukinshippu	(< skinship)	= bonding

5.2 Word classes

5.2.1 Nouns

A defining characteristic of a **NOUN** is that it can function as the subject or object of a clause (these terms are explained in detail in Sections 7.1 and 7.2). Nouns form the most dynamic word class, as new nouns are coined on a daily basis. They are subcategorized into **COMMON NOUNS** and **PROPER NOUNS** (i.e. names of people, places, and things). When a common and a proper noun are combined, English is inconsistent in relative order, e.g. Mono Lake vs. Lake Tahoe, Mammoth Mountain vs. Mount Denali. In Japanese, by contrast, the proper noun always precedes the common noun, e.g. *Aoyama-dōri* ‘Aoyama Street’, *Sumida-gawa* ‘Sumida River’, *Shimogamo-jinja* ‘Shimogamo Shrine’, *Iwai-shima* ‘Iwai Island’, *Takao-san* ‘Mount Takao’.

In Japanese, the singular–plural distinction is not obligatory and normally not specified. When specification of the number is significant, it can be expressed with numeral quantifiers (see Subsection 5.2.7).

When a noun modifies another noun, the **GENITIVE** ($\approx$ possessive) particle *no* is inserted, e.g. *nihon* ‘Japan’ *no kuruma* ‘car’ = ‘Japanese car’, *watashi* ‘I’ *no kuruma* = ‘my car’, *isha* ‘physician’ *no Nobuko* ‘Nobuko, the physician’.

VERBAL NOUNS, a special category, designate actions or events rather than persons or things. As nouns, they can function as the subject or object of clauses. However, unlike ordinary nouns, they can form a verb when combined with the verb *suru* ‘do’. A vast majority of verbal nouns are Sino-Japanese in origin (e.g. (8a)), but virtually all English verbs can function as verbal nouns (e.g. (8b)). Native Japanese nouns are only rarely used as such (8c).

(8) a. Sino-Japanese

hōkoku suru	'to report'
kenkyū suru	'to study'
ryōri suru	'to cook'
sanpo suru	'to take a walk'

b. Foreign

mēru suru	'to email'
ofā suru	'to offer'
ritaia suru	'to retire'
sēbu suru	'to save'

c. Native

hirune suru	'to take a nap'
itoma suru	'to leave'
koi suru	'to love'
kokoro suru	'to attend to'

5.2.2 Verbs

As do verbs of many of the world's languages, Japanese verbs **CONJUGATE**, i.e. change forms according to language-specific grammatical categories. (Details of conjugation will be discussed in Section 6.1.) When analyzing verb conjugations, it is necessary to recognize the invariant part (called the **STEM**) from the variant parts. The stems of Japanese verbs end either in a consonant (e.g. *yom-* as in *yom-u* 'read') or in a vowel (e.g. *mi-* as in *mi-ru* 'see'). Japanese verbs have customarily been categorized into three groups: *u*-verbs (consonant-ending stems), *ru*-verbs (vowel-ending stems), and two irregular verbs (i.e. *kuru* 'come' and *suru* 'do'). According to Kokuritsu Kokugo Kenkyūjo (1964: 64), approximately 63 percent of verbs are *u*-verbs, 32 percent are *ru*-verbs, and the remaining 5 percent includes variations and compounds of the irregular verbs.

There is also a category of words that are collectively referred to as the **COPULA**, i.e. linking words between the subject and the predicate (see Section 7.1). In English, *be* and its variations in tense, person, and number (*am*, *are*, *be*, *been*, *is*, *was*, *were*) serve this purpose. In Japanese, its plain forms are *da* (non-past tense) and *datta* (past tense), while its polite forms are *desu* (non-past tense) and *deshita* (past tense). There is no singular and plural variation. The tenses are explained in Chapter 9, and the plain–polite stylistic distinction in Chapter 20.

5.2.3 Adjectives

Two types of words in Japanese can be categorized as adjectives, i.e. their primary functions are to modify nouns (**ATTRIBUTIVE USE**) and to express the state of affairs of the entity designated by the grammatical subject

(**PREDICATIVE USE**) – see (9) for an example of each. Like verbs, but unlike nouns, adjectives can be modified by a degree adverb, e.g. *totemo* 'very'.

(9) a. Attributive

Omoshiroi	*hon*	*o*	*katta.*
interesting	book	ACC	bought

'(I) bought an interesting book.'

b. Predicative

Kono	*hon*	*wa*	*omoshiroi.*
this	book	TOP	is.interesting

'This book is interesting.'

The first type is referred to as ***I*-ADJECTIVES** because their dictionary forms end in the vowel /i/, e.g. *akarui* 'bright', *kurai* 'dark'. *I*-adjectives conjugate like verbs, which will be discussed in Section 6.3. The inventory of *i*-adjectives is surprisingly meager, and the formation of new *i*-adjectives is not productive. Among the 15,712 distinct words appearing in the selected 13 magazines published during 1953–54, only 232 (1.5%) were *i*-adjectives (Kokuritsu Kokugo Kenkyūjo 1958: 81).

The second type of adjective is the ***NA*-ADJECTIVE**, so called because *na* (derived from the copula) is inserted when this type of adjective modifies a noun. In their predicative use as well, the copula is necessary, as is the case with Japanese nouns and English adjectives (see (10)). Thus, while *i*-adjectives act more like verbs (i.e. they conjugate), *na*-adjectives act more like nouns. Because of this, they are sometimes called **NOMINAL ADJECTIVES** or **ADJECTIVAL NOUNS**.

(10) a. Attributive

Benri	*na*	*jisho*	*o*	*katta.*
useful	COP	dictionary	ACC	bought

'(I) bought a useful dictionary.'

b. Predicative

Kono	*jisho*	*wa*	*benri*	*da.*
this	dictionary	TOP	useful	COP

'This dictionary is useful.'

In contrast to the unproductive nature of *i*-adjectives, virtually any foreign word that is semantically appropriate can be used as a *na*-adjective. Approximately 80 percent of *na*-adjectives are Sino-Japanese or foreign (Tamamura 1975: 93).

(11) a. Native Japanese

suki na	*tabemono*
favorite	food
shizuka na	*heya*
quiet	room

b. Sino-Japanese

kodoku na	*hito*
lonely	person
kirei na	*kuruma*
beautiful	car

c. Foreign

shinikaru na	*iken*
cynical	opinion
rīzunaburu na	*nedan*
reasonable	price

5.2.4 *Adverbs*

ADVERBS form a heterogeneous category in form as well as in meaning. Typically, they modify verbs, adjectives, other adverbs, or the entire sentence.

(12) a. Modifying a verb

Watashi	*wa*	*yoku*	*warau.*
I	TOP	often	laugh

'I laugh often.'

b. Modifying an adjective

Sora	*ga*	*totemo*	*[utsukushii/kirei da].*
sky	NOM	very	beautiful

'The sky is very beautiful.'

c. Modifying another adverb

Watashi	*wa*	*hotondo*	*itsumo*	*kaidan*	*o*	*tsukau.*
I	TOP	almost	always	stair	ACC	use

'I almost always use the stairs.'

d. Modifying a sentence

Tabun	*shiken*	*wa*	*yasashii*	*darō.*
probably	examination	TOP	easy	COP.CNJ

'Probably, the examination will be easy.'

5.2.5 *Pronouns*

The English first- and second-person pronouns, *I/me* and *you*, are like mathematical variables. They refer simply to the speaker and the addressee, respectively. The third-person pronouns – *he*, *she*, *they* – contain more information, encoding (in the singular) the gender of the **REFERENT** (i.e. the entities that are referred to by these expressions). Japanese first- and second-person pronouns are much richer in information, designating the speaker's gender and sometimes his/her age group, some aspects of the relationship between the **INTERLOCUTORS** (i.e. conversation participants), and/or the formality of the speech situation. For the first-person pronoun, (13) shows the words which are commonly employed.

(13)
a. *watakushi* gender-neutral, formal
b. *watashi* When used by a male, the speech situation is formal; when by a female, it can be formal or casual.
c. *atashi* feminine, casual
d. *boku* masculine, casual
e. *ore* masculine, very casual
f. *boku-chan* used by a male infant

The use of the first-person pronoun is often unnecessary for communication and, therefore, customarily avoided in Japanese. Explicitly translating into Japanese each occurrence of *I/me*, as in (14b), will result in a grammatical but culturally unbearable sentence. It sounds so egocentric, like "Me, me, me!" in English. A more natural translation would be (14c).

(14) a. *My friend told me that if I read that book, it would have a great impact on me.*

b.

Watashi	*no*	*tomodachi*	*wa*	*watashi*	*ni,*	*moshi*	*watashi*	*ga*	
I	GEN	friend	TOP	I	to	if	I	NOM	
sono	*hon*	*o*	*yondara,*	*sore*	*wa*	*watashi*	*ni*	*ōkina*	*shōgeki*
that	book	ACC	if.read	that	TOP	I	to	great	impact
o	*ataeru*	*darō*	*to*	*itta.*					
ACC	give	COP.CNJ	QUOT	said					

c.

Tomodachi	*wa*	*moshi*	*sono*	*hon*	*o*	*yondara,*	*ōkina*
friend	TOP	if	that	book	ACC	if.read	great
shōgeki	*o*	*ukeru*	*darō*	*to*	*itta.*		
impact	ACC	receive	COP.CNJ	QUOT	said		

'[Lit. (Literally)] (A) friend told (me) if (I) read that book, (I) would receive a great impact.'

The second-person pronoun is even more restricted than the first, its use possibly creating the impression of pointing to or at the addressee with a finger and saying "YOU!" Again, in most contexts, explicitly specifying the addressee as a referent is unnecessary. When clarification is desired, the addressee's name (e.g. *X-san*), his/her title (e.g. *gichō* 'chairperson', *sensei* 'teacher', *shachō* 'company president'), or a kinship term (e.g. *okāsan* 'mother' when talking to the mother of one's friend) is used. Several variations of the second-person pronoun are listed in (15).

(15) a. *anata* gender-neutral
b. *anta* gender-neutral, casual
c. *otaku* gender-neutral, casual or polite according to the context
d. *kimi* masculine, casual
e. *omae* masculine, very casual and/or intimate
f. *temē* masculine, vulgar

Japanese third-person pronouns include *kare* (masculine, singular), *kanojo* (feminine, singular), *karera* (masculine, plural), and *kanojora* (feminine, plural). However, the Japanese language did not spontaneously develop such pronouns. Rather, they were coined only as translational equivalents of those in European languages. Yanabu (1982: 197) reports that *Haruma wage* (a Dutch–Japanese dictionary compiled in the eighteenth century) included *kare*, a distal demonstrative (*that over there*; see Chapter 26), as a translation of the masculine third-person singular pronoun, whereas the feminine counterpart was translated as a compound word consisting of *kare* and *onna* 'woman'. This word was pronounced *kano onna* 'that woman' until the late nineteenth century when it evolved to the present-day pronunciation *kanojo*.

Derived from demonstratives, Japanese third-person pronouns strongly imply the presence of the speaker/writer as the central entity relative to which another entity is located. Because of this emphasis on the presence of the speaker/writer, third-person pronouns are rarely used in the composing of Japanese legal documents and newspaper articles, which employ objective writing styles.

Unlike European languages Japanese pronouns can be modified in various ways. In (16a), *kono watashi* 'this I' emphasizes the speaker, 'I myself'.

(16) a. *Gichō* *ga* *kono watashi* *o* *kōnin* *ni* *shimei shita.*
chairperson NOM this I ACC successor as appointed
'[Lit.] The chairperson appointed this me as (his/her) successor.'
'The chairperson appointed me as (his/her) successor.'

b. *Waratte iru anata* *wa* *totemo* *miryokuteki* *da.*
smiling you TOP very charming COP
'[Lit.] Smiling you are very charming.'
'You are very charming when smiling.'

c. *Watashi* *wa* *kyūkachū no [kare/kanojo]* *o* *hōmon shita.*
I TOP during.vacation GEN [he/she] ACC visited
'[Lit.] I visited him/her, who was on leave of absence.'
'I visited him/her during his/her leave of absence.'

5.2.6 *Particles*

Particles are short (usually one or two moras) dependent elements, unable to stand independently in a sentence. They are subcategorized into four types.

CASE PARTICLES, the first type, are like English prepositions; however, they follow the noun upon which they depend. They are, therefore, sometimes called **POSTPOSITIONS**. The term **CASE** refers here to a feature that designates the syntactic or semantic function of the constituent with respect to the predicate. (Case particles will be discussed in detail in Chapter 7.) Members of the second type are called **SENTENCE-FINAL PARTICLES**. They occur at the end of a sentence, e.g. *ne*, *sa*, *wa*, *yo*. (Chapter 23 is devoted to dealing with them.) The third type, **ADVERBIAL PARTICLES**, occur after a noun, adverb, or case particle. This type includes *dake* 'only', *made* 'even', *mo* 'also', *sae* 'even', and *shika* 'only'.

(17) a. *Midori* *dake* *kita.*
Midori only came
'Only Midori came.'
b. *Midori* *[made/sae]* *kita.*
Midori even came
'Even Midori came.'
c. *Midori* *shika* *konakatta.*
Midori only came.not
'Nobody but Midori came.'

The fourth type is **CONJUNCTIVE PARTICLES**, e.g. *ga* 'and/but', *kara* 'because', *node* 'because', *noni* 'although', *to* 'and'.

(18) a. *Guai* *ga* *warui* *node* *shusseki* *shimasendeshita.*
health.condition NOM bad because attendance did.not
'Because my health was bad, I didn't attend.'
b. *Guai* *ga* *warui* *noni* *shusseki* *shimashita.*
health.condition NOM bad though attendance did
'Although my health was bad, I attended.'

5.2.7 *Numeral classifiers*

In English, numbers can be added directly to countable nouns, but in Japanese such specification of quantity requires a **NUMERAL CLASSIFIER**, according to the shape and other characteristics of the noun's referent.

(19) a. *nin* for people e.g. *kodomo 3-nin* 'three children'
b. *tō* for large animals e.g. *ushi 3-tō* 'three cows'
c. *hiki* for small animals or fish e.g. *neko 2-hiki* 'two cats'
d. *wa* for birds e.g. *suzume 2-wa* 'two sparrows'
e. *mai* for flat objects e.g. *CD 3-mai* 'three CDs'
f. *hon* for long objects e.g. *ninjin 2-hon* 'two carrots'
g. *dai* for cubic objects e.g. *kuruma 2-dai* 'two cars'

5.2.8 Ideophones

One of the defining characteristics of human language is arbitrariness. That is, there is no logical or natural relationship between the word and its meaning. For example, there is no reason to call the planet we live on the *globe* (English) or *chikyū* (Japanese). The association is a mere convention, and, therefore, we must learn each word on its own. However, some vocabulary in human languages is not so arbitrary. Although vaguely and sometimes synesthetically,[2] we can intuitively perceive some correspondences between sound and meaning. The vocabulary words created as a result of such experience are called **IDEOPHONES** (ideo = idea, phone = sound). Japanese is well known for its rich inventory of ideophones.

The clearest ideophone subtype is onomatopoeia, which mimic actual sounds. However, such a direct correspondence between sound and meaning is occasionally extended to visual, glossal (i.e. taste), tactile (i.e. touching), and other kinds of sensations and impressions.

(20) a. Auditory

wanwan	'bow-wow'	*kokekokkō*	'cock-a-doodle-doo'
piyopiyo	'chirp'	*nyā*	'mew'

b. Visual

meramera	'flare up'	*pikapika*	'glitter'
pechanko	'flattened/crushed'	*hirahira*	'flutter'

c. Glossal

sakusaku	'crisp'	*hirihiri*	'spicy hot'
assari	'simple'	*kotteri*	'rich/heavy'

d. Tactile

subesube	'smooth'	*zarazara*	'rough'
nebaneba	'sticky'	*bichabicha*	'soggy'

Ideophones often reflect universal **SOUND SYMBOLISM**. Voiceless consonants in expressive vocabulary are often associated with smallness and low intensity, whereas voiced consonants are associated with largeness and high intensity: e.g. *kirakira* (twinkling star) vs. *giragira* (sizzling sun); *korokoro* (rolling of a ball) vs. *gorogoro* (rolling of a rock). High front vowels like /i/ are associated with smallness, lightness, brightness, sharpness, etc., whereas low vowels like /a/ are associated with largeness, heaviness, dullness, vigor, etc.: e.g. *pichipichi* (tight) vs. *dabudabu* (loose, sagging); *shitoshito* (gentle rain) vs. *zāzā* (downpour). Long sounds are

[2] Synesthesia is a condition in which one type of sensation (e.g. sound) evokes sensation of different modality (e.g. color).

associated with sustained activities; repetitions of short sounds are associated with repetitive actions: e.g. *bōbō* (burn vigorously) vs. *pachipachi* (clapping).[3]

English has a large number of verbs, many of which express both the action and the manner in which the action is performed. Japanese, by contrast, has fewer such verbs; the manner is instead typically expressed by an ideophone, as the following contrasts demonstrate.

(21)

English	Japanese	
Manner ± Action	Manner	Action
chuckle	*kusukusu*	*warau*
guffaw	*geragera*	*warau*
grin	*niyatto*	*warau*
smile	*nikoniko*	*warau*
howl	*wanwan*	*naku*
sob	*shikushiku*	*naku*
weep	*samezameto*	*naku*

5.3 Word frequencies

As mentioned earlier, Kokuritsu Kokugo Kenkyūjo conducted a survey and analyzed a corpus of Japanese texts sampled from 70 magazines published during 1994.[4] A total of 738,377 instances of 59,222 distinct, independent words were identified. (Also analyzed were 327,240 instances of 175 distinct dependent words (e.g. particles) which are not included in the discussion here.) Because these 70 magazines were carefully selected from a wide variety of interests (e.g. art, automobiles, computers, cooking, the economy, electronics, fashion, finance, games, gardening, graphics, history, hobbies, home-making, literature, medicine, politics, science, sports, travel), the results can be considered representative of the vocabulary size of eloquent, adult native speakers.

In the survey, the most frequently occurring words were the following:

(22)
1. *suru* 'do', 15,981 times
2. *ichi* 'one', 11,299 times
3. *ni* 'two', 8,988 times
4. *iru* 'exist, stay, be', 8,642 times
5. *jū* 'ten', 8,239 times
6. *san* 'three', 7,910 times
7. *go* 'five', 6,716 times
8. *man* 'ten thousand', 6,192 times
9. *nijū* 'twenty', 5,888 times
10. *iu* 'say', 5854 times

[3] For universal sound symbolism, see articles in Hinton *et al.* 1994 and especially Ohala 1994.
[4] www.ninjal.ac.jp/archives/goityosa/goihyo_frq_ver.1.0.txt.

Table 5.1 *Word frequency of use (%).*

Top 40 words	25	Top 500	51	Top 6,000	82
Top 50	28	Top 600	54	Top 7,000	84
Top 60	30	Top 700	55	Top 8,000	85
Top 70	32	Top 800	57	Top 9,000	86
Top 80	33	Top 900	58	Top 10,000	87
Top 90	34	Top 1,000	60	Top 20,000	93
Top 100	35	Top 2,000	69	Top 30,000	96
Top 200	42	Top 3,000	74	Top 40,000	97
Top 300	46	Top 4,000	78	Top 50,000	99
Top 400	49	Top 5,000	80	Top 59,222	100

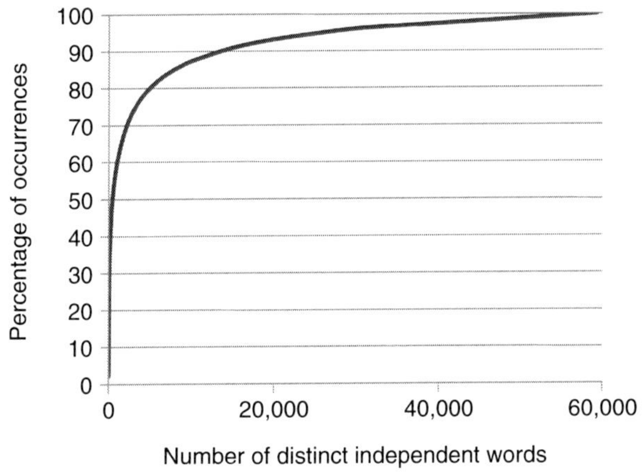

Figure 5.1. Word frequency of use.

These ten words constitute up to 12 percent of the total word count. When we consider the top 20 words, the coverage extends to 18 percent, and the top 30, 22 percent. Table 5.1 and Figure 5.1 provide the word totals ranked by frequency of use and their corresponding percentages based upon the 738,377 total word count.

Suppose that learners of Japanese acquire vocabulary in the order of usage frequency. The first 500 words will enable them to recognize approximately 50 percent of words appearing in common texts. When they learn 3,000 distinct words, their recognition rates rise to 75 percent. Certainly it depends on the text type, but the 80 percent recognition rate enabled by 5,000 words may be sufficient for most casual reading.

By contrast, 42,528 of 59,222 distinct words (72%) occurred no more than three times in the entire corpus.

(23) a. 28,866 words (49%) occurred only once, e.g. *aikurushii* ‘charming, lovely’, *inishie* ‘ancient times’.
b. 9,072 words (15%) occurred only twice, e.g. *yūzora* ‘evening sky’, *warifuru* ‘allot’.
c. 4,590 words (8%) occurred only three times, e.g. *enso* ‘chlorine’, *ōhi* ‘empress’.

Therefore, the lack of such a large vocabulary is unlikely to hinder the reading comprehension of most texts.

6 Word structure

6.1 Verb conjugation

As time passes, all languages change. Such historical changes make it difficult, if not impossible, to enumerate all Japanese verb conjugation forms in a coherent, straightforward paradigm.[1] One possibility is provided below. Although it deviates from the traditional grammar and all hitherto proposed analyses, in formulating it I have striven for simplicity and consistency, while sacrificing reflection on historical change.

I posit ten conjugation categories, beginning with the **NEGATIVE** form, indicated by the negative auxiliary *-(a)nai*. The **ADVERBIAL** form resembles the English gerund (*-ing* form),[2] as it can stand as a noun, and is normally followed by some auxiliary, e.g. *-(i)masu*, which simultaneously indicates politeness as well as the non-past tense (see Chapter 9 for a discussion of tense). The **CONCLUSIVE** form indicates the non-past tense; dictionaries utilize it as a basis for the ordering of entries. The **HYPOTHETICAL** form appears in a conditional construction (see Chapter 18). The **IMPERATIVE** form can be utilized for issuing commands, although it sounds very coarse, and is, therefore, rarely used in modern colloquial Japanese. With the **VOLITIONAL** form, the speaker encourages the addressee and/or the speaker him/herself to perform the action designated by the verb stem. Traditional grammar, however, does not recognize this form in its conjugation paradigm. The volitional form of a *u*-verb is traditionally to be derived from the **MIZEN-KEI** 'irrealis form' (i.e. the negative form without *-nai*) followed by the auxiliary *-u*, which underwent sound change during the Edo period (1603–1868) (Suzuki 1977: 215),

[1] For detailed discussions of the problems involved in a paradigmatic representation of verb conjugation, see Teramura (1984: 19–49), Shibatani (1990: 221–35), and Komatsu (1999/2001: 185–89).

[2] The adverbial form is often identified as *infinitive* or *gerundive*. However, its functions differ from those forms in European languages. The term *adverbial form* captures its range of uses without claiming any such cross-linguistic similarities.

e.g. *kak-a-u* 'I shall write/let's write' became *kak-ō*. There is no explanation as to why *yō* is attached in the case of *ru*-verbs (e.g. *tabe-yō*) and irregular verbs (*ko-yō*, *shi-yō*). Unlike *u*-verbs, deriving *yō* from *ya-u* has no historical precedent. As such, this chapter posits the volitional as a separate verb form. The **TE-FORM** will be explained shortly; the **TA-FORM** indicates the past tense. The **CAUSATIVE** form will be discussed in Chapter 11, and the **PASSIVE** form in Chapter 12.

(1) *U*-verbs, e.g. *kak-* 'write'[3]

a. Negative	*kak-anai*	'not write'
b. Adverbial	*kak-i*	'writing'
c. Conclusive	*kak-u*	'write'
d. Hypothetical	*kak-eba*	'if (someone) writes'
e. Imperative	*kak-e*	'Write!'
f. Volitional	*kak-ō*	'I shall write, let's write'
g. *Te*-form	see below	
h. *Ta*-form	see below	'wrote'
i. Causative	*kak-aseru*	'make (someone) write'
j. Passive	*kak-areru*	'be written'

(2) *Ru*-verbs, e.g. *tabe-* 'eat'

a. Negative	*tabe-nai*	'not eat'
b. Adverbial	*tabe*	'eating'
c. Conclusive	*tabe-ru*	'eat'
d. Hypothetical	*tabe-reba*	'if (someone) eats'
e. Imperative	*tabe-ro*	'Eat!'
f. Volitional	*tabe-yō*	'I shall eat, let's eat'
g. *Te*-form	*tabe-te*	
h. *Ta*-form	*tabe-ta*	'ate'
i. Causative	*tabe-saseru*	'make (someone) eat'
j. Passive	*tabe-rareru*	'be eaten'

(3) *K-* 'come'

a. Negative	*k-onai*	'not come'
b. Adverbial	*k-i*	'coming'
c. Conclusive	*k-uru*	'come'
d. Hypothetical	*k-ureba*	'if (someone) comes'
e. Imperative	*k-oi*	'Come!'
f. Volitional	*k-oyō*	'I shall come, let's come'

[3] In traditional Japanese grammar, the vowels that immediately follow the *u*-verb stem are considered part of the verb conjugation, which are then followed by an auxiliary element. For example, the negative form of *kak-* is analyzed as *kak-a* + *nai* and the hypothetical form as *kak-e* + *ba*. With *ru*-verbs, by contrast, the auxiliaries are attached directly to the verb stem, e.g. *tabe* + *nai* and *tabe* + *reba*. I take the position that the vowels in *u*-verbs are a part of the auxiliary, e.g. *-anai* and *-eba*. This practice of positing two forms of auxiliaries, e.g. *-anai* and *-nai*, makes the description of verb conjunction simpler and more coherent because we need to posit two forms of auxiliaries anyway, e.g. the hypothetical form being *-ba* with *u*-verbs, but *-reba* with *ru*-verbs, and the conclusive form being *-u* with *u*-verbs, but *-ru* with *ru*-verbs.

g.	*Te*-form	*k-ite*	
h.	*Ta*-form	*k-ita*	'came'
i.	Causative	*k-osaseru*	'make (someone) come'
j.	Passive	*k-orareru*	(ungrammatical in English)

(4) *S-* 'do (something)'[4]

a.	Negative	*sh-inai*	'not do'
b.	Adverbial	*sh-i*	'(someone) will do'
c.	Conclusive	*s-uru*	'do'
d.	Hypothetical	*s-ureba*	'if (someone) does'
e.	Imperative	*sh-iro*	'Do!'
f.	Volitional	*sh-iyō*	'I shall do, let's do'
g.	*Te*-form	*sh-ite*	
h.	*Ta*-form	*sh-ita*	'did'
i.	Causative	*s-aseru*	'make (someone) do'
j.	Passive	*s-areru*	'be done'[5]

The *u*-verb *ar-u* 'exist/be' (normally used in modern Japanese for an inanimate entity) is irregular; its negative form is *nai*, not **ar-anai*. Like *ar-u*, the stem of a considerable number of *u*-verbs ends in the consonant /r/, e.g. *ir-u* 'need', *hashir-u* 'run', *kaer-u* 'go home', *kir-u* 'cut', *mamor-u* 'protect', *nor-u* 'ride', *shir-u* 'know', *tor-u* 'take'. When presented in the conclusive form, such verbs cannot be distinguished from *ru*-verbs. In order to identify the stem boundary, another form is needed: for example, *ir-anai* (the *u*-verb *iru*) 'do not need' vs. *i-nai* (the *ru*-verb *iru*) 'do not exist'; *kir-anai* (the *u*-verb *kiru*) 'do not cut' vs. *ki-nai* (the *ru*-verb *kiru*) 'do not wear'.

The *te*-form is also excluded in the traditional conjugation paradigm because it was originally derived from the adverbial form by addition of the conjunctive particle *te*, e.g. *tabe-te* 'eat', *k-i-te* 'come', *sh-i-te* 'do'. Due to historical change (see Subsection 1.2.3), the *te*-forms of *u*-verbs are very complex, varying according to the stem-final consonant:

(5)	a.	*ka-u*[6]	'buy'	*kat-te*
	b.	*kak-u*[7]	'write'	*kak-i-te* > *ka-i-te*

[4] The stem of this verb is uniformly *s-*; the alternation between *s-* and *sh-* is an artifact of the Hepburn Romanization System (see Section 4.6). If written in the Cabinet Ordinance System, these forms would uniformly be written with *s-*, e.g. *s-inai, s-i, s-uru, s-ureba, s-iro, s-iyō, s-aseru*.

[5] According to the traditional grammar, the causative and passive auxiliaries are said to attach to the *mizen-kei* of the verb, and the *mizenkei* of *suru* 'do' is *sh-i-*. This derivation rule wrongly generates the causative and passive forms as **sh-i-saseru* and **sh-i-rareru*.

[6] The stem of the *u*-verbs whose conclusive form ends in a succession of vowels (e.g. *au* 'meet', *iu* 'say', *ou* 'chase', *kau* 'buy', *suu* 'inhale', *mau* 'dance') has /w/ as its final consonant. This consonant, however, appears only in the negative, causative, and passive forms, e.g. *kaw-anai, kaw-aseru, kaw-areru*. In other conjugation forms, the /w/ drops, e.g. *kaw-u* becomes *ka-u*; *kaw-i* becomes *ka-i*; *kaw-eba* becomes *ka-eba*.

[7] Although ending in /k/, *ik-u* 'go' is irregular in *te*-form formation: *ik-i-te* > *it-te*, not **i–i-te*.

c. *oyog-u*	'swim'	*oyog-i-te* > *oyo-i-de*
d. *kas-u*	'lend'	*kash-i-te*
e. *kats-u*[8]	'win'	*kach-i-te* > *kat-te*
f. *shin-u*	'die'	*shin-i-te* > *shin-de*
g. *tob-u*	'fly'	*tob-i-te* > *to-n-de*
h. *nom-u*	'drink'	*nom-i-te* > *no-n-de*
i. *ur-u*	'sell'	*ur-i-te* > *ut-te*

Although the *te*-form can stand by itself, it is typically followed by an auxiliary expression, e.g. *non-de imasu* 'is drinking', *non-de kudasai* 'please drink', *non-de shimau* 'finish drinking'. The *ta*-form can be derived by replacing *-te/de* with *-ta/da*, e.g. *kat-ta* 'bought', *kai-ta* 'wrote', *kashi-ta* 'lent', *non-da* 'drank', *shin-da* 'died'.

Missing in the above conjugation list is the so-called **POTENTIAL** form, which indicates that the action denoted by the verb stem can be performed.

(6) a. *kak-eru*	'can write'	(*u*-verb)
b. *tabe-rareru*	'can eat'	(*ru*-verb)
c. *k-orareru*	'can come'	(irregular)
d. *dekiru*	'can do'	(irregular)

These forms, however, must be considered as separate, albeit derived, verbs because they have their own conjugation paradigms.[9] Two forms, imperative and volitional, are not possible because these **POTENTIAL VERBS** refer to states of affairs, not actions under a person's control. All potential verbs fall into the *ru*-verb category.

(7) *Kak-e-* (derived from *kak-* 'write')

a. Negative	*kak-e-nai*	'cannot write'
b. Adverbial	*kak-e*	'being able to write'
c. Conclusive	*kak-e-ru*	'can write'
d. Hypothetical	*kak-e-reba*	'if (someone) can write'

(8) *Tabe-rare-* (derived from *tabe-* 'eat')

a. Negative	*tabe-rare-nai*	'cannot eat'
b. Adverbial	*tabe-rare*	'being able to eat'
c. Conclusive	*tabe-rare-ru*	'can eat'
d. Hypothetical	*tabe-rare-reba*	'if (someone) can eat'

(9) *Ko-rare-* (derived from *k-* 'come')

a. Negative	*ko-rare-nai*	'cannot come'
b. Adverbial	*ko-rare*	'being able to come'

[8] The *t*-line of the Japanese syllabary is written in the Cabinet Ordinance System as *ta-ti-tu-te-to*, but in the Hepburn system it is written as *ta-chi-tsu-te-to*.

[9] The potential verbs can be found as early as late Middle Japanese (the twelfth–sixteenth centuries), but full-fledged development had to wait until the nineteenth century (Komatsu 1999/2001: 214).

c. Conclusive *ko-rare-ru* 'can come'
d. Hypothetical *ko-rare-reba* 'if (someone) can come'

(10) *Deki-* is not derived from *s-* 'do' but is functionally equivalent to other potential verbs.
a. Negative *deki-nai* 'cannot do'
b. Adverbial *deki* 'being able to do'
c. Conclusive *deki-ru* 'can do'
d. Hypothetical *deki-reba* 'if (someone) can do'

While enabling their users to express the notion of possibility succinctly, these potential verbs impose a burden on Japanese verb usage because the auxiliary *-rareru* also is indicative of two other major functions, passive and honorific.[10] This problem does not arise with *u*-verbs (*kak-eru* 'can write' vs. *kak-areru* 'be written' (passive) or 'will write' (honorific)), but for *ru*-verbs and *kuru* 'come', the newly created potential verbs with *-rareru* underscore the problem. For example, *mi-rareru* (< *miru* 'see') can be interpreted as 'be seen' (passive), 'will see' (honorific), or 'can see' (potential). To remedy this three-way ambiguity, a new formation called the **RA-LESS FORM** (*ra-nuki kotoba*) was invented and has been spreading rapidly in recent years despite the protests of linguistic conservatives and purists who detest the form.[11] In this innovative system, the passive and the honorific are conveyed by *-rareru*, but the potential by *-reru*, e.g. *mi-reru* 'can see', *tabe-reru* 'can eat', *ko-reru* 'can come'.[12]

6.2 Copula conjugation

The copula, which is necessary to form predicates and modifiers with nouns and *na*-adjectives, conjugates as below. The adverbial form is used to modify a verb, while the **ATTRIBUTIVE FORM** modifies a noun. Verbs have the volitional form in their conjugation, but the copula takes the **CONJECTURAL** form instead. The polite version of the conjectural form is *deshō*.

(11) a. Negative *de wa nai, ja nai* 'not be'
b. Adverbial *ni* 'being'
c. Attributive[13] *na, no* 'be'

[10] An additional function of *-rareru* is **INCHOATIVE**, vis-à-vis causative, which indicates that the event happens spontaneously without a causing agent, e.g. *anji-rareru* ≈ 'cannot stop worrying' < *anjiru* 'worry'. This function is rare and not discussed in this book.

[11] See Komatsu (1999/2001) for the development of *-reru* since Old Japanese.

[12] Contrary to the *ra*-less form, the **RE-MORE FORM** (*re-tashi kotoba*), a new potential form that contains an additional *re*, has become noticeable among younger generations (Sunakawa 2011). For example, *iku* 'go' > *ik-e-ru* 'can go' > *ik-e-re-ru* (*re*-more); *miru* 'see' > *mi-rareru* 'can see' > *mi-reru* (*ra*-less) > *mi-re-reru* (*re*-more).

[13] The *na* in *na*-adjectives is the attributive form of the copula. When a noun modifies another noun, *no* appears after the modifying noun. Therefore, this *no* can be considered another attributive form of the copula.

d. Conclusive *da, desu* 'be'
e. Hypothetical *naraba* 'if it is'
f. Conjectural *darō, deshō* 'probably be'
g. *Te*-form *de*
h. *Ta*-form *datta, deshita* 'was, were'

(12) a. *Midori wa kangoshi [de wa/ja]-nai.* [negative]
TOP nurse [COP]-NEG.NPST
'Midori is not a nurse.'

b. *Shizuka ni shi-te kudasai.* [adverbial]
COP.ADV do-TE please
'Please be quiet.'

c. *Midori wa shinsetsu na hito da.* [attributive]
TOP kind COP.ATT person COP.NPST
'Midori is a kind person.'

Like verbs, the conclusive form of the copula, *da*, appears in dictionaries and indicates the non-past tense, (12d), while its polite counterpart is *desu*. The use of the *te*-form to conjoin clauses, as in (12g), will be discussed in Subsection 16.2.1. The polite counterpart of *datta* in (12h) is *deshita*.

d. *Midori wa [kaikeishi/shinsetsu] da.* [conclusive]
TOP [accountant/kind] COP.NPST
'Midori is [an accountant/kind].'

e. *Ashita ame naraba, marason wa chūshi da.* [hypothetical]
tomorrow rain COP.HYP marathon TOP cancellation COP.NPST
'If it rains tomorrow the marathon will be cancelled.'

f. *Ashita ame ga furu darō.* [conjectural]
tomorrow rain NOM fall COP.CNJ
'Probably it will rain tomorrow.'

g. *Midori wa kaikeishi de, Shigeru wa kangoshi da.* [*te*-form]
TOP accountant COP.TE TOP nurse COP.NPST
'Midori is an accountant, and Shigeru is a nurse.'

h. *Kinō wa ame datta.* [*ta*-form]
yesterday TOP rain COP.PAST
'It rained yesterday.'

6.3 *I*-adjective conjugation

Like verbs and the copula, the conclusive form of *i*-adjectives appears in dictionaries and can indicate the non-past tense. Unlike verbs, the negative auxiliary *nai* attaches to the adverbial form. Although *i*-adjectives do not require copula support, *desu* can be added for politeness, as in *omo-i desu* 'it is heavy'. *Desu* can also accompany the *ta*-form, as in *omo-katta desu* 'it was heavy', but this combination might sound awkward in some situations. Therefore, when politeness has to be expressed, other strategies are preferable, one being to place the adjective within a larger verbal phrase, e.g. *omo-katta to omoimasu* 'I think it was heavy'. The conjectural form, e.g. *omo-karō*, is archaic and appears almost exclusively in fixed expressions.

(13)

a.	Adverbial	*omo-ku*	'being heavy'
b.	Conclusive	*omo-i*	'be heavy'
c.	Hypothetical	*omo-kereba*	'if heavy'
d.	Conjectural	*omo-karō*	'probably heavy'
e.	*Te*-form	*omo-kute*	
f.	*Ta*-form	*omo-katta*	'was/were heavy'

(14) a. *Kono rapputoppu wa omoku-nai (desu).* [adverbial]
this laptop TOP heavy.ADV-NEG.NPST COP
'This laptop is not heavy.'

a′. *Akachan wa zuibun omoku natta.* [adverbial]
baby TOP fairly heavy.ADV became
'The baby has become quite heavy.'

b. *Ano rapputoppu wa omoi.* [conclusive]
that laptop TOP heavy.NPST
'That laptop is heavy.'

c. *Omokereba, hoka no rapputoppu o kaimasu.* [hypothetical]
heavy.HYP other laptop ACC buy.NPST
'If (it's) heavy, (I) will buy some other laptop.'

d. *Yasukarō, warukarō.* [conjectural]
cheap.CNJ bad.CNJ
'It's probably cheap, but it's also probably bad.' (i.e. You get what you pay for.)

e. *Kono rapputoppu wa yasukute hayai.* [*te*-form]
this laptop TOP inexpensive.TE fast.NPST
'This laptop is inexpensive and (yet) fast.'

f. *Ano rapputoppu wa omokatta.* [*ta*-form]
that laptop TOP heavy.PAST
'That laptop was heavy.'

Some auxiliaries conjugate as *i*-adjectives, e.g. *na-i* 'not'.

(15)

a.	Adverbial	*(omoku)-na-ku*	'not being heavy'
b	Conclusive	*(omoku)-na-i*	'is not heavy'
c.	Hypothetical	*(omoku)-na-kereba*	'if (it's) not heavy'
d.	Conjectural	*(omoku)-na-karō*	'probably not heavy'
e.	*Te*-form	*(omoku)-na-kute*	'not heavy and'
f.	*Ta*-form	*(omoku)-na-katta*	'was not heavy'

6.4 Casual speech

In everyday casual speech, words tend to be pronounced less clearly than in formal situations. This section explains several casual forms; a more extensive list is available at the book's website (http://hasegawa.berkeley.edu/Cambridge/introduction.php).

The *te*-form of a verb combines frequently with an auxiliary. In such cases, two tendencies are observed: (i) deletion of front vowels (/i/ and /e/), and (ii) avoidance of successive vowels.

a. When the auxiliary begins with /i/, /i/ drops: *yonde* 'read' + *iru* 'exist/be' → *yonderu* 'be reading'; *motte* 'hold' + *iku* 'go' → *motteku* 'take'. However, the auxiliary *ii* 'good' does not undergo this change: *mite* 'see' + *ii* → *mite ii* 'it's allowed to see something'. (One can consider that, in the combination of /e/ and /i/, /e/ wins and /i/ drops.)
b. The final /e/ of the *te*-form drops when the auxiliary begins with /a/ or /o/: *shite* 'do' + *ageru* 'give' → *shitageru* 'do something for someone'; *tsukutte* 'make' + *oku* 'to place' → *tsukuttoku* 'make something in advance'. However, with the auxiliary *aru* 'exist/be' this change does not occur: *katte* 'buy' + *aru* → *katte aru* 'something has been bought'. (In the combination of /e/ and /a/ or /o/, the latter wins and /e/ drops.)
c. With the auxiliary *shimau* 'finish', the final /e/ of the *te*-form drops, resulting in *chimau* or *jimau*: *tabete* 'eat' + *shimau* → *tabechimau* 'finish eating'; *yonde* 'read' + *shimau* → *yonjimau* 'finish reading'.
d. The contracted form *chimau* and *jimau* can be further reduced to *chau* or *jau*, respectively: *tabechimau* → *tabechau*; *yonjimau* → *yonjau*.

The next rule involves front vowel deletion and consonant palatalization (see Section 3.1).

e. In casual speech, the /eb/ part of the hypothetical form of a verb drops, and the consonant preceding /eba/ is palatalized: *hanas-eba* 'if speak out' → *hanasha*; *oyog-eba* 'if swim' → *oyogya*; *mi-reba* 'if see' → *mirya*. When a vowel precedes /eba/, /y/ is inserted: *a-eba* 'if meet' → *aya*. With *i*-adjectives, /kereba/ becomes /kerya/ or /kya/: *taka-kereba* 'if expensive' → *takakerya* → *takakya*.
f. If the vowel before the topic marker *wa* is /i/ or /e/, the vowel and /w/ drop, and the preceding consonant is palatalized: *watashi* 'I' + *wa* → *watasha*; *kore* 'this' + *wa* → *korya*; *yonde* 'reading' + *wa* → *yonja*.

When at the end of a conjugated verb, the syllables /ra/, /ri/, and /ru/ become the moraic nasal under certain circumstances.

g. When followed by /an/, /in/, or /un/, the stem final /r/ becomes a moraic nasal: *kaer-anai* 'not go home' → *kaennai*; *kaer-ina* 'Go home!' → *kaenna*; *kaer-una* 'Don't go home!' → *kaenna*.

Rule (g) can cause serious problems for the hearer. One of my students visited a rural area in Japan for a homestay. She found the house and an elderly man working in the barn. He said *hainna, hainna*. She knew that *hairu* 'enter, the conclusive form' + *na* (a sentence-final particle, to be discussed in

Subsection 23.2.4) means a prohibition, 'don't enter', but his facial expression was inviting. As you see in (g), the affirmative command, *hairi* (the adverbial form) + *na*, and the negative command, *hairu* + *na*, can both be contracted to *hainna* in casual speech. The only difference is pitch accent: the former is *hainná*, whereas the latter is *háinna*.

6.5 Deriving nouns

The adverbial form of a verb can be used as a noun, like the English gerund, e.g. *swimming*.

(16) a. *oyog-u* 'swim'

Midori	*wa*	*oyogi*	*ga*	*jōzu*	*da.*
	TOP	swimming	NOM	good.at	COP.NPST

'Midori is good at swimming.' (i.e. Midori is a good swimmer.)

b. *shirabe-ru* 'investigate'

Shirabe	*ga*	*tari-nai.*
investigation	NOM	adequate-NEG.NPST

'The investigation is inadequate.'

From adjectives, nouns can be derived by the use of the suffix *-sa* or *-mi*. While *-sa* can co-occur with virtually any adjective, *-mi* is limited to a small number of *i*-adjectives. When both suffixes are permitted, *-sa* is generally more abstract than *-mi*.

(17) *I*-adjectives

atataka-i 'warm'	*atataka-sa*	*atataka-mi*	'warmth'
shitashi-i 'familiar'	*shitashi-sa*	*shitashi-mi*	'familiarity'
kura-i 'dark'	*kura-sa*	**kura-mi*	'darkness'
tsumeta-i 'cold'	*tsumeta-sa*	**tsumeta-mi*	'coldness'
uma-i 'tasty'	*uma-sa*	'tastiness'	
	uma-mi	'essence of taste'	
yowa-i 'weak'	*yowa-sa*	'weakness'	
	yowa-mi	'weak point'	

(18) *Na*-adjectives (*-mi* is prohibited)

benri 'convenient'	*benri-sa*	**benri-mi*	'convenience'
kenkō 'healthy'	*kenkō-sa*	**kenkō-mi*	'healthiness'
zeitaku 'lavish'	*zeitaku-sa*	**zeitaku-mi*	'lavishness'

Verbal nouns can be derived from ordinary nouns or from *na*-adjectives by the suffix *-ka* '-ization', and the derived verbal nouns can form verbs with *suru* 'do'.

(19)

Noun	Verbal noun	+ *suru*
nihon 'Japan'	*nihon-ka* 'Japanization'	'Japanize'
taishū 'populace'	*taishū-ka* 'popularization'	'popularize'
toshi 'city'	*toshi-ka* 'urbanization'	'urbanize'

(20)

Na-adjective	Verbal noun	+ *suru*
dejitaru 'digital'	*dejitaru-ka* 'digitization'	'digitize'
fuhen 'general'	*fuhen-ka* 'generalization'	'generalize'
saiteki 'optimum'	*saiteki-ka* 'optimization'	'optimize'

6.6 Deriving verbs

In addition to adding *suru* to verbal nouns, adding the non-past suffix *-ru* to a base noun can generate a verb, although the latter process is much less productive.

(21)

jiko 'accident'	*jiko-ru* 'to have a traffic accident'
kaso 'depopulation'	*kaso-ru* 'to become unpopular' (e.g. Internet bulletin board)
gugu < Google	*gugu-ru* 'to search with Google'
torabu(ru) < trouble	*torabu-ru* 'to be in trouble'

This process can also be used to derive a verb from a proper noun. For example, *Egawa-ru* 'to obtain what one wants in a sneaky way' was derived from Taku EGAWA, the name of a former pitcher of the Yomiuri Giants baseball team, and *Hato-ru* 'to leave one's duties unfinished' from Yukio HATOYAMA, the name of a former prime minister of Japan. In this derivation process, it is interesting to note that the base word is first treated as the stem of a *ru*-verb (a natural process because the word ends in a vowel, considered as a vowel-ending stem), obtaining the suffix *-ru*, but then it behaves as an *u*-verb. For example, the Japanese verb *negu-ru*, derived from the English verb *neglect*, conjugates *negur-anai* (negative), *negur-i(masu)* 'adverbial', *negur-eba* (hypothetical), etc.[14]

Although no longer a productive process, verbs can be derived from adjectives (for the intransitive–transitive distinction, see Section 7.2):

(22)

I-adjectives		intransitive	transitive	
kata-i	'hard'	*kata-maru*	*kata-meru*	'solidify'
tsuyo-i	'strong'	*tsuyo-maru*	*tsuyo-meru*	'strengthen'
kiyo-i	'pure'		*kiyo-meru*	'purify'
kurushi-i	'painful'		*kurushi-meru*	'inflict pain'
futo-i	'fat'	*futo-ru*		'gain weight'
hoso-i	'thin'	*hoso-ru*		'become slender'

(23)

Na-adjectives		intransitive	transitive	
shizuka	'quiet'	*shizu-maru*	*shizu-meru*	'to quiet'
yasuraka	'peaceful'	*yasura-gu*	*yasura-geru*	'have/bring peace of mind'
hanayaka	'gorgeous'	*hanaya-gu*	*hanaya-geru*	'scintillate'
yuruyaka	'gentle'	*yuruya-gu*		'become gentle'

[14] Some older verbs generated by this process persist as *ru*-verbs, e.g. *tasogare* 'dusk' > *tasogare-ru* 'get dark', which conjugate as *tasogare-nai* (negative), *tasogare-(masu)* (adverbial), *tasogare-reba* (hypothetical), etc.

6.7 Deriving adjectives

The auxiliary *-rashii* derives *i*-adjectives from a noun or *i*- or *na*-adjective.[15]

(24) Nouns

haru	'spring'	*haru-rashii*	'typical of spring'
gakusei	'student'	*gakusei-rashii*	'typical of a student'
nihon	'Japan'	*nihon-rashii*	'typically Japanese'

(25) *I*-adjectives (highly limited)

kawai-i	'lovely'	*kawai-rashii*	'lovely looking'
kitana-i	'dirty'	*kitana-rashii*	'dirty-looking'
niku-i	'detestable'	*niku-rashii*	'spiteful-looking'

(26) *Na* adjectives (highly limited)

baka	'fool'	*baka-rashii*	'foolish'
iya	'disagreeable'	*iya-rashii*	'disagreeable-looking'
mottomo	'reasonable'	*mottomo-rashii*	'deceptively reasonable-looking'

The suffix *-ppoi* also derives *i*-adjectives from a noun, verb, or *i*- or *na*-adjective.

(27) Nouns

hokori	'dust'	*hokori-ppoi*	'dusty'
mizu	'water'	*mizu-ppoi*	'watery'
rikutsu	'reason, argument'	*rikutsu-ppoi*	'argumentative'

(28) Verbs (adverbial form)

aki-ru	'lose interest'	*aki-ppoi*	'easily tired of something'
okor-u	'get angry'	*okori-ppoi*	'irritable'
wasure-ru	'forget'	*wasure-ppoi*	'forgetful'

(29) *I*-adjectives (highly limited)

ara-i	'harsh'	*ara-ppoi*	'harsh' (negatively evaluated)
yasu-i	'inexpensive'	*yasu-ppoi*	'cheap-looking'

(30) *Na*-adjectives

aware	'pitiful'	*aware-ppoi*	'pitiful-looking'
hiniku	'sarcastic'	*hiniku-ppoi*	'inclined to be sarcastic'
uwaki	'unchaste'	*uwaki-ppoi*	'habitually betraying one's spouse'

When both *-rashii* and *-ppoi* can attach to the same noun, the former indicates a typical characteristic, whereas the latter indicates a similarity.

(31) *kodomo* 'child', *egao* 'smile', *kagakusha* 'scientist', *kodawari* 'obsession'

kodomo-rashii egao	'a smile that is typical of a child'
kodomo-ppoi egao	'a smile as if the person were a child'
kagakusha-rashii kodawari	'an obsession that is typical of a scientist'
kagakusha-ppoi kodawari	'an obsession as if the person were a scientist'

The suffix *-teki* derives *na*-adjectives from nouns.

[15] For details of this process, see Yamashita (1995).

(32) *geijutsu* 'art' *geijutsu-teki* 'artistic'
kihon 'foundation' *kihon-teki* 'fundamental'
rekishi 'history' *rekishi-teki* 'historical'

6.8 Compounding

Nouns, verbs, and adjectives can be combined to form new words. Some examples below exhibit sequential voicing (see Section 3.7).

(33) Native Japanese
a. Noun + noun → noun
onna 'female' + *oya* 'parent' *onna-oya* 'mother'
kabe 'wall' + *kami* 'paper' *kabe-gami* 'wallpaper'
b. Verb (adverbial) + noun → noun
tōri 'pass' + *ame* 'rain' *tōri-ame* 'passing rain'
kai 'buy' + *mono* 'thing' *kai-mono* 'shopping'
c. Adjective (stem) + noun → noun
naga 'long' + *kutsu* 'shoes' *naga-gutsu* 'rain boots'
ureshi 'happy' + *namida* 'tear' *ureshi-namida* 'joyful tears'
d. Noun + verb (adverbial) → noun
sake 'alcohol' + *nomi* 'drink' *sake-nomi* 'drinker'
tsume 'nail' + *kiri* 'cut' *tsume-kiri* 'nail clipper'
e. Noun + verb → verb
me 'eye' + *sameru* 'wake up' *me-zameru* 'wake up'
tabi 'journey' + *tatsu* 'depart' *tabi-datsu* 'go on a journey'
f. Verb (adverbial) + verb → verb
ki 'wear' + *kaeru* 'change' *ki-gaeru* 'change clothes'
koge 'burn' + *tsuku* 'attach' *koge-tsuku* 'burn food onto the pan'
g. Adjective (stem) + verb (adverbial) → verbal noun
haya 'early' + *oki* 'wake up' *haya-oki* 'early rising'
yasu 'cheap' + *uri* 'sell' *yasu-uri* 'bargain sale'
h. Noun + adjective → adjective
hokori 'pride' + *takai* 'high' *hokori-takai/dakai* 'highly proud'
shio 'salt' + *karai* 'spicy' *shio-karai* 'salty'
i. Verb (adverbial) + adjective → adjective
nebari 'persevere' + *tsuyoi* 'strong' *nebari-zuyoi* 'tenacious'
utagai 'doubt' + *fukai* 'deep' *utagai-bukai* 'distrustful'
j. Adjective (stem) + adjective → adjective
atsu 'hot' + *kurushii* 'uncomfortable' *atsu-kurushii* 'oppressively warm'
zuru 'cunning' + *kashikoi* 'smart' *zuru-gashikoi* 'devious'

(34) Sino-Japanese
a. Noun + noun → noun
en 'lead' + *hitsu* 'writing brush' *en-pitsu* 'pencil'
gyū 'cow' + *niku* 'meat' *gyū-niku* 'beef'
b. Verb + noun → noun
shoku 'eat' + *ki* 'container' *shok-ki* 'tableware'
shoku 'eat' + *taku* 'table' *shoku-taku* 'dinner table'
c. Verb + noun → verbal noun
doku 'read' + *sho* 'book' *doku-sho* 'reading'
to 'climb' + *san* 'mountain' *to-zan* 'mountain climbing'

d. Adjective + noun → noun
kō 'high' + *ri* 'interest' *kō-ri* 'high interest'
tei 'low' + *on* 'sound' *tei-on* 'low tone'
e. Verb + verb → verbal noun
kai 'open' + *shi* 'start' *kai-shi* 'start'
zō 'increase' + *san* 'produce' *zō-san* 'increase in production'
f. Adjective + verb → verbal noun
an 'peaceful' + *min* 'sleep' *an-min* 'sound sleep'
shin 'new' + *chiku* 'build' *shin-chiku* 'new construction'

6.9 Abbreviation

In Japanese, long compounds and borrowed foreign words are customarily shortened as exemplified by some common strategies below:

(35) Combine the first one or two moras of each component.
dejitaru 'digital' + *kamera* 'camera' → *deji-kame* 'digital camera'
dotanba 'last minute' + *kyanseru* 'cancel' → *dota-kyan* 'last-minute cancellation'
kopī 'copy' + *pēsuto* 'paste' → *kopi-pe* 'copy and paste'
sekusharu 'sexual' + *harasumento* 'harassment' → *seku-hara* 'sexual harassment'
shūshoku 'obtaining employment' + *katsudō* 'activity' → *shū-katsu* 'job hunting'

(36) Use only the first component.
keitai 'portable' + *denwa* 'telephone' → *keitai* 'cell phone'
kyūkō 'express' + *densha* 'train' → *kyūkō* 'express train'
sōri 'prime' + *daijin* 'minister' → *sōri* 'Prime Minister'
sūpā 'super' + *māketto* 'market' → *sūpā* 'super market'

(37) Use only first two to four moras.
apartment → *apāto*
appointment → *apo*
convenience store → *konbini*
presentation → *purezen*
Starbucks → *Sutaba* (> *Sutaba-ru* 'to go to Starbucks')

Part III

Grammatical foundations

7 Grammatical relations and case marking

7.1 Introduction

A **CLAUSE** is a linguistic unit which consists, at a minimum, of a **PREDICATE** and its **ARGUMENT(S)**. It is a unit smaller than a **SENTENCE**, for a sentence can consist of more than one clause. In Japanese, a predicate is a verb (**VERBAL PREDICATE**), an *i*- or *na*-adjective plus copula (**ADJECTIVAL PREDICATE**), or a noun plus copula (**NOMINAL PREDICATE**). Arguments typically, but not necessarily, consist of **NOUN PHRASES** (NPs) such as *mado ga*, *heya ga*, *kore ga* in (1).

(1) a. *Mado* *ga* *aita.* [verb = verbal predicate]
window NOM opened
'The window opened.'

b. *Heya* *ga* *hiroi.* [*i*-adjective = adjectival predicate]
room NOM spacious
'The room is spacious.'

c. *Heya* *ga* *kirei* *da.* [*na*-adjective + copula = [adjectival predicate]
room NOM clean COP.NPST
'The room is clean.'

d. *Kore* *ga* *keiyakusho* *da.* [noun + copula = predicate]
nominal.this NOM contract COP.NPST
'This is the contract.'

Each predicate requires a number of arguments for conveying its essential meaning.[1] Generally, adjectival and nominal predicates, as well as some verbal predicates, require only one argument. In Japanese, this mandatory argument is marked by the postpositional particle *ga*, as shown in (1), and the NP is said to be in the **NOMINATIVE** case. The term **GRAMMATICAL RELATION** is also used to identify the grammatical function of the given NP with respect to the predicate. In (1), all of the nominative NPs hold the grammatical relation of **SUBJECT** to their corresponding predicates.

[1] In English, some **METEOROLOGICAL VERBS**, e.g. *rain*, *drizzle*, do not require arguments. In such a case, the semantically empty pronoun *it* is inserted to complete a sentence, e.g. *It rained.*

7.2 Intransitive vs. transitive predicates

In traditional grammars, when a predicate requires only a single nominative argument, it is called **INTRANSITIVE**. Many verbs require more than one argument.[2] For example, to understand the meaning of *yomu* 'read' requires a person (or persons) who can read and something readable, a book, for example, or newspaper or magazine. In Japanese, such a secondary argument is marked by the particle *o*, and said to be in the **ACCUSATIVE** case.

(2) a. *Midori ga hon o yonda.*
NOM book ACC read
'Midori read a book.'
b. *Shigeru ga kabin o watta.*
NOM vase ACC broke
'Shigeru broke the vase.'

If a given predicate requires both nominative and accusative NPs, it is considered **TRANSITIVE**. With a transitive predicate, the accusative NP holds the grammatical relation of **DIRECT OBJECT**.

In English, many, if not most, verbs can be used either intransitively or transitively.[3]

(3) a. *The door opened.* [intransitive]
b. *I opened the door.* [transitive]

(4) a. *I drive a car every day.* [transitive]
b. *This car drives smoothly.* [intransitive]

In Japanese, by contrast, only a small number of verbs can be used both ways, e.g. *hiraku* 'open', *tojiru* 'close', *masu* 'increase', *tomonau* 'accompany'.[4]

(5) a. *Tobira ga hiraita.* [intransitive]
door NOM opened
'The door opened.'
b. *Midori ga tobira o hiraita.* [transitive]
NOM door ACC opened
'Midori opened the door.'

[2] Like verbs, some adjectival and nominal predicates require more than one argument. For example, *tomodachi da* 'be a friend' as in *Watashi wa tomodachi da* 'I'm a friend' is semantically incomplete. In order to understand this sentence, the hearer needs to know with whom the speaker is friends. Therefore, the person that the speaker befriends is considered an argument.

[3] With the exception of some pronouns (e.g. *I* = nominative, *me* = accusative), case in English is not marked formally. It is encoded by the location of words in a clause: typically, the position before the predicate is for the nominative, and the one immediately after the predicate is for the accusative.

[4] See Okutsu (1967), Morita (1994), and Kageyama (1996) for further discussions of transitive *qua* intransitive verbs.

Most Japanese verbs have related yet distinct intransitive and transitive forms.

(6) a. *Tobira* *ga* *aita*. [intransitive]
door NOM opened
'The door opened.'
b. *Midori* *ga* *tobira* *o* *aketa*. [transitive]
NOM door ACC opened
'Midori opened the door.'

(7) a. *Nedan* *ga* *sagatta*. [intransitive]
price NOM dropped
'The price dropped.'
b. *Shigeru* *ga* *nedan* *o* *sageta*. [transitive]
NOM price ACC dropped
'Shigeru dropped the price.'

(8)

	Intransitive	Transitive	Gloss
a.	*mag-aru*	*mag-eru*	bend
	tom-aru	*tom-eru*	stop
b.	*sas-aru*	*sas-u*	pierce
	tsunag-aru	*tsunag-u*	connect
c.	*or-eru*	*or-u*	break
	war-eru	*war-u*	break
d.	*kowa-reru*	*kowa-su*	break
	naga-reru	*naga-su*	flow/drain
e.	*utsu-ru*	*utsu-su*	transfer
	nao-ru	*nao-su*	heal
f.	*kawak-u*	*kawak-asu*	dry
	her-u	*her-asu*	decrease
g.	*k-ieru*	*k-esu*	turn off

Aita-aketa in (6) and *sagatta-sageta* in (7) are obviously related, and some recurring patterns are observable between such intransitive and transitive pairs as shown in (8). Nevertheless, deriving one form from the other by simply applying a rule is not possible. Therefore, each pair of forms must be learned separately.

In both English and Japanese, predicates exist that require three arguments.

(9) *Midori* *ga* *Shigeru* *ni* *kabin* *o* *okutta/ageta*.
NOM DAT vase ACC sent/gave
'Midori sent/gave Shigeru a vase.'

Okuru 'send' and *ageru* 'give' presuppose a recipient in addition to the sender/giver and the item that is transferred. This third argument is marked with the particle *ni*, and called **DATIVE**. The grammatical relation that the dative NP in (9) holds is that of **INDIRECT OBJECT**. The predicates that require a nominative, an accusative, and a dative argument are referred to as **DITRANSITIVE** (*di* = twice).

7.3 Valence

When we consider a wider range of predicates and their associated arguments, the traditional categorization of *intransitive–transitive–ditransitive* proves inadequate. *Iku* 'go', for example, does not require an accusative NP, and, therefore, it is intransitive.[5] Nevertheless, with only a nominative NP, a sentence such as (10a) is semantically incomplete. In order to interpret the sentence, the addressee naturally questions where Midori went. That is, another argument must be supplied with *ni* 'to' as in (10b).[6]

(10) a. *Midori ga itta.*
NOM went
'Midori went.'

b. *Midori ga toshokan ni itta.*
NOM library to went
'Midori went to the library.'

This being the case, a new concept is needed to discuss predicates' obligatory arguments, and linguists have borrowed the useful and widely employed term **VALENCE** from chemistry – where the term refers to the number of bonded electron atoms forming a chemical element – to help them visualize/conceptualize a predicate in relation to its arguments.[7] From this perspective, we can metaphorically conceive of a clause as a nucleus (predicate) surrounded by valence electrons (arguments).

If a predicate requires only one argument, it is called a **ONE-PLACE PREDICATE**; if two, a **TWO-PLACE PREDICATE**; if three, a **THREE-PLACE PREDICATE**.

(11) a. *Midori ga waratta.* [intransitive, one-place]
NOM laughed
'Midori laughed.'

b. *Midori ga densha ni notta.* [intransitive, two-place]
NOM train on rode
'Midori got onto the train.'

[5] Although *iku* 'go' requires two arguments, it is semantically intransitive because it does not indicate the relationship between the subject, e.g. Midori, and the goal, e.g. the library. Rather, *iku* describes the subject's location at two different points in time.

[6] *Ni* in (10b) is the **ALLATIVE** case marker, which indicates the goal of a motion. Whether or not the *ni*-marked NPs in (9) and (10b) should be labeled differently (dative and allative, respectively) is not a settled topic. Some linguists, e.g. Iwasaki (2002), invariably label *ni* as dative, while others, e.g. Shibatani (1990), sometimes label it as dative but at other times as representing various prepositional meanings, e.g. *to*, *in*, *at*. In order to simplify exposition, this book normally provides corresponding English prepositions rather than case names.

[7] The term *valence* was introduced in linguistics circles by Lucien Tesnière (1959/1976).

c. *Midori* *ga* *uchi* *ni* *iru.* [intransitive, two-place]
NOM home at exist
'Midori is at home.'

d. *Midori* *ga* *hako* *ni* *rōsoku* *o* *ireta.* [transitive, three-place]
NOM box to candle ACC put
'Midori put candles into the box.'

Categorization of predicates based on the number of mandatory arguments is a complex task and can therefore vary according to the theoretical framework to which one subscribes. Consider, for example, the sentences in (12).

(12) a. *Shigeru* *ga* *monku* *o* *itta.*
NOM complaint ACC said
'[Lit.] Shigeru said a complaint.'
'Shigeru complained.'

b. *Shigeru* *ga* *tsumaranai* *to* *itta.*
NOM trivial QUOT said
'Shigeru said that (it) was/is trivial.'

In (12a), an accusative NP is obligatory; therefore, it is clearly transitive. But is the sentence semantically complete with only two arguments? When a person complains, should there not be a target person or organization to whom the complaint is made? Or can one complain without addressing anyone? It depends on one's understanding or definition of *monku o iu* 'to complain' as well as of the noun *monku* 'complaint'. The case in (12b), where no accusative NP is involved, is even more problematic. Is the **QUOTATIVE** phrase, marked by *to*, a substitute for the mandatory accusative argument, and if so, should the predicate be considered transitive? This is a difficult question, and most Japanese dictionaries are ambiguous as to whether *iu* 'say' is categorically transitive or intransitive.

7.4 Transitivity

Traditional grammars loosely and metaphorically conceive of the notion of **TRANSITIVITY** in such a way that an activity is "transferred" from one participant to another, and they categorize transitivity according to the presence or absence of the secondary (i.e. accusative) argument. Such a distinction between intransitive and transitive is observed in diverse world languages, and is therefore unlikely to be a purely linguistic (i.e. arbitrary and language specific) phenomenon. Rather, it is more likely to be a reflection of universal human cognition.

Hopper and Thompson (1980) believe the intransitive–transitive dichotomy cannot capture many relevant phenomena, and that transitivity should instead be conceived of in terms of a continuum. That is, it should be meaningful to say that some predicates are *more transitive* than others. They propose to decompose transitivity into ten components:[8]

(13) a. PARTICIPANTS: Situations with two participants are higher in transitivity than those with one participant.
b. KINESIS: Actions (e.g. *Mia hugged Jacob*) are higher than non-actions (e.g. *Mia likes Jacob*).
c. ASPECT: Completed actions (e.g. *I ate all of the pizza*) are higher than non-complete actions (e.g. *I'm eating the pizza*).
d. PUNCTUALITY: Punctual actions (e.g. *Mia kicked the car fender*) are higher than durative actions (e.g. *Mia carried a suitcase*).
e. VOLITIONALITY: Volitional actions (e.g. *Mia wrote your name*) are higher than non-volitional actions (e.g. *Mia forgot your name*).
f. AFFIRMATION: Affirmative clauses (*Mia will attend the meeting*) are higher than negative clauses (*Mia won't attend the meeting*).
g. MODE: Actual events (e.g. *I speak Korean*) are higher than those that are assumed to occur in a non-real world (e.g. *I wish I could speak Korean*).
h. AGENCY (i.e. the capacity of an entity to act or effect): Events whose participants are high in agency (e.g. *Mia startled me*) are higher than those with low agency participants (*The story startled me*).
i. INDIVIDUATION OF THE OBJECT: When the object is clearly distinct from other participants or background (e.g. *I saw Mia in town*), the transitivity is higher than when it is not (*I saw beautiful scenery*).
j. AFFECTIVENESS OF THE OBJECT: Events whereby the object is completely affected (e.g. *I destroyed the gate*) are higher than those with the partially affected object (*I opened the gate*).

According to this conceptualization, certain clauses are extremely high in transitivity. For example, in (14) with *korosu* 'kill', the situation involves (13a) two participants, (13b) action, (13c) completion, (13d) punctuality, (13e) volition,[9] (13f) affirmation, and (13g) an actual event. The subject (the speaker) is (13h) high in agency, and the object, Nobuo, is (13i) distinct from others and (13j) totally affected. In such a high transitivity situation, most languages would be expected to encode it with a transitive verb and accusative case marking.

(14) *Watashi ga Nobuo o koroshita.*
I NOM ACC killed
'I killed Nobuo.'

In contrast, it is predicted that situations with low transitivity are encoded as transitive by some languages and as intransitive by others, as exemplified in (15). *Meet* and *understand*, for example, are transitive in English, but

[8] Hopper and Thompson's ideas are somewhat modified and simplified here to make their relevance clearer within the context of the Japanese language.
[9] Were the event not volitional, the complex predicate *koroshite shimatta* would be preferred.

intransitive in Japanese. (The distinction between the nominative marker *ga* and the topic marker *wa* will be discussed in Chapter 8.)

(15) a. *Midori ga Shigeru ni atta.*
NOM to met
'Midori met Shigeru.'

b. *Midori wa chūgokugo ga wakaru.*
TOP Chinese NOM understand
'Midori understands Chinese.'

Au 'meet' is clearly lower in transitivity than *korosu* 'kill' because the object is not so drastically affected. With *wakaru* 'understand', the object, the Chinese language, is not affected at all. These examples indicate that with low transitivity, accusative marking of the secondary entity in the clause might be inconsistent. This topic will be returned to shortly.

7.5 Arguments vs. adjuncts

Clauses can contain more NPs than mandatory arguments.

(16) a. *Midori ga nichiyōbi ni resutoran de bangohan o tabeta.*
NOM Sunday on restaurant at dinner ACC ate
'On Sunday Midori ate dinner at a restaurant.'

b. *Midori ga Shigeru to denshirenji de kēki o tsukutta.*
NOM with microwave.oven with cake ACC made
'With Shigeru, Midori made a cake using a microwave oven.'

c. *Midori ga Hawai kara kikoku-shita.*
NOM from returned
'Midori came back (returned to her home country) from Hawaii.'

The predicate of (16a) is *tabeta* 'ate', which requires nominative and accusative NPs. Other NPs in (16) provide additional information: *nichiyōbi ni* (time) and *resutoran de* (place). Time and place are broader concepts than the event specified by the predicate because all events occur at a specific time and place. In (16b) and (16c), *Shigeru to* indicates accompaniment, *denshirenji de* the instrument, and *Hawai kara* the origin of the movement. Unlike time and place, these phrases provide event internal information. Such non-obligatory elements are collectively referred to as **ADJUNCTS** vis-à-vis arguments.

The distinction between arguments and adjuncts is not always easy to make. Nevertheless, in most cases, the distinction is psychologically real, and I propose the **QUESTION PULL** (Hasegawa 1988) as an empirical test to justify the distinction. Unlike English, obligatory arguments in Japanese need not be overtly stated; it is even the norm to omit obviously identifiable elements from sentences. For example, an utterance consisting of just a predicate is possible, as in *Michatta* 'saw'. In such a case, unless another entity has been established as the topic of the conversation, the speaker is normally understood to be the default subject. Therefore *Michatta* is interpreted as 'I saw it'. When the hearer is unable to identify the referent of *it*, s/he would likely ask *nani o* 'what (accusative)'. It would sound absurd if the hearer asked at this point for an adjunct, e.g. *itsu* 'when', *doko de* 'where', or *dare to* 'with whom'. That is, identification of adjuncts is not meaningful until all obligatory arguments are clarified. This natural sequence of obtaining (pulling) information supports my contention that certain elements are indispensable for understanding a clause while others contribute non-essential, supplemental information.

Adjuncts are sometimes said to carry a **SEMANTIC CASE**, in contrast to nominative, accusative, and dative, which indicate **GRAMMATICAL CASE**. The cases of adjuncts – e.g. time, place (*at*), accompaniment (*with*), instrument/means (*by*), the origin of movement (*from*) – are semantically more specific than the grammatical cases whose semantics cannot be determined unless the predicate is identified. For example, *Midori* is uniformly marked with *ga* in (17), but its semantic case is **AGENT** (i.e. it intentionally performs the action) in (17a), **EXPERIENCER** (i.e. it undergoes sensory, emotional, or cognitive experience) in (17b), and **PATIENT** (it undergoes a change) in (17c) below.

(17)	a.	*Midori*	*ga*	*shashin*	*o*	*moyashita.*
			NOM	photo	ACC	burnt
		'Midori burnt the photo.'				
	b.	*Midori*	*ga*	*yūrei*	*o*	*mita.*
			NOM	ghost	ACC	saw
		'Midori saw a ghost.'				
	c.	*Midori*	*ga*	*shinda.*		
			NOM	died		
		'Midori died.'				

Likewise, the dative NPs in the two sentences in (18) act in completely opposite ways – i.e. *ni* indicates 'to' or 'from' depending upon the predicate chosen.

(18)	a.	*Midori*	*ga*	*Shigeru*	*ni*	*shashin*	*o*	*ageta.*
			NOM		DAT	photo	ACC	gave
		'Midori gave a photo *to* Shigeru.'						
	b.	*Midori*	*ga*	*Shigeru*	*ni*	*shashin*	*o*	*moratta.*
			NOM		DAT	photo	ACC	received
		'Midori received a photo *from* Shigeru.'						

In (18b), it is clear that *ni* is dative, distinct from the goal adjunct, as in *gakkō ni iku* 'go to school'. The dative NP with *morau* 'receive' – but not with *ageru* 'give' – can be superseded by NP *kara* 'from', which is semantically more explicit.

7.6 Discrepancies between case and grammatical relations

In typical sentences, neat correspondences exist between case marking and grammatical relations: nominative for subject, accusative for direct object, and dative for indirect object. However, as shown in (15b), these canonical agreements can be disrupted, thus becoming problematic. For many speakers, *wakaru* is conceptually transitive, albeit with low transitivity, involving a sentient subject experiencing some phenomenon or entity as direct object. Nevertheless, the NP that is conceptually a direct object is marked with the nominative *ga*. Many linguists (e.g. Martin 1962: 44; 1975: 198–201) consider the nominative NP to be invariably the subject of the clause, whereas others (e.g. Kuno 1973) analyze *ga* in such clauses as marking a direct object.[10]

In any case, the "nominative direct object" appears only in a limited number of constructions, all of which are low in transitivity. Observe the following sentences:

(19) With adjectival predicates

a. *Watashi wa kuruma ga hoshii.* [*i*-adjective]
I TOP car NOM want
'I want a car.'

b. *Watashi wa eiga ga suki da.* [*na*-adjective]
I TOP movie NOM fond COP.NPST
'I like (am fond of) movies.'

(20) *Want-to-do* construction

Watashi wa eiga ga mi-tai.
I TOP movie NOM see-want
'I want to see a movie.'

(21) *Can-do* construction

Watashi wa piano ga hikeru.
I TOP piano NOM can.play
'I can play the piano.'

(22) Non-intentional cognition/perception

a. *Watashi wa tōkei ga wakaru.*
I TOP statistics NOM understand
'I understand statistics.'

b. *Watashi wa yūrei ga mieru.*
I TOP ghost NOM can.see
'I can see ghosts.'

[10] At one time, I, like Martin, equated nominative with subject, but I am now convinced that accepting a nominative-marked direct object is more appropriate when considering the concept of transitivity as discussed above. The reader can likewise select either stance because both are equally persuasive and equally problematic.

Another incongruent situation occurs when the predicate indicates some movement and the accusative NP indicates location. For (23), because *cross* and *climb* are transitive, English speakers are unlikely to find the sentences problematic.

(23) a. *Midori ga michi o watatta.*
NOM street ACC crossed
'Midori crossed the street.'

b. *Midori ga yama o nobotta.*
NOM mountain ACC climbed
'Midori climbed the mountain.'

This pattern extends to many motion verbs, some of which can hardly be conceived of as transitive. In such cases, whether to label the particle *o* as accusative or as a location marker varies from analysis to analysis.

(24) a. *michi o aruku* 'walk along the street'
b. *rōka o hashiru* 'run in the corridor'
c. *yamamichi o iku* 'go along the mountain trail'
d. *kawa o oyogu* 'swim across the river'
e. *kōen o sanpo-suru* 'take a walk in the park'
f. *sora o tobu* 'fly through the sky'

The third problematic case is the so-called **DATIVE SUBJECT**. The *can-do* construction, as introduced in (21), non-intentional cognition/perception, as in (22), **EXISTENTIAL VERBS** *aru* and *iru*, and some other predicates accommodate an NP that can be conceived of as a subject, but marked with the dative *ni* as in the following examples.[11]

(25) a. *Midori ni ronbun ga kak-eru darō ka.*
DAT thesis NOM write-can I.wonder
'I wonder whether Midori can write a thesis.'

b. *Midori ni kono oto ga kikoeru darō ka.*
DAT this sound NOM audible I.wonder
'I wonder if Midori can hear this sound,' or 'I wonder if this sound is audible to Midori.'

c. *Midori ni (wa) kodomo ga iru.*
DAT (TOP) child NOM exist
'Midori has a child.'

d. *Dare ni sonna taikin ga hitsuyō ka?*
who DAT such big.money NOM necessary INT
'Who needs such a great quantity of money?'

In these constructions, the natural word order is "NP-*ni* NP-*ga* Predicate," whereas NP-*ga* normally precedes NP-*ni* in most constructions.

[11] Dative subjects are frequently marked with *wa* as well (see Section 8.13).

7.7 Fluctuation between nominative and accusative markings

One of the constructions that corresponds to the English phrase *want-to-do* employs a verb with the suffix *tai* as shown in (20). In (26a), *nomu* 'drink' is transitive and requires an accusative NP. However, when *-tai* is added, as in (26b), the same object can be marked with the nominative *ga*, and the subject person is normally restricted to the speaker. (This phenomenon is discussed in Subsection 24.2.5.)

(26)	a.	*Watashi*	*ga*	*wain*	*o*	*nomu.*
		I	NOM	wine	ACC	drink
		'I drink wine.'				
	b.	*Watashi*	*wa*	*wain*	*ga/o*	*nomi-tai.*
		I	TOP	wine	NOM/ACC	drink-want
		'I want to drink wine.'				

Many native speakers of Japanese would prefer *ga* to *o* in (26b), but when the transitivity is very high, the preference for *o*-marking increases. According to (13h: agency), for example, (27a) with a human object is higher in transitivity than (26b), which involves a non-human object. Therefore, more native speakers are likely to prefer *o* in (27a). When the transitivity is even higher, as in (27b), most native speakers would select *o*. These examples show that *o*-marking is sensitive to the transitivity of the clause.

(27)	a.	*Kekkon-shiki*	*ni*	*tejinashi*	*ga/o*	*yobi-tai.*
		wedding-ceremony	to	magician	NOM/ACC	hire-want
		'I want to hire a magician for (my) wedding-ceremony.'				
	b.	*Watashi*	*wa*	*buchō*	*ga/o*	*koroshi-tai.*
		I	TOP	section.chief	NOM/ACC	kill-want
		'I want to kill (my) section chief.'				

8 Subjects and topics

8.1 Introduction

One of the most difficult aspects of the study and use of Japanese grammar involves the distinction between *ga* and *wa*. Textbooks commonly explain that the primary function of *ga* is to mark the subject, although, as seen in Chapter 7, *ga*-marked NPs do not always qualify conceptually as subjects. On the other hand, *wa* is said to mark a **TOPIC**. In ordinary language, both *subject* and *topic* can be loosely defined as the focal point of discussion. Therefore, subject and topic do overlap in function – that is, many subjects are also topics, and many topics are commonly expressed as subjects. In linguistics, however, *subject* and *topic* refer to drastically different concepts. Subject is a grammatical relation held between a given constituent, typically an NP, and the predicate. That is, the scope of a subject is limited to a clause, or to a sentence if the sentence is mono-clausal. Topic, on the other hand, references a much broader notion. It is normal to consider the topic of a paragraph, the topic of a chapter, or even the topic of an entire book. In other words, the scope of a topic is a **DISCOURSE** (or a **TEXT**); that is, a sequence of sentences organized by a specific purpose.

This difference in scope between subject and topic makes elucidation of *ga* and *wa* a challenge because they do not necessarily contrast on the same bases. When a sentence is examined in isolation, *ga* and *wa* can often be used interchangeably; however, when that same sentence is embedded in a discourse, either *ga* or *wa* might not be usable. Another reason for difficulty is that the selection criteria for these particles are not mutually exclusive. In the same sentences, *ga* might be appropriate according to one criterion, but *wa* preferable according to another. To put it differently, the distinction between *ga* and *wa* is primarily a matter of **INFORMATION PACKAGING**, i.e. how the message is sent, rather than the content of the message itself (Chafe 1976: 28).

8.2 Identifiability

The following two sentences depict the same situation:

(1) a.

Tsukue	*no*	*ue*	*ni*	*hon*	*ga*	*aru.*
desk	GEN	top	on	book	NOM	exist

'There is a book on [the top of] the desk.'

b.

Hon	*wa*	*tsukue*	*no*	*ue*	*ni*	*aru.*
book	TOP	desk	GEN	top	on	exist

'The book is on [the top of] the desk.'

Nevertheless, these two sentences are not interchangeable. *Hon wa* in (1b) cannot be used unless the speaker believes that the addressee can identify the referent (i.e. the book). This notion of **IDENTIFIABILITY** is indispensable for topichood. A subject, by comparison, need not be identifiable. English has a special sentence pattern referred to as the **THERE-CONSTRUCTION**, which is used to introduce an unidentifiable entity into a discourse, as in (1a). Its Japanese counterpart is the use of the existential verbs *iru* and *aru*. When these verbs are used for this purpose, the subject uniformly occurs with the nominative *ga*, not with the topic-marker *wa*.

In English, identifiable NPs are typically marked with the **DEFINITE ARTICLE** *the*, as in (1b), and unidentifiable NPs by an **INDEFINITE ARTICLE** *a/an*, as in (1a). Notwithstanding such a distinction, identifiability is a supposedly universal cognitive category, whereas **DEFINITENESS** is a grammatical category, which can be idiosyncratic to a given language. In fact, among languages that employ definite articles (e.g. French, German, Greek, Italian), their use or non-use can vary considerably when depicting the same entity in the same situation (Lambrecht 1994: 79–87).

The referent of an interrogative phrase (a form used for questioning) – e.g. *dare* 'who', *nani* 'what', *doko* 'where' – is unknown to the speaker, i.e. unidentifiable, so it cannot be marked by *wa*, although it can be marked by *ga*.

(2) a. [INT = interrogative particle]

Dare	*ga/*wa*	*kimashita*	*ka?*
who	NOM/TOP	came	INT

'Who came?'

b.

Nani	*ga/*wa*	*miemasu*	*ka?*
what	NOM/TOP	visible	INT

'What is visible?'

c.

Doko	*ga/*wa*	*kowarete imasu*	*ka?*
where	NOM/TOP	is.broken	INT

'Where [which part] is it broken?'

Likewise, the referent of an **INDEFINITE** phrase (e.g. *dareka* 'someone', *nanika* 'something', *dokoka* 'somewhere') is supposed to be unidentifiable by the speaker and/or the hearer, and can therefore be marked by *ga*, but not by *wa*. The terms *interrogative* and *indefinite* are frequently confused, and it is crucial to understand the conceptual difference between them. Compare the interrogative expressions of (2) and the corresponding indefinites in (3) to clarify the difference. The sentences in (2) cannot be used unless the corresponding question in (3) is presumed to have an affirmative answer.

(3) a. *Dareka ga/*wa kimashita ka?*[1]
someone NOM/TOP *came* INT
'Did someone come (here)?'

b. *Nanika ga/*wa miemasu ka?*
something NOM/TOP visible INT
'Is something visible?'

c. *Dokoka ga/*wa kowarete imasu ka?*
somewhere NOM/TOP is.broken INT
'[Lit.] Is someplace (of it) broken?'
'Is (it) broken someplace?'

8.3 Anaphoric topics

In a discourse, the usual way to make a referent identifiable is the mechanism of **ANAPHORA**, which refers to the relationship between two expressions co-occurring and co-referring within a single discourse. Anaphora consists of two parts: the preceding part is called an **ANTECEDENT**, and the following part an **ANAPHOR**. The following is the opening passage of *Momotaro*, 'Peach Boy', a popular Japanese folktale (see Section 2.1).

(4) *Mukashi mukashi aru tokoro ni ojīsan to obāsan ga*
old.days certain place in old.man and old.woman NOM
sunde imashita. Aru hi ojīsan wa yama e shibakari
were.living certain day old.man TOP mountain to gather.firewood
ni, obāsan wa kawa e sentaku ni ikimashita.
for old.woman TOP river to washing for went
'A long long time ago, there lived an old man and an old woman. One day, the old man went to the mountain to gather firewood, and the old woman went to the river to wash clothes.'

The old couple is first introduced into the discourse with *ga* (*ojīsan to obāsan ga*), which serves as the antecedent. At this point, they are unidentifiable and translated into English with the indefinite article *an* (*an old man and an old woman*). Although the reader does not know these referents, they are nonetheless registered in his/her mind. They are *hitching posts* for new knowledge, to use Chafe's (1976: 44) metaphor. Once the referents are registered, the NPs can be marked with *wa* (*ojīsan wa . . . obāsan wa . . .*), and in English the use of the definite article *the* is standard.

[1] With an indefinite *dareka*, *nanika*, or *dokoka*, the use of a case particle is optional. For example, *Dareka kimashita ka?* 'Did someone come?' is a well-formed sentence.

8.4 Generic topics

As discussed, topics must be identifiable, and one way to establish identity is through anaphora. Another identifiable case is when the referent is **GENERIC**, i.e. when a class of entities, rather than an individual in the class, is denoted. In Japanese, generic NPs are uniformly marked with *wa*; in English, however, they can be expressed with a plural NP (5a), with a singular NP with *the* (5b), or *a/an* (5c), or with a singular NP without an article (5d).

(5) a. *Ari wa satō o konomu.*
ant TOP sugar ACC like
'Ants like sugar.'

b. *Nō wa ōku no nikutai-kinō o tsukasadoru.*
brain TOP many bodily function ACC control
'The brain controls many bodily functions.'

c. *Rakuda wa mizu nashi de 3-shūkan ikirareru.*
camel TOP water without 3-weeks can.live
'A camel can live for three weeks without water.'

d. *Wain wa kono chihō no jūyō na sanbutsu da.*
wine TOP this region GEN important product is
'Wine is an important product of this region.'

8.5 Unique topics

Some entities are known by the speaker and addressee uniquely and are, therefore, identifiable.

(6) a. *Taiyō wa nishi ni shizumu.*
sun TOP west in set
'The sun sets in the west.'

b. *Midori wa konai to itta.*
TOP not.come QUOT said
'Midori said she won't come.'

Under normal circumstances, *taiyō* 'sun' refers to our sun. In (6b), if Midori is not known by both interlocutors, or if they know more than one person whose name is *Midori*, the referent must be properly introduced into the discourse as happens in this example sentence: *Yesterday, I met Midori, a friend of mine*.

8.6 Non-subject topics

A topic is frequently encoded as a subject, but it does not need to be. When the topic is not a subject, *wa* can be used, though *ga* is ungrammatical. In (7), *yasai* 'vegetable' is the direct object of *tabemasu* 'eat', so it cannot be marked by *ga*.

(7) Yamada: *Tanaka-san wa shōshoku desu ne.* [SFP = sentence-final particle]
TOP light.eater is SFP
'Tanaka-san, you're a light eater.'
Tanaka: *Yasai wa/*ga takusan tabemasu yo.*
vegetable TOP/NOM a.lot eat SFP
'[Lit.] Vegetables, I eat a lot.'
'I eat lots of vegetables, though.'

8.7 Topic–comment vs. event reporting sentences

We can consider two broad classes of sentences: **TOPIC–COMMENT** and **EVENT REPORTING**. In order to interpret a topic–comment sentence, we perform two activities: (i) identify the referent of the *wa*-marked NP, and (ii) construe the comment part as new information about the referent (Kuroda 1972). By contrast, in an event-reporting sentence – e.g. one that is used to respond to the question *What happened?* – we treat all entities in the sentence equally, not designating one for the special status of topic that the balance of the sentence is about. That is, if you answer *What happened?* with *Mia bought a new car*, the sentence is not about Mia, but about her buying a new car.[2] In contrast, if the question is *What happened to Mia?* and the answer is *Mia bought a new car*, the latter sentence is about Mia, designated as the topic. The Japanese language is sensitive to this distinction. *Wa* is used in the topic–comment construction, whereas *ga* is used in the non-topical, event reporting sentence type. Compare the following:

(8) a. *Hito wa shinu.*
human TOP die
'All men die,' or 'Man is mortal.'
b. *Hito ga shinu.*
human NOM die
'People will die.'

In (8a), it is important to first recognize that *hito wa* is referenced generically, and that the comment part of the sentence denotes a constant characteristic of the category of human being. By contrast, (8b) does not assert a universal truth about human beings. Rather, it predicts a specific event in the future with indefinite referents. One might articulate this sentence when a war is rumored.

[2] We normally do not report a new event in a subordinate clause. For example, with *When my father died, I inherited the house*, I report my inheritance, not my father's death. Therefore, event reporting is a main-clause phenomenon.

Similarly, (9a) indicates a permanent property of the sky, whereas (9b) describes a particular scene that the speaker is reporting about at the time s/he witnesses it.

(9) a. *Sora* *wa* *aoi.*
sky TOP blue
'The sky is blue.'
'The sky is an entity that is blue.'
b. *Wā,* *sora* *ga* *aoi.*
wow sky NOM blue
'Wow, the sky is blue!'

8.8 Attribute description

Participants in a reported event need not be identifiable as exemplified in (10):

(10) *Tsūkōnin* *ga* *mado* *o* *kowashita.*
passerby NOM window ACC broke
'A passerby broke a window.'

However, when some **ATTRIBUTE** (a characteristic or quality inherent in the entity) is to be described, the entity must be identifiable. Otherwise, the sentence would sound anomalous, e.g. #*A passerby is tall* (the pound symbol # indicates that the expression is grammatical, and yet unacceptable for various reasons). Therefore, adjectival and nominal predicates normally co-occur with NP-*wa*, rather than NP-*ga*.

(11) a. *Kono* *rapputoppu* *wa* *karui.* [adjectival predicate]
this laptop TOP light
'This laptop is light.'
b. *Shigeru* *wa* *kangoshi* *da.* [nominal predicate]
TOP nurse is
'Shigeru is a nurse.'

8.9 Focus

In contrast with (11), when the subject that is characterized or described is marked by *ga*, it becomes the **FOCUS** of the sentence, the most informative part, because it is unpredictable in the given context (Lambrecht 1994: 207). In English, this notion of focus can be expressed with a **CLEFT CONSTRUCTION** as in (12).[3]

[3] *Cleft sentence* refers to grammatical constructions in which an original single clause, e.g. *Jacob is a student*, is divided into two parts, e.g. *It is Jacob who is a student.*

(12) a. *Kono* *rapputoppu* *ga* *karui.*
this laptop NOM light
'It is this laptop that is light.'
b. *Shigeru* *ga* *kangoshi* *da.*
NOM nurse is
'It is Shigeru who is a nurse.'

When a question consists of an interrogative subject, the portion of the answer that corresponds to this unidentified entity is naturally the most informative part, and, therefore, marked by *ga*. In (13), *watashi wa* in B's utterance sounds unacceptable because the sentence is not about the speaker, but about the event in which the speaker is a mere participant.

(13) A: *Dare* *ga* *kore* *o* *tsukuttan* *desu* *ka?*[4]
who NOM this ACC made is INT
'Who made this?'
B: *Watashi* *ga/#wa* *tsukurimashita.*
I NOM/TOP made
'I made it.'

In English, *I'm going to* and *I'll* are interchangeable in many, if not most, contexts. However, if the lecturer enters your classroom and says, *Oh, I forgot to bring the projector*, and you decide to volunteer to bring it, you should say *I'll go get it*, not #*I'm going to go get it*, because the latter indicates that the activity is pre-planned, not decided on site. This distinction can be captured by the use of *ga* and *wa*. In (14a), the use of *ga* conveys a decision just made at the time of the utterance while the use of *wa* does not. On the other hand, in (14b), *wa*, but not *ga*, is appropriate if answering the question, *Is everybody going to the lecture this evening?*

(14) a. *Watashi* *ga/#wa* *motte-kimasu.*
I NOM/TOP carry-come
'I'll go get it.'
b. *Watashi* *#ga/wa* *ikimasu.*
I NOM/TOP go
'I'm going.'

8.10 Contrastive *wa*

Wa has a contrastive (CNT) function, in which case the NP does not have to be identifiable.

(15) a. *Ōzei no* *hito* *wa* *pātī* *ni* *kimashita* *ga,* *omoshiroi* *hito*
many people CNT party to came but interesting people
wa *hitori* *mo* *imasendeshita.* (Kuno 1973: 47)
CNT one.person even did.not.exist
'Many people came to the party, but there were none who were interesting.'

[4] This type of sentence with the copula *desu* will be discussed in Chapter 15.

b. *Tegami* *wa* *kimashita.*
letter TOP/CNT came
'The letter came.' [non-contrastive] or 'A letter came (but there was nothing else).'

c. *Dare* *wa* *kite,* *dare* *wa* *konakattan* *desu* *ka?*
who CNT came.and who CNT did.not.come is INT
'Who came, and who didn't come?'

The first half of (15a), *ōzei no hito wa pātī ni kimashita* 'many people came', is unacceptable if it stands by itself because *ōzei no hito* is unidentifiable and yet marked by *wa*. However, when a contrast is added by means of the second half, the sentence becomes acceptable. (15b) is ambiguous. If *tegami* 'letter' is identifiable (e.g. when the interlocutors have been talking about a specific letter), the sentence is interpreted as consisting of the topic–comment construction, but if *tegami* is not identifiable, the hearer automatically interprets the sentence as contrastive, implying that something else has not arrived. With a strong emphasis on contrast, even interrogative subject NPs can be marked with *wa* as shown in (15c).

8.11 Negative-scope marker *wa*

Wa can mark the **SCOPE OF NEGATION**, i.e. specifying what is negated.

(16) a. *Kenkyūsho* *wa* *yomimasen.*
research.book TOP/NEG-SCP not.read
'I don't read scholarly books.'

b. *Kenkyūsho* *wa* *kai* *wa* *shimasu* *ga* *yomi* *wa* *shimasen.*
research.book TOP buy CNT do but read NEG-SCP not.do
'As for scholarly books, I buy them, but don't read them.'

In (16a), *kenkyūsho o* 'research book (accusative)' is possible, but when the sentence is negative, *wa*-marking sounds more natural. *Kenkyūsho wa* here is thus ambiguous between the topic and the negative-scope reading. If the interlocutors have already been talking about scholarly books, *wa* is a topic marker. On the other hand, if the speaker of (16a) is responding to someone else's comment that the speaker is a diligent researcher, this utterance would indicate that s/he buys research books but does not read them. It also implies that the speaker possibly reads something other than scholarly books. In this case, the concept of scholarly book is introduced into discourse by this very utterance, like *yasai* 'vegetables' in (7). Put differently, *wa*-marking of an NP can enable the hearer to project negation early on in interpreting an utterance. This function is particularly significant because in Japanese negation does not actually appear until the end of the clause.

In (16b), the first *wa* is normally construed as a topic marker, but the second and third occurrences of NP-*wa* cannot be topics. That is, it is unlikely that the utterance is about buying and reading things in this context. While both the second and the third *wa* can be analyzed uniformly as contrastive, I prefer to mark the third *wa* as negative-scope marking because this function is most saliently perceived here. As shown with these examples, the distinctions among topic, contrast, and negative scope are not clear-cut. They overlap, and when the NP is simultaneously the topic, contrastive, and in a negative sentence, *wa*-marking is most strongly called for.

Negative-scope marking *wa* can appear freely with constituents other than NPs or verbs (McGloin 1987: 173–74).

(17) a. *Kono kyōkasho wa atarashiku wa nai.* [*i*-adjective]
this textbook TOP new NEG-SCP neg
'This textbook is not new.'

b. *Jōzu ni wa kakenai.* [adverbial]
well NEG-SCP cannot.write
'(I can write it, but) I can't write (it) well.'

c. *Zenbu wa dekinakatta.* [adverb]
all NEG-SCP could.not
'(I did some, but) I couldn't do (them) all.'

8.12 Dependent clauses

A sentence can consist of one or more clauses. The one that can stand by itself is called the **MAIN CLAUSE**, and others the **DEPENDENT CLAUSES**. There are three types of dependent clauses: (i) subordinate clauses, (ii) noun-modifying clauses, and (iii) quotative clauses. Subordinate clauses normally augment the main clause with additional information such as time, condition, reason, etc.[5] A sentence asserts the content of the main clause, but not that of a subordinate clause. Therefore, subordinate clauses cannot contain a topic. In (18a), *Midori* is the topic as well as subject, but when the sentence is converted into a subordinate clause, e.g. to specify the time frame of some other event, as in (18b), *Midori* is no longer the topic, although it remains as the subject of *katta* 'bought', and must be marked with *ga*.

(18) a. *Midori wa kabu o katta.*
TOP stock ACC bought
'Midori bought stocks.'

b. *Midori ga/#wa kabu o katta toki, kaisha wa*
NOM/TOP stock ACC bought when company TOP
tōsan sunzen datta.
bankruptcy right.before was
'When Midori bought the stocks, the company was about to go bankrupt.'

[5] When two clauses of equal status are independent of each other, they are said to be in **COORDINATION**, not in subordination. For example, the Japanese connective *ga* 'but/and' forms such a clausal relationship, e.g. *Kore wa yasui ga, are wa takai* 'This is inexpensive, but that is expensive'. Theoretically, the distinction between subordination and coordination is highly complex. See Hasegawa (1996a: 8–16) for detailed discussion.

The underlined part in (19) exemplifies noun-modification clauses, which will be discussed in detail in Chapter 14. Like subordinate clauses, noun-modifying clauses do not assert their contents; therefore, the topic-marker *wa* does not occur in them.

(19) *Watashi ga/#wa kinō mita eiga wa omoshiroku-nakatta.*
I NOM/TOP yesterday saw movie TOP interesting-not
'The movie (I) saw yesterday was not interesting.'

QUOTATIVE CLAUSES (see Chapters 15 and 27), which represent other persons' utterances, are the exception to this rule. When an NP is marked with *wa* in reported speech, *wa* is maintained even when the clause is embedded into a larger reporting sentence. This is due to the fact that in a quotative sentence two voices (those of the original speaker and the reporting speaker) are represented, and each speaker's perspective (e.g. designation of a topic) must be separately maintained. In (20b) *shiken wa muzukashikatta* is a quotative clause, and *Midori wa ... to itta* a reporting clause.

(20) a. *Shiken wa muzukashikatta.*
examination TOP was.difficult
'The examination was difficult.'

b. *Midori wa shiken wa muzukashikatta to itta.*
TOP examination TOP was.difficult QUOT said
'Midori said that the examination was difficult.'

When *wa* marks contrast, rather than mere topic, it can occur in subordinate clauses.

(21) a. *Kuruma ga/#wa kowareta node mukae ni ikemasen.*
car NOM/TOP broke because pick.up for cannot.go
'Because (my) car broke down, (I) can't go pick (you) up.'

b. *Kuruma ga/wa kowarete-mo ōtobai ga aru*
car NOM/CNT broke-though motorcycle NOM exist
node mukae ni ikemasu.
because pick.up for can.go
'Although (my) car broke down, (I) can go pick (you) up because (I) have a motorcycle.'

8.13 The *wa–ga* construction

In English, the notions of subject and topic are difficult, sometimes impossible, to disentangle. In contrast, a single Japanese sentence can have a distinct topic (NP-*wa*) and subject (NP-*ga*). As demonstrated by the four sentences in (22), the topic in this construction delimits the applicability of the statement that includes the subject referent.

(22) a. *Midori wa piano ga aru.*
TOP piano NOM exit
'[Lit.] Midori, there is a piano.'
'Midori has a piano.'

b. *Watashi* *wa* *tomodachi* *ga* *ōi.*
I TOP friend NOM numerous
'[Lit.] Me, friends are numerous.'
'I have many friends.'

c. *Umeboshi* *wa* *Wakayama* *ga* *yūmei* *da.*
pickled.plum TOP Wakayama NOM famous is
'[Lit.] Pickled plums, Wakayama is famous.'
'Wakayama is famous for pickled plums.'

d. *Sakana* *wa* *sake* *ga* *oishii.*
fish TOP salmon NOM delicious
'Of fish, salmon is (the most) delicious.'

A commonly employed translation strategy for the *wa–ga* construction is *as for X*, e.g. *As for Midori, there is a piano* for (22a). However, Chafe (1976: 50) cautions that this strategy is misleading because the original Japanese sentence does not carry contrastive connotation, vis-à-vis someone other than Midori, but *as for X* inevitably does.

8.14 Staging

An explanation of *wa* as a special rhetorical device is appropriate at this point. A written text can begin with an NP-*wa* even when the reader is unable to identify the intended referent. For instance, the text presented in the following section begins with the sentence *The Visor Television Company shipped 1,000 television sets to a large department store chain.* Although *Visor Television Company* is a fictitious name and is therefore unidentifiable, it is nevertheless more natural to mark this name with *wa*, rather than with *ga*. This specialized use of *wa* is limited to written texts. In a spoken discourse, the speaker needs to supply some introductory passage – e.g. *There's a TV manufacturer called Visor Television Company. Have you heard of it?* And then s/he can continue the story about this TV manufacturer. Otherwise, the speech would sound strange, possibly incomprehensible.

Borrowing from Maynard (1987), I label this use of *wa* to mark an unidentifiable entity at the opening of a written text **STAGING**. Maynard defines *staging* as the narrator's selection of an event participant whose point of view is taken as the basis of the narration. That is, the participant is selected as the protagonist, and the narrative is constructed as if the event is perceived by him/her. Although Maynard's definition of the term *staging* is much broader than what is intended here, I nevertheless adopt this term because it provides the most illustrative image of this function of *wa* – the entity marked with *wa* at the beginning of a written discourse is, metaphorically speaking, placed on the theatrical stage as the protagonist. This rhetorical technique of staging occurs only at the beginning of a written text.

8.15 A case study

In this final section, let us consider the distinction between *ga* and *wa* in a real discourse. The following is a text drawn from a logic textbook (Baum 1981); the translation is by me. At each point where either *ga* or *wa* must be chosen, I have placed a blank square. The proper filler of each square is discussed following the passage.

The Visor Television Company shipped 1,000 television sets to a large department store chain. During the next three months, 115 of the sets were returned. In each case, the picture reception was good, but there was no sound. Examining the first group of ten returned sets, a plant inspection supervisor noticed that, in every set, a certain wire to the speaker was improperly soldered. She also noticed that the same person – Bill Evans, a fairly new employee – had done the soldering. The supervisor inspected the next group of returned sets and found the same improperly soldered wire in each. She concluded that Bill Evans' faulty soldering was the cause of the problem.

Baizā-terebi-gaisha	□[1]	*terebi*	*1,000-dai*	*o*	*ōte*	*depāto*
Visor-television-company		TV	1,000-units	ACC	major	department-store

chēn	*ni*	*shukka shita*	*ga,*	*3-kagetsu*	*inai ni*	*sono*	*uchi*	*115-dai*	□[2]
chain	to	shipped	but	3-months	within	that	within	115-units	

henpin sarete kita.	*Sorera*	*no*	*terebi*	□[3]	*gazō*	□[4]	*seijō*	*da*	*ga,*
were.returned	those	GEN	TV		picture		normal	COP	but

onsei	□[5]	*denakatta.*	*Seihin-kanri-kakarichō*	□[6]	*saisho no*	*10-dai*	*o*
sound		did.not.emit	product-control-supervisor		first	10-units	ACC

kensa shita	*tokoro,*	*izure mo*	*supīkā*	*e*	*no*	*haisen*	*no*	*handa-zuke*
inspected	when	everyone	speaker	to	GEN	connection	GEN	soldering

ni	*mondai*	□[7]	*atta.*	*Mata,*	*saikin*	*koyō sareta*	*Biru*	*Ebansu*	□[8]
in	problem		existed	and	recently	was.employed	Bill	Evans	

handa-zuke	*no*	*sagyō*	*o*	*okonatta*	*koto*	*mo*	*kakunin sareta.*	*Kakarichō*
soldering	GEN	operation	ACC	did	fact	also	was.confirmed	supervisor

□[9]	*tsugi ni*	*modotte kita*	*terebi*	*o*	*kensa*	*shi,*	*onaji*	*mondai*	*o*
	next	returned	TV	ACC	inspection	do.and	same	problem	ACC

hakken shita.	*Shitagatte,*	*kakarichō*	□[10]	*Biru Ebansu*	*no*	*sagyō*	*no*	*ochido*
discovered	consequently	supervisor			GEN	operation	GEN	failure

□[11]	*mondai*	*no*	*gen'in*	*da*	*to*	*no*	*ketsuron*	*ni*	*itatta.*
	problem	GEN	cause	COP	QUOT	GEN	conclusion	to	arrived

□[1] *Baizā-terebi-gaisha* 'Visor Television Company' is unidentifiable. Therefore, the use of *ga* is justified (see Section 8.2), and indeed many native speakers of Japanese would likely select *ga* here. Nevertheless, I prefer *wa* in this case for the rhetorical effect of staging. This example illustrates that the choice between *ga* and *wa* can be based on stylistic preference, and not only on grammatical rules.

□[2] *Ga* is more appropriate here than *wa* because *115-dai* '115 units' is unidentifiable. *Wa* would be possible only if a strong contrast were intended, which is unlikely in this case.

□[3] *Wa* must be selected here because *sorera no terebi* 'those TVs' is anaphoric (see Section 8.3). Additionally, it is in the *wa–ga* construction (see Section 8.13), e.g. *Sorera no terebi wa gazō ga kirei da* 'Those TVs, picture is sharp'.

□[4] This clause is in the second part of the *wa–ga* construction, but the use of *ga* is anomalous. This irregularity is due to the salient contrast being expressed (Section 8.10), i.e. the picture reception was normal, *but* something else was not normal. Therefore, *wa* must be selected.

□[5] The use of *wa* is justifiable here because this is the second part of the contrast, indicating what was abnormal. However, I prefer the use of *ga* for focusing (Section 8.9), i.e. it was the sound that was not functioning. Here, again, some native speakers of Japanese are likely to select *wa*.

□[6] *Ga* must be selected because *seihin-kanri-kakarichō* 'plant inspection supervisor' is the subject of the subordinate clause, *X ga Y o kensa shita tokoro* 'when X inspected Y'.

□[7] I prefer *ga* because this is a typical situation corresponding to the English *there* construction (*there was a problem in the soldering*), as shown in (1a). However, the selection of *wa* is also reasonable because *mondai* 'problem' is already implied by the preceding sentence. Therefore, although the word *mondai* has not been explicitly mentioned, it can be construed as an anaphor, which is normally marked by *wa*.

□[8] This must be *ga* because the NP is included in an event reporting clause (Section 8.7), *Bill Evans did the soldering*, as well as in a dependent clause (Section 8.12), *the fact that Bill Evans did the soldering*.

□[9] Anaphoric *wa*.

□[10] Anaphoric *wa*.

□[11] This must be *ga* because the NP is the subject of the dependent clause, *to no ketsuron* 'the conclusion that . . .'.

9 Tense, aspect, and taxis

9.1 Introduction

Time is an intellectual construct necessary to conceive of and to comprehend changes in the world around us. Grammatical notions of time are manifestations of the human experience of time, traditionally characterized in terms of tense, aspect, and taxis. **Tense** frames time linearly as a past–present–future continuum and establishes the relationship between the time of the depicted situation and the moment of speech. **Aspect** is defined as the assessment or characterization of the denoted situation "as it progresses or as it is distributed in time, but irrespective of the moment of speech or . . . of the time of another action, mentioned or implied" (Maslov 1988: 63). **Taxis**, which is less common than tense and aspect, is concerned with the chronological relationship between two situations: i.e. do they occur simultaneously; does one take precedence; is there a perceived sequentiality?

In the modern world, people consider tense to be indispensable for an understanding of reality. Nonetheless, a tense system is not an ontological necessity. Historically, aspect is primary, and tense secondary in Indo-European languages (Kurylowicz 1964; Bybee 1985), and creole languages are inherently aspectual (Givón 1982; Kotsinas 1989).[1] For pre-modern people, more salient than tense *per se* was whether or not a certain change had occurred and whether or not the speaker could ascertain its occurrence with confidence. If the speaker was certain, the hearer would naturally interpret the change to have occurred in the past. Tense has thus emerged as secondary. Tense is abstract, intellectual, and objective; aspect, on the other hand, is definite, impressionistic, and subjective (Izui 1967: 85), involving not only the temporal contour of a situation, but a number of other factors that are not strictly temporal (Michaelis 1993: 17), e.g. modality and evidentiality (Chapter 24), resultativity (Section 9.7), transitivity (Section 7.4), and

[1] Creole languages are developed from pidgin languages. A pidgin language is a simplified language used for communication between speakers of different languages. Unlike pidgin language, however, a creole is a fully fledged language spoken by native speakers.

distribution of focus over sentential constituents (Section 8.9). Ancient Japanese people conceived of time quite differently than their modern Japanese counterparts as evidenced by the fact that the word *toki* 'time' in classical Japanese meant a moment or occasion appropriate to starting a certain action (Wada 1994), e.g. *toki no koe* [Lit. voice of the time] meaning 'a battle cry'.

9.2 Tense

With regard to tense, English makes a three-way distinction (past–present–future), while Japanese makes a two-way distinction (past vs. non-past). As explained in Section 6.1, Japanese has two verbal suffixes, *-ta/-da* (e.g. *hanashi-ta* 'talked', *non-da* 'drank', *tabe-ta* 'ate') and *-u/-ru*, collectively as *-ru*, (e.g. *nom-u* 'drink', *tabe-ru* 'eat').[2] The former is referred to as the **PAST TENSE FORM**, and the latter as the **NON-PAST TENSE FORM**. For adjectives, the past tense form ends in *-katta* (e.g. *samu-katta* 'was cold'), and the non-past tense form in *-i* (e.g. *samu-i* 'is cold'). The past tense form of the copula is *datta*, and the non-past tense form is *da*. Their polite equivalents are *deshita* (past) and *desu* (non-past). (Polite forms will be discussed in Chapter 20.)

The *-ru* form indicates present time only when the predicate is **STATIVE**, which expresses not an event or action, but a state of affairs (i.e. no change is involved): e.g. *ar-u/i-ru* 'exist', *chiga-u* 'differ', *deki-ru* 'is able to do something', *ir-u* 'need'. When the predicate is **DYNAMIC**, expressing some change, *-ru* indicates future time as exemplified in (1a). English has many stative verbs, e.g. *contain*, *know*, *live*, *love*, *own*, *resemble*, whereas most Japanese verbs are dynamic, and cannot be used in the *-ru* form to describe a present state. Instead, the *-te iru* construction must be utilized as in (1b).

(1) a.	*Watashi*	*wa*	*kariforunia*	*ni*	*sum-u.*	
	I	TOP	California	in	live-NPST	
	'I'll live in California.'					
b.	*Watashi*	*wa*	*kariforunia*	*ni*	*sun-de*	*i-ru.*
	I	TOP	California	in	live-TE	exist-NPST
	'I live in California,' or 'I'm living in California.'					

In mono-clausal sentences that occur in isolation, *-ta* and *-ru* mark past and non-past time, respectively.

(2) a.	*Kinō*	*wa*	*ichinichijū*	*uchi*	*ni*	*i-ta/*i-ru.*
	yesterday	TOP	all.day	home	at	exist-PAST/*exist-NPST
	'I stayed home all day yesterday.'					

2 The suffix *-ta* arose in Late Old Japanese (circa ninth–twelfth centuries) from the auxiliary verb *-tari*, which in turn was derived from *-te ari* prior to the Old Japanese era. *Ari* is the primeval form of the existential verb *aru*.

b. *Ashita kaimono ni *it-ta/ik-u.*
tomorrow shopping for *go-PAST/go-NPST
'I'll go shopping tomorrow.'

However, in multi-clausal sentences or sentences embedded in a discourse, *-ta* and *-ru* do not necessarily designate tense as exemplified in (3).

(3) a. *Fushin na nimotsu o mi-ta toki wa, sugu ni keisatsu*
suspicious luggage ACC see-PAST time TOP immediately police
ni tsūhō shite kudasai.
to report do.TE please
'Report to the police immediately when (you) find suspicious luggage.'
b. *Marī wa uchi o deru to eki e mukatta.*
TOP house ACC leave-NPST when station to headed
'After leaving (her) house, Mary headed for the station.'

Nevertheless, in the following sentence types derived from Kunihiro (1967: 56–68) the glosses PAST and NPST are retained as the labels for *-ta* and *-ru*, respectively.

(4) The past tense form
a. A situation that materialized in the past and still exists:
Ōkiku nat-ta ne.
big become-PAST SFP
'You've grown, haven't you?'
b. Sudden discovery that a certain state of affairs has continuously existed:
A, soko ni i-ta no.
oh there at exist-PAST SFP
'Oh, there you are!'
c. Sudden recalling of a future event or plan that the speaker has known as definite:
A, ashita shiken ga at-ta.
oh tomorrow exam NOM exist-PAST
'Oh, I have an exam tomorrow!'
d. A request for hearer's confirmation of a fact (normally only in questions):
Anata wa donata deshita ka? (Mikami 1953)
you TOP who COP.PAST INT
'Who were you?' (English also employs the past tense.)
e. Proclamation or assertion of the realization of a situation which has not been realized:
Yoshi, kat-ta. (Suzuki 1965)
ok buy-PAST
'All right, [I'm sold] I'll buy it!'
f. A command (normally repeated twice):
Doi-ta, doi-ta.
step.back-PAST
'Step back! Step back!'

(5) The non-past tense form
a. A past event:
Kikizute-naranai koto o i-u ne.
ignore-cannot thing ACC say-NPST SFP
'You've said something I can't ignore.'
b. A step-by-step procedure (e.g. in recipes):
Tsugi ni shio o ire-ru.
next salt ACC put-NPST
'Next, add some salt.'

c. A command:
Sugu ni *tabe-ru.*
immediately eat-NPST
'Eat (it) now!'

These examples demonstrate that simply equating *-ta* and *-ru* with English tenses is misleading and confusing.

9.3 Aspect

Compared with tense, aspect is a more subjective notion, in which **PERFECTIVE** and **IMPERFECTIVE** are the most salient concepts. Comrie (1976) describes them as follows.

> [T]he perfective looks at the situation from outside, without necessarily distinguishing any of the internal structure of the situation, whereas the imperfective looks at the situation from inside, and as such is crucially concerned with the internal structure of the situation, since it can both look backwards towards the start of the situation, and look forwards to the end of the situation, and indeed is equally appropriate if the situation is one that lasts through all time, without any beginning and without any end (p. 4).

> Aspect is not concerned with relating the time of the situation to any other time-point, but rather with the internal temporal constituency of the one situation; one could state the difference as one between situation–internal time (aspect) and situation–external time (tense) (p. 5).

Sumu 'reside' in (1a) is perfective, designating the event as a whole, whereas the *-te iru* construction in (1b) indicates the imperfective aspect – i.e. the event in progress. The perfective involves the notion of *completeness* (wholeness), which is sometimes confused with the notion of *completed* (Comrie 1976: 18). Whether or not the situation is actually completed (i.e. has already happened) is expressed by tense, not by aspect.[3]

Unlike dynamic verbs, with stative verbs, e.g. those in (6), it is unclear whether or not *-ru* marks perfective.[4]

(6) a. *Watashi* *wa* *kumērugo* *ga* *deki-ru.*
I TOP Khmer.language NOM can-NPST
'I can (speak) Khmer.'

[3] Miller (1975) claims that *-ta* marks perfective and *-ru* marks imperfective. However, his conceptualization of imperfective differs greatly from that presented here. See Hasegawa (1999b) for further discussion of Miller's idea.

[4] As Kindaichi (1950) points out, Japanese has two types of stative predicates. One cannot occur in the *-te iru* construction, e.g. (6a) **kumērugo ga dekite iru* 'I'm able to speak Khmer', but the other type can, e.g. (6b) *takusan no shima kara natte iru* '(Japan) consists of many islands'. Kindaichi characterizes the latter as depicting a state where the notion of time is not involved.

b. *Nihon wa takusan no shima kara nar-u.*
Japan TOP many island from consist-NPST
'Japan consists of many islands.'

Are these situations depicted as a whole from the outside (perfective) or from the inside (imperfective)? Is this even a meaningful question? It seems more reasonable to conclude that the perfective–imperfective distinction is neutralized when the predicate is stative.

The imperfective aspect, concerned with the internal structure of the situation, is naturally more complex than the perfective. One subtype of imperfective is **HABITUAL**, a situation characterized by extended time (Comrie 1976: 27). In English, the habitual aspect is expressed with the present tense form if the situation exists during speech time, but is expressed with the *used to* construction if the situation no longer holds, as in *Mia used to eat meat.* In Japanese, the former case is expressed with the non-past form, e.g. (7a), and the latter with the past form, e.g. (7b), or with the *mono da* construction, e.g. (7c).

(7) a. *Watashi wa yoku uta-u.*
I TOP often sing-NPST
'I often sing.'
b. *Ano koro wa yoku utat-ta.*
that time TOP often sing-PAST
'(I) used to sing often.'
c. *Ano koro wa yoku utat-ta mono da.*
that time TOP often sing-PAST thing COP.NPST
'[Lit.] It is the case that (I) used to sing often.'

Another subtype of imperfective aspect is **PROGRESSIVE**. It is expressed by the *-te iru* construction.

(8) *Midori wa piano o hii-te i-ta/i-ru.*
TOP piano ACC play-TE exist-PAST/exist-NPST
'Midori was/is playing the piano.'

There are other constructions for expressing various imperfective aspects:

(9) a. Verb (adverbial) + *tsutsu aru* 'about to start'
Midori ga piano o hiki-tsutsu ar-u.
NOM piano ACC play-about.to exist-NPST
'Midori is about to play the piano.'
b. Verb (adverbial) + *hajimeru* 'start' [The situation has just begun.]
Midori ga piano o hiki-hajime-ta.
NOM piano ACC play-begin-PAST
'Midori began to play the piano.'
c. Verb (adverbial) + *tsuzukeru* 'continue' [The situation continues.]
Midori ga piano o hiki-tsuzuke-ta.
NOM piano ACC play-continue-PAST
'Midori continued playing the piano.'

9.4 Taxis

The term *taxis* – expressing the chronological relationship between two situations – is less commonly used than are *tense* and *aspect*, but it is nevertheless a very helpful notion for analyzing time-related concepts in the Japanese language. As mentioned above, *-ta* and *-ru* can be considered the past and the non-past, respectively, when the predicate is in a mono-clausal sentence considered in isolation. However, a sentence normally occurs within a coherent discourse, in which the comprehension of the temporal relationships between events is indispensable. Compare the following two situations:

(10) a. *Fushin na* *nimotsu* *o* *[mi-ta/#mi-ru]* *toki* *wa,*
suspicious luggage ACC [see-PAST/#see-NPST] when TOP
sugu ni *keisatsu* *ni* *tsūhō* *shite* *kudasai.*
Immediately police to report do.TE please
'Report to the police immediately when (you) find suspicious luggage.'

b. *Okane* *o* *[#kashi-ta/kas-u]* *toki* *wa,* *aite* *o* *yoku*
money ACC [#lend-PAST/lend-NPST] when TOP person ACC well
shirabe-nasai.
investigate-IMP
'When (you) lend money, you should thoroughly check the recipient.'

In (10a), suspicious luggage must be found *before* reporting it to the police. With the connective *toki* 'when', such a case requires *-ta* to indicate that the subordinate event is completed *before* the main event. By contrast, in (10b), it is advised to loan money only *after* checking the person. Because *-ta* indicates the opposite order, *-ru* must be used if the subordinate event is yet to be realized when the main event occurs. The notion of completion in taxis should not be confused with the perfective aspect, which refers to the event as a whole. In terms of aspect, both *kashi-ta* and *kas-u* are perfective.

Next, consider the following:

(11) a. *Nihon* *ni* *ik-u* *toki,* *kono* *kamera* *o* *kaimashita.*
Japan to go-NPST when this camera ACC buy-PAST
'When (I) went to Japan, (I) bought this camera.'

b. *Nihon* *ni* *it-ta* *toki,* *kono* *kamera* *o* *kaimashita.*
go-PAST
'When (I) went to Japan, (I) bought this camera.'

(11a) is unambiguous, the camera being bought before the speaker went to Japan. By contrast, (11b) is ambiguous: the camera might have been bought before the speaker's departure or after his/her arrival in Japan. The latter interpretation is in accordance with the explanation of (10), but the former calls upon further explanation. In this interpretation, the event of going to Japan is conceived as a whole (i.e. perfective proper), including its preparatory phase up to its aftermath. Why, then, is such a perfective interpretation precluded in (11a)? Although both *ik-u* and *it-ta* occur in a subordinate clause, which can be free from the concept of tense, in this particular case tense plays a significant role. Because both events occurred in the past, *ik-u* in (11a) permits only the taxis reading, whereas *it-ta* in (11b) permits both tense and taxis readings, resulting in the said ambiguity.

9.5 Reference time

In order to account for various time-related phenomena in language, Reichenbach (1947) introduced the concepts of **EVENT TIME** and **REFERENCE TIME**. Event time refers to the temporal location at which a given situation (i.e. an event, action, or state) takes place; reference time is determined contextually and located between event time and speech time. In his framework, the past tense indicates that the event time is identical with the reference time, which precedes the speech time. Consider the following sentence derived from Somerset Maugham's *Of Human Bondage*:

(12) But Philip ceased to think of her a moment after he had settled down in his carriage.

In a narrative, the series of recounted events determines the point of reference. As exemplified in (12), it normally falls in the past. The subordinate event – Philip's action of settling down in his carriage – is depicted not directly from the point of speech (past tense), but, rather, from the reference time, i.e. when Philip ceased to think of her (past perfect).

Some researchers analyze *-ta* and *-ru* along these lines. Ota (1972), for example, argues that *-ta* indicates event time being prior to reference time, and *-ru* otherwise. If no reference time is explicitly specified, speech time serves as the default reference time, making *-ta* and *-ru* resemble tense markers. In a dependent construction, e.g. a subordinate clause, reference time is supplied by the construction on which it depends.

Miura (1974) points out that, in dependent constructions, not only the main-clause time, but also the speech time can serve as the reference time as in the following example:

(13) *Kanai* *no* *ike-ta* *hana* *ga* *ashita* *no*
my.wife GEN arrange-PAST flower NOM tomorrow GEN
tenrankai *ni* *de-ru.*
exhibition in enter-NPST
'Flowers that my wife [has arranged/will arrange] will be displayed in tomorrow's exhibition.'

In one reading, the flowers have already been arranged before the speech time, and in the other, they will be arranged after the speech time but before the exhibition (i.e. the reference time).

The analysis that *-ta* designates the event time being prior to the reference time and *-ru* otherwise cannot account for some cases straightforwardly. The following is derived from Onoe (1995):

(14) *Naite tanom-u kara kane o kashite-yat-ta no da.*
crying ask-NPST because money ACC lend-give-PAST NMLZ COP.NPST
'Because (you) implored (me), (I) lent (you) the money.'

In (14), the reference time may be the time of lending the money or the speech time, and the *-ru* marked imploration event is normally understood to have occurred before lending the money as well as before the speech time. (Marking with *-ta* is also possible here.) However, as a rule, *-ru* is to indicate that the event is incompleted at the reference time. This irregularity can be explained in such a way that the imploration is understood to be continued while the speaker is handing the money.

Furthermore, unlike the connective *toki* 'when', which permits both *-ta* and *-ru* (as in (10)), some connectives occur with only one or the other, but not both, as in the following sentences.

(15) a. *Mado o [ake-ta/*ake-ru]-ra, kanarazu shimete kudasai.*
window ACC [open-PAST/*open-NPST]-when surely close.TE please
'Please make sure to close it after you open the window.'
b. *Mado o [*ake-ta/ ake-ru]-to, tori ga haitte-ki-ta.*
window ACC [*open-PAST/open-NPST]-when bird NOM enter-come-PAST
'When I opened the window, a bird flew in.'

The connective *-ra* 'when/if' in (15a) allows only *-ta*, whereas the connective *to* in (15b) only *-ru*. Both connectives indicate, among other things, an event sequence: the one in the subordinate clause occurs before the main-clause event. The use of *-ta* in (15a) is consistent with its general meaning of *-ta*, but the use of *-ru* in (15b) is not. These grammatical restrictions are idiosyncratic and cannot be derived by means of any rule.

9.6 *-Ta* and *-ru* in discourse

-Ta and *-ru* frequently alternate in written as well as spoken discourse. This can be regarded as a rhetorical phenomenon, as in the case of English, where the present tense can be used for a past situation – the so-called **HISTORICAL PRESENT**. The historical present is considered by many to be a stylistic device with limited distribution (Wolfson 1979; Schiffrin 1981; Fleischman 1990). Soga (1983: 219) has this to say concerning rhetorical uses of *-ta* and *-ru* in Japanese:

With the exception of the uses of *-ru* required by grammatical restrictions, it is quite possible for an author to use only the *-ta* form regardless of whether an event is "foreground" or "background."[5] Likewise, although it may not be very common, it should be possible to use nothing but the non-past tense form regardless of the types of the events described. In the former case, the story will be perceived only in a matter-of-fact way, while in the latter it will be perceived as if the reader is experiencing the events himself. In this sense, therefore, it seems that proper uses of tense forms constitute an element of the effective specific style of an author or of a story.

9.7 The perfect

The (present) perfect is the most complex category that deals with time-related linguistic phenomena.[6] It differs from the aspects proper (e.g. perfective and imperfective) because the perfect tells us "nothing directly about the situation in itself, but rather relates some state to a preceding situation" (Comrie 1976: 52). In those languages that have both perfect and past-tense forms, the semantics of the two invariably overlap, e.g. *I have eaten breakfast* vs. *I ate breakfast*. The difference is traditionally explained in such a way that, while both refer to a past event, the perfect also signals its present relevance. This characterization is manifestly inadequate because in normal conversation, the very act of mentioning an event guarantees its present relevance, and the use of the perfect does not transform an irrelevant piece of information into a relevant one.

In Reichenbach's framework introduced in Section 9.5, the perfect differs from the past tense in the location of the reference time. In the perfect, e.g. *The door has been open*, the reference time is aligned with the speech time, whereas in the past tense, e.g. *The door was open*, it is aligned with the event time. That is, if in answer to the question *What did you notice when you checked the cellar?* and a witness responds *The door was open*, the reference time is the time at which the witness checked the cellar. The door may have been open for a long time beforehand, and it may still be open, but the witness is making a claim for only a specific time span in the past (the reference time), and the relationship between the speech time and the event time (when the door was opened) is not specified, i.e. the door may still be open (Klein 1992).

[5] Hopper (1979: 213) divides statements in narrative discourse into two categories: those signaling the major thread of the narration and those providing supporting information. He calls the former **FOREGROUND**, and the latter **BACKGROUND**. Foreground statements express events in chronological order, making the completion of one event a necessary condition for the next; as such, verbs that appear in foreground tend to be punctual. Background statements need not be sequential with respect to foreground events, tend to amplify or comment on the main narrative events, and are concurrent with the main events and tend to be stative.

[6] The perfect construction can occur with the past, present, and future tenses. The discussion here is limited to the present perfect.

Comrie (1976: 56–61) divides the perfect into four subcategories: (i) **PERFECT OF RESULT**, (ii) **EXPERIENTIAL PERFECT**, (iii) **PERFECT OF PERSISTENT SITUATION**, and (iv) **PERFECT OF RECENT PAST**. The difference between the first two is exemplified by these two sentences:

(16) a. *Bill has gone to America.*
b. *Bill has been to America.*

In (16a), the perfect of result, the present state that Bill is in America is expressed as the result of a past event – that Bill went to America. In (16b), the experiential perfect, the given event is said to have held at least once during some time in the past leading up to the present, i.e. Bill went to America at least once. Comrie considers the perfect of result to be the clearest manifestation of the present relevance of a past event.

The closest resemblance to English perfect in Japanese is the *-te iru* construction, which also expresses the progressive aspect, e.g. (8). Although both situations in (16) can be expressed by a single construction in Japanese, (17a), the difference between the perfect of result and the experiential perfect emerges with other predicates, as in (17b) and (17c).

(17) a. *Biru wa Amerika ni it-te i-ru.*
Bill TOP America to go-TE exist-NPST
'Bill has [gone/been] to America.'
b. *Bīru ga reizōko ni hait-te i-ru.* [perfect of result only]
beer NOM refrigerator in enter-TE exist-NPST
'There is beer in the refrigerator.'
c. *Biru wa takusan hon o yon-de i-ru.* [experiential perfect only]
Bill TOP many book ACC read-TE exist-NPST
'Bill has read many books.'

The third category, the perfect of persistent situation, describes a situation that began in the past and persists into the present, e.g. *We've lived here for ten years*, which can be expressed by the *-te iru* construction as in (18).

(18) *Watashitachi wa 10-nen koko ni sun-de i-ru.*
we TOP 10-years here in live-TE exist-NPST
'We've lived here for ten years.'

The final category, the perfect of recent past, is expressed in Japanese with the *-ta tokoro da* construction.

(19) *Biru ga tsui-ta tokoro da.*
Bill NOM arrive-PAST place COP.NPST
'Bill has just arrived.'

A vital difference between the perfect and the past in English is the co-occurrence restriction on temporal adverbials, as illustrated in (20).

(20) a. *Bill has left the house.*
b. **Bill has left the house at six o'clock.*
c. *Bill left the house at six o'clock.*

Many languages, including Japanese, impose no such restriction.

(21) a. *Biru wa 6-ji ni ie o de-te i-ru.*
Bill TOP 6-o'clock at house ACC leave-TE exist-NPST
'[Lit.] *Bill has left the house at six o'clock.'
b. *Watashi wa kinō 10-jikan ne-te i-ru.*
I TOP yesterday 10-hours sleep-TE exist-NPST
'[Lit.] *I have slept 10 hours yesterday.'

Most instances of the *-te iru* construction are, in principle, ambiguous between progressive and perfect readings. However, the ambiguity is normally resolved by a co-occurring adverbial and/or other expression.

(22) a. *Biru wa ima hon o yon-de i-ru.*
Bill TOP now book ACC read-TE exist-NPST
'Bill is reading a book now.'
b. *Biru wa 8000-satsu mo hon o yon-de i-ru.*
Bill TOP 8000-volumes as.many.as book ACC read-TE exist-NPST
'Bill has read as many as 8,000 books.'

9.8 The resultative

In the previous section, it was demonstrated that the *-te iru* construction can indicate the perfect of result. In order to understand how the Japanese language articulates temporal notions, it is necessary to recognize the difference between the perfect of result and the **RESULTATIVE** proper as exemplified by the two kinds of *-te aru* constructions. Although both describe a present state as the result of a past event, several differences exist between the two. For example, Nedjalkov and Jaxontov (1988: 15–17) point to the following oppositions (for further discussion, see Hasegawa 1992).

(23) a. The perfect does not alter the valence (see Section 7.3) of the base verb, whereas the resultative is predominantly intransitive.
b. Unlike the resultative, the perfect can be derived from any verb, either transitive or intransitive, including those that denote situations that involve no change of the state of any participant, e.g. *sing* and *laugh*.
c. In the perfect, adverbials of moment, e.g. *at three o'clock*, denote the moment at which the event takes place, whereas in the resultative, they denote only the moment at which the state is in existence.

While the valence of the base verb does not change in the *-te iru* construction, it can be reduced by one in the *-te aru* construction. In (24a), the logical direct object of the transitive verb *tomeru* 'to park' is marked with the accusative *o*, and the logical subject with the nominative *ga*. In (24b), by contrast, the logical direct object is marked with the nominative, and the logical subject cannot be mentioned explicitly. In other words, the valence of the base verb is maintained in (24a), but reduced by one in (24b).

(24) a. *Midori ga michi ni kuruma o tome-te [i-ru/ar-u].*
NOM street in car ACC park-TE exist-NPST
'Midori has parked the car in the street.'
b. *Kuruma ga michi ni tome-te ar-u.*
car NOM street in park-TE exist-NPST
'There is a car parked in the street.'

Because the *-te iru* construction and the *-te aru* construction in (24a) do not change the valence of the base verb, they are both realizations of the perfect of result, according to criterion (23a). On the other hand, because it changes the verb valence, the second type of the *-te aru* construction represented in (24b) is categorized as the resultative proper. In addition, the *-te iru* construction in (24a) can be interpreted either as the perfect of result (Midori's car is being parked in the street at the speech time) or as the experiential perfect (Midori parked her car in the street at least once), but the *-te aru* construction in (24a) must be interpreted only as the perfect of result.

The distinction between the perfect of result and the resultative proper also emerges by applying criterion (23b): the perfect can be derived from any verb, including those that denote situations involving no change of the state of any participant, but the resultative cannot be derived from such verbs. Of course, there are many semantic and pragmatic constraints, but in principle, the perfect of result *-te iru* and *-te aru* accommodate any type of verb, but the resultative proper *-te aru* occurs only with verbs denoting some change of state. In (25b), because taking preventive measures cannot change a non-existent fire, the resultative *-te aru* is unacceptable. As before, *-te iru* in (25a) can be an instance of either the perfect of result or the experiential perfect, while *-te aru* in (25a) must be interpreted only as an instance of the perfect of result.

(25) a. *Kaji o bōshi shi-te [i-ru/ar-u].*
fire ACC prevention do-TE exist-NPST
'(Someone) has taken preventive measures against a fire.'
b. **Kaji ga bōshi shi-te ar-u.*
fire NOM prevention do-TE exist-NPST
'Preventive measures targeted against fire have been taken.'

As predicted by criterion (23c), moment adverbials referring to the event time such as *kinō* 'yesterday' can appear in the perfect of result, but not in the resultative as shown in (26a) and (26b), respectively:

(26) a. *Kinō wairo o watashi-te [i-ru/ar-u].*
yesterday bribe ACC give-TE exist-NPST
'(I) have given a bribe (to someone) yesterday.'[7]
b. **Kinō wairo ga watashi-te ar-u.*
yesterday bribe ACC give-TE exist-NPST
'A bribe was given (to someone) yesterday.'

[7] With *iru*, the subject is likely to be a third person, whereas with *aru* it is likely to be the first person, i.e. the speaker. See Subsection 24.2.5 for this distancing effect of *-te iru*.

Table 9.1 *Semantics of the constructions discussed in this chapter.*

		Past situation	Present situation
Past	*-ta*	asserted	N/A
Experiential perfect	*-te iru*	asserted	N/A
Perfect of result	*-te iru* *-te aru*	asserted	asserted
Resultative	*-te aru*	implied	asserted
Present	*-ru*	N/A	asserted

9.9 Summary

In an isolated sentence in Japanese, the past tense form indicates a past situation, whereas the non-past tense form indicates a present situation when the predicate is stative, but a future situation when the predicate is dynamic. In terms of aspect, both *-ta* and *-ru* are perfective, whereas the prototypical imperfective notion is expressed with *-te iru*. The *-te iru* construction indicates either the imperfective (progressive) or the perfect aspect. In terms of taxis, *-ta* indicates that the situation is completed before the reference time, whereas *-ru* indicates that the situation still exists or has yet to be realized at the reference time.

The experiential perfect indicates that a given situation has occurred in the past, just like the past tense, so that it is compatible with an adverbial referring to a past time, e.g. *kinō* 'yeserday'. The *-te iru* construction that serves this function comes closest to the past tense. The resultative construction describes a present situation, although it implies that it is a result of a past event. The perfect of result falls somewhere between the resultative proper and the experiential perfect. As such, it does permit an adverbial referring to a past time. These concepts are summarized in Table 9.1.

Part IV

Major clause types

10 Measurement and comparison

10.1 Measurement

English numerically measures the characteristics of entities using (i) nouns that designate particular dimensions, e.g. *depth*, *height*, *age* as in (1); (ii) adjectives that express dimensional concepts, e.g. *tall*, *old* as in (2); and (iii) verbs that incorporate the dimension concept, i.e. *cost* and *weigh* as in (3).[1]

(1) a. Entity + *has* + dimension + *of* + measurement
The container has a height of 6 feet.
b. Entity's + dimension + *is* + measurement
The container's height is 6 feet.
c. Dimension + *of* + entity + *is* + measurement
The height of the container is 6 feet.
d. Entity + *is* + measurement + *in/of* + dimension
The container is 6 feet in height.
My sister is 6 years of age.

(2) Entity + *is* + measurement + adjective
My daughter is 5 feet tall.
My son is 13 years old.
My biology textbook is 3 inches thick.

(3) Entity + verb + measurement
My biology textbook costs 100 dollars.
My biology textbook weighs 2 pounds.

Only the "neutral" members of opposite pairs of adjectives can identify scales of linear extent. *Tall*, *old*, and *thick* are neutral adjectives, as opposed to the "marked," or non-neutral, opposite adjectives *short*, *young*, and *thin*. Therefore, *tall*, *old*, and *thick* can appear in sentence pattern (2) while their opposites cannot.

(4) **My daughter is 5 feet short.*
**My son is 13 years young.*
**My biology textbook is 3 inches thin.*

[1] Much of this chapter is derived from Hasegawa *et al.* (2010).

Japanese measures scalar properties with nouns that designate particular dimensions: e.g. *okuyuki* 'horizontal depth', *fukasa* 'vertical depth', *takasa* 'height', and *atsusa* 'thickness'. In many cases, both the copula and the existential verb *aru* can be used to form a predicate for numerical expressions. (5a) is in the *wa–ga* construction discussed in Section 8.13.

(5) a. Entity + *wa* + dimension + *ga* + measurement + copula/existential
Kono tsukue wa okuyuki ga 60cm da/aru.
this desk TOP depth NOM COP/exist
'This desk has a depth of 60 centimeters.'
b. Entity + *wa* + dimension + measurement + copula
Kono tsukue wa okuyuki 60cm da.
this desk TOP depth COP
'This desk has a depth of 60 centimeters.'
c. Entity + *no* + dimension + *wa* + measurement + copula/existential
Kono tsukue no okuyuki wa 60cm da/aru.
this desk GEN depth TOP COP/exist
'The depth of this desk is 60 centimeters.'

(5a) and (5b) may seem to be mere variations of the same construction, (5a) with *ga*, (5b) without it. They are, however, distinct constructions because (5a) permits both the copula and the existential verb *aru*, but (5b) permits only the copula. Furthermore, while (5a) allows different word orders, (5b) prohibits them.

(5) a'. *Kono tsukue wa 60cm da/aru, okuyuki ga.*
a''. *Okuyuki ga, kono tsukue wa 60cm da/aru.*
b'. **Kono tsukue wa 60cm da, okuyuki.*
b''. **Okuyuki, kono tsukue wa 60cm da.*

Many of these dimensional nouns are derived from adjectives by adding *-sa*, e.g. *atsui* 'thick' > *atsu-sa* 'thickness', *fukai* 'deep' > *fuka-sa* 'depth', *takai* 'high' > *taka-sa* 'height', *wakai* 'young' > *waka-sa*, and so forth (see Section 6.5). When the measurement value (e.g. *100 pēji* '100 pages') implies the dimension (e.g. the length of a book), the dimension (e.g. *nagasa* 'length') itself can be omitted:

(6) Entity + *wa* + measurement + copula/existential
a. *Kono hon wa 100 pēji da/aru.*
this book TOP page COP/exist
'This book is/has 100 pages.'
b. *Kono rapputoppu wa 1 kiro da/aru.*
this laptop TOP kilogram COP/exist
'This laptop is (weighs) 1 kilogram.'

As illustrated in (7), when the noun indicating a dimension is derived from an adjective, Japanese exhibits the same constraint that applies in English (e.g. *five feet tall* vs. **five feet short*).

(7) a. *Kono biru wa takasa/*hikusa ga 30m da/aru.*
this building TOP height/*lowness NOM COP/exist
'This building is 30m high/*low.'
b. *Kono pūru wa fukasa/*asasa ga 2m da/aru.*
this pool TOP depth/*shallowness NOM COP/exist
'The pool is 2m deep/*shallow.'

However, the use of marked (vis-à-vis neutral) adjectives is possible when the marked characteristics are significant in a positive way as in (8b, 8d). Note that in (8b, 8d), nouns derived from marked adjectives occur naturally in the copula construction, but not with the existential *aru*.

(8) a. *Kono hon wa atsusa ga 3cm da/aru.* [neutral]
this book TOP thickness NOM COP/exist
'This book has a thickness of 3 centimeters.'
b. *Kono dejikame wa ususa ga 18mm da/*aru.* [marked]
this digital.camera TOP thinness NOM COP/*exist
'*This digital camera has a thinness of 18mm.'
c. *Kono kabin wa omosa ga 2kg da/aru.* [neutral]
this vase TOP heaviness NOM COP/exist
'*This vase has a heaviness of 2kg.'
d. *Kono rapputoppu wa karusa ga 500g da/*aru.* [marked]
this laptop TOP lightness NOM COP/*exist
'*This laptop has a lightness of 500g.'

When the significance of having a marked characteristic is not immediately obvious, the acceptability declines drastically as shown in (9b, 9d) (e.g. it is unclear that a markedly short treatise would be positive).

(9) a. *Kono ronbun wa nagasa ga 30 pēji da/aru.* [neutral]
this treatise TOP length NOM page COP/exist
'This treatise is 30 pages long.'
b. **Kono ronbun wa mijikasa ga 30 pēji da.* [marked]
this treatise TOP shortness NOM page COP
'#This treatise is 30 pages short.' (This sentence does not express the intended meaning.)
c. *Kono isu wa takasa ga 1 mētoru da/aru.* [neutral]
this chair TOP chair NOM meter COP/exist
'This chair is 1 meter high.'
d. **Kono isu wa hikusa ga 1 mētoru da.* [marked]
this chair TOP lowness NOM meter COP
'*This chair is 1 meter low.'

The constraint on marked expressions of characteristics is more prominent in Sino-Japanese compounds (see Section 6.8): for example, the word *sha-kō* 車高 (car + high = the height of a car) exists, but **sha-tei* *車低 (car + low) does not. Other examples are as follows: *shin-chō* 身長 (body + long = body height) vs. **shin-tan* *身短 (body + short); *sui-shin* 水深 (water + deep = the depth of the water) vs. **sui-sen* *水浅 (water + shallow); *tai-jū* 体重 (body + heavy = body weight) vs. **tai-kei* *体軽 (body + light).

10.2 Comparison

English reports scalar equalities and inequalities between two entities as (i) arguments (i.e. obligatory elements, see Section 7.1) of a comparison adjective, which designates the dimension as occurs in (10), or (ii) arguments of a generic comparison verb or adjective, in which case the dimension is introduced in a prepositional phrase, as in (11). The argument denoted as Entity2 is called the **STANDARD OF COMPARISON**.

(10) a. Entity1 + *is* + *as* + adjective + *as* + entity2
Your proposal is as interesting as mine.
b. Entity1 + *is* + comparison adjective + *than* + entity2
Your proposal is better/worse than mine.
Your proposal is longer than mine.
c. Entity1 + *is* + comparison marker + adjective + *than* + entity2
Your proposal is more/less interesting than mine.

(11) a. Entity1 + *is* + identity adjective + *to* + entity2 + *in* + dimension
Your proposal is identical to mine in length.
b. Entity1 + comparison verb + entity2 + *in* + dimension
Your proposal exceeds mine in length.

Japanese reports scalar equalities and inequalities between two entities using a plain adjective that incorporates the dimension. Although there is no comparative form for adjectives, the phrases NP *to onaji kurai/gurai* 'about the same amount as', NP *no hō* (Lit. 'NP's side'), and NP *yori* 'than NP' are unambiguous indicators of comparison semantics.

(12) a. Entity1 + *wa* + entity2 + *to onaji kurai* + adjective

Kore	*wa*	*are*	*to*	*onaji*	*kurai*	*nagai.*
this	TOP	that	with	same	about	long

'This is as long as that.'

b. Entity1 + *no hō ga* + adjective

Kore	*no*	*hō*	*ga*	*nagai.*
this	GEN	side	NOM	long

'This is longer.'

c. Entity2 + *yori* + adjective

Are	*yori*	*nagai.*
that	than	long

'It's longer than that.'

d. Entity1 + *no hō ga* + entity2 + *yori* + adjective

Kore	*no*	*hō*	*ga*	*are*	*yori*	*nagai.*
this	GEN	side	NOM	that	than	long

'This is longer than that.'

Under the right circumstances, *ga*-marked subjects alone can make a clause comparative, especially when only two items are under discussion as in (13). *Wa*-marked subjects do not convey comparison as shown in (13B').

(13) A: *Dotchi/Dore* *ga* *takai?*
which.side/which NOM expensive
'*Which one is more expensive?*'
B: *Kotchi/Kore* *ga* *takai.*
this.side/this NOM expensive
'This one is more expensive.'
B': *Kotchi/Kore* *wa* *takai.*
this.side/this TOP expensive
'This one is expensive.'

In English, the standard of comparison can be expressed in several ways: e.g. *than her, than she is, than expected, than is expected*. However, when the standard is a numerical value, it cannot be encoded as a clause:

(14) a. *John is taller than Bill is.*
b. **John is taller than 6 feet is.*

When the standard is a numerical value, Japanese employs totally different constructions, with *ijō* 'equal to or more than' as in (15c).[2]

(15) a. *Kono* *kuruma* *wa* *watashi* *no* *yori* *takai.*
this car TOP mine GEN than expensive
'This car is more expensive than mine.'
b. ??*Kono* *kuruma* *wa* *30,000* *doru* *yori* *takai.*[3]
this car TOP dollar than expensive
'This car is more expensive than $30,000.'
c. *Kono* *kuruma* *wa* *30,000* *doru* *ijō* *da/suru.*
this car TOP dollar more.than COP/do
'This car is (equal to or) more than $30,000.'

Ijō follows a numerical expression and forms an NP, which in turn can modify another NP.

(16) a. *30,000* *doru* *ijō* *no* *kuruma*
dollar more.than GEN car
'a car that is (equal to or) more than $30,000'
b. *500-nin* *ijō* *no* *hito* *ga* *sanka shita.*
more.than GEN people NOM participated
'(Equal to or) More than 500 people participated.'

As in English, adverbs can occur in comparison constructions in Japanese.

(17) a. *Kono* *hon* *wa* *motto* *nagai.*
this book TOP more long
'This book is even longer. [Lit. more long]'
b. *Kono* *hon* *wa* *haruka ni* *nagai.*
this book TOP by.far long
'This book is much longer.'

[2] When *ijō* follows a numerical expression, the number is included. That is, *2 ijō* means '2 or more', not 'more than 2'.

[3] This type of expression can occur freely in noun-modification constructions, e.g. *30,000 doru yori takai kuruma* 'a car (that is) more expensive than $30,000'.

c. *Kono* *hon* *wa* *wazuka ni* *nagai.*
this book TOP slightly long
'This book is slightly longer.'

10.3 Measured difference

English reports differences between two entities measured against the same scale with an adjectival comparison construction, introducing the value of the difference as (i) a modifier of the adjective as in (18), or (ii) an argument of *by* as in (19).

(18) Entity1 + *is* + measurement + comparison adjective + *than* + entity2
Harry is 2 years older than Emily.
My refrigerator is 6 degrees colder than yours.

(19) Entity1 + *is* + comparison adjective + *than* + entity2 + *by* + measurement
Harry is older than Emily by 2 years.
My refrigerator is colder than yours by 6 degrees.

Japanese reports differences between two entities measured against the same scale as arguments of a comparative construction with the measurement modifying the adjective as in (20).

(20) Entity1 + *no hō ga* + entity2 + *yori* + measurement + adjective
Kore *no* *hō* *ga* *are* *yori* *100* *pēji* *nagai.*
this GEN side NOM that than page long
'This is 100 pages longer than that.'

Measured difference can also be expressed by juxtaposition of a measurement and an adjective.

(21) a. *Kono* *hon* *wa* *nagai.*
this book TOP long
'This book is long.'
b. *Kono* *hon* *wa* *100* *pēji* *nagai.*
this book TOP page long
'This book is 100 pages *longer.*'
NOT 'This book is 100 pages long.'

While (21a) translates 'this book is long', (21b) does not mean 'this book is 100 pages long'. Rather, it means 'this book is 100 pages *longer*' than some unnamed referent, even though no overt comparative marker is present. That is, Japanese scalar adjectives do not permit an explicit measurement-value to co-occur with them. Here are some additional examples:

(22) a. *Kono* *hako* *wa* *5 kg* *omoi.*
this box TOP heavy
'This box is 5 kg *heavier.*'
b. *Kono* *pen* *wa* *2,000 en* *takai.*
this pen TOP 2,000 yen expensive
'This pen is 2,000 yen *more expensive.*'

In English, the measurement construction concerns measurements from a scalar zero, whereas the measured-difference construction represents measurements from some implicit or explicit reference point by means of a *than*-phrase. Unlike the measurement construction, the measured-difference construction allows not only both members of polar adjective pairs, but also a wider set of attributes.

(23) Measurement construction
*2 feet tall/*short, 2 inches thick/*thin, 2 years old/*young, *2 pounds heavy, *2 degrees cold, *2 dollars expensive, *20 percent likely, *20 IQ points intelligent*

(24) Measured-difference construction
2 inches taller/shorter, 2 years older/younger, 2 pounds heavier, 2 degrees colder, 2 dollars more expensive, 20 percent more likely, 20 IQ points more intelligent

Some measurement expressions are "hidden" comparisons: *ten minutes late* means ten minutes later than some appointed time, and *ten minutes early* means ten minutes earlier than some appointed time. Therefore, these sentences can be paraphrased as *X was late/early by ten minutes*. Similarly, *five miles ahead* and *five miles behind* mean, respectively, five miles ahead of or behind some fixed reference point or moving object. Such appointed time and reference point/object must be recoverable from a prior discourse.

In fact, all evaluative adjectival expressions involve hidden comparisons. For example, in *That building is tall*, the standard of comparison is implicit but generally understood, e.g. tall for buildings with its function, tall for buildings in the neighborhood, etc. Such an implicit standard can be made explicit.

(25) a. *He is short for a Swede.*
b. *He is tall even for a Swede.*

One way to account for the Japanese measured-difference construction would attribute the difference between English and Japanese to the idea that adjectives are inherently ambiguous: those that render an implicit comparison (α-reading) and those without such a comparison (β-reading) as in the examples in (26).

(26) a. *A dissertation that is 100 pages* $long_{\beta}$ *is not* $long_{\alpha}$ *at all.*
b. *How* $long_{\beta}$ *is her dissertation?*

From this perspective, the differences between English and Japanese would be summarized as follows:

(27)

		English	Japanese	
α.	Implicit comparison	*long*	*naga-i*	(adjective)
β.	No comparison	*long*	*naga-sa*	(noun)
γ.	Explicit comparison	*long-er*	*naga-i*	(adjective)

In terms of this analysis, in English, the base form (i.e. more basic form, e.g. *long*) is ambiguous between the α- and β-readings. By contrast, the base form in Japanese always implies comparison; the non-comparison β-reading must be expressed by a more complex, derived form, e.g. *naga-sa* 'length'. The problem with this is that only limited, neutral adjectives permit β-readings, thus making the generalization rather restricted.

(28) a. **A dissertation that is 100 pages short*$_{\beta}$ *is not short*$_{\alpha}$ *at all.*
b. **A car that goes 50 miles per hour fast*$_{\beta}$ *is not fast*$_{\alpha}$ *at all.*

Another perspective on the difference between the two languages might offer the generalization that in the measurement construction, English adjectives only identify a relevant scale. For example, *long* in *Her dissertation is 100 pages long* is not evaluative, evoking only the length scale and a location on that scale without communicating whether a length of 100 pages is considered long or short. By contrast, *long* in non-measurement construction (e.g. *Her dissertation is long/short*) evaluates the length of the dissertation as compared against an implicit standard of quantity as represented in (29).

(29) Length scale

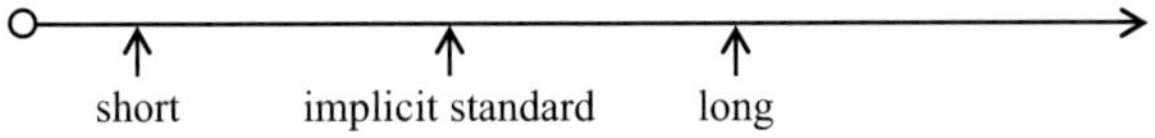

The relevant scale is associated with an implicit standard for a given type of entity. When the measurement value of the entity is above such a standard, the entity is judged as long; when its value is below the standard, it is judged as short. In this view, Japanese adjectives are necessarily evaluative and unable to serve a mere scale-identifying function, which must be attained by an appropriate noun such as *naga-sa* 'length'.

Notice that the scale in (29) has one end closed and the other open. This asymmetrical configuration explains the commonly observable neutral vs. marked distinction in regard to adjectives with polar opposition. Because there is no limit on the larger end of the scale, wherever the implicit standard is, *long* by nature has greater coverage. The applicability of *short*, on the other hand, is limited, and thus less usable.

10.4 Less/fewer

Japanese possesses fairly productive means of expressing scalar equalities as well as positive inequalities that correspond to English *more/-er* as shown in (12). However, conveying negative inequalities in Japanese is problematic, and normally expressed by negating equality as is demonstrated in (30) below:

(30) Standard + *hodo* + feature-*nai*

a. *Kono rapputoppu wa sono hako hodo omoku-nai.*
this laptop TOP that box as.much heavy-not
'[Lit.] This laptop is not as heavy as that box.'
'This laptop is less heavy than that box.'

b. *Watashi wa anata hodo tomodachi ga inai.*
I TOP you as.much friend NOM not.exist
'[Lit.] With me, friends do not exist like you.'
'I have fewer friends than you do.'

c. *Yōki ni wa mizu ga 20 rittoru mo nokotte-inai.*
container in TOP water NOM 20 liter as.much remain-not
'[Lit.] Not as much as 20 liters of water remain in the container.'
'Less than 20 liters of water remain in the container.'

d. *Yosōshita hodo ōkuno dōbutsu wa higai o uke-nakatta.*
expected as.much numerous animal TOP harm ACC receive-not.PAST
'[Lit.] Not as many animals were harmed as was expected.'
'Fewer animals than expected were harmed.'

In (15), the Sino-Japanese comparison noun *ijō* 'equal to or more than' was introduced. Its counterpart in descending order *ika* 'equal to or less/fewer than' is comparatively limited in utility. When, for example, the standard of comparison is a numerical value as in (31a), *ika* is usable. However, when the standard is another entity, the compared characteristic must be specified as in (31b–31c).

(31) a. *Kono rapputoppu wa 1 kg ika da.*
this laptop TOP less.than COP
'This laptop is (equal to or) less than 1kg.'

b. *Kono rapputoppu wa omosa ga sono hako ika da.*
this laptop TOP weight NOM that box less.than COP
'[Lit.] This laptop, the weight is (equal to or) less than that box.'

c. *Kono rapputoppu no omosa wa sono hako ika da.*
this laptop GEN weight TOP that box less.than COP
'The weight of this laptop is (equal to or) less than that of that box.'

Further, as illustrated by (30b), what is compared must be numbers of friends rather than the friends themselves. Therefore, (32a) is ungrammatical as a paraphrase of (30b).[4] When this distinction is made clear, *ika* can be used grammatically as in (32b), but its use does not sound as idiomatic as (30b).

(32) a. #*Watashi wa anata ika no tomodachi ga iru.*
I TOP you less.than GEN friend NOM exist

b. *Watashi no tomodachi no kazu wa anata ika da.*
I GEN friend GEN number TOP you less.than COP
'The number of my friends is (equal to or) less than yours.'

[4] (32a) can be interpreted only as 'I have friends whose (humanistic) quality is less than that of yours'.

Converting (30c) using *ika* is possible, but sounds natural only in limited contexts.

(33) a. *Yōki ni nokotteiru mizu wa 20 rittoru ika da.*
container in remaining water TOP 20 liter less.than COP
'The water remaining in the container is (equal to or) less than 20 liters.'

b. ?*20 rittoru ika no mizu ga yōki ni nokotte iru.*
20 liter less.than GEN water NOM container in remain
'(Equal to or) Less than 20 liters of water remain in the container.'

(33b) is grammatical, but its pragmatic function is unclear. The use of *ijō* assures that at least twenty liters of water remains, but *ika* guarantees only that the water remaining is twenty liters or less – in fact, there might be no water at all. Therefore, (33b) is usable only when storing more than twenty liters of water is prohibited.

Ika can combine with the verbal noun *yosō/yosoku* 'anticipation/expectation' to express 'less than anticipated/expected'. Such a phrase sounds unnatural when occurring in a subject NP.

(34) a. *Higai o uketa dōbutsu wa yosō ika datta.*
harm ACC received animal TOP anticipation less.than COP.PAST
'The animals that were harmed was (equal to or) fewer than anticipated.'

b. ?*Yosō ika no dōbutsu ga higai o uketa.*
anticipation less.than GEN animal NOM harm ACC received
'Fewer animals than expected were harmed.'

10.5 Modifying nouns

English makes frequent use of noun modification when comparing numbers or quantities as happens in (35a). Although noun modification with the idea of "more" is possible in Japanese, e.g. (35b), quantification generally occurs more naturally in applications involving a predicate as happens in (35c).

(35) a. *More people participated than last year.*

b. *Kyonen yori ōku no hito ga sanka shita.*
last.year than numerous people NOM participated
'[Lit.] People more numerous than last year participated.'

c. *Sanka shita hito wa kyonen yori ōkatta.*
participated people TOP last.year than be.numerous.PAST
'[Lit.] The number of people who participated was more numerous than last year.'

Although Japanese provides the adjectives *ōi* 'many/numerous' and *sukunai* 'few/little', both can be used only predicatively (e.g. (36a) and (37a)), not attributively (e.g. (36b) and (37b)).

(36) a. *Watashi wa tomodachi ga ōi.*
I TOP friend NOM many
'[Lit.] With me, friends are numerous.'
'I have many friends.'

b. **Watashi wa ōi tomodachi ga aru.*
I TOP many friend NOM exist
'I have many friends.' (intended)

c. *Watashi* *wa* *tomodachi* *ga* *aru.*
I TOP friend NOM exist
'[Lit.] With me, there are friends.'
'I have friends.'

(37) a. *Watashi* *wa* *tomodachi* *ga* *sukunai.*
I TOP friend NOM few
'[Lit.] With me, friends are few.'
'I have (only) few friends.'

b. **Watashi* *wa* *sukunai* *tomodachi* *ga* *aru.*
I TOP few friend NOM exist
'I have (only) few friends.' [intended]

The extreme case of the preference toward noun modification in English involves the use of *no* as in (38). Unthinkable in Japanese, the meaning conveyed by this sequence must be formulated by negating the existence of something (friends, object, etc.) by means of negative predicate form as illustrated in (39).

(38) a. *I have no friends.*
b. *There is no printer in this room.*

(39) a. *Watashi* *wa* *tomodachi* *ga* *inai.*
I TOP friend NOM not.exist
'[Lit.] Regarding myself, friends do not exist.'

b. *Kono* *heya* *ni* *wa* *purintā* *wa* *nai.*
this room in TOP printer NEG-SCP not.exist
'[Lit.] In this room, a printer does not exist.'

11 Causatives

11.1 Introduction

The **CAUSATIVE CONSTRUCTION** is prototypically used to indicate that someone (encoded as the subject in the nominative case or as the topic with the marker *wa*) makes someone else do something. The causing agent is referred to as the **CAUSER**, and the person who is made to act is the **CAUSEE**. The causee is marked with the accusative marker *o* if the verb is intransitive as in (1b), or with the dative *ni* if the verb is transitive as is the case in (2b).

(1) a. *Shigeru* *ga* *oyoi-da.* [intransitive]
NOM swim-PAST
'Shigeru swam.'

b. *Midori* *wa* *Shigeru* *o* *oyog-ase-ta.*
TOP ACC swim-CAUS-PAST
'Midori made Shigeru swim.'

(2) a. *Shigeru* *ga* *tegami* *o* *kai-ta.* [transitive]
NOM letter ACC write-PAST
'Shigeru wrote a letter.'

b. *Midori* *wa* *Shigeru* *ni* *tegami* *o* *kak-ase-ta.*
TOP DAT letter ACC write-CAUS-PAST
'Midori made Shigeru write a letter.'

The causative forms of verbs are derived as follows.

(3) a. *U*-verbs: the stem + *-ase-ru* (the derived causative verb becomes a *ru*-verb)

aw-ase-ru 'meet', *kizuk-ase-ru* 'recognize', *hanas-ase-ru* 'talk', *mat-ase-ru* 'wait', *shi-nase-ru* 'die', *tob-ase-ru* 'fly', *yom-ase-ru* 'read', *kaer-ase-ru* 'return'
or the stem + *-as-u* (the derived causative verb remains as a *u*-verb)[1]
aw-as-u 'meet', *kizuk-as-u* 'recognize', *nug-as-u* 'take off', *mat-as-u* 'wait', *shin-as-u* 'die', *tob-as-u* 'fly', *yom-as-u* 'read', *kaer-as-u* 'return'

When the stem is intransitive, e.g. *hashir-* 'run', the short form *hashir-as-u* can be considered as a separate (i.e. not derived) transitive verb referred to as a **LEXICAL CAUSATIVE**.

[1] According to the causative-verb derivation rules, the past tense of the long form is *-ase-ta* (e.g. *aw-ase-ta* 'cause to meet'), whereas that of the short form is *-ashi-ta* (e.g. *aw-ashi-ta*). However, the short form is less common than the long form, or it does not exist for some verbs.

b. *Ru*-verbs (e.g. *tabe-* 'eat'): the stem + *-sase-ru*
ake-sase-ru 'open', *tabe-sase-ru* 'eat', *i-sase-ru* 'stay', *mi-sase-ru* 'see'
or the stem + *-sas-u* (the derived causative verb becomes a *ru*-verb)
ake-sas-u 'open', *tabe-sasu* 'eat', *i-sas-u* 'stay', *mi-sas-u* 'see'
c. *K-* 'come': *k-osase-ru* or *k-osas-u*
d. *S-* 'do (something)': *s-ase-ru*

The causative construction is schematically represented in (4), with the square-bracketed portion representing the caused event:

(4) CAUSER-*ga/wa* [CAUSEE-*o/ni* (DIRECTOBJECT-*o*) VERBSTEM] *-(s)ase-* TENSE

11.2 Case marking of the causee

When used with an intransitive verb, the causee can optionally be marked with *ni* rather than with *o*.

(5) *Midori* *wa* *Shigeru* *ni* *oyog-ase-ta.*
TOP DAT swim-CAUS-PAST
'Midori made Shigeru swim.'

However, some intransitive verbs, such as those in (6), prohibit *ni*-marking.

(6) *akiru* 'lose interest', *kanashimu* 'feel sad', *konran-suru* 'get confused', *kurushimu* 'suffer', *kuruu* 'go insane', *madou* 'get lost', *nageku* 'lament', *naku* 'cry', *naoru* 'recover', *nemuru* 'sleep', *neru* 'go to bed', *odoroku* 'be surprised', *okiru* 'wake up', *shinu* 'die', *warau* 'laugh', *yorokobu* 'be delighted'

These verbs in (6) refer to an event over which the causee has little control. By contrast, the following verbs allow both *o-* and *ni*-marking.

(7) *aruku* 'walk', *asobu* 'play', *funki-suru* 'be stirred up', *hagemu* 'strive', *hairu* 'enter', *iku* 'go', *iru* 'stay', *jisatsu-suru* 'commit suicide', *katsu* 'win', *makeru* 'lose', *modoru* 'return', *nigeru* 'escape', *sawagu* 'make noise', *shirizoku* 'retreat', *shitagau* 'obey', *taeru* 'endure', *tomaru* 'stop', *unazuku* 'nod', *yaseru* 'lose weight', *yoru* 'stop by'

The verbs in (7) represent actions controllable by the causee. Shibatani (1990: 309–410) compares the following sentences to illustrate when the use of *o* but not *ni* is appropriate:

(8) a. *Hana* *ga* *migoto ni* *sai-ta.*
flower NOM beautifully bloom-PAST
'The flowers bloomed beautifully.'
b. *Tarō* *ga* *hana* *o/*ni* *migoto ni* *sak-ase-ta.*
NOM flower ACC/DAT beautifully bloom-CAUS-PAST
'Taro made the flowers bloom beautifully.'

(9) a. *Hanako* *ga* *kizetsu* *shi-ta.*
NOM faint do-PAST
'Hanako fainted.'
b. *Kūfuku* *ga* *Hanako* *o/*ni* *kizetsu* *s-ase-ta.*
hunger NOM ACC/DAT faint do-CAUS-PAST
'Hunger made Hanako faint.'

In (8b), because flowers do not bloom of their own free will, *ni*-marking is impossible. In (9b), although the causee is a human, fainting is not usually a controllable act; therefore, *Hanako* cannot be marked with *ni*. That is, *ni* indicates the agency of the causee. Tsujimura (2007: 288) makes the same point with the adverbial *muriyari* 'forcibly', which sounds awkward when it co-occurs with *ni* as in (10b):

(10) a.	*Tarō*	*ga*	*Hanako*	*o*	*muriyari*	*aruk-ase-ta.*
		NOM		ACC	forcibly	walk-CAUS-PAST

'[Lit.] Taro forcibly made Hanako walk.'
'Taro forced Hanako to walk.'

b.	??*Tarō*	*ga*	*Hanako*	*ni*	*muriyari*	*aruk-ase-ta.*
		NOM		DAT	forcibly	walk-CAUS-PAST

Iwasaki (2002: 145) generalizes these facts as follows: in the case of a causative making use of an intransitive verb, *o* is the default particle to mark the causee; however, when the causee's volition or ability to perform becomes an issue, it can be highlighted by the use of *ni*.

Notwithstanding such a distinction, Tokashiki (2006) cautions that this characterization of the *o*/*ni* alternation does not necessarily capture native speakers' intuitions. Using a questionnaire, she asked 40 Japanese native speakers to select a particle in five intransitive-causative sentences, including the two following sample sentences:

(11) a.	*Chichioya*	*wa*	*kodomo ()*	*mainichi*	*hashir-ase-masu.*
	father	TOP	child	everyday	run-CAUS-NPST

'The father makes the child run every day.'

b.	*Hahaoya*	*wa*	*kodomo ()*	*juku*	*ni*	*ik-ase-mashita.*
	mother	TOP	child	cram.shool	to	go-CAUS-PAST

'The mother made the child go to a cram school.'

For (11a), 32 respondents (80%) selected *o*, while eight (20%) selected *ni*. For (11b), 35 (87.5%) selected *o*, and five (12.5%) selected *ni*. Differences here can be interpreted as being due to ambiguity with respect to the willingness of the causees. However, in the second section of her questionnaire, Tokashiki asked whether or not (12) is grammatical.

(12)	*Oya*	*wa*	*kodomo*	*ni*	*kaimono*	*ni*	*ik-ase-ta.*
	parent	TOP	child	DAT	shopping	for	go-CAUS-PAST

'The parent made the child go shopping.'

26 (65%) answered *yes*, 13 (32.5%) answered *no*, and one answered that it sounds odd, but not necessarily ungrammatical. These numbers show that the fluctuation between *o* and *ni* is not based solely on the ambiguity of the causee's willingness. Grammaticality is also a factor: one third of the native speakers in the experiment considered the use of *ni* to be ungrammatical.

In the third section of the questionnaire, Tokashiki asked the participants to explain the difference between *o*- and *ni*-marking in (13).

(13)	*Oya*	*wa*	*kodomo*	*o/ni*	*suwar-ase-mashita.*
	parent	TOP	child	ACC/DAT	sit-CAUS-PAST

'The parent made the child sit down.'

21 (52.5%) responded that *o* is more coercive, seven (14%) that *ni* is more so, four (10%) that the use of *ni* is ungrammatical, and three (7.5%) did not respond at all. These results imply that, although the tendency for *ni* to mark volition/ability on the part of the causee – as exemplified in (8b), (9b) and (10b) – is persuasive to a point, this tendency is not significantly salient for native speakers to select *ni* consistently to highlight the causee's willingness or ability to comply with the causer's demand.

A more salient difference involving *o* and *ni* appears when marking focus or contrast (Chapter 8). To me, sentences like (5) without context are only marginally acceptable.

(5)	*Midori*	*wa*	*Shigeru*	*ni*	*oyog-ase-ta.*
		TOP		DAT	swim-CAUS-PAST

'Midori made Shigeru swim.'

However, if Midori happens to be a swimming coach selecting which team member is to swim in the relay race, the use of *ni* in (5) becomes more natural, conveying the idea that "It was Shigeru who Midori made/chose to swim."

Unlike the causative with an intransitive verb, the causative with a transitive verb permits only *ni*-marking because postpositional particles with the same function cannot occur more than once in a single clause.

(14) a.	*Midori*	*to*	*Shigeru*	*ga*	*tegami*	*o*	*kai-ta.*		
		and		NOM	letter	ACC	write-PAST		
	'Midori and Shigeru wrote a letter.'								
b.	**Midori*	*ga*	*Shigeru*	*ga*	*tegami*	*o*	*kai-ta.*		
		NOM		NOM	letter	ACC	write-PAST		
(15) a.	*Midori*	*wa*	*ginkō*	*to*	*toshokan*	*ni*	*it-ta.*		
		TOP	bank	and	library	to	go-PAST		
	'Midori went to the bank and to the library.'								
b.	**Midori*	*wa*	*ginkō*	*ni*	*toshokan*	*ni*	*it-ta.*		
		TOP	bank	to	library	to	go-PAST		
(16) a.	*Midori*	*wa*	*denshi-renji*	*to*	*ōbun*	*de*	*kēki*	*o*	*tsukut-ta.*
		TOP	microwave-oven	and	oven	with	cake	ACC	make-PAST
	'Midori baked a cake using a microwave oven and a conventional oven.'								
b.	**Midori*	*wa*	*denshi-renji*	*de*	*ōbun*	*de*	*kēki*	*o*	*tsukut-ta.*
		TOP	microwave-oven	with	oven	with	cake	ACC	make-PAST
(17) a.	*Shigeru*	*ga*	*tegami*	*o*	*kai-ta.*				
		NOM	letter	ACC	write-PAST				
	'Shigeru wrote a letter.'								
b.	**Midori*	*wa*	*Shigeru*	*o*	*tegami*	*o*	*kak-ase-ta.*		
		TOP		ACC	letter	ACC	write-CAUS-PAST		
	'Midori made Shigeru write a letter.'								

Because the accusative case does not appear in an intransitive clause, the causee can be marked with *o*. In contrast, *o* necessarily occurs in a transitive clause, e.g. (17a), and as a result the causee must be marked with a different case marker, namely the dative *ni*.

11.3 Animate vs. inanimate causers and causees

While the causative construction prototypically is used to describe a situation in which a person makes another person carry out some act, the causer can be an inanimate entity as well, as is the case with *uwasa* 'rumor' in (18b):

(18) a. *Hitobito wa mura kara nigedashi-ta.*
people TOP village from escape-PAST
'People escaped from the village.'

b. *Sono uwasa ga hitobito o mura kara nigedas-ase-ta.*
that rumor NOM people ACC village from escape-CAUSE-PAST
'The rumor caused the people to escape from the village.'

However, Japanese generally disfavors inanimate subjects with transitive verbs, including (or even especially) with causative verbs. In fact, causatives with an inanimate subject became possible only when Western texts began to be translated during the Meiji period (1868–1912) (see Section 4.2). The possibility of encoding an inanimate entity as the subject was a shocking discovery. In the 1930s, a silent movie titled *Nani ga kanojo o sō saseta ka* 'What made her do it?' created a sensation in Japan. This box-office success was reportedly due in great part to its linguistically eccentric title: it used familiar vocabulary and a familiar grammatical structure, but it juxtaposed an inanimate, abstract subject (*nani* 'what') to the causative verb (*saseta*), which simply did not happen in normal Japanese. Even today, after many decades of noticeable rhetorical–stylistic changes influenced mainly by English, this type of sentence continues to sound peculiar to many Japanese ears.[2]

Not only the causer, but also the causee can be inanimate, as exemplified below.

(19) a. *Oyu ga futtō shi-ta.*
hot.water nom boiling do-past
'The water has boiled.'

b. *Midori ga oyu o futtō s-ase-ta.*
NOM hot.water ACC boiling do-CAUS-PAST
'Midori boiled the water.'

(20) a. *Tsukue ga idō shi-ta.*
desk NOM movement do-PAST
'The desk has moved.'

[2] See Hasegawa (2011) for further discussion and examples.

b. *Midori* *ga* *tsukue* *o* *idō* *s-ase-ta.*
NOM desk ACC movement do-CAUS-PAST
'Midori moved the desk.'

Other verbs that take an inanimate causee are as follows:[3]

(21) *afureru* 'overflow', *au* 'match', *fukuramu* 'inflate', *hazumu* 'bounce', *hikaru* 'shine', *kōsa-suru* 'cross', *kumoru* 'cloud', *shigeru* 'grow thick', *yasumu* 'rest'

11.4 Causative vs. transitive verbs

A subset of transitive verbs are semantically causative counterparts of intransitive verbs (see Section 7.2). Therefore, they are sometimes called LEXICAL CAUSATIVES. A listing of commonly used pairs appears in (22).

(22)

Intransitive	Transitive	Gloss
aku	*akeru*	open
hairu	*ireru*	enter
hirogaru	*hirogeru*	widen
kawaru	*kaeru*	change
kieru	*kesu*	disappear (not a transitive verb in English)
magaru	*mageru*	bend
tomaru	*tomeru*	stop

While the causative form with *(s)aseru* is highly productive, these lexical intransitive–transitive pairs cannot be derived by rules; therefore, they must be listed separately in the lexicon. Furthermore, when an intransitive verb has no transitive counterpart, as exemplified in (23), only the causative form can express that the event is not spontaneous, but is, instead, brought about by a causer.[4]

(23)

Intransitive	Gloss	Causative	Gloss
aruku	walk	*aruk-aseru*	make someone walk
hikaru	shine	*hikar-aseru*	make something shine
isogu	hurry up	*isog-aseru*	hurry someone up
kusaru	decay	*kusar-aseru*	let something decay
kōru	freeze	*kōr-aseru*	freeze something
odoroku	be surprised	*odorok-aseru*	surprise someone
tsukareru	feel tired	*tsukare-saseru*	make someone feel tired

Finally, when the caused event can only be described with a transitive verb, the causative construction is the only way to express causation external to the transitive event.

[3] For an extensive list of causative as well as transitive verbs each with an inanimate causee, see Hayatsu and Ko (2012: 11–52).

[4] As explained in Section 11.1, the short forms – e.g. *aruk-asu*, *isog-asu*, *kōr-asu*, *odorok-asu* – can be considered transitive counterparts of the original verbs, and they are listed as such in many dictionaries.

For a transitive verb to qualify as a lexical causative, it must indicate nothing more than that the agent (i.e. the subject of the transitive verb) causes the event that the intransitive verb would designate. For example, *Mia broke the vase* means that Mia was the cause of the vase breaking. If a transitive verb includes more information than the mere occurrence of the intransitive event, these verbs do not form a pair. *Smash* in *Mia smashed the vase*, for example, is not a lexical causative of *break* because it also denotes the manner of breaking.

To provide another example, the English verb *kill* can be analyzed as the lexical causative of *die*, i.e. *cause someone to die*. In Japanese, by contrast, *korosu*, which is routinely translated as *kill*, normally encodes intentionality. Therefore, (24b) is anomalous or perceived figuratively, as an instance of personification: i.e. the inanimate *sensō* 'war' serves as the actor that killed Noboru. (24c) is an idiomatic way to describe the event.

(24) a. *Noboru ga shin-da.*
NOM die-PAST
'Noboru died.'
b. #*Sensō ga Noboru o koroshi-ta.*
war NOM ACC kill-PAST
'The war killed Noboru.'
c. *Noboru ga sensō de shin-da.*
NOM war in die-PAST
'Noboru died in the war.'

If the causer is a human being, but the killing is unintended, *korosu* must be accompanied by *-te shimau*, which cancels any encoded agency.

(25) a. #*Yuki ga hazumi de Noboru o koroshi-ta.*
NOM unintentionally ACC kill-PAST
'Yuki unintentionally killed Nobuo.'
b. *Yuki ga hazumi de Noboru o koroshi-te shimat-ta.*
NOM unintentionally ACC kill-TE finish-PAST
'Yuki unintentionally killed Nobuo.'

A question arises here regarding the difference between the lexical causative (i.e. transitive) and the *(s)aseru* causative. The former depicts a situation as being caused by the subject referent. Whether the referent of the direct object is capable of performing the action or not is normally immaterial as shown in (26c).

(26) a. *Shigeru ga uchi ni kaet-ta.*
NOM home to return-PAST
'Shigeru went home.'
b. *Midori ga Shigeru o uchi ni kaeshi-ta.* [transitive]
NOM ACC home to return-PAST
'[Lit.] Midori returned Shigeru home.'
'Midori sent Shigeru home.'
c. *Midori ga hon o toshokan ni kaeshi-ta.* [transitive]
NOM book ACC library to return-PAST
'Midori returned the book to the library.'

Kaesu in (26b) is the lexical causative of *kaeru* 'return' in (26a). In (26b), Shigeru is capable of going home by himself, but the direct object of *kaesu* can be inanimate as in (26c). When the direct object is incapable of performing the act, e.g. (26c), the causer must manipulate the object physically. On the other hand, when the object has such a capacity, e.g. (26b), the event can be accomplished by the causer's directing the causee to perform the act without physical manipulation. When both lexical and *(s)aseru* causatives are available, the former is more likely to imply manipulative or more forceful causation, while the latter is more likely to indicate directive causation. In (27a), for example, Midori put clothes on, or dressed, the child; in (27b), however, it is more likely that Midori directed the child to wear the clothes.

(27) a. *Midori ga kodomo ni fuku o kise-ta.* [transitive]
NOM child DAT cloth ACC wear-PAST
'Midori made the child wear the clothes.'
b. *Midori ga kodomo ni fuku o ki-sase-ta.* [causative]
NOM child DAT cloth ACC wear-CAUS-PAST

With some exceptions – see for example (19–21) – the causee in the *(s)aseru* causative is normally an animate being as in (28a). Thus, (28b) is unacceptable because the direct object causee is the inanimate object *hon* 'book'.

(28) a. *Midori ga Shigeru o uchi ni kaer-ase-ta.* [causative]
NOM ACC home to return-CAUS-PAST
'Midori made Shigeru go home.'
b. **Midori ga hon o toshokan ni kaer-ase-ta.* [causative]
NOM book ACC library to return-CAUS-PAST
'*Midori made the book return to the library.'

11.5 The permissive causative

A person can bring about an event or a state of affairs not only by performing a causing act, but also by not preventing the event from happening. This type of causative is called the **PERMISSIVE (CAUSATIVE)**, or ***let*-CAUSATIVE** (i.e. the subject lets the event take place).

(29) a. *Tamago o kusar-ase-te shimat-ta.*
egg ACC rot-CAUS-TE finish-PAST
'(I unintentionally) allowed the eggs to go bad/rotten.'
b. *Tamago o fuka-sase-ta.*
egg ACC hatch-CAUS-PAST
'(I) hatched the eggs.' [e.g. by placing them in an incubator]
c. *Midori wa niwa ni rōzumarī o shiger-ase-te i-ru.*
TOP garden in rosemary ACC grow-CAUS-TE exist-NPST
'Midori is growing rosemary in the garden.'

The distinction between the permissive causative and the regular causative is frequently not clear-cut. Because every organic creature eventually decays,

(29a) is easy to classify as a case of the permissive. However, the spontaneous process involved in eggs hatching or rosemary growing is unclear with regard to causation. Even if the speaker in (29b) and Midori in (29c) actively engaged in some action to bring about the caused event, the outcomes are ultimately dependent on the causees' potential. Therefore, the interpretations of (29b) and (29c) with respect to the effectiveness as the causer varies from situation to situation. When the causee is a human being, as in (28a), the distinction between causative and permissive readings is even more blurred and more context dependent.

The permissive occurs frequently with the *-te kudasai* construction, which is commonly used for requesting permission, as in (30a), or even for volunteering to do something for the addressee's sake, as in (30b).

(30) a. *Kyō wa hayaku kaer-ase-te kudasai.*
today TOP early return-CAUS-TE please.let.me.receive
'Please let me go home early today.'
b. *Watashi ni haraw-ase-te kudasai.*
I DAT pay-CAUS-TE please.let.me.receive
'Please let me pay.'

11.6 The intermediary causative

In some transitive sentences the subject is not the direct causer of the event, but a mere initiator; such constructions are called **INTERMEDIARY CAUSATIVES**.

(31) a. *Midori wa i o shujutsu shi-ta.*
TOP stomach ACC surgery do-PAST
'[Lit.] Midori did surgery on (her) stomach.'
'Midori had surgery done on (her) stomach.'
b. *Midori wa ie o tate-ta.*
TOP house ACC build-PAST
'Midori built a house.'

In (31a), because no one can perform stomach surgery on oneself, it is understood that a doctor operated on Midori. In (31b), by contrast, it could be the case that Midori herself built a house, but it is more likely that she had some contractor do the job. Nevertheless, the simple transitive (i.e. lexical causative) construction can be used in both Japanese and English. This encoding is possible only when the result of an action is involved, rather than the process of the action. In this case, the transitive cannot encompass causative events (Sato 2005: 94).

(32) a. *Midori ga doresu o tsukut-ta.*
NOM dress ACC make-PAST
'Midori had a dress made.'

b. *Midori*	*ga*	*doresu*	*o*	*dezain*	*shi-ta.*
	TOP	dress	ACC	design	do-PAST

'Midori designed a dress.'
Cannot mean: 'Midori had a dress designed.'

While (32a) can indicate that Midori initiated the event in which someone else actually made the dress, (32b) cannot indicate the situation in which Midori had someone design her dress. It can only mean that Midori herself designed the dress. This is because the intermediary causative cannot focus on the process of actions involved in the event. That is, while (32a) indicates the event as a whole, (32b) concerns its process. Other expressions that can be used in the intermediary causative are:

(33) *kami o kiru* 'cut hair', *ki o ueru* 'plant a tree', *kuruma o naosu* 'repair a car', *me o kensa suru* 'examine eyes', *megane o tsukuru* 'make eyeglasses', *oiru o irekaeru* 'change oil', *tatami o kaeru* 'change a tatami mat', *yane o harikaeru* 'recover the roof'

11.7 The structure of the causative construction

Although the causative construction is not a complex sentence with a subordinate or embedded clause, it is semantically complex. A common way to illustrate this point is by means of the interpretation of the reflexive pronoun *jibun* 'self'. The antecedent of *jibun* is normally restricted to the subject of the sentence:

(34) a. *Midori*$_i$	*ga*	*Shigeru*$_j$	*o*	*jibun*$_i$	*no*	*uchi*	*ni*	*manei-ta.*
	NOM		ACC	self	GEN	house	to	invite-PAST

'Midori invited Shigeru to her [Lit. self's] house.'

b. *Midori*$_i$	*ga*	*Shigeru*$_j$	*o*	*jibun*$_{i,j}$	*no*	*heya*	*de*	*benkyō*	*s-ase-ta.*
	NOM		ACC	self	GEN	room	in	study	do-CAUS-PAST

'Midori made Shigeru study in her/his room.'

In non-causative (34a), *jibun* must be **COREFERENTIAL** (i.e. referring to the same entity) only with the subject, *Midori*, not with the direct object, *Shigeru*. By contrast, in causative (34b), *jibun* is ambiguous; it can be coreferential with either *Midori* or *Shigeru*. That is, although *Shigeru* is the direct object, it is also the subject of *benkyō suru* 'study', while *Midori* is the subject of the causative verb *saseru*. Therefore, the structure of the causative is bi-clausal at an abstract level, which can be represented graphically as follows (S = sentence, V = verb).

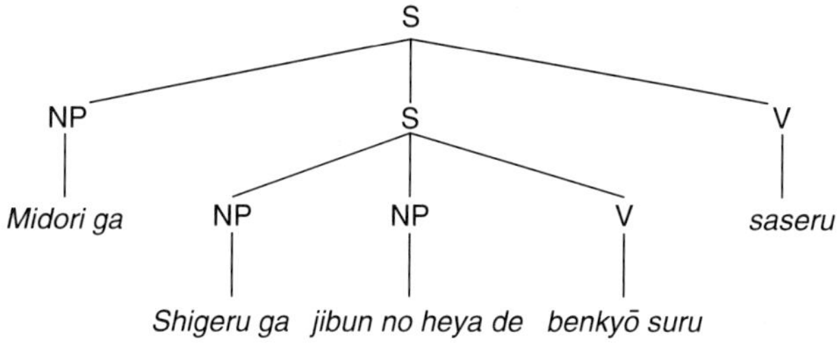

12 Passives

12.1 Introduction

The quintessential distinction between the **ACTIVE** and **PASSIVE VOICES** in the world's languages is that the direct object of the active clause undergoes a "transformation" (metaphorically speaking) to assume the subject position in the corresponding passive clause, while the subject of the active clause is optionally encoded as an incidental agentive phrase (e.g. a *by*-phrase in English) in the passive clause. Here, **AGENT** can be defined broadly as an initiator of an event. (A narrower definition of agent limits it to entities that perform an act of their own will.) As a rule, English passive clauses have corresponding active clauses as in example (1).

(1) a. *The board hired her.* [active]
b. *She was hired (by the board).* [passive]

In Japanese, the passive voice is expressed by the **PASSIVE FORM** of the verb, which is derived as in (2).

(2) *U*-verbs: Stem + *-areru*

a. *Dareka ga mado o kowashi-ta.* [active]
someone NOM window ACC break-PAST
'Someone broke the window.'

b. *Mado ga kowas-are-ta.* [passive]
window NOM break-PASS-PAST
'The window was broken.'

(3) *Ru*-verbs: Stem + *-rareru*

a. *Dareka ga piza o todoke-ta.* [active]
someone NOM pizza ACC deliver-PAST
'Someone delivered pizza.'

b. *Piza ga todoke-rare-ta.* [passive]
pizza NOM deliver-PASS-PAST
'Pizza was delivered.'

(4) *Kuru*: *k-orareru* (This construction will be discussed in the next section.)

(5) *Suru*: *s-areru*

a. *Dareka ga kaigi o kyanseru shi-ta.* [active]
someone NOM meeting ACC cancellation do-PAST
'Someone cancelled the meeting.'

b. *Kaigi ga kyanseru s-are-ta.* [passive]
meeting NOM cancellation do-PASS-PAST
'The meeting was cancelled.'

Not only the direct object, but also the indirect object of many ditransitive verbs (see Section 7.2) can appear as the subject of a passive clause.

(6) a. *Chichioya wa kodomo ni nusumi o oshie-ta.*
father TOP child to stealing ACC teach-PAST
'The father taught the child how to steal.'
b. *Kodomo wa chichioya ni nusumi o oshie-rare-ta.*
child TOP father by stealing ACC teach-PASS-PAST
'The child was taught how to steal by his father.'

However, the indirect object of the typical ditransitive verbs *ageru* 'give' and *kureru* 'give' cannot be rendered in the passive voice.

(7) a. *Shigeru wa Midori ni kamera o age-ta.*
TOP to camera ACC give-PAST
'Shigeru gave Midori a camera.'
b. **Midori wa Shigeru ni kamera o age-rare-ta.*
TOP by camera ACC give-PASS-PAST
'Midori was given a camera by Shigeru.'

(8) a. *Shigeru wa imōto ni kamera o kure-ta.*
TOP younger.sister to camera ACC give-PAST
'Shigeru gave my younger sister a camera.'
b. **Imōto wa Shigeru ni kamera o kure-rare-ta.*
younger.sister TOP by camera ACC give-PASS-PAST
'My younger sister was given a camera by Shigeru.'

12.2 Direct vs. indirect passives

The type of passive in Japanese that corresponds to the English passive, in which the subject is identical to the direct object of the corresponding active clause, is called the **DIRECT PASSIVE**. Japanese additionally permits two types of passives that are not available in English. The first type contains the passive form of an intransitive verb, with the subject of the active verb encoded with the **AGENTIVE MARKER** *ni* 'by', along with an extra NP which is introduced as the subject (normally marked by *wa*). Let us call this type the **INTRANSITIVE PASSIVE**.

(9) a. *Midori no kodomo ga abare-ta.* [active]
GEN child NOM behave.violently-PAST
'Midori's child behaved violently.'
b. *Midori wa kodomo ni abare-rare-ta.* [passive]
TOP child by behave.violently-PASS-PAST
'Midori was adversely affected by her child's violent behavior/child behaving violently.'

(10) a. *Midori no otto ga nige-ta.* [active]
GEN husband NOM run.away-PAST
'[Lit.] Midori's husband ran away (from her)'
'Midori's husband left her.'

b. *Midori wa otto ni nige-rare-ta.* [passive]
TOP husband by run.away-PASS-PAST
'Midori was adversely affected by her husband leaving her.'

In the direct passive, the agentive NP is optional, but it is obligatory in the intransitive passive, e.g. *kodomo* 'child' in (9b) and *otto* 'husband' in (10b). That is, while the valence (Section 7.3) of the verb in the direct passive is reduced by one, the valence is increased by one in the intransitive passive. The extra subject entity is portrayed by the speaker as having been adversely affected by the described event.

The second type of passive that is unavailable in English involves a transitive verb, but the direct object of the active clause remains as direct object of its passive counterpart. Let us call this type the **DIRECT-OBJECT PASSIVE**.

(11) a. *Tenchō ga iyami na guchi o it-ta.*
manager NOM sarcastic complaint ACC say-PAST
'The manager made sarcastic remarks.'
b. *Watashi wa tenchō ni iyami na guchi o iw-are-ta.*
I TOP manager by sarcastic complaint ACC say-PASS-PAST
'I was adversely affected by my manager's sarcastic remarks (to me).'

(12) a. *Dareka ga kūkō de Midori no rapputoppu o nusun-da.*
someone NOM airport at GEN laptop ACC steal-PAST
'Someone stole Midori's laptop at the airport.'
b. *Midori wa kūkō de rapputoppu o nusum-are-ta.*
TOP airport at laptop ACC steal-PASS-PAST
'Midori was adversely affected by her laptop being stolen while at the airport.'

Again, this passive construction increases the verb's valence, and the extra entity is understood as having suffered in or as a result of the described event. Because of these shared characteristics, the intransitive and direct-object passives are categorized together and referred to by the term **INDIRECT PASSIVE** or **ADVERSITY PASSIVE**.[1]

Adversity created by the indirect passive must be separated out from that implied by the verb itself. For example, if someone is fired, it is very likely that s/he is negatively affected. However, this sense of adversity is lexical and borne by both active (13a) and passive (13b) sentences.

(13) a. *Midori ga shain o kaiko shi-ta.*
NOM employee ACC dismissal do-PAST
'Midori fired an employee.'

[1] Shibatani (1994: 481) contends that, across languages, whether the extra subject entity is predominantly associated with an adversity or adverse reading depends to a great extent upon whether a given language has a distinct benefactive construction. Japanese does, as will be discussed in Chapter 13, so its indirect passive typically cannot have a positive reading.

b. *Shain* *ga* *Midori* *ni* *kaiko* *s-are-ta.*
employee NOM by dismissal do-PASS-PAST
'An employee was fired by Midori.'

By contrast, the indirect passive can generate adversity when its active counterpart does not have such a connotation as illustrated below.

(14) a. *Midori* *ga* *uchi* *ni* *ki-ta.*
NOM house to come-PAST
'Midori came to (my) house.' [The speaker might be grateful.]
b. *Midori* *ni* *uchi* *ni* *k-orare-ta.*
by house to come-PASS-PAST
'I was adversely affected by Midori's coming to (my) house.'

(15) a. *Midori* *ga* *wain* *o* *non-da.*
NOM wine ACC drink-PAST
'Midori drank the wine.' [No negative connotation is accompanied.]
b. *Midori* *ni* *wain* *o* *nom-are-ta.*
by wine ACC drink-PASS-PAST
'I was adversely affected by Midori's drinking the wine.'

The primary motivation for employing the passive voice can be stated in either of two ways: (i) to "promote" the direct object of the active clause to the more prominent subject position in the passive clause, or (ii) to "defocus" the subject of the active clause by effacing it completely, or by expressing it as an optional, peripheral element. Because there is no direct object to promote in the case of the intransitive passive, and because the direct object remains as such in the direct-object passive, Shibatani (1985: 834) cogently concludes that the primary function of the passive voice is (ii) to defocus the subject, rather than (i) to promote the direct object.

12.3 Adversity in the indirect passive

Not all indirect passive clauses connote adversity. Alfonso (1971), for example, provides numerous examples in which adversity is not implied.

(16) a. *Pāma* *o* *kake-te* *soto* *ni* *detara* *hito* *ni*
perm ACC have-TE outside to when.go people by
furimuk-are-te *chotto* *ureshi-katta.*
turn.look.at-PASS-TE a.little happy-PAST
'When I had a perm and went outdoors, I was pleased when people turned to look at me.'
b. *Ame* *ni* *fur-are-te* *kaeru* *no* *mo* *omoshiro-i.*
rain by fall-PASS-TE go.home NMLZ also interesting-NPST
'Going home in the rain is somehow attractive/pleasant/comforting.'

However, all indirect passives in Alfonso's examples occur in subordinate clauses. Wierzbicka (1979/1988: 262) argues convincingly that passive verbs have different effects depending upon whether they occur in a subordinate clause or in the main clause, and that the connotation of adversity is basically a main-clause phenomenon. For example, (17a) sounds natural because the adversity induced by the indirect passive and the content of the sentence cohere, but (17b) sounds odd because the content is inherently positive. This oddity, however, disappears when the passive is embedded in a subordinate clause as happens in (17c).

(17) a. *Jon* *wa* *tsuma* *ni* *shin-are-ta.*
TOP wife by die-PASS-PAST
'John was adversely affected by his wife's death.'

b. ?*Jon* *wa* *tsuma* *ni* *naor-are-ta.*
TOP wife by recover-PASS-PAST
'John was affected by his wife recovering from her illness.'

c. *Jon* *wa* *tsuma* *ni* *naor-are-te* *yorokon-de* *i-ru.*
TOP wife by recover-PASS-TE please-TE exist-NPST
'His wife having recovered, John is pleased.'

Nevertheless, some main-clause indirect passives do not give rise to adversity.

(18) a. *Pāma* *o* *kake-te* *soto* *ni* *detara* *hito* *ni* *furimuk-are-ta.*
perm ACC have-TE outside to when.go people by turn.look.at-PASS-PAST
'After I had a perm and went out, people turned to look at me.'

b. *Eigakan* *de* *kawaii* *ko* *ni* *tonari* *ni* *suwar-are-ta.*
movie.theater in pretty girl by next at sit-PASS-PAST
'In a movie theater, a pretty girl sat next to me (and I was affected by it).'

Comparing (18) with typical adversity passives, e.g. (17a), Wierzbicka hypothesizes that when the subject referent (i.e. the affected person) is directly involved in the described event, the passive construction does not result in an adverse connotation. However, in (17a), John has nothing to do with his wife's death; therefore, the adverse reading is unavoidable. By contrast, the speakers (who are the implicit subjects) in (18) were directly involved in the described situations: s/he was looked at by the people in (18a), and s/he was sitting next to the girl in (18b). Thus, the situations in (18) are not interpreted as adverse.

Adopting Wierzbicka's analysis, Shibatani (1990: 330) argues that involvement cannot be characterized merely in terms of binary oppositions; it is better understood as the unfolding of a process based upon a continuum. For example, the object referent of *kill* is more involved than that of *see* (i.e. high and low in transitivity; see Section 7.4). Shibatani goes on to assert that the less involved the passive subject referent is in the described event, the stronger the adversity connotation.

Wierzbicka (1979/1988: 273) also observes that when the referent of the direct object is a body part, the adversity reading does not arise.

(19) a. *Kanja* *wa* *ashi* *o* *shōdoku* *s-are-ta.*
patient TOP leg ACC disinfection do-PASS-PAST
'The patient's leg was disinfected (and the patient was affected by it).'

b. *Jon wa inu ni ashi o name-rare-ta.*
TOP dog by leg ACC lick- PASS-PAST
'A dog licked John's leg (and John was affected by it).'

Shibatani (1990: 328) argues that *o*-marked body parts in the indirect passive are not direct objects proper; rather, they are locations. Therefore, when they are to be identified, they are accompanied by *doko* 'where', not *nani* 'what'.

(20) a. *Tarō wa atama o nagur-are-ta.*
TOP head ACC hit-PASS-PAST
'Taro was hit on/in the head.'
b. *Tarō wa doko o nagur-are-ta?*
TOP where ACC hit-PASS-PAST
'Where was Taro hit?'
c. **Tarō wa nani o nagur-are-ta?*
TOP what ACC hit-PASS-PAST
'With what was Taro hit?'

However, Wierzbicka's account of involvement as regards adversity cannot explain the difference between the two sentences in (21).

(21) a. *Jon wa sensei ni kodomo o shikar-are-ta.*
TOP teacher by child ACC scold-PASS-PAST
'John was adversely affected by the teacher scolding his child.'
b. *Jon wa sensei ni kodomo o home-are-ta.*
TOP teacher by child ACC praise-PASS-PAST
'The teacher praised John's child (and John was affected by it).'

While the construction and the content both point to an adversity reading in (21a), (21b) can hardly be interpreted negatively. This difference cannot be directly attributed to the lexical difference between *shikaru* 'scold' and *homeru* 'praise'. Recall the anomaly of (17b), which contains the semantically positive verb *naoru* 'recover'. There, the indirect passive construction does not accommodate this positive verb, resulting in marginal acceptability. By contrast, (21b) is perfectly acceptable. One might suspect that the difference is due to *naoru* being an intransitive verb as opposed to *homeru* being a transitive verb. However, this is not the case, because the following sentences involve transitive verbs and yet their semantic components sound odd just as with (17b).

(22) a. ?*Jon wa musume ni Akademī-shō o tor-are-ta.*
TOP daughter by Academy-award ACC obtain-PASS-PAST
'John's daughter won an Academy award (and John was affected by it).'
b. ?*Jon wa tsuma ni oishii ryōri o tsukur-are-ta.*
TOP wife by delicious dish ACC make-PASS-PAST
'John's wife made a delicious meal (and John was affected by it).'

Because no compelling explanation readily covers these multifarious linguistic phenomena, Wierzbicka hypothesizes two types of indirect passive constructions – one invariably adversative, e.g. (17b) and (22), the other compatible with neutral or positive interpretations, e.g. (21b). Her solution, while certainly not the most elegant, encourages continuing research into the phenomenon.

12.4 Agency in passives

When a speaker intends to describe an event empathetically – in regard to the subject referent that the speaker believes has been affected – the indirect passive is employed. As such, the subject must refer to a human or some other sentient being. The examples in (23), derived from Wierzbicka (1979/1988: 275), illustrate this point.

(23) a. *Jon* *wa* *inu* *ni* *ashi* *o* *name-rare-ta.*
        TOP dog by leg ACC lick- PASS-PAST
    'A dog licked John's leg (and John was affected by it).'
    b. **Tēburu* *wa* *inu* *ni* *ashi* *o* *name-rare-ta.*
        table TOP dog by leg ACC lick- PASS-PAST
    'A dog licked a leg of the table (and the table was affected by it).'

Furthermore, the agentive NP also typically refers to a person. In (24), for example, having one's house burn down or having toothache doubtlessly negatively impacts the victim, but these situations cannot be expressed using the indirect passive.

(24) a. *Jon* *no* *ie* *ga* *moe-ta.*
        GEN house NOM burn-PAST
    'John's house burned down.'
    a′. **Jon* *wa* *ie* *ni* *moer-are-ta.* (p. 264)
        TOP house by burn-PASS-PAST
    'John's house burned down on him.'
    b. *Ha* *ga* *itam-u.*
        tooth NOM ache-NPST
    'My tooth aches.'
    b′. **Watashi* *wa* *ha* *ni* *itam-are-ta.*
        I TOP tooth by ache-PASS-PAST
    'My tooth ached (and I was affected by it).'

On the other hand, many natural phenomena (e.g. weather events) may appear as the agentive entity in this construction.

(25) a. *Midori* *wa* *tsunami* *ni* *ie* *o* *nagas-are-ta.*
        TOP by house ACC wash.away-PASS-PAST
    'The tsunami washed Midori's house away on her.'
    b. *Midori* *wa* *taiyō* *ni* *senaka* *o* *yak-are-ta.*
        TOP sun by back ACC burn-PASS-PAST
    'The sun burned Midori's back (and she was affected by it).'

Iwasaki (2002: 128–29) points out that the choice between active and passive encoding depends upon where the speaker's empathy falls. (The subject is the default position for empathy.) Therefore, the passive construction is particularly appropriate when the subject of the active verb is non-human and its object is human, as occurs in (26a).

(26) a.	*Basu*	*ga*	*Tarō*	*o*	*hane-ta.*
	bus	NOM		ACC	hit-PAST
	'A bus hit Taro.'				
b.	*Tarō*	*ga*	*basu*	*ni*	*hane-rare-ta.*
		NOM	bus	by	hit-PASS-PAST
	'Taro was hit by a bus.'				

12.5 Stative verbs in passives

Stative verbs (i.e. their non-past tense can refer to the present state) cannot appear in the passive voice as in (27).

(27) a.	**Jon*	*wa*	*kodomo*	*ni*	*okane*	*ga*	*ir-are-te*	*komat-ta.*	
		TOP	child	by	money	NOM	need-PASS-TE	be.troubled-PAST	
	'John was troubled because money was needed by/for his child.' (Kuno 1973: 144)								
b.	**Jon*	*wa*	*seito*	*ni*	*jibun*	*yori*	*umaku*	*nihongo*	*ga*
		TOP	student	by	self	than	better	Japanese	NOM
	deki-rare-te	*yowa-tta.*	(p. 144)						
	can-PASS-TE	be.troubled-PAST							
	'John had a difficult time because his students could (speak) Japanese better than he could.'								

The only exception to this rule is *iru* 'exist/stay', which can appear in the passive voice as in (28).

(28)	*Tomodachi*	*ni*	*osoku*	*made*	*i-rare-te*	*koma-tta.*
	friend	by	late	until	stay-PASS-TE	be.troubled-PAST
	'My friend stayed (at my house) until late, and I was worried.'					

Iwasaki (2002: 135–36) divides all passive sentences into the **EVENTIVE PASSIVE** (including both the direct and indirect passives), which depicts incidents, and the **STATIVE PASSIVE**, which describes a characteristic of the subject entity. While incidents can be instantaneous, characteristics must range over a period of time. Therefore, the active counterparts of stative passive sentences generally occur in the *-te iru* construction (Section 9.3) as shown in the following examples. The eventive passive is usually more natural when the subject is animate, whereas the stative passive does not have such a preference.

(29) a.	*Takusan no*	*ki*	*ga*	*kono*	*kōen*	*o*	*kakon-de*	*i-ru.*
	many	tree	NOM	this	park	ACC	surround-TE	exist-NPST
	'Many trees surround this park.'							
b.	*Kono*	*kōen*	*wa*	*takusan no*	*ki*	*ni*	*kakom-are-te*	*i-ru.*
	this	park	TOP	many	tree	by	surround-PASS-TE	exist-NPST
	'This park is surrounded by many trees.'							

(30) a. *Kono kudamono wa bitamin shī o takusan fukun-de*
this fruit TOP vitamin C ACC much contain-TE
i-ru.
exist-NPST
'This fruit contains a lot of vitamin C.'

b. *Kono kudamono ni wa bitamin shī ga takusan fukum-are-te*
this fruit in TOP vitamin C ACC much contain-PASS-TE
i-ru.
exist-NPST
'There is a lot of vitamin C in this fruit.'

12.6 The *ni-yotte* passive

In the discussion so far, the agentive NP has invariably been marked with *ni*, but it can also be marked by *ni-yotte*, a combination of *ni* and the *te*-form of *yoru* 'be due to/caused by'.[2] *Ni-yotte* was appropriated as a translational equivalent for the Dutch agentive marker *door* 'through' (Kinsui 1997: 771).[3] Due to its origin, *ni-yotte* does not induce adversity readings, unlike the indigenous agentive marker *ni*. Therefore, it can freely appear with non-sentient agentive entities.

Some passive clauses permit both *ni* and *ni-yotte*, while others permit only one or the other. Generally, the direct passive permits both.

(31) a. *Sukaipu ga Maikurosofuto [ni/ni-yotte] baishū s-are-ta.*
Skype NOM Microsoft [by] acquisition do-PASS-PAST
'Skype was acquired by Microsoft.'

b. *Sutoraiki-ken wa hō [ni/ni-yotte] hoshō-sare-te i-ru.*
strike-right TOP law [by] guarantee-PASS-TE exist-NPST
'The right to strike is guaranteed by law.'

However, when the agentive NP is non-human or unidentifiable, the acceptability of *ni-yotte* declines.

(32) a. *Tarō ga basu [ni/??ni-yotte] hane-rare-ta.*
NOM bus [by] hit-PASS-PAST
'Taro was hit by a bus.'

b. *Ie ga tsunami [ni/*ni-yotte] nomikom-are-ta.*
house NOM [by] swallow-PASS-PAST
'The house was engulfed by a tsunami.'

c. *Haka ga dareka [ni/?ni-yotte] horiokos-are-ta.*
grave NOM someone [by] uncover-PASS-PAST
'The grave was uncovered by someone.'

[2] The third possibility of agentive marking is the use of *kara* 'from', e.g. *Sensei kara homer-are-ta* '(I) received praise by (from) the teacher'. However, *kara* as an agentive marker is limited to transitive verbs with low transitivity, e.g. *aisu* 'love', *chūi suru* 'warn', *iu* 'say', *kiku* 'ask', *kirau* 'hate', *mitomeru* 'recognize', *motomeru* 'want', *oshieru* 'teach'.

[3] Kinsui (1997: 772) found the first occurrence of *ni-yotte* in a Dutch grammar book published in 1822.

By contrast, when the subject is non-human, *ni-yotte* can be more fitting than *ni*.

(33) a. *Kono konsāto wa shimin [?ni/ni-yotte] kikaku s-are-ta.*
this concert TOP resident [by] plan do-PASS-PAST
'This concert was planned by residents.'
b. *Kyōbai wa dīrā [*ni/ni-yotte] okonaw-are-ta.*
auction TOP dealer [by] carry.out-PASS-PAST
'The auction was conducted by a dealer.'

When the verb denotes a creation of some sort, only *ni-yotte* can mark the agent (Teramura 1982: 223), e.g. (*tonneru o*) *horu* 'dig (a tunnel), (*hashi o*) *kakeru* 'build (a bridge)', *kaku* 'write', *tateru* 'build', *tsukuru* 'make'.

(34) a. *Hōjōki wa Kamo no Chōmei [*ni/ni-yotte] kak-are-ta.*
TOP [by] write-PASS-PAST
'*Hōjōki* (The Ten Foot Square Hut) was written by Kamo no Chōmei.'
b. *Kono kōen wa shimin [*ni/ni-yotte] tsukur-are-ta.*
this park TOP citizen [by] make-PASS-PAST
'This park was constructed by citizens.'

In the stative passive, as discussed in the previous section, agency seems irrelevant to the judgment of acceptability.

(35) a. *Kono kōen wa takusan no ki [ni/ni-yotte] kakom-are-te i-ru.*
this park TOP many tree [by] surround-PASS-TE exist-NPST
'This park is surrounded by many trees.'
b. *Sono furukabe wa ippon no bō [ni/ni-yotte] sasae-rare-te i-ru.*
that old.wall TOP one rod [by] support-PASS-TE exist-NPST
'That old wall is supported by one rod.' (Iwasaki 2002: 137)

The impersonal nature of *ni-yotte* does not harmonize well with the indirect passive, which is inherently emphatic.

(36) a. *Jon wa tsuma [ni/*ni-yotte] shin-are-ta.*
NOM wife [by] die-PASS-PAST
'John was adversely affected by his wife's death.'
b. *Midori wa otto [ni/*ni-yotte] nige-rare-ta.*
TOP husband [by] run.away-PASS-PAST
'Midori was adversely affected by her husband running away (from her).'

When the verb is intransitive, *ni-yotte* in the indirect passive is completely banned; with a transitive verb, the acceptability varies.

(37) a. *Midori wa tsunami [ni/ni-yotte] ie o nagas-are-ta.*
TOP [by] house ACC wash.away-PASS-PAST
'The tsunami washed away Midori's house.'

b. *Kodomo wa chichioya [ni/ni-yotte] nusumi o oshie-rare-ta.*
child TOP father [by] stealing ACC teach-PASS-PAST
'The child was taught how to steal by his father.'

c. *Kanja wa kangoshi [ni/ni-yotte] ashi o shōdoku s-are-ta.*
patient TOP nurse [by] leg ACC disinfection do-PASS-PAST
'The patient's wounded leg was disinfected (and the patient was affected by it)'

d. *Jon wa inu [ni/?ni-yotte] ashi o name-rare-ta.*
TOP dog [by] leg ACC lick-PASS-PAST
'A dog licked John's leg (and John was affected by it).'

e. *Midori wa dareka [ni/*ni-yotte] rapputoppu o nusum-are-ta.*
TOP someone [by] laptop ACC steal-PASS-PAST
'Midori was adversely affected by her laptop being stolen by someone.'

f. *Jon wa sensei [ni/*ni-yotte] kodomo o shikar-are-ta.*
TOP teacher [by] child ACC scold-PASS-PAST
'John was adversely affected by the teacher scolding his child.'

12.7 The structure of the passive constructions

In Section 11.7, it was demonstrated that the reflexive pronoun *jibun* 'self' must be coreferential with the subject. The interpretation of *jibun* can be used to differentiate direct and indirect passive constructions.

(38) a. *Kodomo*$_i$ *wa hahaoya*$_j$ *ni jibun*$_i$ *no heya de shikar-are-ta.*
TOP by self GEN room in scold-PASS-PAST
'The child$_i$ was scolded by his mother in his$_i$ [Lit. self's] room.'

b. *Kodomo*$_i$ *wa hahaoya*$_j$ *ni jibun*$_{i/j}$ *no heya de nak-are-ta.*
TOP by self GEN room in cry-PASS-PAST
'The child$_i$ was adversely affected by his mother$_j$'s crying in his$_i$/her$_j$ room.'

In (38a), which is in the direct passive, *jibun* is coreferential only with the subject *kodomo*, not with the agentive *hahaoya*. By contrast, in indirect

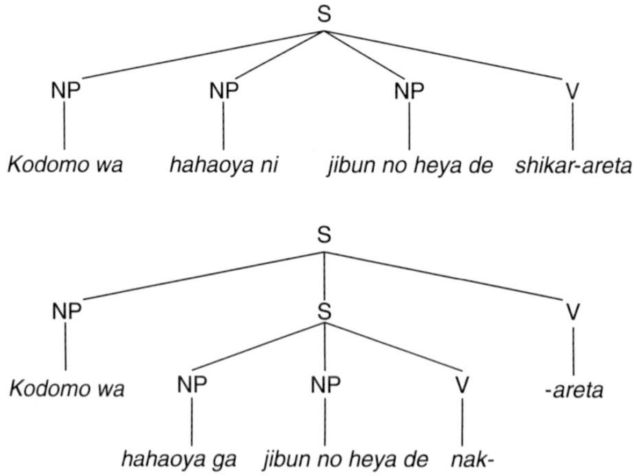

Figure 12.1.

passive as in (38b), *jibun* can be coreferential with either the subject *kodomo* or the agentive *hahaoya*. Therefore, while the direct passive has a simple, mono-clausal structure, the indirect passive – upon analysis – manifests an additional clause embedded at an abstract level of representation. In this structure, the indirect passive has two subjects at the abstract level, giving rise to ambiguity in the interpretation of *jibun*.

12.8 The causative passive

The causative and passive constructions can be combined:

(39) a.

Watashi	*wa*	*hōkokusho*	*o*	*kai-ta.*
I	TOP	report	ACC	write-PAST

'I wrote a report.' [active]

b.

Buchō	*wa*	*watashi*	*ni*	*hōkokusho*	*o*	*kak-ase-ta.*
manager	TOP	I	DAT	report	ACC	write-CAUS-PAST

'The manager made me write a report.' [causative]

c.

Watashi	*wa*	*buchō*	*ni*	*hōkokusho*	*o*	*kak-ase-rare-ta.*
I	TOP	manager	DAT	report	ACC	write-CAUS-PASS-PAST

'I was required by the manager to write a report.' [causative-passive]

When combined, the causative always precedes the passive. With a *u*-verb, the shorter form of the causative (see Section 11.1) is more frequently used than the longer form.

(40) a. *U*-verbs: Stem + *-ase* (causative) + *rare* (passive) or stem + *-as* + *-are*

kak-ase-rare-ru	*kak-as-are-ru*	to be made to write
hanas-ase-rare-ru	*hanas-as-are-ru*	to be made to speak
mat-ase-rare-ru	*mat-as-are-ru*	to be made to wait
yom-ase-rare-ru	*yom-as-are-ru*	to be made to read
kaer-ase-rare-ru	*kaer-as-are-ru*	to be made to go home
iw-ase-rare-ru	*iw-as-are-ru*	to be made to say

b. *Ru*-verbs: Stem + *-sase* + *rare*

tabe-sase-rare-ru	to be made to eat
mi-sase-rare-ru	to be made to watch

c. *Kuru*: *ko-sase-rare-ru* to be made to come

d. *Suru*: *s-ase-rare-ru* to be made to do

13 Benefactives

13.1 Introduction

One of the salient differences between Japanese and English language use occurs in the expression of one's subjective evaluation of a conveyed event. Such expressions are sometimes mandatory in Japanese, but never in English. For example, the language of the speaker of (1a) sounds indifferent and is, potentially, socially inappropriate. Its English translation, on the other hand, exhibits none of these negative qualities.

(1) a.	*Chichi*	*wa*	*watashi*	*ni*	*kuruma*	*o*	*katta.*
	father	TOP	I	DAT	car	ACC	bought

'My father bought me a car.'

If the speaker is grateful for his/her father's buying a car for him/her, it is idiomatic to add the auxiliary verb *kureru* 'give' to express this feeling of gratefulness.

b.	*Chichi*	*wa*	*watashi*	*ni*	*kuruma*	*o*	*kat-te*	*kureta.*
	father	TOP	I	DAT	car	ACC	buy-TE	gave

'[Lit.] My father gave me a favor of buying a car.'

Because this type of construction describes actions or events from which someone receives benefit, it is called a **BENEFACTIVE (CONSTRUCTION)**. This chapter explores the structure and usage of Japanese benefactive constructions.

13.2 Donatory verbs

Benefactives employ verbs that convey meanings of giving and receiving, collectively referred to as **DONATORY VERBS**. There are three kinds: the AGERU-type (*ageru, yaru, sashiageru*), KURERU-type (*kureru, kudasaru*), and MORAU-type (*morau, itadaku*).[1] In the case of AGERU and KURERU,

[1] *Sashiageru* and *itadaku* are *humilific* (humbling) verbs, which linguistically lower the subject referent in order to show respect to the referent of the direct or indirect object NP. By contrast, *kudasaru* is an *honorific* verb, which indicates the speaker's deference towards the subject referent. See Chapter 20 for details.

the giver occupies the subject position of the clause, and the receiver is marked with the dative particle *ni* (Section 7.2); for MORAU, these positions are reversed: the giver is marked with either the dative *ni* or the particle *kara* 'from', and the receiver moves into the subject slot. AGERU and KURERU can be translated into English as 'give', and MORAU as 'receive'.

(2)	a.	*Chiyoko*	*wa*	*Eiji*	*ni*	*mikan*	*o*	*ageta.*
			TOP		DAT	tangerine	ACC	gave

'Chiyoko gave Eiji (some) tangerines.'

b.	*Chiyoko*	*wa*	*watashi*	*ni*	*nashi*	*o*	*kureta.*
		TOP	I	DAT	pear	ACC	gave

'Chiyoko gave me (some) pears.'

c.	*Chiyoko*	*wa*	*Eiji*	*ni*	*kuri*	*o*	*moratta.*
		TOP		DAT	chestnut	ACC	receive

'Chiyoko received (some) chestnuts from Eiji.'
'Chiyoko was given (some) chestnuts by Eiji.'

Two mutually independent factors are involved in the selection of a particular donatory verb: (i) the direction of transfer with respect to the in-group/out-group distinction; and (ii) the relative status of the giver and receiver. If rules regarding (i) are violated, the sentence will be ungrammatical and thus unacceptable. On the other hand, if rules regarding (ii) are violated, the sentence itself will be grammatical, but one's judgment of the relative statuses of the participants may be rejected as inappropriate.

13.2.1 Directions of transfer

To clarify the transfer direction, consider Figures 13.1 and 13.2 below. The speaker is located in the center of the universe of discourse, and surrounding him/her are the **IN-GROUP** (e.g. his/her family members and close friends) and **OUT-GROUP** individuals.[2]

(3) a. AGERU cannot be used for inward transfer.

OK:	Speaker ⇒ In-group	NO:	In-group ⇒ Speaker
	Speaker ⇒ Out-group		Out-group ⇒ Speaker
	In-group ⇒ Out-group		Out-group ⇒ In-group
	In-group ⇒ In-group		
	Out-group ⇒ Out-group		

[2] The in-group is flexibly defined according to the speech situation. For example, when an employee talks with a colleague about their CEO, the CEO is treated as a member of their out-group, and normally honorific expressions are employed. However, when an employee represents his/her company and talks with a client about the CEO, the CEO is conventionally considered to be a member of the in-group. Therefore, the use of honorifics is prohibited or discouraged. For further discussion, see Wetzel (1984: 231–32) and Hasegawa and Hirose (2005: 227–28).

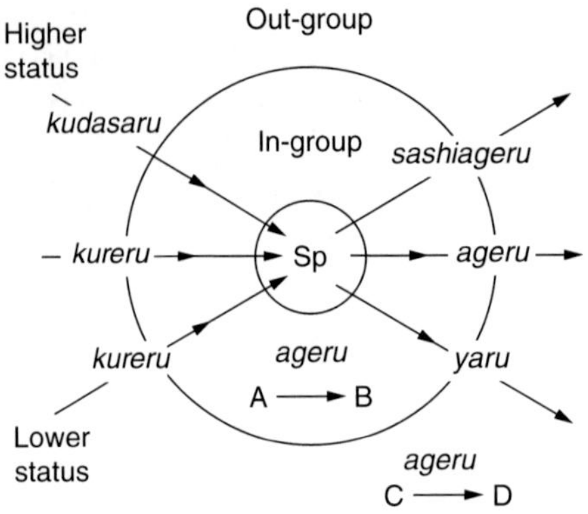

Figure 13.1. AGERU and KURERU.

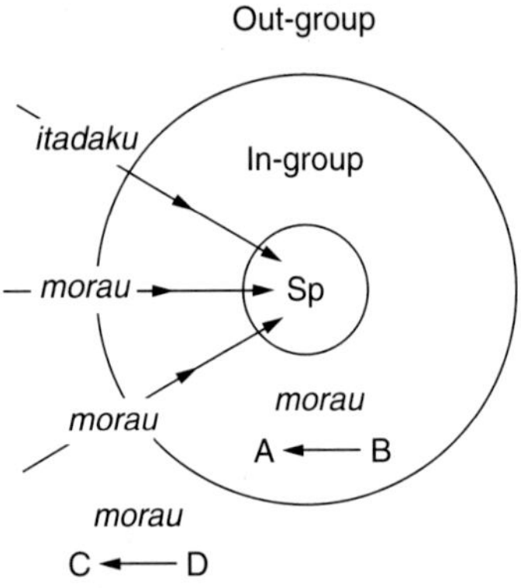

Figure 13.2. MORAU.

b. KURERU can be used only for inward transfer.

OK:	In-group ⇒ Speaker	NO:	Speaker ⇒ In-group
	Out-group ⇒ Speaker		Speaker ⇒ Out-group
	Out-group ⇒ In-group		In-group ⇒ Out-group
	In-group ⇒ In-group		

When the recipient is the speaker him/herself, *watashi ni* 'to me' is usually omitted. Within the in-group, the speaker may feel someone is closer to him/her than the others. In this case, the speaker can use KURERU when the receiver is closer to him/her than is the giver or AGERU when the giver is closer to him/her.

c. MORAU verbs cannot be used for outward transfer.

OK:	Speaker ⇐ In-group	NO:	In-group ⇐ Speaker
	Speaker ⇐ Out-group		Out-group ⇐ Speaker
	In-group ⇐ Out-group		Out-group ⇐ In-group
	In-group ⇐ In-group		
	Out-group ⇐ Out-group		

13.2.2 Relative status of giver and receiver

Relative status is highly conventional; that is, to a great extent, status is socioculturally determined, and the speaker normally does not have total freedom to set or alter it. In most cultures, certain people are regarded as higher in status. Criteria can include age, body size/shape, ethnicity, lineage, occupation, sex, skin color, wealth, wisdom, and so forth. However, differing hierarchies usually exist within a single culture, and one need not observe the dominant one. Take, for example, the status of educators and the fact that in Japanese society education is highly regarded. *Sensei* 'teacher/professor' is a term that signals respect, so when it is used in combination with the humilific *sashiageru* in (4a), the professor is elevated linguistically, which is consistent with conventional language practice. However, (4b) does not encode respect for the professor.

(4) a. *Shiga-sensei* *ni* *o-tegami* *o* *sashiageta.*
to letter.HON ACC gave.HON
'I gave a letter to Professor Shiga.'
b. *Shiga-sensei* *ni* *tegami* *o* *ageta/yatta.*
to letter ACC gave
'I gave a letter to Professor Shiga.'

Naturally, not all people respect their teachers, and those who do not must use a different, even derogatory addressing term when they wish to show their contempt. *Senkō* can serve this purpose. *Senkō ni tegami o yatta* is linguistically flawless. However, some native speakers of Japanese might claim that this sentence is unacceptable. What they think is unacceptable is, however, the speaker's attitude towards his/her teacher as conveyed by the utterance, but not the utterance or sentence in and of itself.

Yaru is used when the speaker considers the receiver to be inferior to the giver as well as to the speaker. Because of this discriminating nuance, *yaru* is used infrequently, especially by female speakers. The existence of a hierarchical attitude towards animals is also worthy of comment. If, for example, one thinks of a pet animal/bird/etc. as a family member, *ageru*, rather than *yaru*, is more likely to be employed, as in *Maiasa neko ni iwashi o ageru* 'I feed (my) cat sardines every morning'. When the pet, however, is a tropical fish, the utility of *yaru* increases, and when the receiver is a plant, e.g. when watering (giving water to) a plant, many select *yaru*.

13.3 Benefactive constructions

Donatory verbs appear as auxiliaries in benefactive constructions, which encode a **BENEFACTOR** (a person who confers a favor of performing some act) and a **BENEFICIARY** (a person who receives the benefit).

The action that the benefactor performs is encoded as the main verb in the *te*-form as in (5).

(5) a.	*Chiyoko*	*wa*	*Eiji*	*ni*	*tebukuro*	*o*	*an-de*	*ageta.*
		TOP		DAT	glove	ACC	knit-TE	gave

'Chiyoko knitted gloves for Eiji.'

b.	*Chiyoko*	*wa*	*(watashi*	*ni)*	*jagaimo*	*o*	*yude-te*	*kureta.*
		TOP	(I	DAT)	potato	ACC	boil-TE	gave

'Chiyoko boiled a potato for me.'

c.	*Chiyoko*	*wa*	*Eiji*	*ni*	*sōgankyō*	*o*	*naoshi-te*	*moratta.*
		TOP		DAT	binocular	ACC	repair-TE	received

'[Lit.] Chiyoko received from Eiji the favor of repairing (her) binoculars.'

When *-te ageru* and *-te kureru* are used, the subject referent is the benefactor, and the dative NP (Section 7.2) designates the beneficiary. In the case of *-te morau*, the subject referent is the beneficiary, and the dative NP designates the benefactor.

13.3.1 Two types of beneficiary

There are two kinds of beneficiary: one who benefits by receiving something, and one who benefits by having someone do something on his/her behalf. The former is referred to as a **RECIPIENT BENEFICIARY**, and the latter as a **DEPUTATIVE BENEFICIARY**. A recipient beneficiary need not receive a tangible object as is illustrated by the sentences in (6).

(6) a.	*Chiyoko*	*wa*	*Eiji*	*ni*	*piano*	*o*	*hii-te*	*ageta.*
		TOP		DAT	piano	ACC	play-TE	gave

'Chiyoko played the piano for Eiji.'

b.	*Chiyoko*	*wa*	*(watashi*	*ni)*	*ryōri*	*o*	*oshie-te*	*kureta.*
		TOP	(I	DAT)	cooking	ACC	teach-TE	gave

'Chiyoko taught me how to cook.'

c.	*Chiyoko*	*wa*	*Eiji*	*ni*	*jogen*	*o*	*shi-te*	*moratta.*
		TOP		DAT	advice	ACC	do-TE	received

'[Lit.] Chiyoko received from Eiji a favor of giving (her) advice.'

Unlike a recipient beneficiary, a deputative beneficiary cannot be marked with the dative particle *ni*; instead, *no tame ni* 'for the sake of' must be employed.

(7) a.	*Chiyoko*	*wa*	*Eiji*	*[*ni/no tame ni]*	*rirekisho*	*o*	*kai-te*	*ageta.*
		TOP		[*DAT/for.the.sake.of]	CV	ACC	write-TE	gave

'Chiyoko prepared [Lit. wrote] a (Eiji's) *curriculum vitae* for Eiji.'

b.	*Chiyoko*	*wa*	*watashi*	*[*ni/no tame ni]*	*ginkō*	*ni*	*it-te*	*kureta.*
		TOP	I	[*DAT/for.the.sake.of]	bank	to	go-TE	gave

'Chiyoko went to the bank for me.'

In the *-te morau* construction, as in (7c), the particle *ni* marks the benefactor, not the beneficiary. Therefore, a *ni*-marked NP can always occur with *-te morau*, regardless of the type of benefit.

c.	*Chiyoko*	*wa*	*Eiji*	*ni*	*ginkō*	*ni*	*it-te*	*moratta.*
		TOP		DAT	bank	to	go-TE	received

'Chiyoko had Eiji go to the bank for her.'

13.3.2 The event benefactive

While *-te ageru* and *-te morau* require, explicitly or implicitly, the presence of a benefactor, *-te kureru* can be used to express gratitude or relief for the occurrence of an event that need not have an agent.

(8) a.	*Jishin*	*ga*	*yatto*	*osamat-te*	*kureta.*
	earthquake	NOM	finally	cease-TE	gave

'The earthquake finally ceased (and I'm grateful for it).'

b.	*Kabuka*	*ga*	*jōshō shi-te*	*kureta.*
	stock.price	NOM	rise-TE	gave

'The stock price has risen (and I benefitted from it).'

c.	*Kodomo*	*ga*	*yatto*	*ne-te*	*kureta.*
	child	NOM	finally	sleep-TE	gave

'The kids finally fell asleep (and I'm thankful for that).'

This type is called the **EVENT BENEFACTIVE** (Smith 2005: 41). In this case, the beneficiary must be the speaker him/herself, but *watashi ni* 'for me' cannot be expressed overtly. Because there is no human benefactor to be honored, the honorific *kudasaru* cannot be used in this construction.

13.4 Implicit meanings of donatory verbs

Donatory verbs are problematic if the speaker wishes to show respect equally to both giver and receiver. When grateful to their teachers, for example, adult native speakers of Japanese feel uneasy using (9), which lacks an honorific expression.

(9)	*Shiga-sensei*	*wa*	*Fujita-sensei*	*ni*	*hon*	*o*	*ageta.*
		TOP		DAT	book	ACC	gave

'Professor Shiga gave a book to Professor Fujita.'

The humilific version of AGERU, *sashiageru*, cannot be used here because it automatically places Professor Shiga (the subject) lower than Professor Fujita (the indirect object).

Furthermore, donatory verbs are not translational equivalents of 'give/receive' in English. Rather, they are closer in meaning to 'donate/bestow/make a present of'.[3] That is, they describe situations of someone well off (i.e. of

[3] Donatory verbs are different from English *give* in another respect. While *give* does not necessarily indicate transfer of ownership (i.e. it can be used as a synonym of *hand over*), Japanese donatory verbs encode a change in ownership.

superior status) giving something to someone who is less fortunate (i.e. of inferior status).[4] Therefore, (9) might be (mis)interpreted as Professor Shiga having more resources than Professor Fujita. In such difficult situations, tactful speakers use less "colorful" verbs such as *okuru* 'present' and its honorific version *o-okuri ni naru*.

(10)	*Shiga-sensei*	*wa*	*Fujita-sensei*	*ni*	*hon*	*o*	*o-okuri ni natta.*
		TOP		DAT	book	ACC	presented.HON

'Professor Shiga gave a book to Professor Fujita.'

Similarly, many native speakers feel uncomfortable with (11a) because the sentence lacks an honorific. *Uketoru* 'receive', which is more neutral than *morau*, and its honorific version *o-uketori ni naru* are preferable.

(11) a.	*Fujita-sensei*	*wa*	*Shiga-sensei*	*ni*	*hon*	*o*	*moratta.*
		TOP		DAT	book	ACC	received

'Professor Fujita received a book from Professor Shiga.'

b.	*Fujita-sensei*	*wa*	*Shiga-sensei*	*kara*	*hon*	*o*	*o-uketori ni natta.*
		TOP		from	book	ACC	received.HON

'Professor Fujita received a book from Professor Shiga.'

The problem with AGERU is more pronounced in the *-te ageru* construction.

(12) a.	*Sensei,*	*otetsudai*	*shi-te*	*sashiagemashō*	*ka?*
	teacher	help	do-TE	give.HUM.CNJ.POL	INT

'Professor, shall I give you a hand?'

Sashiageru is the humilific version of AGERU, showing deference to the non-subject referent, in this case the professor. Therefore, (12a) should be appropriate. Nevertheless, it sounds insolent due to the proprietary overtone of donatory verbs as explained above: that is, in using such a verb, the speaker bestows a favor to the person in need. More acceptable alternatives are the following.

b.	*Sensei,*	*otetsudai*	*shimashō*	*ka?*
	teacher	help	do.CNJ.POL	INT

'Professor, shall I help you?'

c.	*Sensei,*	*otetsudai*	*s-ase-te*	*kudasai.*
	teacher	help	do-CAUS.TE	please.give

'Professor, please let me help you.'

13.5 The *-te morau* causative

Inherently coarse, causative constructions (Chapter 11) are usually appropriate only in the following situations: (i) when the causer has total control over the causee, e.g. (13a); (ii) when exercising power is part of the causer's

[4] With KURERU, the receiver is the speaker or his/her in-group member. Lowering oneself or one's in-group is not risky behavior; therefore, the problem discussed here does not apply to KURERU.

responsibility, e.g. (13b); (iii) when the sentence depicts an event as an objective fact, e.g. (13c).

(13) a. *Saibankan wa mokugekisha o shuttō-sase-ta.*
judge TOP witness ACC appear-CAUS-PAST
'The judge made the witness appear in the court.'

b. *Hahaoya wa kodomo ni ha o migak-ase-ta.*
mother TOP child DAT tooth ACC polish-CAUS-PAST
'The mother made the child brush his teeth.'

c. *Yoron wa kaisha ni seihin o kaishū s-ase-ta.*
public.opinion TOP company DAT product ACC recall do-CAUS-PAST
'Public opinion made the company recall its product.'

Because the *saseru* causative can sound arrogant in certain situations, many people avoid it in favor of the *-te morau* construction, which softens the sense of demanding associated with causatives.

(14) a. *Denkiya-san ni kūrā o naos-ase-ta.*
electrician DAT air.conditioner ACC repair-CAUSE-PAST
'(I) made the electrician repair the air conditioner.'

b. *Denkiya-san ni kūrā o naoshi-te morat-ta.*
electrician DAT air.conditioner ACC repair-TE receive-PAST
'[Lit.] (I) received a favor of repairing the air conditioner from the electrician.'
'(I) had the electrician repair the air conditioner.'

The use of *saseru* as in (14a) emphasizes the demanding nature of the causer (the speaker), and thus that sentence, and ones like it, are viewed as less than ideal. In (14b), the speaker asked the electrician to repair the air conditioner, and, consequently, the electrician complied. The sentence, therefore, is semantically causative, but it is still preferable because it frames the event in a more humble fashion. For another example, consider (15):

(15) a. *Raigetsu Yoshida-san o yame-sase-ru.*
next.month ACC quit-CAUS-NPST
'[Lit.] (I) will make Yoshida quit (the company) next month.'
'(I) will fire Yoshida next month.'

b. *Raigetsu Yoshida-san ni yame-te mora-u.*
next.month DAT quit-TE receive-NPST
'[Lit.] (I) will receive a favor of quitting (the company) from Yoshida next month.'
'(I) will ask Yoshida to resign from (the company) next month.'

No matter how it is expressed, the situation and its outcome remain the same. That is, if the speaker of (15) has the authority to dismiss Yoshida, and if the decision has already been made, Yoshida will have no choice but to comply. The speaker of (15b) does not intend to give Yoshida discretion to make a choice; rather, the speaker wishes to appear non-autocratic and in compliance with the requirements of refined linguistic taste.

Examining a speech corpus consisting of transcribed telephone conversations, Smith (2005: 219–22) found 178 instances of the *-te morau* construction, of which 114 (64%) were semantically causative:

(16) a. *Un, kai-te moraō.*
yeah write-TE receive.VOL
'Yeah, let's have (him) write (a letter).'

b. *Shirabe-te morat-ta?*
examine-TE receive-PAST
'Have (you) had (your doctor) examine (your lungs)?'

Her findings confirmed the tendency of speakers to use the *-te morau* construction in order to avoid explicitly causative sentences.

13.6 The causative + *-te itadaku*

The causative followed by *-te itadaku* is frequently used as an intensely humble expression. The following two sentences involve contrasting expressions used in regard to making an entrance.

(17) A: *Dōzo hait-te kudasai.*[5]
please enter-TE give
'Please come in.'

B: *Hair-ase-te itadakimasu.*
enter-CAUS-TE receive.POL
'[Lit.] I receive the favor of your making me enter.'
'Thank you for letting me in.'

When an interlocutor of higher status requests something be done, as in (17A), the interlocutor of lower status typically must comply. Therefore, such a request exerts a causative force, which is acknowledged by the humble tone of (17B).

However, in many instances, the causative + *-te itadaku* is used merely to express one's own determination as illustrated in the following examples:

(18) a. Posted on a bulletin board in a store window:
Teikyūbi ni tsuki, kyūgyō s-ase-te itadakimasu.
regular.holiday because suspension.of.operation do-CAUS-TE receive
'Because it is a regular holiday, our store is closed.'

b. *Heisha no atarashii jigyō no go-setsumei o*
company.HUM GEN new project GEN explanation.HON ACC
s-ase-te itadakimasu.
do-CAUS-TE receive.POL
'Let me explain our company's new project.'

[5] *Kudasai* is the request (command) form of *kudasu* 'hand down'.

In (18a), the store does not need the customer's consent regarding when to close; in (18b), no one has asked the speaker to explain the project. These utterances pretend or presume that the given act is performed in compliance with the addressee's request/demand. Those who use this construction as a more-or-less fixed expression regard it as a mere humble expression, but those who are aware of the meanings of each of its constituents consider it pretentious or even arrogant (Bunkachō 2007: 40–41).

13.7 *-Te kureru* vs. *-te kuru*

The *-te kureru* construction is commonly utilized when the speaker is appreciative of an event in which s/he is involved. When, on the other hand, the speaker evaluates an event negatively, such negativity can be expressed with a *-te kuru* construction. *Kuru* literally means 'come', and *-te kuru* is used to convey a variety of meanings (Hasegawa 1996b). Compare the following sentences derived from Tokunaga (1986: 130).

(19) a.

Tomu	*wa*	*watashi*	*ga*	*komatte ita*	*node,*	*okane*	*o*
	TOP	I	NOM	was.in.trouble	because	money	ACC
kashi-te		*kureta.*					
lend-TE		gave					

'Tom lent me money because I was troubled [financially] (and I'm grateful to him).'

b.

Tomu	*wa*	*watashi*	*ga*	*ir-anai*	*to*	*iu*	*noni,*	*okane*
	TOP	I	NOM	need.neg	QUOT	say	although	money
o	*kashi-te*		*kita.*					
ACC	lend-TE		came					

'Tom lent me money although I said I didn't need it (and I'm annoyed).'

Note, however, that *-te kuru* in (20) does not carry a negative connotation.

(20)

Ginkō	*ga*	*(yatto)*	*okane*	*o*	*kashi-te*	*kita.*
	NOM	(finally)	money	ACC	lend-TE	came

'(Finally,) the bank lent me the money.'

This difference is due to differing expectations based on human nature and social norms. It is routine business for a bank to lend money, but it is exceptional for a friend to do so. Therefore, when a friend lends money to the speaker, the speaker is typically grateful. The use of *-te kuru* indicates that this normal interpretation of the situation does not hold. On the other hand, it is not necessary to show appreciation when a bank lends money; that is, expressing gratitude or annoyance becomes irrelevant, and, consequently, *-te kuru* does not imply the speaker's annoyance. *Kuru* in this case simply indicates that the movement of the object is towards the speaker.

13.8 Malefactive rendering

The benefactive constructions utilizing *yaru*, *kureru*, and *morau* can also be used to convey adversative nuances as exemplified in (21), wherein the agent performs an action with the effect of negatively impacting a second party. A grammatical construction specialized to express such an event is called a **MALEFACTIVE**.

(21) a. *Hara ga tatta node, oikaeshi-te yatta.*
stomach NOM stiffen because turn.away-TE gave
'Because I got angry, I turned (him) away.'

b. *Yatsura o korashime-te kureru.*
they ACC punish-TE give
'I'll give them punishment.'

c. *Uteru mono nara, ut-te moraō.*
Shoot thing if shoot-TE receive.VOL
'[Lit.] If you can shoot me, I'd receive the favor of shooting me.'
'If you dare shoot me, go ahead and do it!'

Whether or not Japanese benefactive constructions also serve as malefactives merits further consideration. Is it not absurd to characterize a given grammatical construction as both benefactive and malefactive? Smith (2005: 2) factors out positive and negative evaluations from the characterizations of constructions employing donatory verbs, categorizing them more abstractly as **AFFECTEDNESS CONSTRUCTIONS**. That is, some participants are affected, but whether to evaluate an event positively or negatively is not specified and depends upon the context within which the construction is situated. This is a reasonable outcome, but I should point out that these constructions are predominantly benefactive. In fact, it took me some time to create the malefactive examples in (21). This suggests to me that these constructions are indeed benefactives, and that benefactives can be used *ironically* to express malefaction. An extreme case is exemplified in (22), which can be and has been used in *yakuza* 'gangster' movies.

(22) *Shin-de itadakimasu.*
die-TE receive
'[Lit.] I honorably receive your favor of dying.'
'Thank you for dying.'

14 Noun modification and complementation

14.1 Introduction

Nouns in Japanese can be modified by (i) another noun, (ii) a *na*-adjective, or (iii) an *i*-adjective as shown in the three examples in (1). In (1a), the genitive particle *no* is inserted after the modifying noun, in (1b), *na*, the attributive form (i.e. noun-modifying form; see Section 6.2) of the copula, is used before a noun, and in (1c), the *i*-adjective modifies the noun directly.

(1) a. *watashi* *no* *uchi* [noun]
I GEN house
'my house.'

b. *kirei* *na* *uchi* [*na*-adjective]
beautiful COP.ATT house
'a beautiful house'

c. *hiroi* *uchi* [*i*-adjective]
spacious house
'a spacious house'

Nouns can also be modified by a clause termed a **RELATIVE CLAUSE** (RC). In Japanese, all modifying elements must precede the modified noun.

14.2 The gapped externally headed relative clause

Sentence (2) contains a RC and the **HEAD** noun phrase (NP), *the apple*, which is located outside the RC. Inside the RC, *the apple* functions as the direct object of the verb *bought*; however, it cannot be expressed overtly: **I ate the apple that/which Joan bought the apple/it*. This obligatory gap inside the RC that corresponds to the head NP is marked by "Ø".

(2) *I ate* *the apple* *[that/which Joan bought Ø].*
HEAD RELATIVE CLAUSE

English allows only this type of RC, which is called a **GAPPED EXTERNALLY HEADED RELATIVE CLAUSE**. This type is common in Japanese as well.

Unlike in ordinary clauses, the subject inside a Japanese RC can be marked with the genitive particle *no* in addition to regular nominative marking with *ga* as shown in (3b). Although it is possible for the polite form (*desu/masu* form; see Subsection 20.2.1) to appear in a RC, the predicate in a RC is normally in plain form even when the entire sentence is considered polite speech. The relative pronouns (*that*, *who*, *whom*, *which*) which appear at the beginning of RC constructions in English do not exist in Japanese. Therefore, no overt marker punctuates the boundary between the RC and the head NP.

(3) a.	*Ichirō*	*ga*	*ringo*	*o*	*katta.*			
		NOM	apple	ACC	bought			

'Ichiro bought an apple.'

b.	*[Ichirō*	*ga/no*	*Ø*	*katta]*	*ringo*	*o*	*tabemashita.*
	[	NOM/GEN		bought]	apple	ACC	ate.POL
		RELATIVE CLAUSE			HEAD		

'I ate the apple that Ichiro bought.'

The gap in a RC can be the subject as in (4a) or the direct object as in (4b).

(4) a.	*[Ø*	*kinō*	*watashi*	*ni*	*denwa shita]*	*hito*
	[	yesterday	I	to	telephoned]	person

'the person who called me yesterday'

b.	*[watashi*	*ga/no*	*Ø*	*sonkei suru]*	*hito*
	[I	NOM/GEN		respect]	person

'a person whom I respect'

When the gap functions as the indirect object as in (4c) or as the genitive (i.e. possessor) as in (4d), *no*-marking of the subject is prohibited. If *no* were employed, the subject NP would be confused as the possessor of the following direct object, e.g. *watashi no hon* 'my book' in (4c) and *watashi no namae* 'my name' in (4d).

c.	*[watashi*	*ga/*no*	*Ø*	*hon*	*o*	*todoketa]*	*hito*
	[I	NOM/GEN		book	ACC	delivered]	person

'the person to whom I delivered the book'

d.	*[watashi*	*ga/*no*	*Ø*	*namae*	*o*	*wasureta]*	*hito*
	[I	NOM/GEN		name	ACC	forgot]	person

'a person whose name I forgot'

Expressions of time or location/goal can also become the head NP as in (5) and (6).

(5) a.	*Watashi*	*wa*	*sono*	*hi*	*saibansho*	*ni*	*itta.*
	I	TOP	that	day	courthouse	to	went

'I went to the courthouse on that day.'

b.	*[watashi*	*ga*	*Ø*	*saibansho*	*ni*	*itta]*	*hi*
	[I	NOM		courthouse	to	went]	day

'the day on which I went to the courthouse'

(6) a.	*Watashi*	*wa*	*machi*	*ni*	*kita.*
	I	TOP	town	to	came

'I came to the town.'

b. *[watashi* *ga/no* *Ø* *kita]* *machi*[1]
[I NOM/GEN came] town
'the town to/from which I came'

Although the attributive and conclusive forms of *i*-adjectives and verbs are identical in Modern Japanese, except for the copula, they were distinct in classical Japanese. For example, the modern adjective *furui* 'old' had an attributive form, *furuki* (e.g. *furuki miyako* 'old capital city'),[2] and a conclusive form, *furushi*. Verbs also had two distinct forms; for the modern verb *ukeru* 'receive', the attributive form was *ukuru* (e.g. *[Ø jihi o ukuru] mono* 'a person who receives mercy'), and the conclusive form was *uku*. However, these two forms merged, and by the fourteenth century, the old attributive form had been established as the new conclusive form in the spoken language (Komatsu 1999/2001: 184). When attributive forms existed, the boundary between the RC and its head NP was clearly identified as coming after the attributive form of the predicate.

This merger of the attributive and conclusive forms has made noun modification with an adjective structurally ambiguous. For example, (1b–1c) can be analyzed as the *na*-adjective *kirei* 'beautiful' and the *i*-adjective *hiroi* 'spacious' modifying the noun *uchi* 'house', as in (1b–1c), or as involving a RC as in (7a–7b).

(1) b. *kirei* *na* *uchi* [*na*-adjective]
beautiful COP.ATT house
'a beautiful house'

c. *hiroi* *uchi* [*i*-adjective]
spacious house
'a spacious house'

(7) a. *[Ø* *kirei* *na]* *uchi*
[beautiful COP.ATT] house
'a beautiful house'

b. *[Ø* *hiroi]* *uchi*
[spacious] house
'a spacious house'

By contrast, when the head corresponds to a genitive NP within the RC, e.g. *uchi no daidokoro* 'the house's kitchen', the modifying constituent unambiguously involves a RC.

c. *[Ø* *daidokoro* *ga/no* *kirei* *na]* *uchi*
[kitchen NOM/GEN beautiful COP.ATT] house
'the house whose kitchen is beautiful'

[1] When a location/goal NP becomes the head, the post-positional particle attached to it is obligatorily deleted. Therefore, (6b) is potentially ambiguous between the readings 'the town *to which* I came' and 'the town *from which* I came' although the goal interpretation (the former) is much more prevalent.

[2] The old attributive forms of *i*-adjectives are still in use in poetic expressions.

d. *[Ø daidokoro ga/no hiroi] uchi*
[kitchen NOM/GEN spacious] house
'the house whose kitchen is spacious'

14.3 The internally headed relative clause

In Japanese, the head NP can be situated *inside* a RC. This construction, which is rare among the world's languages,[3] is referred to as an **INTERNALLY HEADED RELATIVE CLAUSE.**

(8) a. *Ringo ga tēburu no ue ni atta.*
apple NOM table GEN top on existed
'There was an apple on the table.'

b. *[Ringo ga tēburu no ue ni atta] no o tabeta.*[4]
[apple NOM table GEN top on existed] NMLZ ACC ate
'I ate the apple that was on the table.'

The main clause in (8b) asserts that the speaker ate something, and that what was eaten is a *ringo* 'apple', which appears inside the RC. Structurally, (8b) is equivalent to *I ate that there was an apple on the table*, which, of course, is nonsensical in English. More examples follow below:

(9) a. *[Tomodachi ga CD o kashite kureta] no o nakushite shimatta.*
[friend NOM ACC lend.TE gave] NMLZ ACC lose.TE finished
'[Lit.] I lost that a friend of mine lent me a CD.'
'A friend of mine lent me a CD, which I lost.'

b. *[Hahaoya ga ginkō ni okane o furikonde kureta] no*
[mother NOM bank to money ACC transfer.TE gave] NMLZ
o Ichirō wa kyō hikidashita.
ACC TOP today withdrew
'[Lit.] Ichiro withdrew today that (his) mother transferred money to (his) bank.'
'Today Ichiro withdrew the money that (his) mother had transferred to (his) bank.'

Because the head NP is not specially marked as such in the RC, this construction may create ambiguity:

(10) a. *[Keikan ga dorobō o oi kakete ita] no ga kawa ni ochita.*
[police NOM thief ACC was.chasing] NMLZ NOM river to fell
'A police officer was chasing a thief, and the police officer fell into the river.'
'A police officer was chasing a thief, and the thief fell into the river.'
'A police officer was chasing a thief, and they both fell into the river.'

3 It has been reported that the following languages have internally headed RCs: Diegueño (spoken by native Americans in the southwestern US and northwest Mexico), Korean, Lakota (North and South Dakota), Navajo (the southwestern US), Quechua (the central Andes), and Wappo (northern California) (Ohara 1996: 27–31).

4 The status of *no* in this construction is controversial. Although I label it *nominalizer*, it can be analyzed as a pronoun head like *one* in English *the one (that) I ate*.

In the RC of (10a), two persons are mentioned, a police officer and a thief. The sentence can mean that either one fell into the river, or both of them did. In contrast, the semantics of (10b) prevent an ambiguous rendering.

b. *[Otonari ga daiku-san o yonda] no o uchi ni mawashite moratta.*
[neighbor NOM carpenter ACC called] NMLZ ACC house to send.around received
'(My) neighbor called a carpenter, and I had (him/her) sent around to (my) house.'

The internally headed RC occurs mostly in narratives to advance the story line (Ohara 1996: 82). Consider the following English RCs.

(11) a. *I gave the letter to the clerk who was wearing a blue jacket.*
b. *I gave the letter to the clerk, who was insolent, and left the bank.*
c. *I gave the letter to the clerk, who then copied it.*

In the (11a) situation, there were several clerks, and *who was wearing a blue jacket* designates the one to whom the speaker handed the letter; this type is called a **RESTRICTIVE RELATIVE CLAUSE**. In (11b), there may have been only one clerk or several, but the relevant clerk has already been identified in the preceding discourse, and *who was insolent* provides supplemental information about the clerk; this type is called a **NON-RESTRICTIVE RELATIVE CLAUSE**.[5] The RC in (11c) functions differently from either type: it effects narrative progress rather than identifying the referent or supplying additional information. Thus, it is labeled a **NARRATIVE-ADVANCING RELATIVE CLAUSE**. (11c) can be paraphrased as (11d); *and s/he* here is considered to be conflated into *who* in (11c).

d. *I gave the letter to the clerk, and s/he then copied it.*

Likewise, the function of the internally headed RC in Japanese is to advance narration, and it can be paraphrased as follows (compare with (9a–9b)):

(9) a′. *Tomodachi ga CD o kashite kureta ga, nakushite shimatta.*
friend NOM ACC lend.TE gave but lose.TE finished
'A friend of mine lent me a CD, but (I) lost (it).'

b′. *Hahaoya ga ginkō ni okane o furikonde kureta ga,*
mother NOM bank to money ACC transfer.TE gave and
Ichirō wa kyō hikidashita.
TOP today withdrew
'(Ichiro's) mother transferred money to (his) bank, and he withdrew (it) today.'

[5] Japanese does not make a formal distinction between restrictive and non-restrictive RCs. However, demonstratives can co-occur with a non-restrictive relative clause but not with a restrictive one: e.g. *kinben na nihonjin* 'the diligent Japanese' (ambiguous) vs. *sorera no kinben na nihonjin* 'those Japanese, who are diligent' (the non-restrictive reading only).

14.4 The gapless relative clause

The third type of RC that Japanese permits is the **GAPLESS RELATIVE CLAUSE**.[6] It has an external head NP, but the RC contains no corresponding gap. In other words, the head NP is neither structurally nor semantically integrated into the RC.

(12) a.	*[dareka*	*ga*	*kaidan*	*o*	*orite-kuru]*	*oto*
	[someone	NOM	stairs	ACC	descend-come]	sound

'the sound of someone descending the stairs'

In (12a), the RC has no missing constituent; hence, the term *gapless* RC applies. In (12b), the RC lacks the subject of *katta* 'bought', but it must be a person, not the change, which is referred to by the externally located head. The omission of the subject here is an instance of stylistic preference, quite normal in Japanese, and has nothing to do with the RC formation.

b.	*[Ø*	*kōhī*	*o*	*katta]*	*otsuri*
	[	coffee	ACC	bought]	change

'the change from buying coffee'

The subject of the RC is also absent in (12c–12d), but it cannot be the book or the TV commercial, respectively, referred to by the corresponding head. (12c) interpreted fully means 'a book such that if one reads it, one can become (learn to be) more considerate to others'; and (12d) is understood as 'a TV commercial such that it is so interesting/exciting/etc. that one cannot leave for the bathroom while it is showing'.

c.	*[Ø*	*hito*	*ni*	*yasashiku*	*nareru]*	*hon*
	[	people	to	kind	can.become]	book

'a book that (helps you) become more considerate to others'

d.	*[Ø*	*toire*	*ni*	*ikenai]*	*komāsharu*
	[	toilet	to	cannot.go]	commercial

'a TV commercial that is (too interesting/exciting/etc.) to leave for the bathroom'

In (13a), the head indicates the time when the RC event took place. Therefore, one can consider the head in (13a) to be a spatiotemporal constituent of the RC, an instance of the gapped externally headed RC.

(13) a.	*[Jirō*	*ga*	*taiho sareta]*	*hi*
	[	NOM	was.arrested]	day

'the day when Jiro was arrested'

However, (13b) clearly involves a gapless RC because *yokujitsu* 'day after' cannot be a constituent of the RC.

[6] For detailed discussion of the gapless RC, see Matsumoto (1988).

b. *[Jirō ga taiho sareta] yokujitsu*
[NOM was.arrested] day.after
'the very next day of the day when Jiro was arrested'

14.5 Extraction from adverbial clauses

The gapless RC can be analyzed as an instance of extraction from an adverbial (subordinate) clause. For example, (12c) can be analyzed as (14b):

(14) a. *[Sono hon o yomu to]*$_{Adv}$ *hito ni yasashiku nareru.*
[that book ACC read if] people to kind can.become
'If you read that book, you can become more considerate to others.'

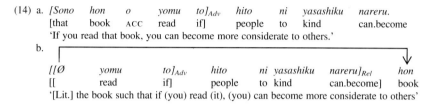

b. *[[Ø yomu to]*$_{Adv}$ *hito ni yasashiku nareru]*$_{Rel}$ *hon*
[[read if] people to kind can.become] book
'[Lit.] the book such that if (you) read (it), (you) can become more considerate to others'

The adverbial clause can then be omitted completely. Another example of this type of RC is provided below:

(15) a. *[Sono hito ga yameta node]*$_{Adv}$ *minna hotto shita.*
[that person NOM stepped.down because] everyone became.relieved
'Because s/he stepped down from the position, everyone was relieved.'

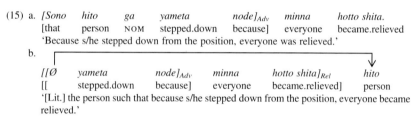

b. *[[Ø yameta node]*$_{Adv}$ *minna hotto shita]*$_{Rel}$ *hito*
[[stepped.down because] everyone became.relieved] person
'[Lit.] the person such that because s/he stepped down from the position, everyone became relieved.'

14.6 Extraction from relative clauses

Japanese also permits extraction of an NP from a RC. Consider the following:

(16) a. *Kodomo ga shatsu o kite iru.*
child NOM shirt ACC is.wearing
'The child is wearing a shirt.'

In both English and Japanese, *shatsu* 'shirt' can be extracted from this clause, e.g. (16b), and the resulting phrase can be embedded in a larger clause, e.g. (16c):

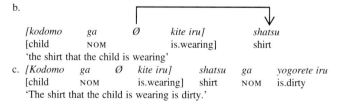

b. *[kodomo ga Ø kite iru] shatsu*
[child NOM is.wearing] shirt
'the shirt that the child is wearing'

c. *[Kodomo ga Ø kite iru] shatsu ga yogorete iru*
[child NOM is.wearing] shirt NOM is.dirty
'The shirt that the child is wearing is dirty.'

English does not allow further extraction from the original RC, but Japanese does:

d.

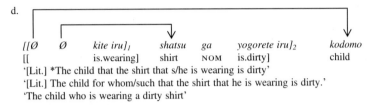

[[Ø	*Ø*	*kite iru]$_1$*	*shatsu*	*ga*	*yogorete iru]$_2$*	*kodomo*
[[		is.wearing]	shirt	NOM	is.dirty]	child

'[Lit.] *The child that the shirt that s/he is wearing is dirty'
'[Lit.] The child for whom/such that the shirt that he is wearing is dirty.'
'The child who is wearing a dirty shirt'

One explanation for this constraint on the English RC formation is that extraction cannot cross more than one clause boundary, called the **SUBJACENCY CONDITION** (Chomsky 1973). Here, in (16d), *kodomo* 'child' crosses two boundaries, hence ungrammaticality in English. Japanese does not have such a constraint on extraction from RCs.

14.7 Questioning a constituent inside relative clauses

Questions are of two types: **YES–NO QUESTIONS** and **WH-QUESTIONS**. In Japanese, a Yes–No question is formed by adding the interrogative particle *ka* at the end of the corresponding declarative sentence.

(17) a.

Ashita	*wa*	*yasumi*	*desu.*	
tomorrow	TOP	holiday	COP	

'Tomorrow is a holiday.'

b.

Ashita	*wa*	*yasumi*	*desu*	*ka?*
tomorrow	TOP	holiday	COP	INT

'Is tomorrow a holiday?'

In English, Wh-words are "moved" (metaphorically speaking) from their original position (Ø) to clause initial position.

(18) a. *Who/Whom did Joan invite Ø to the party?*
b. *What did she buy Ø?*
c. *Where did she go Ø?*
d. *When did she go there Ø?*
e. *How did she make the cake Ø?*

In Japanese, interrogative words remain in their original position:

(19) a.

Jōn	*wa*	*dare*	*o*	*shōtai shimashita*	*ka?*
	TOP	who	ACC	invited	INT

'[Lit.] Joan invited who?'
'Who/Whom did Joan invite?'

b.

Kanojo	*wa*	*nani*	*o*	*kaimashita*	*ka?*
she	TOP	what	ACC	bought	INT

'[Lit.] She bought what?'
'What did she buy?'

c. *Kanojo wa doko ni ikimashita ka?*
she TOP where to went INT
'[Lit.] She went to where?'
'Where did she go?'

d. *Kanojo wa itsu soko ni ikimashita ka?*
she TOP when there to went INT
'[Lit.] She went to there when?'
'When did she go there?'

e. *Kanojo wa dō yatte kēki o tsukurimashita ka?*
she TOP how cake ACC made INT
'[Lit.] She made the cake how?'
'How did she make the cake?'

Unlike English, Japanese permits constituents of a RC to be questioned. Consider (20).

(20) a. *Ōno-kyōju ga kōhosha o suisen shita.*
Professor Ono NOM candidate ACC recommended
'Professor Ono recommended the candidate.'

b. *[Ōno-kyōju ga Ø suisen shita] kōhosha*
[NOM recommended] candidate
'the candidate that Professor Ono recommended'

The recommender in (20b) can be queried:

c. *[Dare ga Ø suisen shita] kōhosha ga saiyō saremashita ka?*
[who NOM recommended] candidate NOM was.hired INT
'[Lit.] #The/A candidate that who recommended was hired?' (Possible only as an echo question.)
'Whose candidate was hired?'
'Who recommended the hired candidate?'

Like extraction from a RC discussed in Section 14.5 above, English does not allow this type of questioning. However, if the focus of the query is shifted slightly, it can be expressed in English:

d. *Who recommended the candidate that was hired?*

Note that (20d) requests the identification of the successful recommender, but (20c) requests the identification of the successful candidate in terms of his/her recommender. Therefore, the two sentences may not be interchangeable.[7] This type of question is very common in Japanese as exemplified below.

(21) a. *[Ø nani-iro no fuku o kite iru] hito ga suki?*
[what-color GEN clothes ACC is.wearing] person NOM like
'[Lit.] The person wearing what-color clothes do you like?'

b. *[Ø doko ni suwatte iru] hito o shitte iru no?*
[where in is.sitting] person ACC know SFP
'[Lit.] The person sitting where do you know?'

[7] See Hasegawa (1989) for further discussion.

14.8 Tense in relative clauses

This book refers to the *ta*-form as the past tense marker, and the *ru*-form as the non-past tense marker, but, as discussed in Chapter 9, these tense markers behave very differently than their English counterparts. Recall the following sentence discussed in Section 9.5, repeated here as (22).

(22) *[Kanai no Ø ike-ta] hana ga ashita no tenrankai*
[my.wife GEN arrange-PAST] flower NOM tomorrow GEN exhibition
ni de-ru.
in enter-NPST
'Flowers arranged by my wife will be displayed in tomorrow's exhibition.'

The flowers had already been arranged at the speech time, or they would be arranged after the speech time but before the exhibition. As this example illustrates, the *ta*-form in a RC indicates that the event takes place prior to the reference time, which may equate with the speech time (rendering a past tense interpretation) or the time supplied by the main clause. Similarly, in (23), the *ru*-form version indicates that the person had not provided the funds as of the day before speech time, whereas the *ta*-form version indicates that the funds had been provided prior to the meeting.

(23) *[Ø shikin o dashite kureru/kureta] hito ni kinō atta.*
[fund ACC provide.TE give/gave] person with yesterday met
'I met the person who [will provide/had provided] funds.'

In a RC, the *ta*-forms of certain predicates are normally interpreted as resultative (see Section 9.7), referring to a state which resulted from a preceding event, as exemplified in (24).

(24) a. *[Ø yaseta] hito*
[lose.weight.PAST] person
'[Lit.] a person who has lost (his/her) weight'
'a thin person'
b. *[Ø megane o kaketa] hito*
[eye.glass ACC put.on.PAST] person
'[Lit.] a person who has put on eyeglasses'
'a person wearing eyeglasses'

When the predicate in a RC is stative (Section 9.2) rather than dynamic, the *ta*-form cannot be employed if the state of affairs continues to exist at the reference time:

(25) a. *[Ø se ga/no takai/*takakatta] hito ni michi o kikareta.*
[height NOM/GEN is.high/*was.high person by way ACC was.asked
'[Lit.] I was asked by a person who is/was tall how to get (to a certain place).'
b. *[Ø betonamugo ga/no hanaseru/*hanaseta] hito o sagashimashita.*
[Vietnamese NOM/GEN can.speak/*could.speak] person ACC looked.for
'I looked for a person who can/could speak Vietnamese.'

In (25a), the person was tall when s/he asked the speaker about a route (i.e. the reference time); therefore, *takai* but not *takakatta* must be selected. *Takakatta* here would indicate that the person used to be tall, but no longer was at the reference time. Likewise, in (25b), *hanaseta* would indicate that the speaker is looking for a person who was once able to speak Vietnamese, but not any longer – an odd situation.

The progressive form provides a different interpretation from pure stative verbs exemplified in (25).

(26) a. *Nami wa [Ø IBM ni tsutomete iru/tsutomete ita] hito to*
TOP [at is.working/was.working] person with
kekkon shita.
married
'Nami married a person who was working/used to work for IBM.'

In (26a), *tsutomete iru hito* indicates that the bridegroom was working for IBM when they married, but *tsutomete ita hito* indicates that he had worked for IBM but had left the company before the marriage. (In the former, whether or not he was still working for IBM at the speech time cannot be determined from the utterance.)

However, the tense in a RC is not always completely relative to the time of the main clause. If a temporal adverbial phrase that refers to a past time occurs inside the RC, *-te iru* cannot be used:

b. *Nami wa [Ø kyonen IBM ni *tsutometeiru/tsutomete ita] hito to kekkon shita.*
TOP [last.year at *is.working/was.working] person with married
'Nami married a person who was working for IBM last year.'

By contrast, in (27a), *yonde ita* and *yonde iru* are interchangeable, although the former can also mean that Nami confiscated the book that the child used to read:

(27) a. *Nami wa [kodomo ga/no Ø yonde iru/yonde ita] hon o toriageta.*
TOP [child NOM/GEN is.reading/was.reading] book ACC confiscated
'Nami took the book that the child was reading away from the child.'

Josephs (1972: 113–14) analyzes the difference between *-te iru* and *-te ita* in such a way that, while *-te iru* simply describes the action in progress at the time of the main-clause action, *-te ita* implies that the speaker has paid attention to or has at least been aware of the RC action for some time prior to the main-clause action taking place. The difference is very subtle. Here is Josephs' original example and his translations:

b. *Watakushi wa densha no naka de [Ø kasa o*
I TOP train GEN inside in [umbrella ACC
motte iru/motte ita] hito ni hanashikaketa.
is.carrying/was.carrying] person to accosted
'In the train, I struck up a conversation with a man [who happened to be carrying/who I (had) noticed was carrying] an umbrella.'

Kuno (1973: 268) supports Josephs by providing (27c):

c. *Densha ni tobinoru to, [Ø kasa o motte iru/??motte ita]*
train to jump.into when [umbrella ACC is.carrying/was.carrying]
hito ga hanashikakete kita.
person NOM accosted.TE came
'When I jumped onto a train, a person who was carrying an umbrella started talking to me.'

The connective *to* in (27c) marks a temporal subordinate clause and indicates that immediately after the subordinate-clause event occurs, the speaker recognizes the main-clause event (see Subsection 16.2.6). This construction is compatible with *-te iru*, but it contradicts *-te ita* because, as Josephs claims, it describes a temporal sequence in which a new situation arises. Because *-te ita* necessarily implies that the speaker has paid attention for some time to some situation, the person carrying an umbrella in this case, it is incompatible.

14.9 Noun complementation

Certain nouns require some kind of modification or supplementation. Consider *tendency* for example. *There is a tendency* does not in itself sound complete; it requires a phrase like *for people to eat too fast* to describe what is referred to by *tendency*. Such semantically necessary modifiers are called **NOUN COMPLEMENTS**. Noun complements in Japanese are commonly marked with *to iu* 'saying that' as exemplified below:

(28) a. *[Takamine-san ga yūshō shita] to iu shirase*
[NOM won] that message
'the message that Takamine won the championship'

b. *[kaisha ga tōsan shita] to iu jijitsu*
[company NOM went.bankrupt] that fact
'the fact that the company has gone bankrupt'

Some noun complements do not require *to iu* and thus have the appearance of a RC. The following examples are derived from Teramura (1984: 207–08):

(29) a. *Watashi ni wa [hatsugen suru] shikaku ga nai.*
I in TOP [voice] qualification NOM not.exist
'[Lit.] I don't have qualifications for voicing (my thoughts).'
'I'm not qualified to speak.'

b. *[Raigetsu made ni kono shigoto o shiageru] yotei da.*
[next.month by this project ACC complete] plan COP
'I plan to complete this project by next month.'

c. *[100-man en o damashi totta] utagai de taiho-sareta.*
[one.million yen ACC defraud] charge for was.arrested
'(S/he) was arrested on the charge of defrauding (the person) one million yen.'

The same nouns can be modified by a RC as shown in (30).

(30) a. *[Watashi ga 2-nen kakete Ø totta] shikaku wa*
[I NOM 2-years spending obtained] qualification TOP
kachi ga nakatta.
value NOM not.existed
'[Lit.] The qualification I obtained by spending two years was useless.'
'The qualification I spent two years to obtain was useless.'

b. *[Takamine-san ga Ø tateta] yotei o ginmi shita.*
[NOM made] plan ACC scrutinized
'(I) scrutinized the plan that Takamine made.'

c. *Kare wa kurō shite [Ø kakerareta] utagai o harashita.*
he TOP having.trouble [was.imposed] charge ACC cleared
'[Lit.] Undergoing hardships, he cleared the charge that was imposed (on him).'
'He cleared the charge (on himself) but with great difficulty.'

There are clear examples of noun modification and noun complementation functioning as opposing constructions. However, there are also numerous cases that resist unequivocal categorization. Thus, noun modification and complementation are considered to form a cline (a scale of continuous gradation) rather than a dichotomy.

15 Nominalization

15.1 Introduction

One of the defining characteristics of a noun (strictly speaking, a noun phrase, NP, rather than a bare noun) is its ability to serve as either the subject or the object of a clause (see the discussion in Subsection 5.2.1).

(1) a. *The news brought much needed optimism to dejected Japanese people.* [NP subject]
    b. *I saw a car accident.* [NP object]

However, it is sometimes necessary to use a clause as a subject or an object as exemplified in (2).

(2) a. *That abundant reservoirs of methane hydrate exist in the seabed surrounding the Japanese archipelago brought much needed optimism to dejected Japanese people.* [clause subject]
    b. *I saw a car hit a pedestrian.* [clause object]

In Japanese, clauses that function as nouns or NPs are formed by attaching the **FORMAL NOUN** *koto* 'fact, thing' (*koto* is designated "formal" because, while it is a noun, it does not identify a specific class of referents, unlike nouns like *person, desk, apple*, etc.) or the particle *no*. This process is called **NOMINALIZATION**, and *koto* and *no* are referred to as **NOMINALIZERS** or **COMPLEMENTIZERS**.

(3) a.

Nihon	*kinkai*	*no*	*kaitei*	*ni*	*bōdai na*	*ryō*	*no*
Japan	coastal water	GEN	seabed	in	abundant	amount	GEN

metan haidorēto	*ga*	*maizō sarete iru*	*koto*	*wa*	*shitsui no*
methane hydrate	NOM	is buried	NMLZ	TOP	dejected

nihon	*kokumin*	*ni*	*nagaku*	*machi nozomareta*	*akarusa*	*o*	*motarashita.*
Japan	people	to	long	expected	cheerfulness	ACC	brought

'That an abundant amount of methane hydrate is buried in the seabed of Japanese coastal waters brought long-awaited optimism to the dejected Japanese people.'

b.

Watashi	*wa*	*kuruma*	*ga*	*hokōsha*	*o*	*haneru*	*no*	*o*	*mita.*
I	TOP	car	NOM	pedestrian	ACC	hit	NMLZ	ACC	saw

'I saw a car hit a pedestrian.'

Some predicates take only *koto* as their nominalizer, others take *no*, and still others take both. This chapter examines the conditions and constraints on nominalization.

15.2 *No* vs. *koto*

No is used to reference a concrete situation (i.e. action, event, or state) perceivable by the five senses, whereas *koto* pertains to situations that involve abstract cognition (Kuno 1973: 220–21):

(4) a. *Watashi wa Chiyoko ga piano o hiku [no/*koto] o mita.*
I TOP NOM piano ACC play NMLZ ACC saw
'I saw Chiyoko playing the piano.'

b. *Watashi wa Chiyoko ga piano o hiku [no/koto] o kiita.*
NMLZ heard
'I heard [Chiyoko playing/that Chiyoko plays] the piano.'

In (4a), only *no* is possible. In (4b), on the other hand, both *no* and *koto* can be used, but they depict different scenes. With *no*, the speaker actually heard Chiyoko playing the piano, but with *koto*, the speaker heard from someone that Chiyoko is able to play the piano. This difference can be accounted for by the perception vs. cognition distinction mentioned above.

However, for some non-perception predicates, *no* serves as the sole nominalizer:

(5) a. *Watashi wa Chiyoko ga piano o hiku [no/*koto] o shashin ni totta.*
photo to take
'I took a photo of Chiyoko playing the piano.'

b. *Watashi wa Chiyoko ga piano o hiki-owaru [no/*koto] o matta.*
finish.playing waited
'I waited for Chiyoko to finish playing the piano.'

Hashimoto (1990) characterizes *no* as a nominalizer of simultaneity. That is, the nominalized situation and the main-clause situation must occur simultaneously. A prototypical case is perception. On the other hand, *koto* indicates that the nominalized situation is detached in time from the main-clause situation. These characteristics are illustrated in (6), derived from Noda (1995: 427):

(6) a. *Chichi wa niwa no kaki ga minotta [no/koto] o yorokonda.*
father TOP garden GEN persimmon NOM bore.fruits NMLZ ACC was.delighted
'(My) father was delighted (to see) that the persimmon (tree) in the garden bore fruit.'

b. *Chichi wa ima made no kurō ga minotta [?no/koto] o yorokonda.*
father TOP now until GEN hardship NOM bore.fruits NMLZ ACC was.delighted
'(My) father was delighted that all (his) hard work bore fruit.'

In (6a), when *no* is used, the speaker is depicting his/her father's delight in watching the persimmon tree bear fruit, i.e. the two situations co-occur. On the other hand, when *koto* is used, the father is no longer watching the scene, but probably hearing from someone the fact about the persimmon tree fruit. That is, the two situations are separated in time. In (6b), the father's accomplishments occurred prior to his contentment.

This co-temporality, or lack thereof, can predict to a considerable extent whether a given predicate takes *no* or *koto*, although there are many unpredictable idiosyncrasies such as those included in the following list, based on Kudo (1985):

(7) Predicates that take *no* exclusively
kenbutsu suru 'view', *kikoeru* 'be audible', *kiku* 'hear (perception)', *matsu* 'wait', *mieru* 'be visible', *mimamoru* 'watch', *miru* 'see', *nagameru* 'look on', *naoru/naosu* 'repair', *saegiru* 'interrupt', *tasukeru* 'help', *tetsudau* 'help', *tomaru/tomeru* 'stop'

(8) Predicates that take *koto* exclusively
a. Thinking (cognitive) verbs
kangaeru 'consider', *omou* 'think', *rikai suru* 'understand', *satoru* 'realize', *shinjiru* 'believe', *utagau* 'doubt'
b. Communication verbs
hanasu 'talk', *iu* 'say', *kaku* 'write', *kiku* 'hear (hearsay)', *shiraseru* 'notify', *tsutaeru* 'communicate', *yomu* 'read'
c. Directive verbs
kinjiru 'prohibit', *meijiru* 'command', *nozomu* 'desire', *kimeru* 'decide', *yakusoku suru* 'promise', *yurusu* 'permit'
d. Indicating verbs
honomekasu 'imply', sasu 'point to', shimesu 'indicate', shiteki suru 'point out', shōmei suru 'prove'

(9) Predicates that take both *no* and *koto*
a. Cognitive verbs
hakken suru 'discover', *oboeru* 'memorize', *omoidasu* 'recall', *shiru* 'find out', *wakaru* 'understand'
b. Attitude verbs
akirameru 'give up', *kanashimu* 'feel sad', *kitai suru* 'expect', *odoroku* 'be surprised', *sansei suru* 'approve', *yorokobu* 'rejoice'
c. Miscellaneous
fusegu 'protect', *sakeru* 'avoid', *yameru* 'quit', *yosu* 'quit'

15.3 *No/koto* vs. *to*

Another grammatical construction which resembles nominalization is that involving the **QUOTATIVE PARTICLE** *to*. (This topic will be discussed further in Chapter 27). *To* and *koto o* are frequently interchangeable, as shown in (10). Note that *to* can be categorized as a complementizer (i.e. forming a complement clause), but not a nominalizer (forming an NP); therefore, the accusative particle *o*, which attaches only to NPs, does not follow *to*.

(10) a.

Midori	*wa*	*chikyū*	*ga*	*6,000*	*nen*	*mae ni*	*tanjō shita*	*[koto o/to]*	*shinjite iru.*
	TOP	earth	NOM		year	ago	was.born		believe

'[Lit.] Midori believes that the earth was born 6,000 years ago.'
'Midori believes that the earth is 6,000 years old.'

b.

Midori	*wa*	*tsukaikomi*	*o*	*shita*	*[koto o/to]*	*kokuhaku shita.*
	TOP	embezzlement	ACC	did		confessed

'Midori confessed that (she) committed embezzlement.'

In (10), both *koto o* and *to* depict the same situation, but the selection of *koto o* reveals the speaker's **PRESUPPOSITION** that the content of the embedded clause is true.[1] This is the reason why the use of *koto o* in (10a) sounds odd, for it is a generally accepted fact that the earth came into being much earlier than 6,000 years ago. *To*, on the other hand, does not convey such a presupposition; the speaker might or might not believe the truth of the embedded content. Regarding (10b), because the legitimacy of the claim that Midori committed embezzlement remains unknown, both *koto o* and *to* sound conceivable. Nevertheless, there is a difference regarding the speaker's presuppositions which should be recognized.

This phenomenon of revealing presupposition is discussed in linguistics in terms of **FACTIVITY**. Compare the following structurally identical sentences:

(11) a. *George Price believes that the earth is 6,000 years old.*
b. *George Price knows that the earth is 6,000 years old.*

In (11a), the speaker is merely reporting Price's belief; however, (11b) implies that the speaker also believes that the earth is 6,000 years old. The difference is due to the selection of the predicates. Those that encode the speaker's presupposition that the given content is true are called **FACTIVE PREDICATES**, and those that do not are **NON-FACTIVE PREDICATES** (Kiparsky and Kiparsky 1970).[2]

(12) a. Factive predicates
be significant, be exciting, bother, make clear, make sense, suffice, be aware (of), deplore, forget (about), ignore, keep in mind, regret, resent, take into consideration
b. Non-factive predicates
be possible, be likely, be true, happen, seem, turn out, allege, assert, believe, charge, conclude, conjecture, deem, maintain, suppose

English provides various means to covertly express factivity. For example, only factive predicates can take as their objects the noun *fact* with a gerund or *that*-clause (Kiparsky and Kiparsky 1970).

(13) Factive predicates
a. *You have to keep in mind the fact of his having proposed several alternatives.*
b. *I want to make clear the fact that I don't intend to participate.*

(14) Non-factive predicates
a. **We may conclude the fact of his having proposed several alternatives.*
b. **I assert the fact that I don't intend to participate.*

[1] Many students are often confused about whose presupposition is implied by *koto*. It is that of the speaker, not of the subject referent – Midori in this case. Midori believes the embedded content, but this state of affairs is asserted by the verb *shinjite iru* 'believe', not implied by the nominalizer.

[2] To examine factivity, the complement must be verifiable, i.e. referring to a past or present situation. If the complement refers to a future situation, the speaker's presupposition of its factivity is deemed immaterial.

For another example, the grammatical construction called **EXTRAPOSITION** (*It ... that ...*) is optional for factive predicates, but it is obligatory for non-factive predicates:

(15) Factive predicate
 a. *That there are porcupines in our basement makes sense to me.*
 b. *It makes sense to me that there are porcupines in our basement.*

(16) Non-factive predicate
 a. **That there are porcupines in our basement seems to me.*
 b. *It seems that there are porcupines in our basement.*

In Japanese, factivity is encoded not only in predicate selection, but also in complementizer selection. *Shinjiru* 'believe' and *kokuhaku suru* 'confess' in (10) are non-factive. With such predicates, the embedded content is normally expressed with non-factive *to*, and can optionally be expressed with factive *no* or *koto*. When, on the other hand, the predicate is categorized as factive, the use of *to* is prohibited, as illustrated in (17).

(17) a.

Midori	*wa*	*jikan*	*ga*	*sugite iru*	*[no o/koto o/*to]*	*mushi shita.*
	TOP	time	NOM	has.passed		ignored

'Midori ignored the fact that the time has (already) passed.'

b.

Midori	*wa*	*tsukaikomi*	*o*	*shita*	*[no o/koto o/*to]*		*kōkai shita.*
	TOP	embezzlement	ACC	did	NMLZ/QUOT	ACC	regretted

'Midori regretted that (she) committed embezzlement.'

c.

Midori	*wa*	*Shigeru*	*ni*	*tegami*	*o*	*dashita*	*[no o/koto o/*to]*	*wasurete ita.*
	TOP		to	letter	ACC	sent		forgot

'Midori forgot that she had sent a letter to Shigeru.'

15.4 The *n(o)* + copula construction

The construction consisting of *no* (or its abbreviated form *n*) followed by the copula (*da*, *desu*, *datta*, *deshita*; see Subsection 5.2.2) 'it is the case that ~' frequently appears in Japanese discourse. This section discusses several functions of this construction.

15.4.1 External negation

In English, the sentence *He isn't promoted because he is kind to his staff* is ambiguous between interpretations involving internal and external negation: (i) because he is kind to his staff, he is not promoted (**INTERNAL NEGATION**, negating only *is promoted*); (ii) it is not the case that he is promoted because he is kind to his staff, or the reason why he is promoted is not that he is kind to his staff (**EXTERNAL NEGATION**).

(18) a. [[*He is promoted*]$_{\text{-NOT}}$ [*because he is kind to his staff*]]
 b. [[*He is promoted*] [*because he is kind to his staff*]]$_{\text{-NOT}}$

In Japanese, placing a cause or reason clause (Chapter 17) after the main clause is impossible. Instead, the idea is typically expressed by the construction appearing in (19a). Note that when the order of the main and subordinate clauses changes in English, the ambiguity disappears.

(19) a. *Kare* *wa* *buka* *ni* *shinsetsu* *da* *kara* *shōshin* *shi-nai.*
he TOP staff to kind is because promotion do-not
'Because he is kind to (his) staff, he is not promoted.'

In order to express external negation in Japanese, nominalization of the two clauses by means of *n(o)* + copula is required (Hasegawa 1996a: 43). *No de wa nai* in (19b) is the negation of *no da*.

b. *Kare* *wa* *buka* *ni* *shinsetsu* *da* *kara* *shōshin* *shita* *no* *de* *wa* *nai.*
he TOP staff to kind is because promotion did NMLZ COP NEG-SCP not
'[Lit.] It is not the case that he is promoted because he is kind to (his) staff.'
'He was promoted not because he is kind to (his) staff.'

Another example of external negation, taken from Noda (1997: 35), is provided in (19c), where *n ja nai* is an abbreviated form of *no de wa nai* (see Section 6.4). This sentence does not negate the speaker's crying, but, rather, his/her reason for crying:

c. *Kanashiku-te* *naite iru* *n* *ja* *nai.* *Ureshiku-te* *naite iru* *n* *da.*
be.sad-TE is.crying NMLZ TOP.COP not be.happy-TE is.crying NMLZ COP.NPST
'[Lit.] It is not the case that (I'm) crying because (I'm) sad; it is the case that (I'm) crying because (I'm) happy.'
'(I'm) not crying because (I'm sad). (I'm) crying because (I'm) happy.'

15.4.2 Metalinguistic negation

Another context in which the *n(o) da* construction plays a significant role is **METALINGUISTIC NEGATION**, characterized by Horn (1985) and exemplified by (20):

(20) a. Lauren Bacall's TV commercial for High Point decaffeinated coffee
Around here, we don't like coffee – we love it!
b. *Max doesn't have three children – he has four.*

In (20a), what is negated is the word choice of *like*, not the speaker's fondness of coffee, as *like* normally indicates a lesser degree of fondness than *love*. The utterance conveys, *I wouldn't say I like coffee; rather, I'd say I love it.* In (20b), if Max has four children, it is true that he has three. However, *Max has three children* normally implies that he has no more than three, an implication that does not strictly follow logical inference but which is common in conversation.[3] This sentence negates the "illogical" but common implication concerning the upper boundary. In these cases, what is negated is not the linguistic constituent to which *not* is attached. *I don't like coffee* normally means that the speaker does not like coffee; *Max doesn't have three children* normally means that he has two, one, or no children. Rather, the negation takes place at a meta level of language use, i.e. at a level appropriate for the formation or selection of certain linguistic expressions. Hence, the label *metalinguistic negation* is applied.

In Japanese, metalinguistic negation must employ the *n(o) da* construction.[4]

(21) a.

#Watashi-tachi	*wa*	*kōhī*	*ga*	*suki*	*de*	*wa*	*arimasen.*
we	TOP	coffee	NOM	like	COP	TOP	not

Kōhī	*o*	*aishite iru*	*no*	*desu.*
coffee	ACC	love	NMLZ	COP.NPST

'We don't like coffee. The fact is that (we) love coffee.'

b.

Watashi-tachi	*wa*	*kōhī*	*ga*	*suki*	*na*	*no*	*de*	*wa*	*arimasen.*
we	TOP	coffee	NOM	like	COP	NMLZ	COP	NEG-SCP	not

Kōhī	*o*	*aishite iru*	*no*	*desu.*
coffee	ACC	love	NMLZ	COP.NPST

'It is not the case that we like coffee. The fact is that (we) love coffee.'

(22) a.

#Makkusu	*wa*	*kodomo*	*ga*	*3-nin*	*imasen.*	*4-nin*	*iru*	*no*	*desu.*
Max	TOP	child	NOM	3-persons	not.exist	4-persons	exist	NMLZ	COP.NPST

'Max doesn't have three children. The fact is that (he) has four.'

b.

Makkusu	*wa*	*kodomo*	*ga*	*3-nin*	*iru*	*no*	*de*	*wa*	*arimasen.*
Max	TOP	child	NOM	3-persons	exist	NMLZ	COP	NEG-SCP	not

4-nin	*iru*	*no*	*desu.*
4-persons	exist	NMLZ	COP.NPST

'It is not the case that Max has three children. The fact is that (he) has four.'

15.4.3 N(o) da *as a nominal predication*

Compare the two sentences in (23) that depict an identical scene.

(23) a.

Kōji	*genba*	*no*	*ashiba*	*ga*	*kuzureta.*
construction	site	GEN	scaffolding	NOM	collapsed

'The scaffolding on the construction site collapsed.'

b.

Kōji genba no ashiba ga kuzureta	*no*	*da.*
	NMLZ	COP.NPST

'It is the case that the scaffolding on the construction site collapsed.'

[3] This "illogical" but nonetheless common interpretation is accounted for in linguistics as the speaker's observation of a **Maxim of quantity** (i.e. one makes one's contribution as informative as is required for the purposes of the exchange, and one does not make one's contribution more informative than is required) in the **Gricean Theory of Implicature**. Refer to any pragmatics textbook for further information about Gricean Theory.

[4] For further discussion of the scope of negation in Japanese, see Masuoka (1991).

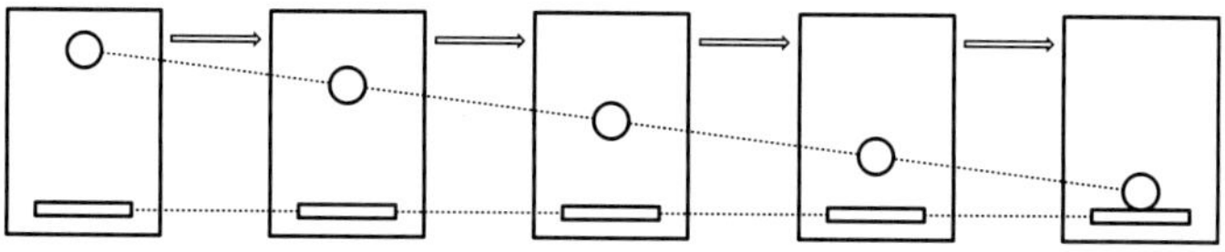

Figure 15.1. Sequential scanning.

(23a) is an ordinary event-reporting sentence, whereas (23b) presents the event in terms of nominalization. The semantic difference between the two may be intuitive for native speakers of Japanese, but it is very difficult to articulate precisely.

Langacker (1987) explains that these constructions reflect two modes of cognitive processing that apply to the conceptualization of a complex scene. A verb is a symbolic expression of a **PROCESS** (i.e. a situation that changes over time), which can be represented as a series of schematic conceptions of states aligned in time (which he terms **SEQUENTIAL SCANNING**). Figure 15.1 demonstrates such a cognitive process regarding an object falling onto a flat surface. In this diagram, the circle indicates the falling object, the rectangular shape the flat surface, and the arrows the flow of time. The dotted lines indicate that the items are the same from one state to the next.

Humans are also capable of conceptualizing a complex array of cognitive events simultaneously as a coherent **GESTALT** (i.e. a structure of a physical or psychological phenomenon so integrated as to constitute a unit not derivable by summation of its parts). This type of conceptualization, which Langacker calls **SUMMARY SCANNING**, is expressed by nominalization, graphically represented in Figure 15.2.

To provide an analogy, the first type (Figure 15.1) can be likened to a motion picture, the second type (Figure 15.2) to a long-exposure photograph. Note that in the first type, time is involved both in the depicted situation (e.g. the falling event in the real world) and when it is conceptualized in the speaker's mind and expressed as a sentence like (23a). Contrastively, in the second type, time is relevant in the depicted situation, but not in cognitive processing.[5] In this respect, nominalized expressions are static and, therefore, resemble nouns.

[5] Langacker (1987: 262) convincingly argues for these two distinct notions of time. The antithesis of nominalization involves describing a static scene in such a way as this: *This road is winding through the mountains*. Here, in characterizing the road as winding, the speaker mentally compares various parts of the path one at a time as if s/he is driving along the road. In this case, the notion of time is not involved in the depicted situation, but it is involved in cognition – just opposed to nominalization.

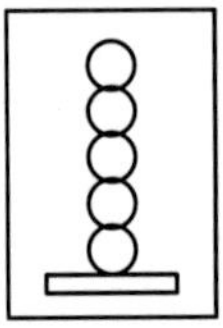

Figure 15.2. Summary scanning.

15.4.4 N(o) da *to supply background information*

What does this insight into nominalization tell us about how (23a) and (23b) differ? As an atemporal expression, the *n(o) da* construction cannot be used to advance a **NARRATIVE** (i.e. a retelling of what happened, normally in chronological order). A narrative characteristically consists of foreground and background information (see Section 9.6). The foreground consists of events sequentially arranged to form the primary story line, whereas the background is everything else, including descriptions of involved entities or scenes and knowledge prerequisite to comprehending the given narrative. For example, (23b) cannot appear as part of the story line as in (24), but can supply background information as in (25):

(24) *Totsuzen gō to iu oto ga shite, jimen ga yure dashita.*
suddenly roaring sound NOM do-TE ground NOM started.shaking
Me no mae de kōji genba no ashiba ga
eye GEN front at construction site GEN scaffolding NOM
[kuzureta/#kuzureta no da]. Watashi wa tetsu-paipu no
[collapsed/collapsed-NMLZ-COP.NPST] I TOP steel-pipe GEN
nadare ni makikomare sō ni natta.
avalanche to be.caught as.if to became
'Suddenly, there was a roaring sound. In front of (my) eyes, the scaffolding on the construction site collapsed. I was almost caught in the avalanche of steel pipes.'

(25) *Bakuhatsu no yō na gōon ni Chiyoko wa gyotto shite*
explosion GEN like roar.sound to TOP be.astonished-TE
furikaetta. Kōji genba no ashiba ga
looked.back construction site GEN scaffolding NOM
[kuzureta/kuzureta no da].
collapsed/collapsed-NMLZ-COP.NPST
'Chiyoko was astonished by a blast-like roar, and looked back. [The scaffolding on the construction site collapsed/It was the collapse of the scaffolding on the construction site].'

In (25), if the non-nominalized *kuzureta* is used, the collapsing event is understood as taking place after Chiyoko looked back. On the other hand, if the nominalized version *kuzureta no da* is used, the collapse of the scaffolding is explained as, or is understood to be, the cause of the blast-like sound.

15.4.5 N(o) da *and the expression of spontaneity*

When expressing one's future action, Section 8.9 noted that the English expression *be going to* ~ can be used only if the action is pre-planned while *will* must be selected if the action is determined spontaneously at the time of the utterance. Such spontaneity can be expressed in Japanese by *ga*, as was also discussed, and exemplified in (26).

(26) To the professor who forgot to bring a video projector:

Watashi	*[ga/#wa]*	*motte-kimasu.*
I	[NOM/TOP]	carry-come

'I'll go get it.'

Watashi <u>*wa*</u> *motte-kimasu* 'I'm going to bring it' is appropriate when responding to the question below, in which case the use of *ga* is inappropriate.

(27)

Minna	*obentō*	*o*	*motte-kuru*	*n*	*desu*	*ka.*
everyone	box.lunch	ACC	carry-come	NMLZ	COP.NPST	INT

'[Lit.] Is it the case that everyone will bring a box lunch?'
'Will everyone bring a box lunch?'

Like *wa*, *n(o) da* is also unable to express spontaneity. In (28), *n(o) da* cannot be used:

(28)

Watashi	*ga*	*[motte-kimasu/#motte-kuru n desu].*
I	NOM	[carry-come]

'I'll go get it.'

This inability of *n(o) da* can be accounted for by Langacker's conceptualization of nominalization as depicting a cognitive event as an atemporal gestalt, and not as a time-bound phenomenon.

Part V

Clause linkage

16 Temporal clauses

16.1 Introduction

Section 9.4 discusses the notion of taxis, which concerns the chronological relationship between a pair of situations (i.e. events, actions, and states), and this chapter considers how taxis is manifested in Japanese. The two situations in question are encoded as two clauses and arranged in a sentence with various connectives appearing between them. Such connected clauses will be schematically represented as P and Q, where clause P precedes clause Q in a sentence. In Japanese, subordinate clauses always precede the main clause; therefore, P is invariably a subordinate clause, whereas Q is a main clause. The following three temporal relationships will be explored in this chapter.

(1) a. After P, Q.
    b. Before P, Q.
    c. While P, Q.

Because its clause order is iconic with the event order, (1a) is easier to comprehend than (1b), in which the clause order reverses the event order. Consequently, more patterns are available to express (1a).

The two connected situations referred to by P and Q will be represented as P' and Q', respectively. Be sure to keep in mind that P and Q are linguistic objects, whereas P' and Q' stand for the situations to which they refer.

(2) a. $P' \prec Q'$ — P' precedes Q'.
    b. $Q' \prec P'$ — Q' precedes P'; P' follows Q'.
    c. $P' \approx Q'$ — P' and Q' occur simultaneously or overlap.

Although the *ta*-form is labeled as the marker of the past tense and the *ru*-form as the non-past tense, tense marking occurs only in the main clause; the *ta*- and *ru*-forms do not mark tense *per se* in temporal subordinate clauses.

16.2 P′ ≺ Q′

16.2.1 P-te *Q*

The P′ ≺ Q′ sequence is frequently expressed with P in the *te*-form (see Section 6.1), especially when the subjects of P and Q are identical as in (3a).

(3) a. *Watashi wa kinō kaimono o shi-te eiga o mita.*
I TOP yesterday shopping ACC do-TE movie ACC saw
'Yesterday, I went shopping and saw a movie.'

b. *Taifū ga ki-te, hashi ga nagasareta.*
typhoon NOM come-TE bridge NOM was.washed.away
'A typhoon came, and the bridge was washed away.'

Note that, like the English conjunction *and*, this pattern does not explicitly *assert* a temporal sequence, but merely *implies* it by virtue of its iconic clause order.[1] Nevertheless, in actual communication, merely implying a sequence is often sufficient, and sometimes an explicit mention of the sequence might even sound like excess verbiage – hence, widespread use of the "P-*te* Q" pattern.

It is, however, important to recognize that "P-*te* Q" cannot express a pure (i.e. merely incidental) temporal sequence such as exemplified in (4).

(4) a. #*Maki ga mado o ake-te, doa no beru ga natta.*
NOM window ACC open-TE door GEN bell NOM chimed
'Maki opened the window, and the doorbell chimed.'

b. #*Watashi ga kaijō ni tsui-te, kōen ga hajimatta.*
I NOM meeting.place at arrive-TE lecture NOM started
'I arrived at the meeting place, and the lecture began.'

In order for "P-*te* Q" to imply a temporal sequence, some conceivable connection beyond a mere temporal alignment between the two situations must exist: for example, the speaker's recognition of the event sequence as a series of planned action as in (3a), or his/her recognition of a causal relationship between the stated events as in (3b) (see Chapter 6 of Hasegawa 1996a for further discussion).

16.2.2 P-te kara *Q*

Unlike "P-*te* Q," the verb *te*-form followed by the particle *kara* 'from' explicitly denotes a temporal sequence; therefore, it can be used to express sequences of events lacking any causal or other relationship(s), including those prohibited in (4).

[1] Due to the iconicity between the clause and the event order, this sequential interpretation is accounted for in linguistics as the speaker's observation of a **MAXIM OF MANNER** (i.e. the drive to be clear and orderly in order to communicate cooperatively), a part of the Gricean Theory of Implicature. Refer to any pragmatics textbook for further information on Gricean Theory.

(5) a. *Maki ga mado o ake-te kara, doa no beru ga natta.*
NOM window ACC open-TE.after door GEN bell NOM chimed
'After Maki opened the window, the doorbell chimed.'
b. *Watashi ga kaijō ni tsui-te kara, kōen ga hajimatta.*
I NOM meeting.place at arrive-TE.after lecture NOM started
'After I arrived at the meeting place, the lecture began.'

16.2.3 *P*-ta ato (de) *Q*

The $P' \prec Q'$ sequence can also be expressed with the pattern wherein P is in the *ta*-form, followed by the connective *ato* 'behind' or *ato de* '[Lit.] at behind'.

(6) a. *Kono jitensha wa, katta ato (de) totemo kōkai shita.*
this bicycle TOP buy.PAST after very regretted
'[Lit.] Speaking of this bicycle, I regretted it a lot after buying (it).'
b. *Itsu mo tabeta ato (de) ha o migaku.*
always eat.PAST after tooth ACC polish
'(I) always brush (my) teeth after eating.'

"P-*ta ato (de)* Q" is often interchangeable with "P-*te kara* Q." Martin (1962: 156) argues, however, that while both patterns indicate $P' \prec Q'$, *-te kara* emphasizes immediate sequentiality. By contrast, *-ta ato (de)* simply indicates that Q′ occurs any time after P′. Therefore, *-ta ato (de)* is anomalous in (7), in which the time is counted beginning immediately after P′.

(7) *Daigaku o sotsugyō [shite kara/#shita ato de], 10-nen tachimashita.*
college ACC graduation [after.doing] 10-years passed
'Ten years have passed since (I) graduated from college.'

Kuno (1973: 161) provides the following example to support Martin's analysis:

(8) a. *Roku-ji ni Biru to atte kara shichi-ji ni eiga o mi ni itta.*
6-o'clock at Bill with after.meeting 7-o'clock at movie ACC see for went
'After meeting with Bill at six o'clock, (I) went to see a movie at seven.'
b. *#Roku-ji ni Biru to wakarete kara shichi-ji ni eiga o mi ni itta.*
after.parting
'After parting with Bill at six o'clock, (I) went to see a movie at seven.'

(8a) sounds natural because it suggests that the meeting lasted for one hour, and that the speaker went to see a movie immediately afterward. By contrast, (8b) sounds anomalous due to the one-hour gap between the speaker parting with Bill and going to see the movie, thus supporting Martin's analysis.

However, Kuno also points out that the notion of immediate sequentiality cannot account for many objectionable cases, as shown in the examples in (9).

(9) a. *Jon ga gohan o [#tabete kara/tabeta ato de], Marī ga yatte kita.*
NOM meal ACC [after.eating] NOM arrived
'After John had eaten, Mary arrived.'
b. *Jon wa sensō ga [#owatte kara/owatta ato de] shinda.*
TOP war NOM [after.ending] died
'After the war had ended, John died.'

Kuno contends that "P-*te kara* Q" implies that the immediate timing of P′ and Q′ is planned by the subject referent of Q. In (9a) and (9b), it is unlikely that Mary and John, respectively, controlled the timing of Q′, thus resulting in anomaly. On the other hand, "P-*ta ato de* Q" does not carry such a controllability connotation and can thus be used appropriately in those examples.

Adachi (1995) amends Kuno's analysis by considering cases in which, contrary to Kuno, Q represents an event that is uncontrollable by its subject referent, as in (10).

(10)

Uchi	*o*	*dete*	*sukoshi*	*aruite kara*	*kuchibeni*	*o*
house	ACC	leave.TE	a.little	after.walking	lipstick	ACC

tsuke-wasureta	*koto*	*ni*	*ki ga tsuita.*
wear-forgot	NMLZ	to	realized

'After leaving (my) house and walking for a while, (I) realized that I had forgotten to put on lipstick.'

Adachi, who does not consider *-te kara* in (9) to be anomalous, asserts that while *-ta ato de* contrasts with *-ru mae ni* 'before' as in (11), *-te kara* contrasts with *made* 'until' combined with negation of Q, the construction that conveys Q′ not occurring until P′ has occurred, as illustrated in (12).

(11) a.

Jon	*ga*	*gohan*	*o*	*tabeta ato de,*	*Marī*	*ga*	*yatte kita.*
	NOM	meal	ACC	after.eating		NOM	arrived

'After John had eaten, Mary arrived.'

b.

Jon	*ga*	*gohan*	*o*	*taberu mae ni,*	*Marī*	*ga*	*yatte kita.*
	NOM	meal	ACC	before.eating		NOM	arrived

'Before John had eaten, Mary arrived.'

(12) a.

Jon	*ga*	*gohan*	*o*	*tabete kara,*	*Marī*	*ga*	*yatte kita.*
	NOM	meal	ACC	after.eating		NOM	arrived

'After John had eaten, Mary arrived.'

b.

Jon	*ga*	*gohan*	*o*	*taberu made,*	*Marī*	*wa*	*yatte konakatta.*[2]
	NOM	meal	ACC	until.eating		TOP	did.not.arrive

'Until John had eaten, Mary did not arrive.'

Thus, (10) imparts the nuance that the speaker had forgotten to apply lipstick until she had walked away from home. When such a suspended condition is to be emphasized, the use of *-te kara* is justified even when Q refers to an uncontrollable event.

16.2.4 *P*-ta ato ni *Q*

Instead of the location particle *de* 'at', another location particle *ni* 'in' can follow *ato* 'behind'. Comparing such sentences as in (13), Kuno (1973: 164–65) argues that the use of *ato ni* is appropriate only when Q′ fills the conceptual "vacuum" created by P′ as exemplified in (13a).

[2] In (12b), the topic marker *wa*, rather than the nominative *ga* is used because of the negative context of Q (see Section 8.11).

(13) a. *Jon ga kaetta [ato de/ato ni], Marī ga yatte kita.*
NOM leave.PAST [after] NOM arrived
'After John left, Mary arrived.'

In contrast, in (13b), because Mary's leaving the place does not fill the "vacuum" resulting from John's having left the place, the use of *ato ni* is unacceptable.

b. *Jon ga kaetta [ato de/#ato ni], Marī ga kaetta.*
NOM leave.PAST [after] NOM leave
'After John left, Mary left.'

However, contrary to Kuno's analysis, creation and fulfillment of a "vacuum" is not mandatory. As demonstrated in (14), if P indicates a termination of some sort, *ato ni* is normally acceptable:

(14) a. *Zankin no shiharai ga sunda [ato de/ato ni] teitōken o masshōs uru.*
balance GEN payment NOM finish.PAST [after] mortgage ACC revoke
'After payment of the balance is completed, (we) will revoke the mortgage.'
b. *Shikei ga shikkō sareta [ato de/ato ni], enzai da to hanmei shita.*
execution NOM conduct.PAST [after] false.charge COP QUOT Proved
'After the execution was carried out, the charge was proven to be false.'

Furthermore, if the predicate of Q can co-occur with a *ni*-marked location NP, the sentence is again normally acceptable:

(15) a. *Ōame ga futta [ato de/ato ni], jishin ga kita.*
torrential.rain NOM fall.PAST [after] earthquake NOM came
([Lit.] an earthquake came)
'After a torrential rain, an earthquake occurred.'
b. *Kono ki wa hana ga saita [ato de/ato ni]*
this tree TOP flower NOM blossom.PAST [after]
mi o tsukeru.
fruit ACC produce
'This tree produces fruit after flowers blossom.'

Kuru 'come' in (15a) takes a *ni*-marked goal NP, and the sentence can be interpreted as 'an earthquake came to the place that had had torrential rain'. *Mi o tsukeru* 'produce fruit' in (15b) can also take a *ni*-marked location as in *miki ni mi o tsukeru* 'produce fruit to (on) its branches'.

16.2.5 P-tara *Q*

This pattern – consisting of the verb's *ta*-form plus the connective particle *ra* – indicates that Q′ takes place only after P′ is realized or completed. ("P-*tara* Q" can also be used as a conditional sentence, which will be discussed in Chapter 18.)

(16) a. *Yon-dara koko ni modoshite kudasai.*
after.reading here to return.TE please
'After reading, please return (it) here.'

b. *Uchi o de-tara, ame ga futte kita.*
house ACC after.leaving rain NOM started.falling
'After/When (I) left (my) house, rain started.'

As Kuno (1973: 180–83) points out, when "P-*tara* Q" refers to a sequence that has occurred in the past, i.e. a factual statement, self-controllable timing cannot exist between P′ and Q′ as demonstrated in (17).

(17) a. *#Marī wa uchi o de-tara eki e mukatta.*
TOP house ACC after.leaving station to Headed
'After leaving (her) house, Mary headed for the station.'
b. *#Marī wa tegami o kai-tara tomodachi ni miseta.*
TOP letter ACC after.writing friend to showed
'After writing a letter, Mary showed (it) to a friend.'

When the sequence does not occur in the past, this constraint of self-controllability does not apply; therefore, (18) is appropriate:

(18) *Uchi ni kaet-tara denwa shimasu.*
house to after.returning telephone do
'When I get home, I'll call you.'

16.2.6 P-ru to *Q*

Like "P-*tara* Q," "P-*ru to* Q" can also be used as a conditional expression; it will therefore be discussed again in Chapter 18. When used as a temporal-sequence indicator, Q must be in the past tense; otherwise, "P-*ru to* Q" must be interpreted as a conditional sentence. This pattern is most suitable when the speaker intends to objectively portray that two situations occurred in sequence, without interpreting any possible causal or other connections. Therefore, the pairs of situations in (4), which are incompatible with "P-*te* Q," can be expressed naturally with "P-*ru to* Q."

(19) a. *Maki ga mado o akeru to, doa no beru ga natta.*
NOM window ACC when.opening door GEN bell NOM chimed
'Maki opened the window, and the doorbell chimed.'
b. *Watashi ga kaijō ni tsuku to, kōen ga hajimatta.*
I NOM meeting.place at when.arriving lecture NOM started
'I arrived at the meeting place, and the lecture began.'

As a purely objective indicator of a sequence of situations, "P-*ru to* Q" can be used where "P-*tara* Q" is forbidden. Compare (17) and (20).

(20) a. *Marī wa uchi o deru to eki e mukatta.*
TOP house ACC after.leaving station to headed
'After leaving (her) house, Mary headed for the station.'
b. *Marī wa tegami o kaku to tomodachi ni miseta.*
TOP letter ACC after.writing friend to showed
'After writing a letter, Mary showed (it) to a friend.'

Because no logical or other perceivable relationship is implied between P' and Q', "P-*ru to* Q" is commonly employed when P' designates a condition under which Q' is unexpectedly discovered. This is exemplified in (21).

(21) a. *Doa o akeru to, kozutsumi ga oite atta.*
door ACC after.leaving parcel NOM was.left
'When (I) opened the door, there was a parcel left (there).'

b. *Uma wa ike ni kuru to mizu o nomi-dashita.*
horse TOP pond to after.coming water ACC drinking-started
'When the horse came to the pond, it began to drink water.'

The situation in (21b) can be stated also with "P-*te* Q" as in (21c):

c. *Uma wa ike ni ki-te mizu o nomi-dashita.*
horse TOP pond to come-TE water ACC drinking-started
'The horse came to the pond, and started drinking water.'

However, while the speaker of (21b) reports the two events from an indifferent observer's viewpoint, (21c) implies that the speaker has interpreted the sequence as purposeful/planned acts on the part of the horse. That is, the speaker considers that the horse came to the pond to drink water.

This characteristic of "P-*ru to* Q" of emphasizing the speaker as a mere observer makes it inconsistent when used to narrate the speaker's own actions:

(22) *Watashi wa eiga o [mi-te/#miru to] kaimono o shita.*
I TOP movie ACC after.seeing shopping ACC did
'I saw a movie and did some shopping."

*16.2.7 P-*ta toki *Q*

This pattern, which indicates the temporal relationship of $P' \prec Q'$, was discussed in Section 9.4.

16.3 $Q' \prec P'$

In the following sentence patterns, Q' precedes P'; that is, the event sequence is the opposite of the clause order.

*16.3.1 P-*ru mae ni *Q*

As mentioned earlier, this pattern expresses the sequence opposite to "P-*ta ato de* Q."

(23) a. *Taberu mae ni te o arai-nasai.*
before.eating hand ACC wash-IMP
'Wash your hands before eating!'

b. *Hiro ni au mae ni ginkō ni itta.*
with before.meeting bank to went
'Before meeting with Hiro, (I) went to the bank.'

c.	*Taifū*	*ga*	*kuru mae ni,*	*hashi*	*o*	*shūfuku*	*shita.*
	typhoon	NOM	before.coming	bridge	ACC	restoration	did

'Before the typhoon came, (we) restored the bridge.'

16.3.2 *P*-nai uchi ni *Q*

This is a perplexing way to express $Q' \prec P'$, wherein *uchi* 'within the interval' is attached to a verb negative form (see Figure 16.1). This pattern literally means 'during the interval that P' is yet to happen, Q' occurs/occurred'. Therefore, strictly speaking, it designates simultaneity rather than temporal succession. Nevertheless, because it is frequently interchangeable with "P-*ru mae ni* Q," it is considered within this section.

Unlike *-ru mae ni*, *-nai uchi ni* implies the speaker's evaluation of, or expectation concerning, the $P' \prec Q'$ sequence.

A. The speaker thinks that the order of $P' \prec Q'$ is undesirable

(24) a.	*Kuraku*	*[nara-nai uchi ni/naru mae ni],*	*kaetta hō ga ii.*		
	dark	before.becoming	better.go.home		

'(You)'d better go home before it gets dark.'

b.	*Oya*	*ni*	*[mitsukara-nai uchi ni/mitsukaru mae ni]*	*tabako*	*wa*	*yamemashita.*
	parent	DAT	before.being.caught	cigarette	TOP	quit

'(I) quit smoking before (I was) caught by (my) parents.'

In this case, *-nai uchi ni* is preferred to *-ru mae ni*. It seems that the negation in *-nai uchi ni* indirectly signals the undesirability of the sequence.

B. The speaker thinks that the order of $P' \prec Q'$ is expected or desirable, but contrary to this expectation, $Q' \prec P'$ occurs:

(25) a.	*Kaisha*	*wa*	*ninka*	*ga*	*[ori-nai uchi ni/oriru mae ni]*	*kōji*
	company	TOP	permission	NOM	[before.being.granted]	construction
	o	*hajimeta.*				
	ACC	started				

'The company started construction before a permit was granted.'

b.	*Uriage*	*ga*	*antei*	*[shi-nai uchi ni/suru mae ni],*	*jigyō*	*o*
	sale	NOM	stable	[before.achieving]	business	ACC
	kakuchō suru	*koto*	*wa*	*kangaete inai.*		
	expand	NMLZ	TOP	be.not.thinking		

'(I'm) not thinking about expanding the business before sales are stabilized.'

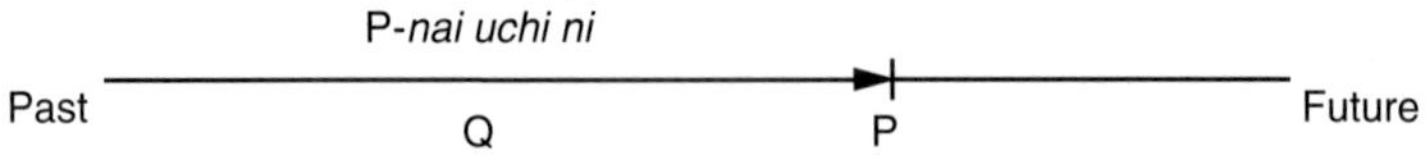

Figure 16.1. P-*nai uchi ni* Q.

In this case, *-nai uchi ni* and *-ru mae ni* are truly interchangeable. Unlike Case A, the relationship between P′ and Q′ in Case B can be expressed with the concessive connector *noni* 'although', which will be examined in Subsection 17.3.2.

C. Rather than expressing the Q′ ≺ P′ sequence, P′ emphasizes how soon Q′ occurs; the particle *mo* 'even' routinely appears in this usage:

(26) a. *10-pun mo [aruka-nai uchi ni/#aruku mae ni], ashi ga itaku natta.*
10-minutes even [before.walking] foot NOM painful became
'(My) feet started aching even before (I'd) walked for 10 minutes.'

b. *Shūshoku shite hantoshi mo [tata-nai uchi ni/#tatsu mae ni],*
getting.employed.TE half.year even [before.passing]
kare wa mō yametagatte iru.
he TOP already want.to.quit
'It had not been even half a year before he began to want to quit (his job).'

In Case C, *-nai uchi ni* can be replaced with the concessive *noni*, but it cannot be replaced with *-ru mae ni*.

Kuno (1973: 156–58) argues that P in "P-*nai uchi ni* Q" cannot refer to a definite event that is known to have happened in the past, and provides the following example:

(27) *#Jon wa kyonen Tōkyō ni ikimashita ga, Tōkyō ni*
TOP last.year to went but to
ika-nai uchi ni byōki ni narimashita.
before.going sick became
'John went to Tokyo last year but, even before he went, he'd gotten sick.'

This analysis, however, is invalid. Consider the following, which is parallel to the construction in (27).

(28) *Jon wa kyonen sotsugyō shimashita ga, sotsugyō shi-nai uchi ni*
TOP last.year graduated but before.graduating
shūshoku ga kimarimashita.
employment NOM secured
'John graduated last year, but, even before graduation, he got a job offer.'

Therefore, the anomaly of (27) must be attributed to some factor other than what Kuno identifies. It can, seemingly, be attributed to the common understanding that becoming sick normally leads to cancellation of a planned event. In fact, "P-*nai uchi ni* Q" can be used to deny the actualization of P′ as exemplified by (24b), quitting smoking before being caught by one's parents. If there is no natural incompatibility between P′ and Q′, as in (28), P can be used to refer to an event that is known to have occurred in the past.

16.3.3 P-ru toki *Q*

This pattern, which can indicate Q′ ≺ P′, was discussed in Section 9.4.

16.4 P′ ≈ Q′

In English, this temporal relationship is expressed idiomatically with the conjunction *while*. In Japanese, different patterns are employed depending upon whether or not (i) the subjects of P and Q are identical, and (ii) the depicted situations are actions or events/states.

16.4.1 P-nagara *Q*

In this construction, (i) the subject of P and Q must be identical, and (ii) *nagara* 'while' attaches to the adverbial form of an action verb, indicating that the subject referent performs the two actions simultaneously.[3] With the English *while*, it is normally implied that the main-clause event takes place within the time frame of the event denoted by the subordinate clause (Leonard 2001). Therefore, (29a) is natural, but (29b) is odd.

(29) a. *While I took a shower, I sang a song.*
b. ??*While I sang a song, I took a shower.*

This restriction does not apply to *nagara*; both sentences in (30) are natural, meaning that the two activities overlap in time.

(30) a.

Watashi	*wa*	*shawā*	*o*	*abi-nagara*	*uta*	*o*	*utatta.*
I	TOP	shower	ACC	taking.while	song	ACC	sang

'While taking a shower, I sang a song.'

b.

Watashi	*wa*	*uta*	*o*	*utai-nagara*	*shawā*	*o*	*abita.*
I	TOP	song	ACC	singing.while	shower	ACC	took

'While singing a song, I took a shower.'

16.4.2 P-ru aida/uchi ni *Q*

Unlike *nagara*, the subject of P and Q with *while* can be distinct, as exemplified below:

(31) *The control tower had a very old computer. One day, when the computer crashed, the air traffic controllers were forced to halt all take-offs while the manager got the backup computer going.*

When the subjects of P and Q are different, "P-*ru aida ni*" or "P-*ru uchi ni*" (in the interval of P′) can be employed.

(32) a.

Kachi	*ga*	*aru*	*[aida/uchi] ni*	*utta*	*hō*	*ga*	*ii.*
value	NOM	exist	[while]	sell	side	NOM	good

'While (it) still has value, (you)'d better sell (it).'

b.

Kodomo	*ga*	*nete iru*	*[aida/uchi] ni*	*hon*	*o*	*yomō.*
I	NOM	sleeping	[while]	book	ACC	read.VOL

'I'll read a book while (my) child is sleeping.'

[3] If the predicate of P is stative, *nagara* is interpreted as a concessive connective (*although, even though*). See Section 17.3 for the concessive relation.

Unlike "P-*nai uchi ni*" discussed above, P in this construction must be stative (see Section 9.2) or in the *-te iru* construction. That is, verbs which refer to a punctual event or action cannot be used in this pattern. This is a semantic requirement because P′ must specify a duration of time within which Q′ takes place.

16.4.3 P-ru aida/aida-jū *(*zutto*) Q*

If P′ and Q′ totally overlap, *aida* 'during the duration of P′' or *aida-jū* 'during the entire duration of P′' is used. Additionally, the verb in P must be stative or in the *-te iru* construction. Q is frequently modified with *zutto* 'all the time/ throughout' as exemplified below:

(33) a. *Watashi ga kōgi o shite iru aida(jū), gakusei wa*
I NOM lecture ACC doing while student TOP
zutto inemuri shite ita.
throughout was.dozing
'The entire time I was lecturing, students were dozing.'

b. *Kare ga bakkuappu konpyūtā o tachiagete iru aida(jū),*
he NOM backup computer ACC booting while
watashi wa tonari no heya ni ita.
I TOP next GEN room in was
'I was in the next room while he booted up the backup computer.'

17 Causal and concessive clauses

17.1 Introduction

A **CAUSAL RELATION** exists between two situations when one (**CAUSE**) brings about the other (**EFFECT**). A **CONCESSIVE RELATION** is one in which one situation (introduced by *although*, *even though*, *despite*, etc.) denotes a circumstance that is expected to preclude another situation (expressed by the main clause), but, contrary to this expectation, does not. This chapter will examine these two clause-linkage types. Continuing the convention introduced in Chapter 16, the connected clauses are represented as P and Q as in (1), and the situations they reference as P′ (cause) and Q′ (effect).

(1) a. Because P, Q or Q because P [causal relation]
  b. Although P, Q or Q although P [concessive relation]

In English, as in (2a), a causal relation is commonly marked by the conjunction *because*. However, *because* is also frequently employed to express a **REASON RELATION** as in (2b).

(2) a. *She lost her job because she posted on Facebook a rant on the restaurant customers.*
  b. *I've decided not to take the position because the duties seem impossible.*

Prototypically, causation applies to the world of tangible entities and natural laws, whereas reasons concern human actions and intentions (i.e. motivation or justification for an action). However, it has often been argued that reasons are themselves causal in nature (e.g. Davidson 1980: 3–19). Languages sometimes employ a word corresponding to *cause* and frequently a word corresponding to *because*, even when reasons and not causes are involved. Furthermore, there are apparent regularities obtaining between reasons and actions, similar to those regularities that lie at the heart of the causal relation in the Humean conception of causation.[1] Therefore, to determine whether a certain

[1] In his *An Enquiry Concerning Human Understanding*, David Hume (1748) claimed that causal relations exist only in human cognition, not between situations themselves. He defined causal

relationship should be uniquely categorized as a cause or a reason is not always easy. Donnellan (1967: 86), who argues that these two concepts must be kept distinct, nevertheless acknowledges that *because* is commonly used to emphasize metaphorically the compelling nature (force) of the reason.

Cause and reason are each distinct in essential ways. Consider this example: if arsenic is found in a corpse, this is likely the cause of the person's death. However, further explanation is usually sought, and if it is discovered that someone deliberately put the poison in the victim's food, then the poisoner's action becomes the cause of this death. The presence of arsenic in the body is now perceived simply as the way in which the poisoner produced the effect. Once this point is reached, a sense of finality is achieved as regards the causal relation. Greed or the desire for revenge may have motivated the poisoner to place arsenic in the victim's food, but such motivations are not regarded as the cause of the victim's death. That is, causes are not traced through to the motive of the deliberate act (Hart and Honoré 1959: 39–40).

Cause and reason differ also in terms of the temporal order of P and Q. In a causal relation, the cause must exist prior to the effect, whereas this chronological arrangement is not mandatory in a reason relation.

(3) a. ^{Q}*Now you're relieved* ^{P}*because I told you the story.* [$P' \prec Q'$; cause]
b. ^{Q}*I've renewed my passport* ^{P}*because I'm going to Japan this summer.* [$Q' \prec P'$; reason)

Awareness of this distinction between cause and reason is beneficial for examination of Japanese causal connectives.

The conjunction *because* can also be used in the following manner:

(4) a. ^{Q}*John smokes* ^{P}*because he has cigarettes in his house.* (Haegeman and Wekker 1984: 54)
b. ^{Q}*John smokes,* ^{P}*because he has cigarettes in his house.*
c. ^{Q}*What are you doing tonight,* ^{P}*because there's a good movie on.* (Sweetser 1990: 77)

Sweetser provides an analysis in which sentences may depict causation in different domains. Sentences like (4a) depict a causation (a reason in this case) in the **CONTENT DOMAIN** (i.e. real-world or external-world) in which the cause (P': John's keeping cigarettes in his house) must exist prior to the effect (Q': his smoking cigarettes). The circumstance is quite different in (4b). P' is the basis from which the speaker has derived the conclusion Q'. This is

relations as *invariable sequences*. Two spatially contiguous changes, A and B, are in a causal relation if A is immediately followed by B and if situations similar to A are always immediately followed by situations similar to B. The notion of similarity is crucial here because without it the human conception of a causal link between specific situations cannot be accounted for. Suppose, for example, that Smith was beheaded and died. This particular sequence of situations occurred only once in history, and yet we recognize a causal relation because we "know" that anyone who is beheaded invariably dies. As Russell (1917) cautions, however, similarity is itself a difficult concept to define. For further discussion on cause and reason, see Hasegawa (1996a: 184–88, 191–94).

claimed to be a causal relation, but operative in the **EPISTEMIC** (i.e. inferential) **DOMAIN**. In (4c), P′ (a good movie was showing) signifies the reason the speaker makes the question Q′ (what the addressee would do on that night). Sweetser asserts that this "causal" relation is effective in the **SPEECH-ACT DOMAIN**.[2, 3] (Speech acts are acts performed and understood linguistically – i.e. by means of utterances – e.g. advising, apologizing, congratulating, greeting, ordering, promising, warning, etc. See Chapter 19 for further explanation.)

These three domains can be identified by whether the *because*-clause can be used to respond to the following questions:

(5) a. *Why does John smoke?*
Because he has cigarettes in his house. [content domain]
b. *Why do you think John smokes?*
Because he has cigarettes in his house. [epistemic domain]
c. *Why do you say it (e.g. ask that question)?*
Because there's a good movie on. [speech-act domain]

17.2 Causal connections in Japanese

Causal relations in Japanese are commonly expressed by use of the conjunctive particles *kara* and *node* or the conjunctive phrase *tame ni* 'for the sake of'.[4]

17.2.1 Kara

The conjunction *kara* can be used to express causal or reason relations in all of the content, epistemic, and speech-act domains.

(6) Content domain [cause]

a.

Koko	*wa*	*umi*	*ni*	*chikai*	*kara,*	*kuruma*	*ga*	*sugu ni*	*sabiru.*
here	TOP	ocean	to	near	because	car	NOM	quickly	rust

'Because it's close to the ocean here, cars rust quickly.'

b.

Kinō	*nomi-sugita*	*kara,*	*atama*	*ga*	*itai.*
yesterday	over.drank	because	head	NOM	hurt

'Because (I) drank too much yesterday, (I) have a headache [Lit. my head aches].'

2 *Since*, another conjunction of causation, tends strongly towards an epistemic or a speech-act reading rather than a content-domain reading (Sweetser 1990: 82). *While* as a concessive conjunction can operate only in the epistemic and speech-act domains. When employed in the content domain, it must be interpreted as a conjunction of simultaneity (p. 155).

3 In French, *parce que* 'because' is used for the content domain, whereas *puisque* is specialized for the epistemic or speech-act domain: *Il va l'épouser parce qu'il l'adore* 'He's going to marry her because he adores her'; *(Mais si,) il va l'épouser puisqu'il l'adore* '(But of course,) he's going to marry her, since he adores her' (Sweetser 1990: 82, 156).

4 Other causal connectors include *okage de* 'thanks to' (used when the speaker is appreciative of the occurrence of Q′) and *sei de* 'as a consequence' (used when the speaker is annoyed by Q′).

(7) Content domain [reason]

a. *Ame ga futta kara, pikunikku wa chūshi shita.*
rain NOM fell because picnic NEG-SCP cancelled
'Because it rained, (we) cancelled the picnic.'

b. *Tsukareta kara, ashita wa shigoto o yasumu.*
tired because tomorrow TOP work ACC rest
'Because (I'm) tired, (I'll) take the day off tomorrow.'

(8) Epistemic domain

a. *Kanojo wa waratte iru kara, kitto gōkaku shita no da.*
she TOP is.smiling because certainly passed NMLZ COP.NPST
'Because she is smiling, it's certain that (she) passed the exam.'

b. *Kuruma ga tomatte iru kara, kare wa kaette iru darō.*
car NOM is.parked because he TOP has.come.home COP.CNJ
'Because (his) car is parked (there), he must be at home.'

(9) Speech-act domain

a. *Koko de matte iru kara, ki-te kudasai.*
here at is.waiting because come-TE please
'Please come here, because I'll be waiting (for you).'

b. *Tenki ga ii kara, dokoka ni ikimasen ka?*
weather NOM good because somewhere to not.go INT
'Because the weather is fine, shouldn't we go somewhere?'

Although *kara* can be used for causal expressions in the content domain, it is more compatible with the reason relation than with the causal relation (the judgments in causal sentences in (10) are from Masuoka 1997: 123):

(10) a. *?Yuki ga hageshiku futta kara, Shinkansen ga tomatta.*
snow NOM heavily fell because NOM stopped
'Because the snow fell so deeply, the Shinkansen bullet train stopped.'

b. *?Jikan ga amari nakatta kara, ketsuron wa denakatta.*
time NOM much there.was.not because conclusion NEG-SCP not.come.about
'Because there was not enough time, a conclusion was not reached.'

Despite a significant number of analyses available for the differences between *kara* and *noda*, the distinction remains unclear largely due to the fluctuation of grammatical and/or appropriateness judgments by analysts (Iwasaki 1995). For example, many native speakers of Japanese would not detect any anomaly in (10). However, (10a) sounds, at the least, ineloquent to me while (10b) sounds better than (10a). By contrast, the causal examples (6a–6b) I constructed sound perfectly natural. It seems that the acceptability increases when the depicted situation pertains to a personal experience (e.g. when the speaker is involved in the depicted situation). On the other hand, when *kara* appears inside a nominalized clause (Chapter 15), its use for causal relations is completely acceptable.

(11) a. *Yuki ga hageshiku futta kara, Shinkansen ga tomatta no da.*
NMLZ COP.NPST
'[Lit.] It is the case that the Shinkansen bullet train stopped because the snow had fallen so deeply.'

b. *Jikan ga amari nakatta kara, ketsuron wa denakatta* *no* *da.*
NMLZ COP.NPST
'[Lit.] It is the case that no conclusion was reached because there was not enough time.'

This fact reveals that *kara* is not intrinsically incongruous with causal relations; rather, the subtle incompatibility in (10) lies in the mental process of tracking a situation as it unfolds in event-reporting sentences (Langacker 1987: 144; 2008: 111; see also Subsection 15.4.3). That is, when constructing and/or interpreting causal sentences like (10), the connected situations are tracked in time as well as for their causal connections, whereas for nominalized sentences like (11), all information is atemporal and simultaneously available. It seems that *kara* is not well-suited to expressing temporal sequentiality and causality simultaneously. This is an interesting topic that awaits further investigation.

Kara is thoroughly compatible with reason relations in the content and epistemic domains. (Note that such sentences are atemporal, and do not narrate sequences of events.) *Kara* also occurs routinely as a conjunction in the speech-act domain (which is also atemporal), as discussed in Shirakawa (1995). However, as with *because*, *kara* cannot mark motivations for many kinds of speech acts:

(12) a. *#Omoshiroi eiga o yatte iru kara, konban nani o*
interesting movie ACC showing because tonight what ACC
shite imasuka?
is.doing INT
'What are you doing tonight, because there's a good movie on.'

b. *#Sotsugyō nasatta kara, omedetō gozaimasu.*
graduation do.HON because congratulations
'[Lit.] Congratulations, because you have graduated.'

c. *#Otōsama ga onakunari ni natta kara,*
father.HON NOM died.HON because
goshūshōsama de gozaimasu.
there.is.lamentation
'(I offer) my deepest condolences, because your father has passed away.' [intended]

The use of *because* is possible in (12a), performing a speech act of questioning, but *kara* cannot be used for genuine questions. Note that (9b), repeated below, which permits *kara*, is also interrogative; however, its speech act must be recognized as an invitation, not as an information-seeking question like (12a).

(9) b. *Tenki ga ii kara, dokoka ni ikimasen ka?*
weather NOM good because somewhere to not.go INT
'Because the weather is fine, shouldn't we go somewhere?'

In (12b–12c), although the addressee's graduation and his/her father's death, respectively, are apparently the reasons for the speaker to congratulate and condole, neither *because* nor *kara* is usable.

17.2.2 Node

Like *kara*, the conjunction *node* can be used to express causal relations in the content, epistemic, and speech-act domains. Unlike *kara*, however, *node* is thoroughly compatible with causal relations in the content domain as shown in (13):

(13) Content domain [cause]

a. *Yuki ga hageshiku futta node, Shinkansen ga tomatta.*
snow NOM heavily fell because NOM stopped
'Because the snow fell deeply, the Shinkansen bullet train stopped.'

b. *Jikan ga amari nakatta node, ketsuron wa denakatta.*
time NOM much there.was.not because conclusion NEG-SCP not.come.about
'Because there was not enough time, a conclusion was not reached.'

(14) Content domain [reason]

a. *Ame ga futta node, pikunikku wa chūshi shita.*
rain NOM fell because picnic NEG-SCP cancelled
'Because it rained, (we) cancelled the picnic.'

b. *Tsukareta node, ashita wa shigoto o yasumu.*
tired because tomorrow TOP work ACC rest
'Because (I'm) tired, (I'll) take the day off tomorrow.'

Node is compatible also with the epistemic domain; however, in such cases, the use of *kara* sounds more natural and idiomatic.

(15) a. *Kanojo wa waratte iru [kara/node], kitto gōkaku shita no da.*
she TOP is.smiling because certainly passed NMLZ COP.NPST
'Because she is smiling, it's certain that (she) passed the exam.'

b. *Kuruma ga tomatte iru [kara/node], kare wa kaette iru darō.*
car NOM is.parked because he TOP has.come.home COP.CNJ
'Because (his) car is parked (there), he must be at home.'

Node can occur in the speech-act domain as well; however, again, *kara* sounds more appropriate in many, if not most, cases:

(16) a. *Koko de matte iru [kara/node], ki-te kudasai.*
here at is.waiting because come-TE please
'Please come here, because I'll be waiting.'

b. *Tenki ga ii [kara/?node], dokoka ni ikimasen ka?*
weather NOM good because somewhere to not.go INT
'Because the weather is fine, shall we go somewhere?'

In (16a), when making a request, *kara* and *node* are equally appropriate, but *node* sounds less assertive and, consequently, more polite. In (16b), an invitation, many native speakers of Japanese would feel the use of *node* somewhat unnatural.

c. *Kitanai [kara/??node], sōji o shi-nasai.*
dirty [because] cleaning ACC do-IMP
'Clean (the room), because it's dirty.'

d.	*Shūchū*	*dekinai*	*[kara/#node],*	*shizuka ni*	*shiro.*
	concentration	cannot	[because]	quiet	do-IMP

'Be quiet, because (I) can't concentrate!'

Both sentences in (16c–16d) make commands, which is a more forceful speech act than a request or invitation. The tone of (16d), with the imperative form of the verb, is more dominant and authoritative than (16c) with the imperative suffix *nasai*. Most native speakers would likely find *node* in (16c) marginal, and in (16d) unacceptable. That is, *node* is incompatible with brusque speech acts. In fact, in (16a), the use of *kara* emphasizes the speaker's reason for making the request, namely that s/he will be waiting for the addressee. Used in this way, *kara* can suggest the forcefulness of the speaker's request, so that the addressee understands s/he should come promptly.

This firm assertiveness of *kara* is likely to be received unfavorably by hearers when the intended speech act is an apology or excuse. In (17), for instance, if *kara* is selected, it conveys the idea that all the blame should be attributed to the computer's breaking down, not the speaker him/herself. *Node*, by contrast, merely states a causal relation more objectively, although explicitly stating such a fact by itself can be received negatively in Japanese culture, attributable to the speaker's lack of emergency-preparedness.

(17)	*Konpyūtā*	*ga*	*kowareta*	*[kara/node],*	*ma ni aimasen deshita.*
	computer	NOM	broke	[because]	not.meet.the.deadline

'Because (my) computer broke down, the deadline couldn't be met.'

Finally, when P is conjectural, the use of *node* is prohibited. That is, when using *node*, P′ must be presented as a fact.

(18) a.	*Dōse*	*ukaranai*	*darō*	*[kara/*node],*	*ukenakatta.*		
	anyway	not.pass	COP.CNJ	[because]	did.not.take		

'Because I thought that (I) wouldn't pass, (I) didn't take (the exam).'

b.	*Otsukare*	*deshō*	*[kara/*node],*	*kōhī*	*wa*	*ikaga desu*	*ka?*
	tired.HON	COP.CNJ.POL	[because]	coffee	TOP	how.about	INT

'How about (some) coffee, because (I) guess you're tired.'

There are grammatical constraints on *kara*, which requires the preceding predicate to be in the conclusive form (used for listing dictionary entries). In contrast, *node* requires the attributive form (used to modify nouns). As explained in Subsection 1.2.4, the conclusive and attributive forms merged during the Middle Japanese period, remaining distinct only for the copula (Section 6.2). The copula's conclusive form is *da*, and its attributive form is *na*.

(19)	*Hima*	*[da kara/na node],*	*shōsetsu*	*o*	*kaita.*
	free	[because]	novel	ACC	wrote

'[Lit.] Because (I was) free, I wrote a novel.'

However, *na* has neither past-tense nor polite counterparts, so if tense or politeness is expressed in P, both *kara* and *node* take the same form.

(20) *Hima datta/deshita [kara/node], shōsetsu o kaita/kakimashita.*
free COP.PAST [because] novel ACC wrote
'Because (I) had plenty of free time, I wrote a novel.'

17.2.3 Tame ni

Unlike *kara* and *node*, the conjunctive phrase *tame ni* is compatible only with causal relations and marginally with reason relations in the content domain; it cannot be used in the epistemic or the speech-act domain.

(21) a. Content domain [cause]
Yuki ga hageshiku futta [?kara/node/tame ni], Shinkansen ga tomatta.
snow NOM heavily fell [because] NOM stopped
'Because the snow fell heavily, the Shinkansen bullet train stopped.'

b. Content domain [reason]
Tsukareta [kara/node/??tame ni], ashita wa shigoto o yasumu.
tired [because] tomorrow TOP work ACC rest
'Because (I'm) tired, (I'll) take the day off tomorrow.'

c. Epistemic domain
*Kanojo wa waratte iru [kara/node/*tame ni], kitto gōkaku shita*
she TOP is.smiling [because] certainly passed
no da.
NMLZ COP.NPST
'Because she is smiling, it's certain that (she) passed the exam.'

d. Speech-act domain
*Tenki ga ii [kara/?node/*tame ni], dokoka ni ikimasen ka?*
weather NOM good [because] somewhere to not.go INT
'Because the weather is fine, shall we go somewhere?'

The appropriate uses of *kara*, *node*, and *tame ni* are summarized schematically in Table 17.1, where O indicates total compatibility, Δ partial compatibility, and × incompatibility. Causal relations in the content domain can be considered as the most objective because the actual relationship between P′ and Q′ is the main factor in this type of linguistic encoding. At the other extreme, "causal" relations in the speech-act domain are most subjective because no causal relation whatsoever exists in the real world between P′ and Q′. "Causal" relations in the epistemic domain fall somewhere between these two extremes.

17.3 Concessive connections

17.3.1 English

Like the causal subordinate conjunction *because*, *although* is used for concession in the three domains. Examples in (22b–22d) are derived from Sweetser (1990: 79):

Table 17.1 Kara, node, *and* tame ni *compared.*[5]

	Content domain		Epistemic domain	Speech-act domain
	Cause	Reason		
kara	Δ	O	O	O
node	O	O	Δ	Δ
tame ni	O	Δ	×	×

(22) a. Content domain (cause)
Although a 6.0 magnitude earthquake hit the region, no casualties were claimed.
b. Content domain (reason)
Although he didn't hear me calling, he came and saved my life.
c. Epistemic domain
Although he came and saved me, he hadn't heard me calling for help. (The fact that he didn't hear me is true in spite of the fact that he came, which might reasonably have led me to conclude that he had heard.)
d. Speech-act domain
Although I sympathize with your problem, please turn in the paper tomorrow!

A concessive relation can be defined as *denial of expectation*, which is commonly expressed not only with subordinate conjunctions like *although*, but also with the coordinate conjunction *but* (Sweetser 1990: 100–11):

(23) a. *Although France is Catholic, it's socialist.*
b. *France is Catholic, but it's socialist.*

(24) a. *Although John is wealthy, he is not smart about his money.*
b. *John is rich but unwise (about how he uses his money).*

But is also used to express **OPPOSITION** (i.e. dissimilarity according to a particular feature), where the use of *although* for this purpose is deemed marginal.

(25) a. *John is rich, but Bill is poor.*
b. *?Although John is rich, Bill is poor.*

This difference is due to the fact that sentences like (25) do not involve any clash between an expectation and reality: it is well within expectation, for example, that some people are rich and some are poor. Therefore, there is opposition, but not concession. However, when additional information is

5 The Dutch language exhibits an interesting distinction among its causal connectives *dus*, *daarom*, and *daardoor*. *Dus* most often expresses epistemic causation and can secondarily be used for reason relations in the content domain. By contrast, *daarom* most often expresses reason relations and can also be used for epistemic causation. These characteristics indicate that reason relations and epistemic causality have common traits and thus can be categorized together. Like *tame ni*, *daardoor* has a strong preference for cause (not reason) relations in the content domain, and its use is totally banned from the epistemic and speech-act domains (Sanders *et al.* 2009: 21).

provided – e.g. John and Bill are brothers – (25b) can become perfectly acceptable because, then, both can be expected to be equally poor or equally rich.

17.3.2 *Japanese*

In Japanese, concessive relations are marked by the conjunctives *keredo(mo)* (and its colloquial variation *kedo*) and *noni*.[6] Both are compatible with the content domain as shown in (26a–b).

(26) a. Content domain [cause]

Magunichūdo	*6.0*	*no*	*jishin*	*ga*	*kita*	*[keredo/noni],*
magnitude		GEN	earthquake	NOM	came	although
fushōsha	*wa*	*hitori*	*mo*	*denakatta.*		
casualty	TOP	one.person	even	did.not.exist		

'Although a magnitude 6.0 earthquake took place, not even a single person was injured.'

b. Content domain [reason]

Watashi	*no*	*sakebi-goe*	*wa*	*todokanakatta*	*[keredo/noni],*
I	GEN	scream	NEG-SCP	did.not.reach	although
kare	*wa*	*tasuke*	*ni*	*ki-te*	*kureta.*
he	TOP	help	for	come-TE	gave

'Although my scream didn't reach (him), he came to help me.'

However, in the epistemic and speech-act domains, *noni* cannot be used:

(27) Epistemic domain

a.

Kare	*wa*	*tasuke*	*ni*	*ki-te*	*kureta*	*[keredo/*noni],*	*watashi*
he	TOP	help	for	come-TE	gave	[although]	I
no	*sakebi-goe*		*wa*		*todokanakatta*	*no*	*da.*
GEN	scream		NEG-SCP		did.not.reach	NMLZ	COP.NPST

'Although he came to help me, it is the case that my scream had not reached (him).'

b.

Kare	*wa*	*yoku natta*	*[keredo/*noni],*	*susumeta*	*kusuri*	*wa*
he	TOP	recovered	[although]	recommended	medicine	NEG-SCP
nomanakatta	*no*	*da.*				
did.not.take	NMLZ	COP.NPST				

'Although he recovered, he didn't take the medicine that (I) recommended.'

(28) Speech-act domain

a.

Anata	*no*	*jijō*	*wa*	*yoku*	*wakarimasu*	*[keredo/*noni],*
you	GEN	circumstance	TOP	well	understand	[although]
shukudai	*wa*	*ashita*	*dashite*	*kudasai.*		
homework	TOP	tomorrow	submit-TE	please.do		

'Although I understand your situation, please submit (your) assignment tomorrow.'

b.

Mada	*hayai*	*[keredo/*noni],*	*dekakemashō.*
still	early	[although]	GO.POL.VOL

'Although it's still early, let's go (now).'

[6] Other concessive connectors include *ni mo kakawarazu* 'in spite of ~', *mono no* 'although', *nagara* 'while'.

Furthermore, *keredo* can be used for opposition although *noni* cannot. For example, *noni* in (29) is acceptable only when John and Bill are expected to be equally affluent or to major in the same academic field, but *keredo* does not have such a restriction.

(29) a. *Jon wa kanemochi [da keredo/#na noni], Biru wa binbō da.*
TOP rich [COP.although] TOP poor COP.NPST
'John is rich, but Bill is poor.'

b. *Jon wa gengogaku o senkō shite iru [keredo/#noni], Biru wa*
TOP linguistics ACC is.majoring [although] TOP
butsurigaku o senkō shite iru.
physics ACC is.majoring
'John is majoring in linguistics, but Bill is majoring in physics.'

Parallel to the situation with causal *kara* and *node*, *keredo* takes the conclusive form (*da*), whereas *noni* takes the attributive form (*na*), as shown in (29a). This difference does not surface with non-copula predicates, e.g. (29b). As discussed earlier, the conclusive form can be replaced with the past-tense or the polite counterpart. This indicates that, although being categorized as subordinate, clauses marked with *kara* or *keredo* are linguistically more independent (i.e. coordination-like) than those marked with *node* or *noni* (pure subordination). This provides a partial explanation as to why *keredo* can be used to signify not only concession but also simple opposition, which is normally expressed by a coordinate conjunction like *but*.

This difference in degree of subordination creates the following contrast:

(30) a. *Shikaku ga nai [?keredo/noni] ōbo shita n desu ka?*
qualification NOM not.exist [although] applied NMLZ COP INT
'[Lit.] Is it the case that (you) applied (for the position) although (you're) not qualified?'

As the translation indicates, the concessive clause in this sentence should be embedded inside the nominalization, and the entire nominalized clause is questioned. That is, the intended meaning is not as *You're not qualified, but have you nevertheless applied?*, but as *Have you applied even though you are not qualified?* While the genuine subordination *node*-clause can comfortably appear within the nominalized clause, the more independent (lower degree of subordination) *kara*-clause can only marginally do so.

18 Conditional clauses

18.1 Introduction

Conditional constructions pose some of the most difficult problems in comparing the grammars of English and of Japanese, especially when attempting to elucidate grammatical contrasts to non-native speakers. It is understandably so because conditional thoughts are among the most complex of mental activities. Compare, for example, conditionals with temporal (Chapter 16) and causal connections (Chapter 17). Although temporal statements involve the speaker's subjective assessment of the temporal alignment of subordinate and main-clause situations, they are nonetheless the simplest among these three types of clause linkage. Causals are more complex, for causality is interpreted in the speaker's mind, and is not overtly present in situations in the real world. Conditionals are even more complex and elusive, dealing not only with actual situations in the real world, but also imagined situations in a hypothetical world and comparing how a given situation might arise.

As evidence of the complexity of conditionals, I have been writing academic articles in English for more than two decades. And yet, as a non-native speaker, I have not grasped all subtleties pertaining to English conditional constructions. And when I ask native speakers of English about my uncertainty regarding problematic conditional sentences, it is frequently unclear whether or not the informant and I are talking about the same situation. I therefore utilize diagrams, rather than verbal characterizations about conditional statements. The diagrams in the following discussion are inspired by Fillmore (1990), wherein ω_0 stands for the real world, ω_1 for a possible (alternative) world, *S* for the speaker (located in the slot "Now" in the real world when the tense is relevant), -P′ for "not P′" (i.e. denial of the factuality of P′) used to represent counterfactual conditionals.

In Japanese, the most common conditional connectives are *ba*, *ra*, *nara*, and *to*. *Ba* attaches to the hypothetical form of the subordinate predicate (e.g. *tabere-ba* 'if eat'), *ra* to the predicate's *ta*-form (e.g. *tabeta-ra*; hereafter, referred to as *tara*), and *to* to the conclusive form (e.g. *taberu-to*). (See Section 6.1 for these conjugation forms.) Because the verb form is uniquely fixed for each connective, such subordinate clauses are tenseless, and their temporal interpretations are totally dependent on the interpretation of the main clause. By contrast, *nara* can take both the past tense form (*-ta nara*) and the non-past tense form (*-ru nara*). Therefore, *nara*-clauses are tensed, although the interpretation of these tense markers are often different from those when they occur in a main clause (Suzuki 1993: 137; Arita 2007: 102–05). To simplify the exposition, this chapter deals mainly with *-ru nara* with only occasional mention of *-ta nara*.

Ba is the most authentic conditional connective, rarely used for other purposes.[1] As discussed in Chapter 16, *tara* and *to* are used also as temporal connectives without implying conditionality. Furthermore, *ba* can co-occur with *tara* (*tara-ba*) and *nara* (*nara-ba*). Masuoka (1993b), therefore, argues that, while *ba* is a conditional connective proper, *tara*, *nara*, and *to* mark conditionality only as an extension of their core functions. Nevertheless, there is no instance in which only *ba* is permitted and other three are prohibited (Maeda 1995: 489).

In (1), where both P and Q refer to present (i.e. speech time) situations, all four connectives can in principle be employed. When P′ and Q′ are placed in a single cell in a diagram, at least one, possibly both, must be stative (see Section 9.2 for stativity) because P′ and Q′ must occur simultaneously or partially overlap. Normally, non-stative situations can occur only consecutively. $P' \approx Q'$ indicates such simultaneity.

(1)

	Past	Now	Future
ω_0		S	
ω_1		$P' \approx Q'$	

ba	*tara*	*nara*	*to*
✓	✓	✓	✓

a. ^{P}*If you're a member,* ^{Q}*you're eligible for a discount.*

b. ^{P}*Kaiin* *[de areba/dattara/(de aru) nara/da to],* ^{Q}*waribiki* *ga* *arimasu.*
member [if.be] discount NOM there.is
'If you're a member, there is a discount.'

The selection of these connectives involves a magnitude of idiosyncrasies and context dependencies, and grammaticality and/or acceptability judgments of conditional sentences vary significantly among native speakers of Japanese. Describing this variation in detail is beyond the scope of this book.[2] Therefore, this chapter attempts to provide a brief overview of Japanese conditional

[1] Exceptional cases are exemplified by *Haru ga kure-ba, sakura ga saku* 'When spring comes, cherry trees blossom', which involves only temporal sequentiality, not the possibility that spring might not come.

[2] For further discussions, see Akatsuka (1985), Arita (1993; 2007), Fujii (1993; 2004), Hinds and Tawa (1975), Kuno (1973), Maeda (1995), and Masuoka (1993a; 1997).

constructions and noticeable differences when they are compared with their English counterparts.

18.2 Content conditionals

Conditional connectives can in principle be operative in the content, epistemic, and speech-act domains. Conditionals in the content domain indicate that the realization of P' is a sufficient condition for the realization of Q' (Sweetser 1990: 114) due to an underlying causal, enablement, or reason (i.e. motivation for an action) relationship between P' and Q'.[3] In diagram (2), $P' \prec Q'$ indicates that P' occurs before Q'.

(2)

	Past	Now	Future
ω_0		S	
ω_1			$P' \prec Q'$

ba	*tara*	*nara*	*to*
✓	✓	✓	✓

a. ^{P}*If the development is approved,* ^{Q}*wild animals will become extinct.*

b. ^{P}*Kaihatsu* *ga* *ninka* *[sarereba/saretara/sareru nara/sareru to],*
development NOM approval [if.be.PASS]
^{Q}*yasei* *dōbutsu* *wa* *shinitaete shimau.*
wild animal TOP will.be.extinct
[When the translation is identical with the a-sentence, it is not repeated.]

In (2), there is a causal relation between P' and Q'. For an example of enablement conditional, consider (1) above. Sentences like (3) represent reason conditionals. Note that, unlike reason relations in causal statements (e.g. ^{P}*Because I'll go to Japan,* ^{Q}*I renewed my passport*), the order of P and Q in reason conditionals cannot differ from the events' temporal order. That is, in all content conditionals, Q' cannot occur and become complete prior to P'.

(3)

	Past	Now	Future
ω_0		S	
ω_1		P'	Q'

ba	*tara*	*nara*	*to*
✓	✓	✓	×

a. ^{P}*If the wage is low,* ^{Q}*I won't apply.*

b. ^{P}*Kyūryō* *ga* *[yasukereba/yasukattara/yasui nara/*yasui to],* ^{Q}*watashi* *wa*
wage NOM [if.low] I TOP
ōbo shinai.
apply.not

[3] A sufficient condition P' for some state of affairs Q' is a condition that, if satisfied, guarantees that Q' also occurs.

In (3), the use of *to* is prohibited not because it is incompatible with this temporal configuration of P' and Q', but because, as explained in Subsection 16.2.6, *to* must convey objective statements. Therefore, the speaker as an active agent cannot appear or be implied in the main clause. All sentences with *to* in (4) are ungrammatical.

(4) a. ^{P}*[Omoshirokereba/omoshirokattara/omoshiroi nara/*omoshiroi to],* ^{Q}*yomimasu.*
[if.interesting] read
'If (it's) interesting, (I'll) read (it).'

b. ^{P}*[Oishikereba/oishikattara/oishii nara/*oishii to],* ^{Q}*tabetai.*
[if.delicious] want.to.eat
'If (it's) delicious, I want to eat (it).'

c. ^{P}*[Wakaranakereba/wakaranakattara/wakaranai nara/*wakaranai to],*
[if.understand.not]
^{Q}*benkyō shiro.*
study.IMP
'If (you) don't understand (it), study!'

In (3) and (4a), Q indicates the speaker's decision to not apply for the position or read the given material, respectively. Therefore, the statements are construed to be subjective. If the subject of Q in (3) and (4a) were a non-speaker, for example *kanojo* 'she', the sentences would be objective and, therefore, acceptable with *to*. The agentivity in (4b) can be questioned; however, this issue does not concern us here. (4c) is an instance of the speech-act conditional, which is discussed later.

Consider (5). The diagram is identical to (3), but the statement is based on an objective standpoint, which makes *to* legitimate:

(5)

	Past	Now	Future
ω_0		S	
ω_1		P'	Q'

ba	*tara*	*nara*	*to*
✓	✓	✓	✓

a. ^{P}*If you're a member,* ^{Q}*you'll receive an invitation to the lecture.*

b. ^{P}*Kaiin [de areba/dattara/(de aru) nara/da to],* ^{Q}*kōen no shōtaijō*
member [if.be] lecture GEN invitation
ga todokimasu.
NOM will.arrive
'If (you're) a member, an invitation to the lecture will be forthcoming.'

To is prohibited when P' occurs in the past and P' and Q' are sequentially aligned. In such cases, the use of *-ru nara* is also prohibited:

(6)

	Past	Now	Future
ω_0		S	
ω_1	$P' \prec Q'$		

ba	*tara*	*nara*		*to*
		-ta	*-ru*	
✓	✓	✓	×	×

a. ^{P}*If she received a scholarship,* ^{Q}*she probably went to a graduate school.*

b. ^{P}*Moshi shōgakukin o [moraeba/morattara/moratta nara/*morau nara/*
if scholarship ACC [if.receive]
**morau to],* ^{Q}*kanojo wa daigakuin ni itta darō.*
she TOP graduate.school to went COP.CNJ
'If she received a scholarship, (I deduce that) she went to a graduate school.'

(7)

	Past	Now	Future
ω_0		S	
ω_1	P′	Q′	

ba	*tara*	*nara*		*to*
		-ta	*-ru*	
✓	✓	✓	×	×

a. ^{P}*If she finished work early,* ^{Q}*she is playing a video game now.*

b. ^{P}*Moshi shigoto ga hayaku [owareba/owattara/owatta nara/*owaru nara/*
if work NOM early [if.finish]
**owaru to],* ^{Q}*kanojo wa imagoro wa bideo gēmu o yatte imasu yo.*
she TOP now TOP video.game ACC is.playing SFP

(8)

	Past	Now	Future
ω_0		S	
ω_1	P′		Q′

ba	*tara*	*nara*		*to*
		-ta	*-ru*	
✓	✓	✓	×	×

a. ^{P}*If he understood the instructions we gave him yesterday,* ^{Q}*he'll arrive on time.*

b. ^{P}*Moshi kinō no setsumei ga [wakareba/wakattara/wakatta nara/*
if yesterday GEN explanation NOM [if.understand]
**wakaru nara/*wakaru to],* ^{Q}*kare wa jikoku dōri ni kimasu yo.*
he TOP time on come SFP
'If he understood the instructions (given to him) yesterday, he'll arrive on time.'

Recall that, in Subsection 16.2.6, we said that for *to* to be interpreted as a temporal connective, the predicate of the main-clause Q must be in the past tense.

(9) *Maki ga mado o akeru to, doa no beru ga natta.*
NOM window ACC when.opening door GEN bell NOM chimed
'Maki opened the window, and the doorbell chimed.'

The converse is not true. That is, even if the Q clause is past tense, this does not guarantee that the *to*-marked subordinate clause is temporal. It can be conditional, though only when P or Q (or both) is stative. In such a case, *-ru nara is also possible*:

(10)

	Past	Now	Future
ω_0		S	
ω_1	P′ ≈ Q′		

ba	*tara*	*nara*		*to*
		-ta	*-ru*	
✓	✓	✓	✓	✓

a. ^{P}*If the applicants satisfied all requirements,* ^{Q}*they were eligible to have an interview.*
b. ^{P}*Moshi subete no jōken o mitashite [ireba/itara/ita*
if all GEN requirement ACC fulfill.TE [if.be]
nara/iru nara/iru to], ^{Q}*ōbosha wa mensetsu o ukeru shikaku ga atta.*
applicant TOP interview ACC take eligibility NOM there.was
'[Lit.] If the applicants satisfied all requirements, they had the right to have an interview.'

To summarize, *to* cannot be used (i) when the statement is subjective (i.e. the speaker is actively involved in the depicted situation or speech act), e.g. (3b) and (4), and (ii) when P' and Q' are sequentially aligned and P' occurs in the past, e.g. (6b), (7b), and (8b). The use of *to* is legitimate if P' and Q' are simultaneous, e.g. (10b), or if P' does not occur in the past, e.g. (1b), (2b) and (5b). *-Ru nara* is prohibited in (ii).

18.3 Epistemic conditionals

18.3.1 $P' \approx Q'$ *or* $P' \prec Q'$

In epistemic conditionals, the condition P' provides the speaker with a reliable basis upon which to conclude the possible realization of Q': i.e. *If I know P′, then I conclude Q′.*

(11)

	Past	Now	Future
ω_0		S	
ω_1		$P' \approx Q'$	

ba	*tara*	*nara*	*to*
✓	✓	✓	×

a. ^{P}*If the lights are on,* ^{Q}*he's at home.*
b. ^{P}*Moshi denki ga tsuite [ireba/itara/iru nara/*iru to],* ^{Q}*kare wa*
if light NOM turned [if.be] he TOP
uchi ni iru (darō).
home at stay COP.CNJ

In (11), P' (the lights are on) does not cause or enable Q' (he is at home), nor does it identify the possible reason for his being at home. Rather, if P' is true, the speaker can derive Q' by inference.

Compare (11b) with the content conditional (1b).

(1)

	Past	Now	Future
ω_0		S	
ω_1		$P' \approx Q'$	

ba	*tara*	*nara*	*to*
✓	✓	✓	✓

b. ^{P}*Kaiin [de areba/dattara/(de aru) nara/da to],* ^{Q}*waribiki ga arimasu.*
member [if.be] discount NOM there.is
'If you're a member, there is a discount.'

Although the temporal alignments of P′ and Q′ are identical in these two cases, the use of *to* is allowed in (1b), but not in (11b). That is, *to* can operate only in the content domain. Another contrast supporting this domain constraint on *to* is between (5b) in the content domain and (12b) in the epistemic domain:

(5)

	Past	Now	Future
ω_0		S	
ω_1		P′	Q′

ba	*tara*	*nara*	*to*
✓	✓	✓	✓

b. ^{P}*Kaiin* *[de areba/dattara/(de aru) nara/da to],* ^{Q}*kōen* *no* *shōtaijō*
member [if.be] lecture GEN invitation
ga *todokimasu.*
NOM will.arrive
'If (you're) a member, an invitation to the lecture will be forthcoming.'

(12)

	Past	Now	Future
ω_0		S	
ω_1		P′	Q′

ba	*tara*	*nara*	*to*
✓	✓	✓	×

a. ^{P}*If he's honest,* ^{Q}*he'll tell the truth.*
b. ^{P}*Moshi* *kare* *ga* *shōjiki* *[de are ba/dattara/(de aru) nara/*da to],*
if he NOM honest [if.be]
^{Q}*hontō* *no* *koto* *o* *iu* *deshō.*
true GEN matter ACC say COP.CNJ

Unlike the case with causal linkage, the distinction between content and epistemic conditionals may be nebulous. For example, (13) below can be categorized as a content conditional because there is a causal relation between P′ and Q′ in the real world. Nevertheless, it can also be considered as an epistemic conditional because Q′ is the speaker's inference should P′ be realized. This ambiguity between content and epistemic interpretations is particularly problematic in an analysis of Japanese, in which conditionals tend to contain epistemic or inferential expressions in Q.

(13)

	Past	Now	Future
ω_0		S	
ω_1			P′ ≈ Q′

ba	*tara*	*nara*	*to*
✓	✓	✓	✓

a. ^{P}*If this heat wave continues tomorrow,* ^{Q}*the air conditioner will break down.*
b. ^{P}*Moshi* *kono* *mōsho* *ga* *ashita* *mo* *[tsuzukeba/tsuzuitara/*
if this heat.wave NOM tomorrow also [if.continue]
tsuzuku nara/tsuzuku to], ^{Q}*eakon* *wa* *kowareru* *darō.*
air.conditioner TOP break COP.CNJ

As discussed in Section 9.2, Japanese utilizes a two-way tense system (past and non-past), rather than three-way (past, present, and future). Therefore, conjectural (i.e. epistemic) expressions are occasionally employed to emphasize futurity. Compare (13) with (14), which is clearly epistemic, and, therefore, prohibits *to*:

(14)

	Past	Now	Future
ω_0		S	
ω_1			$P' \approx Q'$

ba	*tara*	*nara*	*to*
✓	✓	✓	×

a. ^{P}*If he comes back to work tomorrow,* ^{Q}*that will be an expression of his apology.*

b. ^{P}*Moshi ashita kare ga shigoto ni dete [kureba/kitara/kuru nara/*
if tomorrow he NOM work to enter [if.come]
**kuru to],* ^{Q}*sore wa kare no shazai no hyōmei darō.*
that TOP he GEN apology GEN expression COP.CNJ
'If he comes to work tomorrow, that will constitute his expression of apology.'

In (14), P′ and Q′ are clearly cotemporal. However, in the speaker's mind, they can be sequential; i.e. "If he comes back to work tomorrow, I will then conclude that he will be expressing his apology."

Strictly speaking, all content conditionals are also inferential because conditionality is itself inferential. Nevertheless, I maintain the distinction between content and epistemic domains because, as illustrated above, it captures nicely the constraints on *to* as a conditional marker.

18.3.2 $Q' \prec P'$

A salient difference between epistemic and content conditionals is that the chronological order of P and Q may be reversed in epistemic conditionals. There are five possible temporal alignments, as illustrated below. Because *to* is categorically incompatible with epistemic conditionality, it cannot appear in $Q' \prec P'$ configuration either.

(15)

	Past	Now	Future
ω_0		S	
ω_1	Q′	P′	

ba	*tara*	*nara*	*to*
✓	✓	✓	×

a. ^{P}*If she's asleep now,* ^{Q}*the medicine worked.*

b. ^{P}*Moshi ima kanojo ga nete [ireba/itara/iru nara/*iru to],* ^{Q}*kusuri*
if now she NOM sleeping [if.be] medicine
ga kiita [to iu koto da/koto ni naru/hazu da].
NOM worked [it.is.supposed.to.be]
'If she's asleep now, it means that the medicine worked.'

This reversed temporal order must be signaled in Q with such nominalization expressions as *to iu koto da* 'it means that', *koto ni naru* 'it becomes the case that', and *hazu da* 'must be'. (In the following, only *to iu koto da* will be mentioned to save space.) It would hardly be interpretable as intended if the sentence ends in an indicative predicate *kiita* 'worked', which is possible in English as in (15a).

Consider next (16). *Nara* is acceptable in (15b), but not in (16b).

(16)

	Past	Now	Future
ω_0		S	
ω_1	Q′		P′

ba	*tara*	*nara*	*to*
✓	✓	×	×

a. ^{P}*If she recovers quickly,* ^{Q}*we gave her the right medicine.*

b. ^{P}*Moshi kanojo ga sugu ni yoku [nareba/nattara/*naru nara/*naru to],*
if she NOM soon better [if.become]
^{Q}*watashitachi wa tadashii kusuri o ataeta to iu koto da.*[4]
we TOP right medicine ACC gave it.is.supposed.to.be
'If she recovers quickly, it means that we gave her the right medicine.'

This difference reveals an important factor when analyzing conditional constructions. Speakers utilize conditionals when they are uncertain about the validity of P′. Funk (1985: 375–76) points out that there are two sources of uncertainty. One is that the situation in question has not (yet) been realized, i.e. it is a future situation, so no one is certain of its validity. The other is that the realization of the situation is verifiable, but the speaker does not have that information at the time of utterance. P′ in (16) is an instance of the former (a yet to be realized situation), whereas P′ in (15) is an instance of the latter (speaker's ignorance). The generalization is that the use of *nara* is appropriate only when P′ is verifiable but the speaker lacks such information.

In (17), *nara* is illegitimate because the person's passing the examination in the future cannot be verified at the time of utterance. If, however, in a highly unlikely situation, the speaker has some basis to assume that the event will likely occur (e.g. speaking with a fortune teller), *nara* is possible.

(17)

	Past	Now	Future
ω_0		S	
ω_1		Q′	P′

ba	*tara*	*nara*	*to*
✓	✓	×	×

[4] *-Ta nara* is also possible in this case as well as in (19b), which is not discussed in this chapter because it requires an elaborate argument involving intricate scrutiny of tense, aspect (see Section 9.3), and nominalization (see Chapter 15). Although it is an interesting topic, it is beyond the scope of this book.

a. ^{P}*If he passes the exam,* ^{Q}*he's smarter than we think.*
b. ^{P}*Moshi gōkaku [sureba/shitara/*suru nara/*suru to],* ^{Q}*kare wa watashitachi*
if pass [if.do] he TOP we
ga kangaete iru yori atama ga ii to iu koto da.
NOM are.thinking more.than head NOM good it.is.supposed.to.be
'If he passes the exam, it shows that he is smarter than we think.'

When both P′ and Q′ refer to future time, the acceptability of conditional connectives is as follows:

(18)

	Past	Now	Future
ω_0		S	
ω_1			$Q' \prec P'$

ba	*tara*	*nara*	*to*
✓	✓	×	×

a. ^{P}*If she resigns as chair next week,* ^{Q}*she'll be successful in appointing a satisfactory successor at tomorrow's meeting.*
b. ^{P}*Moshi raishū kanojo ga gichō o jinin [sureba/*
if next.week she NOM chairperson ACC resign [if.do]
*shitara/*suru nara/*suru to],* ^{Q}*ashita no kaigi de nattoku no iku*
tomorrow GEN meeting at satisfactory
kōninsha ga kimatta [to iu koto da/koto ni naru].
successor NOM selected it.is.supposed.to.be
'If she resigns from the chairpersonship next week, it is likely that a satisfactory successor will be selected at tomorrow's meeting.'

Now consider (19b), which appears to be a reification of the diagram in (16).

(16)

	Past	Now	Future
ω_0		S	
ω_1	Q′		P′

ba	*tara*	*nara*	*to*
✓	✓	×	×

(19) a. ^{P}*If she ends up going to Japan,* ^{Q}*I was successful in persuading her.*
b. ^{P}*Moshi kanojo ga nihon ni [ikeba/ittara/iku nara/*iku to],*
if she NOM Japan to [if.go]
^{Q}*watashi no settoku ga kiita [to iu koto da/koto ni naru].*
I GEN persuasion NOM effective [it.is.supposed.to.be]
'If she goes to Japan, it means that my persuasion was effective.'

While *ba* and *tara* in (19b) are purely hypothetical, *nara* strongly implies that the subject referent has already decided to go to Japan, and that the speaker has some means to obtain that information, for example, hearing it from the addressee.[5] Therefore, *nara* in (19b) is actually an instance of the diagram in (15). This is why *nara* in (19b) is acceptable.

[5] Newly acquired information takes time to be incorporated in the person's brief system, and, therefore, the use of conditionals to express uncertainty is the norm. See Akatsuka (1985) for further discussion.

(15)

	Past	Now	Future
ω_0		S	
ω_1	Q′	P′	

ba	*tara*	*nara*	*to*
✓	✓	✓	×

This verifiability constraint applies even when *nara* appears in content conditionals. Consider (2b):

(2)

	Past	Now	Future
ω_0		S	
ω_1			P′ ≺ Q′

ba	*tara*	*nara*	*to*
✓	✓	✓	✓

b. ^{P}*Kaihatsu* *ga* *ninka* *[sarereba/saretara/sareru nara/sareru to],*
development NOM approval [if.be.PASS]
^{Q}*yasei* *dōbutsu* *wa* *shinitaete shimau.*
wild animal TOP will.be.extinct
'If the development is approved, wild animals will become extinct.'

If *ninka sarereba*, *saretara*, or *sareru to* 'if (it is) approved' is used, the implicit message is that no one is certain about the realization of P′. In contrast, *ninka sareru nara* guarantees that at least some people consider P′ to be verifiable.

This verifiability of *nara* is to some extent similar to the use of *will* in English conditionals. *Will* is normally prohibited from occurring in P, as in (20a). However, when the sentence carries "assumed likelihood"-meaning, *will* is accepted as in (20b–20c) (Haegeman and Wekker 1984: 46–48):

(20) a. *^{P}*If it will rain tomorrow,* ^{Q}*the match will be cancelled.*
b. ^{P}*If it will rain tomorrow,* ^{Q}*we might as well cancel the match now.*
c. ^{P}*If you will smoke a pack a day,* ^{Q}*you will never get rid of that cough.*

18.3.3 Counterfactual conditionals

Conditionals are used not only when the speaker is uncertain about the validity of P′, but also when the speaker knows/believes that P′ is false. Such sentences are called **COUNTERFACTUAL CONDITIONALS**. The distinction between the content and the epistemic domain seems to have no importance in counterfactual conditionals. Nevertheless, because they are highly inferential, and because the order of P′ and Q′ can be reversed, counterfactuals can be categorized as a subtype of the epistemic conditional.

There is no special counterfactual marker in Japanese. Normally, counterfactual ideas are implied by the conjectural form of the copula (*darō* and its polite variation *deshō*) and/or a concessive connective (e.g. *ni*, *noni*, *keredo*). The implication is such that *if P, then Q, but (because it is not P, it is not Q).*

Because counterfactuals are operative in the epistemic domain, the use of *to* is prohibited. This constraint is derivable from the salient characteristic of *to* to express objective reality. Counterfactual thoughts are genuinely subjective – no observable traits whatsoever exist in the reality. In the following diagrams, -P′ marks counterfactuality.

(21)

	Past	Now	Future
ω_0	-P′	S	
ω_1	$P' \approx Q'$		

ba	*tara*	*nara*	*to*
✓	✓	✓	×

a. *[P]If he had had talent, [Q]he would have continued his career as a pianist.*
b. *[P]Moshi sainō ga [areba/attara/aru nara/*aru to], [Q]kare wa pianisuto*
if talent NOM [if.exist] he TOP pianist
o tsuzukete ita darō (ni).
ACC was.continuing COP.CNJ although

(22)

	Past	Now	Future
ω_0		S, -P’	
ω_1		$P' \approx Q'$	

ba	*tara*	*nara*	*to*
✓	✓	✓	×

a. *[P]If I were you, [Q]I'd be satisfied with it.*
b. *[P]Moshi watashi ga anata [de areba/dattara/(de aru) nara/*da to], [Q]sore*
if I NOM you [if.be] that
de manzoku [shita/suru] (noni).
with satisfaction [do] although
'[Lit.] If I were you, (I'd) be satisfied with it, but . . .'
c. *[P]If she had a pleasant personality, [Q]she would be liked by everyone.*
d. *[P]Moshi seikaku ga [yokereba/yokattara/ii nara/*ii to], [Q]kanojo wa*
if personality NOM [if.good] she TOP
minna ni [sukareta/sukareru] darō (kedo).
everyone by [was.liked/is.liked] COP.CNJ although
'[Lit.] If her personality were pleasant, she would be liked by everyone, but . . .'

It is not obligatory, but in counterfactuals, the tense of Q can be shifted towards the past. For example, in (22b, 22d), *manzoku shita* 'got satisfied' and *sukareta* 'was liked' can be used to refer to the unrealized present situation Q′. If these sentences were in the content domain, the use of the *-ta* form in Q would be prohibited. For example, (23) below, which is a content conditional (as shown by the acceptability of *to*) does not allow the use of *-ta*.

(23)

	Past	Now	Future
ω_0		S	
ω_1		$P' \approx Q'$	

ba	*tara*	*nara*	*to*
✓	✓	✓	✓

a. ^{P}*If her personality is pleasant,* ^{Q}*she is liked by everyone.*

b. ^{P}*Moshi* *seikaku* *ga* *[yokereba/yokattara/ii nara/ii to],* ^{Q}*kanojo* *wa*
   if personality NOM [if.good] she TOP
   minna *ni* *[*sukareta/sukareru].*
   everyone by [was.liked/is.liked]

As in the case of content conditionals, when P′ and Q′ are sequential and P′ is in the past, *-ta nara*, not *-ru nara*, is employed.

(24)

	Past	Now	Future
ω_0	-P′	S	
ω_1	$P' \prec Q'$		

ba	*tara*	*nara*		*to*
		-ta	*-ru*	
✓	✓	✓	×	×

a. ^{P}*If you had listened to my advice,* ^{Q}*you wouldn't have made such mistakes.*

b. ^{P}*Moshi* *watashi* *no* *chūkoku* *o* *[kikeba/kiitara/kiita nara/*kiku nara/*
   if I GEN advice ACC [if.listen]
   **kiku to],* ^{Q}*sonna* *shippai* *wa* *shinakatta* *darō* *(ni).*
   such mistake NEG-SCP did.not COP.CNJ although

(25)

	Past	Now	Future
ω_0	-P′	S	
ω_1	$Q' \prec P'$		

ba	*tara*	*nara*		*to*
		-ta	*-ru*	
✓	✓	✓	×	×

a. ^{P}*If she had recovered,* ^{Q}*it would have been because we gave her the right medicine.*

b. ^{P}*Moshi* *kanojo* *ga* *yoku* *[nareba/nattara/natta nara/*naru nara/*naru to]*
   if she NOM well [if.listen]
   ^{Q}*watashitachi* *wa* *tadashii* *kusuri* *o* *ataeta* *to iu koto datta*
   we TOP right medicine ACC gave it.was.supposed.to.be
   noni.
   although

18.4 Generic (tenseless) conditionals

Some conditional sentences do not refer to specific situations; instead, they express general truths or repetitive situations (i.e. whenever P′ happens, Q′ also happens). Such conditionals are called **GENERIC** or **TENSELESS CONDITIONALS**. Being tenseless, the past–now–future sequence is not designated in the diagrams below. The speaker is, of course, present in the speech situation, but his/her location is also not encoded because *S* in our diagrams is tied to the speech time (i.e. Now). What is retained is only taxis (sequential or simultaneous relationships; see Section 9.4) between P′ and Q′. *Moshi* 'if' can accompany generic conditionals, but it is less frequent than in tensed conditionals. There are three possible settings:

(26)

ω_0	
ω_1	$P' \approx Q'$

ba	*tara*	*nara*	*to*
✓	✓	×	✓

a. ^{P}*If you divide 63 by 3,* ^{Q}*you get 21.*

b. ^{P}*63 o 3 de [wareba/wattara/*waru nara/waru to],* ^{Q}*21 ni naru.*
ACC by [if.divide] to become
'If you divide 63 by 3, it will become 21.'

c. ^{P}*If you have a car,* ^{Q}*it's convenient.*

d. ^{P}*Kuruma ga [areba/attara/*aru nara/aru to],* ^{Q}*benri da.*
car NOM [if.exist] convenient COP.NPST

(27)

ω_0		
ω_1	P'	Q'

ba	*tara*	*nara*	*to*
✓	✓	×	✓

a. ^{P}*If you drink coffee at night,* ^{Q}*you can't sleep.*

b. ^{P}*Yoru kōhī o [nomeba/nondara/*nomu nara/nomu to],* ^{Q}*nemure-nai.*
night coffee ACC [if.drink] can.sleep-not

c. ^{P}*If/Whenever he says yes,* ^{Q}*she always says no.*

d. ^{P}*Kare ga ii to [ieba/ittara/*iu nara/iu to],* ^{Q}*kanojo wa*
he NOM ok QUOT [if.say] she TOP
kanarazu dame da to iu.
always no COP QUOT say
'If he says ok, she always says no.'

(28)

ω_0		
ω_1	Q'	P'

ba	*tara*	*nara*	*to*
✓	✓	×	×

a. ^{P}*If a tsunami occurs,* ^{Q}*there has been an earthquake somewhere.*

b. ^{P}*Moshi tsunami ga [okoreba/okottara/*okoru nara/*okoru to],* ^{Q}*dokoka*
if NOM [if.occur] somewhere
de jishin ga atta to iu koto da.
at earthquake NOM there.was it.is.supposed.to.be
'If a tsunami occurs, it means that there has been an earthquake somewhere.'

From these examples, we can conclude that *nara* is incompatible with generic conditionals.[6] This is in accordance with the verifiability requirement of *nara*. All instances of P' in generic conditionals are not verifiable collectively; therefore, *nara* is incompatible. *To* is harmonious with generics if the statement is in the content domain as in (26b, 26d) and (27b, 27d), but it is not when in the epistemic domain (evidenced by $Q' \prec P'$), as exemplified in (28b).

[6] The use of *-ta nara* is grammatical, but when *-ta nara* is used, the sentence is normally interpreted to be concerned with a specific situation, rather than generically.

18.5 Speech-act conditionals

In speech-act conditionals, P expresses a justification or precondition for performing the speech-act, namely Q. Because the speaker accomplishes a given speech act by merely uttering a sentence, the speech act occurs at the time when Q is uttered. Nevertheless, Q itself can refer to a future situation. For example, *I'll pay you back tomorrow* normally constitutes a speech act of promise, but the act of paying-back is supposed to occur in the future. As a connective for expressing objective relationships between situations, *to* is totally prohibited in speech-act conditionals.[7]

When the predicate of P is stative, e.g. (29) and (30), *ba*, *tara*, and *nara* can be employed:

(29)

	Past	Now	Future
ω_0		S	
ω_1		$P' \approx Q'$	

ba	*tara*	*nara*	*to*
✓	✓	✓	×

a. ^{P}*If you don't mind (my asking),* ^{Q}*how old are you?* (questioning)

b. ^{P}*Moshi shitsurei de [nakereba/nakattara/nai nara/*nai to],* ^{Q}*oikutsu desu ka.*
if rudeness COP [if.not] how.old.HON COP.NPST INT
'If it is not impolite (to ask), how old are you?'

(30)

	Past	Now	Future
ω_0		S	
ω_1		P′	Q′

ba	*tara*	*nara*	*to*
✓	✓	✓	×

a. ^{P}*If you want to,* ^{Q}*eat it!* (permitting)

b. ^{P}*Moshi [tabetakereba/tabetakattara/tabetai nara/*tabetai to],* ^{Q}*tabenasai.*
if [if.want.to.eat] eat.IMP
'If (you) want to eat (it), eat (it)!'

When the predicate of P is dynamic, P is interpreted as referring to a future situation (i.e. it is unverifiable), and the use of *nara* is prohibited.

(31)

	Past	Now	Future
ω_0		S	
ω_1		Q′	P′

ba	*tara*	*nara*	*to*
✓	✓	×	×

[7] An exception is when the utterance is meant to be threatening or warning, e.g. *Ugoku to, utsu zo* 'If (you) move, (I'll) shoot (you)' (McGloin 1976).

a. ^{P}*if you get hungry,* ^{Q}*there are biscuits on the sideboard.* (offering)
b. ^{P}*Moshi onaka ga [sukeba/suitara/*suku nara/*suku to],* ^{Q}*todana ni*
if stomach NOM [if.become.empty] sideboard in
bisuketto ga arimasu yo.
biscuit NOM there.is SFP
c. ^{P}*If a bill collector comes,* ^{Q}*I've left the money here.* (informing)
d. ^{P}*Moshi shūkinnin ga [kureba/kitara/*kuru nara/*kuru to],* ^{Q}*koko ni*
If bill.collector NOM [if.come] Here at
okane o oite okimasu.
money ACC leave

When the predicate of P is dynamic and P′ precedes Q′, only *tara* is compatible.

(32)

	Past	Now	Future
ω_0		S	
ω_1	P′	Q′	

ba	*tara*	*nara*	*to*
×	✓	×	×

a. ^{P}*If I offended you,* ^{Q}*I apologize.* (apologizing)
b. ^{P}*Oki ni [*sawareba/sawattara/*sawaru nara/*sawaru to],* ^{Q}*ayamarimasu.*
nerve to [if.touch] apologize
'[Lit.] If (what I said) irritated (your) nerve, (I) apologize.'

When P′ is verifiable by the addressee and P′ follows Q′, only *nara* is appropriate.

(33)

	Past	Now	Future
ω_0		S	
ω_1			Q′ ≺ P′

ba	*tara*	*nara*	*to*
×	×	✓	×

a. ^{P}*If you (want to) become a police officer,* ^{Q}*learn judo.* (advising)
b. ^{P}*Moshi keikan ni [*nareba/*nattara/naru nara/*naru to],* ^{Q}*jūdō*
if police.officer to [if.become] Judo
O narae.
ACC learn.IMP
c. ^{P}*If you go to the bank,* ^{Q}*please stop by my office.* (requesting)
d. ^{P}*Moshi ginkō ni [*ikeba/*ittara/iku nara/*iku to],* ^{Q}*watashi no jimusho*
if bank to [if.go] I GEN office
ni yotte kudasai.
to please.stop.by

18.6 Summary

A. In the content domain, all four connectives can in principle be employed.
B. In all content conditionals, P′ must occur prior to or simultaneously with Q′.
C. *To* must accompany an objective statement. Because the epistemic and speech-act domains are inherently subjective, *to* can be used only in the content domain.

D. *To* cannot be used in the content domain when
   (i) the statement is subjective (i.e. the speaker is actively involved in the depicted situation), e.g. (3b).
   (ii) P′ occurs in the past and P′ and Q′ are sequentially aligned, e.g. (6b), (7b), (8b).
   (iii) However, when P′ and Q′ are cotemporal, *to* is compatible with P′ in the past.
E. Like *to*, *-ru nara* is prohibited when P′ occurs in the past and P′ and Q′ are sequential, e.g. (6b), (7b), (8b). However, also like *to*, when P′ and Q′ are cotemporal, *-ru nara* is compatible with P′ in the past.
F. In the epistemic domain, Q′ can precede P′, (16b), (17b), (18b). In this reversed sequence, Q must be marked with such nominalization expressions as *to iu koto da* 'it means that', *koto ni naru* 'it becomes the case that', and *hazu da* 'must be'.
G. Uncertainty can be due to futurity (no one is certain) or ignorance (verifiable by someone).
H. *Nara* is appropriate only when P′ is verifiable although the speaker lacks such information, cf. (16b), (17b), (18b).
I. Counterfactual ideas are implied in Japanese by the conjectural form of the copula *darō* (and its polite variation *deshō*) and/or a concessive connective (e.g. *ni*, *noni*, *keredo*).
J. In counterfactual conditionals, as well as content conditionals, when P′ is in the past and P′ and Q′ are sequential, *-ta nara* is used but *-ru nara* is prohibited.
K. *Nara* is prohibited in generic conditionals because P′ is not verifiable.
L. In speech-act conditionals, P expresses a justification or precondition for performing the speech-act that is construed with Q.
M. *To* is prohibited in speech-act conditionals.
N. When the predicate of P is stative, e.g. (29) and (30), *ba*, *tara*, and *nara* can be employed.
O. When the predicate of P is dynamic and refers to a future situation that the addressee cannot verify, the use of *nara* is prohibited, e.g. (31b, d).
P. When the predicate of P is dynamic and P′ precedes Q′, only *tara* is compatible, e.g. (32b).
Q. When P′ is verifiable by the addressee and P′ follows Q′, only *nara* is appropriate, e.g. (33b, d).

Part VI

Pragmatics (language usage)

19 Speech acts

19.1 Introduction

What if someone says the following to you.

(1) *Anata* *tomodachi* *i-nai* *deshō.*
you friend exist-not COP.CNJ
'You don't have friends, do you?'

How would you respond? You are able to literally understand this utterance, but that in itself is insufficient to determine how to react reasonably. In verbal interaction, the addressee needs to understand not only the meaning of the sentence, but also *what the speaker intends to accomplish by saying it*. In this regard, John Austin (1962) recognized that when we speak, we simultaneously perform three types of acts. One is a **LOCUTIONARY ACT**, the act of uttering a sentence and, by so doing, conveying what the sentence literally means.

The second kind is an **ILLOCUTIONARY ACT**, i.e. what we intend to accomplish by the utterance. The term *speech act* is normally used to refer exclusively to illocutionary acts, of which numerous types exist: advising, agreeing, answering, apologizing, asserting, begging, complimenting, condoling, confirming, congratulating, declaring (e.g. war), declining (e.g. an offer), disagreeing, excusing, forbidding, greeting, inviting, making an excuse, offering, ordering, prohibiting, promising, pronouncing (e.g. someone guilty), permitting, questioning, requesting, refusing, swearing, thanking, warning, and so on.

The third is a **PERLOCUTIONARY ACT**, the reaction of the addressee to the utterance. More specifically, does the addressee consider the utterance to be amusing, convincing, distracting, encouraging, irritating, persuading, realizing, threatening, etc.? Because perlocutionary acts depend solely on the addressee's interpretation of the utterance, they may be identical or different in meaning from that which the speaker intends.

With (1), the illocutionary act might be a genuine question, i.e. the speaker wants to know nothing more than whether or not the addressee has any friends. However, this interpretation might well be unrealistic. Even if it is genuinely motivated, one still wonders why the speaker is eliciting such information. A more realistic interpretation might be that it is meant to be hurtful or even insulting. The speaker may be implying that the addressee fails to appeal to him/her, is not likable, and therefore has no friends. (If, however, the tone is playful and light-hearted, then the utterance would be interpreted to be ironically humorous.) If the addressee interprets (1) as an insult, s/he will possibly not respond at all or respond accordingly as in (2a–2c).[1]

(2) a. *Dōyū* *imi* *desu* *ka?*
what.kind.of meaning COP INT
'What do you mean (by that)?'
b. *Zuibun* *shitsurei* *desu* *ne.*
quite impolite COP SFP
'(You're) really rude, aren't you?'
c. *Anata* *mo* *deshō?*
you also COP.CNJ
'Neither do you!'

Another possible scenario, although requiring strong contextual support (e.g. a sympathetic tone), is that the speaker assumes the addressee does not have friends and s/he is willing to become one. The addressee might then respond differently as in (2d).

d. *Arigatō.*
'Thanks.'

In order to make the differences clearer, some researchers use the terms **ILLOCUTIONARY FORCE** and **PERLOCUTIONARY EFFECT** rather than *act* for all three kinds of speech acts. If someone asks a question, the addressee may automatically feel obliged to answer, but when s/he is unable to do so, the tendency is to say *I'm sorry, but . . .* That is, the illocutionary act of questioning has some potential *force* on the addressee. On the other hand, perlocution is more befittingly characterized as an *effect* rather than an *act* because an act is typically conceived of as a deed controllable by the actor. The addressee's emotional reaction is most likely impulsive rather than controlled by reasoning.

Many speech acts prompt a speaker to respond in either one way or another. Offers can be accepted or refused, opinions can be agreed with or disagreed with, and requests can be granted or declined. Accepting, agreeing, and granting are **PREFERRED ACTS** and expressed systematically in different ways than their negative alternatives. Preferred actions can be articulated straightforwardly, but performance of non-preferred acts typically requires indirectness (evasiveness) and considerable tact.

[1] Strictly speaking, an insult is likely to be perlocutional, rather than illocutional. However, such a theoretical issue does not concern us here. For our purposes, an illocutionary act can be understood as what the speaker intends to accomplish by his/her locutionary act.

The execution of such verbal dexterity inevitably results in utterances that highlight cultural differences. A well-known anecdote concerns the speech-act interpretation of *Zensho shimasu* 'I'll do my best' when said to Richard Nixon by Eisaku SATO, the then prime minister of Japan, during his visit to Washington, DC in 1969. At that time, the US–Japan textile industry trade imbalance was aggravated, and Nixon insisted that Japan restrain its textile export to the US. Sato responded, *Zensho shimasu. Zensho* is a Sino-Japanese noun (see Section 5.1), meaning 'an appropriate measure'. Nixon took this as an agreement or promise. However, the phrase simply guarantees that the speaker will make a best effort, without necessarily entailing its success. When he learned that Japan had not moderated its textile export, Nixon reportedly called Sato a liar (Haberman 1988).

Uncertainty in the determination of an intended illocutionary act, as illustrated by this episode, can be a major hindrance in intercultural and international communication. The following sections discuss illocutionary acts that exhibit considerable differences between English and Japanese.

19.2 Apologies

An apology is made when the speaker acknowledges his/her fault or offence caused by performing or not performing some act. In order to restore their good relationship, s/he requests pardon from the addressee. Blum-Kulka and Olshtain (1984) identify the following five apology strategies:

(3) a. Use an illocutionary force indicator (*sorry, apologize, regret, excuse*).
b. Acknowledge responsibility (*I'm so forgetful; It's my fault/mistake*).
c. Explain the cause of the offence (*The bus was late; Traffic is always so heavy in the morning*).
d. Offer reparation (*I'll pay for the damage; I'll see what I can do*).
e. Promise non-recurrence (*This won't happen again*).

The speaker selects an appropriate strategy according to (i) the severity of the offence, and (ii) the relationship with the addressee in terms of psychological distance, power, age, etc. The degree of seriousness of the offence is frequently determined by cultural norms. For example, not arriving at the scheduled starting time for a meeting is a more serious offence in some cultures than in others. Japanese examples corresponding to these strategies in (3) are provided in (4).

(4) a. *(Osoku nat-te)* *sumimasen.*
being.late-TE sorry
'I'm sorry (for being late).'

b. *Subete* *watashi* *no* *sekinin* *desu.*
all I GEN responsibility COP.NPST
'[Lit.] It's all my responsibility.'
'It's all my fault.'

c. *Basu* *ga* *okure-ta* *mono* *desu* *kara . . .*
bus NOM be.delayed-PAST thing COP.NPST because
'Because the bus was delayed . . .'

d. *Baishō* *sase-te* *itadaki-masu.*
compensation do.CAUS-TE receive-NPST.POL
'Please let me compensate you (for the damage).'

e. *Kono* *yō na* *fushimatsu* *wa* *nido to* *okashi-masen.*
this kind mistake TOP second.time commit-NPST.POL
'(I promise you) I'll never make this kind of mistake again.'

(4b–4e) are normally preceded by *sumimasen* or some other formulaic apologetic expression. Those sentences that serve as apologies in terms of explanation of cause, such as (4c), are almost always left incomplete. If the sentence were completed, it would sound like a mere excuse without a genuine sense of apology.

Many non-native speakers of Japanese believe that Japanese people, in general, apologize frequently and on occasions when, in their perception, no apology is needed. For example, in his translation of TANIZAKI Jun'ichirō's *Sasameyuki* (*The Makioka Sisters*), Edward Seidensticker ignored the apologetic *shitsurei de gozaimasu keredo* 'it's rude to ask but' in the following passage:

(5) *Shitsurei* *de gozaimasu* *keredo* *Sagara-san* *wa* *dochira* *ni*
rude COP.POL but TOP where at
osumai-de *irasshaimasu* *no?*
live.HON-TE exist.NPST.HON SFP
'(It's rude to ask you, but) where do you live, Mrs. Sagara?'

On this omission Seidensticker commented:

> Phrases like "it's rude to ask you, but . . ." in this situation are rarely used because English speaking people are less likely to consider asking where a person lives to be rude. Therefore, a faithful translation of such phrases would sound ridiculous. If one prefers to include it, "May I ask where you live?" will be sufficient (Seidensticker and Nasu 1962: 67, translation mine).

In Japanese culture, it is indeed considered rude to ask questions regarding matters that are considered private. These typically include the addressee's name, occupation, family structure, and place of residence. One might attribute this degree of Japanese sensitivity to privacy as simply being greater than that of English-speaking people. Some types of information, e.g. the amount and source of one's income, are likewise regarded as confidential in both Japanese and Western cultures. Generally, confidentiality appears to apply in more areas of Japanese culture than of Western cultures.

As might be suggested by the above, information appears to be a more precious commodity in Japanese culture than it is in Western cultures. Under normal circumstances, when interlocutor A wants to obtain some information and believes that the addressee, interlocutor B, has access to it, A expects B to be cooperative and to supply the information insofar as s/he is able.[2] If B does not cooperate, then A will infer that B considers releasing the information to be indiscreet, impolite, unethical, or discourteous. However, Ochs Keenan (1976) reports that in Malagasy society (in Madagascar, an island nation in the Indian Ocean, off the southeastern coast of Africa), people routinely provide less information than requested. For example, if asked *Where is your mother?*, the likely response is *She is either in the house or at the market* even when the respondent knows her exact location (p. 70). Ochs Keenan contends that such meager responses are motivated by information scarcity: that is, new information rarely surfaces in Malagasy villages, so if one manages to gain access to some, one is reluctant to share it with others.

Japanese society is flooded with new information, but until the late nineteenth century, most people lived their entire lives in small villages, so it is not surprising that there are many similarities between Malagasy and Japanese cultures, e.g. avoiding personal reference in conversation, changing one's name during one's lifetime, and making weaker statements using the double negative *nakereba naranai* 'if not X, then not Y' to express '(you) must do'. If this comparative analysis is valid, then the Japanese also tend to be reluctant to release information to others.

19.3 Commands

For commands, Japanese has designated verbal forms, although naked commands are rarely used.

(6) a. *Kaer-e.*
return.IMP
'Go home!'

The verb *kaere* 'return' in (6a) is in the imperative form (see Section 6.1), which carries very strong illocutionary force. In English, by contrast, the imperative form can be used in a broad spectrum of situations, from issuing coarse command to offering a suggestion or advice. For example, if you encounter your colleague, even your supervisor, becoming sick, you can say *Go home!* But in Japanese, the imperative form cannot be used in such a situation; some other expression, e.g. *Kaetta-ra (ikaga desu ka)* 'what if you go home?', must be used. The imperative is normally used only when the speaker is higher in status than the addressee and commands the addressee to do something against his/her will.

[2] This idea of cooperative behavior was theorized by Paul Grice in his seminal paper (1975) and is referred to as Gricean Theory of Implicature (already mentioned in Chapter 15, footnote 3 and Chapter 16, footnote 1). Refer to any Pragmatics textbook for further information about it.

b. *Kaer-i* *nasai.*
return.ADV do.HON.IMP
'Go home!'

The sentence in (6b) exhibits another form of the imperative, this time the adverbial form of the verb being followed by *nasai*, the imperative form of the honorific verb *nasaru* 'do'. This is softer than (6a), but it can nevertheless be used only to an addressee who is lower in status, e.g. a mother to her child.

As discussed in Section 9.2, the simple past or non-past tense forms can be used for a command.

(7) a. *Doi-ta,* *doi-ta.*
step.back-PAST
'Step back! Step back!'
b. *Sugu ni* *tabe-ru.*
immediately eat-NPST
'Eat (it) now!'

In providing instructions, English uses the imperative form, but in Japanese, the non-past form is the norm.

(8) a. *Tsugi-ni* *monitā* *o* *tsunagi-masu.*
next monitor ACC connect-POL.NPST
'Next, connect the monitor.'
b. *Nitatta-ra* *shio* *o* *kuwaeru.*
when.boiled salt ACC add-NPST
'When boiled, add salt.'

Strong negative commands can be issued with the negative imperative forms, illustrated in (9). As discussed in Section 6.4, in casual speech when the stem of an *u*-verb ends with /r/, except for pitch accent the positive and negative imperatives become identical:

(9) *hairi-na*	*hairu-na*	→	*hain-na*
enter	don't enter		
kaeri-na	*kaeru-na*	→	*kaen-na*
return	don't return		
tsukuri-na	*tsukuru-na*	→	*tsukun-na*
make	don't make		

19.4 Compliments and responses

The Japanese are said to give compliments less frequently than do Americans. Therefore, Japanese people may be troubled, even overwhelmed, by Americans' frequent compliments. Americans, on the other hand, can be equally confused by the absence of positive comments while in the company of Japanese (Barnlund and Araki 1985: 25). According to Barnlund and Araki,

Americans regard most positive comments as compliments, whereas the Japanese tend to regard many as flattery.

Americans tend to praise appearance, skills, personal traits, and taste, in that order, whereas Japanese attach the greatest importance to skills, and then appearance, taste, and personal traits (Barnlund and Araki 1985: 23). Americans offer explicit praise, while Japanese praise is tentative and cautious. Interestingly, the closer the relationship, the more likely Americans are to praise their interlocutors, but the less likely Japanese are to do the same.

Barnlund and Araki also report that, in their study, both Americans and Japanese subjects indicated positive feelings towards giving and receiving compliments (p. 15). I am, however, cautious about this finding. As just discussed, many Japanese people feel uncomfortable when complimented. Furthermore, even in American culture, compliments, especially about aspects of the addressee's appearance and physique, might be evaluated as (sexual) harassment. However positive the evaluation, it might be perceived as a violation of privacy, an area about which outsiders should not comment.

Ishihara and Cohen (2010: 59–60) categorize common types of response to compliments into the following five types:

(10) a. Acceptance
- Token of appreciation (*Thanks; Thank you.*)
- Acceptance by means of a comment (*Yeah, it's my favorite, too.*)
- Upgrading the compliment by self-praise (*Yeah, I can play other sports well too.*)

b. Mitigation
- Comment about history (*I bought it for the trip to Arizona.*)
- Shifting the credit (*My brother gave it to me; It really knitted itself.*)
- Questioning or requesting reassurance or repetition (*Do you really like them?*)
- Reciprocating (*So's yours.*)
- Scaling down or downgrading (*It's really quite old.*)

c. Rejection
- Disagreeing (A: *You look good and healthy.* B: *I feel fat.*)

d. No response

e. Request for interpretation
- Addressee interprets the compliment as a request (*You wanna borrow this one too?*)

Because the Japanese tend to consider positive comments as flattery rather than compliments, accepting them may be judged inappropriate. Daikuhara (1986: 119–20) reports that 95 percent of Japanese responses to compliments are avoidance of self-praise, and only 5 percent evince acceptance and appreciation, restricted to interaction between close friends. The most common responses are rejection, e.g. *ie, ie* 'no, no' and *sonna koto nai* 'that's not true', accounting for 35 percent of all self-praise avoidance responses. The second most frequent response is a smile or no response at all (27%). The third type questions the validity, e.g. *sō?* 'you really think so?' (13%).

Rejecting a compliment appropriately can be difficult for some American learners of Japanese. In an intermediate Japanese course at the University of

California, Berkeley, some students, in desperation, provided these strange-sounding responses:

(11) A: [Looking at the homework assignment returned to B]
Ii *seiseki* *desu* *ne.*
good grade COP.NPST SFP
'You got a good grade, didn't you?'
B: *Īe,* *watashi* *wa* *baka* *desu.*
no I TOP idiot COP.NPST
'No, I'm an idiot.'

(12) A: *Ii* *kutsu* *desu* *ne.*
good shoes COP.NPST SFP
'Nice shoes, aren't they?'
B: *Chūko* *o* *kai-mashita.*
pre-owned ACC buy-PAST
'(I) bought pre-owned ones.'

(11B) is inappropriate because it completely and too explicitly denies A's compliment. It gives the impression that B is unwilling to converse with A. (12B) is more acceptable than (11B). In fact, if A's compliment were about B's car, many native speakers of Japanese would say something like (11B). However, if the item is not very expensive, mentioning it to be second-hand may be a little out of place for Japanese tastes.

19.5 Invitations and requests

Invitation in its technical sense includes advising, suggesting, etc. Both inviting and requesting someone to do something are intended to induce an action that will be performed by the addressee. However, the addressee is the beneficiary in the former (e.g. *Please have some cookies*), while the speaker is in the latter (e.g. *Please clean the room*). In English, both speech acts can be expressed by the same grammatical constructions, e.g. (13).

(13) a. *Please sit down.*
b. *Will you sit down?*
c. *Would you like to wait here?*

By contrast, in Japanese, invitations and requests rarely overlap formally. Himeno (1991) contrasts the following.

(14) a. *Dōzo* *suwat-te* *kudasai.*
please sit-TE give.me
'Please sit down.'
b. *Sumimasen* *ga,* *suwat-te* *kudasai.*
sorry but sit-TE give.me
'I'm sorry, but please be seated.'

While the *-te kudasai* 'please do' construction can be used for both invitation and request, *dōzo* 'please' can occur only with an invitation, and *sumimasen ga*

'I'm sorry, but' only with a request. That is, in (14a), the speaker is advising the addressee to sit down for the addressee's sake, whereas in (14b), the speaker is requesting the addressee to sit down because, for example, the speaker is unable to see the stage when the addressee is standing in front of him/her.

Himeno also points out that most learners of Japanese are taught that *-te kudasai-masen ka* 'would you not' is a politer form of *-te kudasai* (p. 76). However, *-te kudasai-masen ka* is used only for requesting, not for inviting. Therefore, non-native speakers tend to make such errors as (15a). For an invitation, *suwatte kudasai* or simple verb + *masen ka*, without *kureru* 'give', must be used, as in (15b). If more politeness is called for, the honorific form of the verb should be selected as in (15c).

(15) a. [Offering a chair]
#*Suwat-te* *kudasai-masen* *ka?*
sit-TE give.me-POL.NEG INT
'Would you please sit down?'
b. *Suwari-masen* *ka?*
sit.POL.NEG INT
'Why don't [you/we] sit down?'
c. *Osuwari-ni* *nari-masen* *ka?*
sit.HON become-POL.NEG INT
'Would you please sit down?'

Similarly, learners of Japanese are informed that the translational equivalent of "May I ~" is *-te mo ii desu ka*. While the former can be used both for requesting permission and offering a favor, the latter can be used only for requesting permission (pp. 76–77). Therefore, (16a) is natural, but (16b) is unacceptable. For making an offer, (16c) is appropriate.

(16) a. *May I help you?*
b. #*Tetsudat-te* *mo* *ii* *desu* *ka?*
help-TE also good COP.NPST INT
'May I help you?'
c. *Tetsudai-mashō* *ka?*
help-VOL INT
'Shall I help you?'

19.6 Refusal

Refusal is undoubtedly one of the least preferred acts. Therefore, direct refusals (e.g. *I refuse*, *I can't do it*) are rather rare. Beebe *et al.* (1990: 73) propose the following classification of indirect refusals.

(17) a. Statement of regret (*I'm sorry ...; I feel terrible ...*)
b. Wish (*I wish I could help you ...*)
c. Excuse, reason, explanation (*My children will be home that night.*)
d. Statement of alternative (*I'd rather ...; Why don't you ask someone else?*)

e. Set condition for future or past acceptance (*If you had asked me earlier, I would have . . .*)
f. Promise of future acceptance (*I'll do it next time*; *I promise I'll . . .*)
g. Statement of principle (*I never do business with friends.*)
h. Statement of philosophy (*One can't be too careful.*)
i. Attempt to dissuade interlocutor
    - Threat or statement of negative consequences to the requester (to refuse an invitation: *I won't be any fun tonight.*)
    - Guilt trip (waitress to customers who want to sit a while: *I can't make a living from people who just order coffee.*)
    - Criticize the request/requester, insult/attack (*Who do you think you are?*)
    - Request for help, empathy, and assistance by dropping or holding the request
    - Let the interlocutor off the hook (*Don't worry about it; That's okay.*)
    - Self-defense (*I'm trying my best*; *I'm doing all I can do.*)
j. Acceptance that functions as a refusal (unspecific or indefinite reply, lack of enthusiasm)
k. Avoidance
    - Non-verbal (silence, hesitation, do nothing, physical departure)
    - Verbal (topic switch, joke, repetition of part of request (*Monday?*), postponement (*I'll think about it*), hedging (*Gee, I don't know; I'm not sure.*))

In order to investigate whether or not knowledge of speech-act strategies in one's native language is transferred when one communicates in a foreign language (**PRAGMATIC TRANSFER**), Beebe *et al.* (1990) conducted a study with native speakers of Japanese answering in Japanese (JJs), native speakers of Japanese answering in English (JEs), and native speakers of American English answering in English (AEs). Their research subjects were asked by means of a written role-play questionnaire to complete conversations in which they responded with refusals to requests, invitations, offers, and suggestions directed at higher-, equal-, and lower-status interlocutors. Analyzing the acquired data in terms of sequence, frequency, and content, they found that pragmatic transfer does occur frequently. Consider first examples of refusal sequences for declining an invitation to dinner: *I'm sorry* (regret), *but I already have plans* (reason). *Maybe next time* (promise of future acceptance). Conversing with persons of both higher and lower status, AEs tended to begin by expressing a positive feeling (e.g. *thank you, I'd love to go*), then regret, followed by reasons, whereas with a person of equal status, AEs usually began with regret, followed by a reason. With a person of higher status, JJs and JEs also began with an expression of regret, followed by a reason. When refusing someone of lower status, the JJs and JEs tended to be more direct, not using apology or regret. Beebe *et al.* also found that the JJs and JEs frequently used statements of an alternative, but AEs never used this strategy.

Lee (1998: 154–55) reports that native speakers of Japanese tend to use interrogative sentences in refusing requests when speaking in Japanese or in English, confirming pragmatic transfer.

(18) A:	*Warui*	*kedo*	*konban*	*zangyō*	*shi-te*	*kure-nai?*
	bad	but	tonight	overtime	do-TE	give-NEG.NPST

'Sorry, but would you work overtime tonight?'

B: *E,* *konban* *desu* *ka?*
eh tonight COP.NPST INT
'Oh, tonight?'

(19) A: *Kōgi* *no* *nōto* *kashi-te.*
lecture GEN note lend-TE
'Please lend me (your) lecture notes.'
B: *Dō* *shi-te?*
how do-TE
'Why?'

Lee (pp. 160–61) contends that such questions are raised in order to find a convincing reason for refusal and/or to criticize the interlocutor indirectly for making such a request.

19.7 Thanking

The designated expressions for thanks in Japanese are *arigatō* 'thank you' and its polite variation *arigatō gozaimasu.* Additionally, expressions of apology, e.g. (20), are frequently used. This selection aims to reflect the speaker's feeling of indebtedness.

(20) a. *Okokoro-zukai* *osore-irimasu.*
thoughtfulness feel.overwhelmed'
[Lit.] I feel overwhelmed by your thoughtfulness.'
'Thank you for your thoughtfulness.'
b. [Returning a pen]
Dōmo *suimasen* *deshita.*
very sorry COP.PAST'
[Lit.] I was very sorry.'
'Thank you very much.'
c. [Thanking a person who gave you a cake]
Warui *wa-nē.*
bad SFP
'[Lit.] I feel bad.'
'I appreciate it.'
d. [Thanking a person who comes to help you move furniture]
Gomen!
'[Lit.] I'm sorry!'
'Thanks a lot!'

However, expressions of apology cannot always substitute for thanks when the person commenting is not directly involved in the situation of gratitude. For example, apology expressions are inappropriate when responding to the following utterances.

(21) a. *Gōkaku* *omedetō-gozaimasu.*
passing.exam congratulations-POLITE
'Congratulations on your passing the exam!'

b. *Ogenki-ni nat-te, yokatta desu ne.*
healthy become-TE good COP.NPST SFP
'I'm glad to see you've recovered.'

c. *Yoi goryokō o.*
nice trip ACC
'Have a great trip!'

In response to (21a) and (21b), *osore-irimasu* 'I feel embarrassed' can be used, but no other expressions of apology. With (21c), none of the apologetic expressions are appropriate responses. Furthermore, when the indebtedness is very serious – e.g. giving thanks for a mountain rescue – *Arigatō gozaimasu* is appropriate, but expressions of apology cannot be used.

20 Politeness and honorifics I

20.1 Introduction

Linguistic politeness is considered "political" behavior because it is an immediate means to avoid conflict, tone down potential aggression, and ensure smooth interaction. When polite expressions are systematized and incorporated into the grammar of a language, they are termed **HONORIFICS**. (Honorifics are sometimes characterized as *fossilized politeness.*) Japanese is well-known for its elaborate honorific system, which encodes two orthogonal dimensions. One is **ADDRESSEE HONORIFICS**, conveying esteem to the addressee; the other is **REFERENT HONORIFICS**, when showing esteem to the referent person.[1] By "referent person" is meant the person(s) picked out by an expression such as *Alice Thompson* in *Alice Thompson is studying Japanese* (see Figure 20.1). In this sentence, *Alice Thompson* refers to the person whose name is Alice Thompson. Different expressions can be used to refer to the same person, e.g. *Ms. Thompson*, *Alice*, *the person I met yesterday*, etc.

Two methods are used to show respect to the addressee or to the referent. One linguistically exalts the person, while the other depreciates someone (typically the speaker) with respect to the target (honored) person. The former is referred to as an honorific proper, and the latter variously as *humilifics*, *humble forms*, or *non-subject honorifics*, which will be discussed in Section 20.5.

The addressee and the referent can be identical as in *Will you come to the meeting?*, with the referent of *you* also being the addressee. In such a case, addressee and referent honorifics can be employed simultaneously. In fact, these two types of honorifics are frequently intertwined in actual conversation, and some honorific expressions cannot function properly unless the other type is also present in a single sentence, an issue which will be discussed shortly.

As will be seen in this chapter, the Japanese honorific system is extremely complex yet purposeful in terms of actual language practice, reminding me of Sampson's (1985: 173) remark in Chapter 4, regarding the Japanese writing

[1] See Hasegawa (2006) for further discussion of these two types of honorifics.

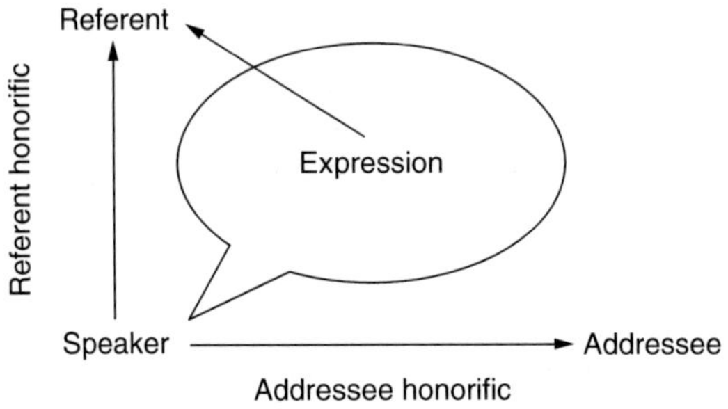

Figure 20.1. Addressee vs. referent honorifics.

system: "One reason why Japanese script deserves its place in this [Sampson's] book is as an illustration of just how cumbersome a script can be and still serve in practice." For most non-native speakers of Japanese, the honorific system appears to be nothing more than pointless complication. However, according to the survey conducted by the Agency for Cultural Affairs in 2004, 96 percent of native-speaker respondents answered that honorifics are an indispensable part of the Japanese language, and, therefore, should be maintained (Bunkachō 2004).

20.2 Addressee honorifics

20.2.1 Verbs

Addressee honorifics are primarily manifested in the **POLITE FORM** (or **DESU-MASU FORM**) of the predicate, vis-à-vis the **PLAIN FORM**. The plain form is appropriate when talking with a friend. When talking with one's superior, the use of a polite form is the norm. (The copula is included in the verb category in this chapter.) Table 20.1 provides examples.

(1) *Watashi ga renraku [suru/shimasu].*
I NOM contact [do.NPST/do.POL.NPST]
'I'll contact (them).'

20.2.2 I-*adjectives*

I-adjectives conjugate like verbs, but they do not have polite forms. It used be that, in order to show respect to the addressee, *gozaimasu*, the polite form of the existential verb *aru*, was added to the adverbial form of *i*-adjectives (see Section 6.3). For example, the adverbial form of *hayai* 'early' is *hayaku*. When *hayaku* is followed by *gozaimasu*, the /k/ in the adverbial suffix *-ku* drops, and the resulting succession of vowels /au/ undergoes a euphonic change and

Table 20.1 *Plain vs. polite forms of verbs.*

Non-past		Past		
Plain	Polite	Plain	Polite	Gloss
da (copula)	*desu*	*datta*	*deshita*	be
iku (*u*-verb)	*ikimasu*	*itta*	*ikimashita*	go
kaeru (*u*-verb)	*kaerimasu*	*kaetta*	*kaerimashita*	return
taberu (*ru*-verb)	*tabemasu*	*tabeta*	*tabemashita*	eat
kariru (*ru*-verb)	*karimasu*	*karita*	*karimashita*	borrow
kuru (irregular)	*kimasu*	*kita*	*kimashita*	come
suru (irregular)	*shimasu*	*shita*	*shimashita*	do

Table 20.2 *Plain vs. polite forms of* i-*adjectives (a).*

Plain	Polite	Gloss	Plain	Polite	Gloss
atarashii	*atarashū gozaimasu*	new	*koi*	*kō gozaimasu*	thick
chikai	*chikō gozaimasu*	near	*nurui*	*nurū gozaimasu*	tepid
kanashii	*kanashū gozaimasu*	sad	*ureshii*	*ureshū gozaimasu*	delighted

becomes *hayō gozaimasu. O-hayō gozaimasu* 'good morning' is derived from this polite expression. When the resultant vowel succession is /uu/, it becomes a long /u/, e.g. *hikui* 'low' > *hikuku* > *hikuu* >*hikū gozaimasu*. When the succession is /ou/, it becomes a long /o/, e.g. *hosoi* 'thin' > *hosoku* > *hosou* > *hosō gozaimasu.*[2] The vowel succession /iu/ results in palatalization (see Section 3.1) of the preceding consonant plus a long /u/, e.g. *ōkii* 'big' > *ōkiku* > *ōkiu* > *ōkyū gozaimasu*. When the preceding consonant is already palatalized, e.g. /sh/, no change occurs on the consonant, e.g. *oishii* 'delicious' > *oishiku* > *oishiu* > *oishū gozaimasu*. Other examples are provided in Table 20.2.

Today, because this type of polite form sounds old-fashioned, the copula is commonly added to *i*-adjectives to express politeness, e.g. *omoshiroi* 'interesting' becomes *omoshiroi desu* (see Table 20.3). This copula support originated during the Meiji period (1868–1912) and spread rapidly, although for some time it was marginalized and even considered ungrammatical. In 1952, the Deliberative Council of the National Language, which had been proposing various linguistic reforms to the government (see Section 4.3), recommended that copula support for *i*-adjectives be accepted as grammatically legitimate.

[2] The stem of the *i*-adjective *tōi* 'far' already contains a long vowel. Therefore, it creates a succession of three /o/s: *tōi* > *tōku* > *tōu* > *tooo gozaimasu*.

Table 20.3 *Plain vs. polite forms of* i*-adjectives (b).*

Non-past		Past		
Plain	Polite	Plain	Polite	Gloss
kuyashii	*kuyashii desu*	*kuyashikatta*	*kuyashikatta desu*	vexing
oishii	*oishii desu*	*oishikatta*	*oishikatta desu*	delicious
takai	*takai desu*	*takakatta*	*takakatta desu*	expensive

Nevertheless, even today, some speakers still feel uncomfortable adding the copula to *i*-adjectives, especially to their past-tense forms, e.g. (2a), and they utilize different constructions, e.g. (2b).

(2) a. *Kōgi wa [nagakatta/nagakatta desu].*
lecture TOP [long.PAST/long.POL.PAST COP.NPST]
'The lecture was long.'
b. *Kōgi wa nagakatta to [omoimasu/omoimashita].*
lecture TOP long.PLAIN.PAST QUOT [think.POL.NPST/think.POL.PAST]
'I [think/thought] the lecture was long.'

When the copula is followed by a sentence-final particle, the unnaturalness vanishes. That is, no one would consider (3) to be a marginal construction.

(3) *Sore wa takai desu [yo./ka?]*
that TOP expensive COP.NPST [SFP/INT]
'That's expensive. / Is that expensive?'

20.3 Referent honorifics

Referent honorifics, the expression of which is more complex than addressee honorifics, are expressed in verbs, adjectives, and/or nouns.

20.3.1 Verbs

When the honored person is encoded as the subject, special honorific verbs or complex forms derived from regular verbs are used.

A. **Honorific verbs**: There are few verbs of this type, in which a separate verb replaces a regular verb.[3] Although few in number, these honorific verbs are frequently used in conversation.

(4) a. *Okada-san wa hogaraka [da/de irassharu].*
TOP cheerful [COP.NPST/COP.HON.NPST]
'Ms. Okada is cheerful.'

[3] This phenomenon is referred to as **SUPPLETION** in linguistics.

Table 20.4 *Honorific verbs.*

Regular	Honorific	Gloss	Regular	Honorific	Gloss
da (copula)	*de irassharu*	be	*taberu*	*meshiagaru*	eat
iu/yuu	*ossharu*	say	*iru*	*irassharu*	stay
suu	*meshiagaru*	smoke	*miru*	*goran ni naru*	see
iku	*irassharu*	go	*kuru*	*irassharu*	come
nomu	*meshiagaru*	drink		*omie ni naru*	
kureru	*kudasaru*	give	*suru*	*nasaru*	do

Table 20.5 O-*V* ni naru.

Regular	Honorific	Gloss	Regular	Honorific	Gloss
iu	*o-ii ni naru*	say	*nomu*	*o-nomi ni naru*	drink
kau	*o-kai ni naru*	buy	*aru*	*o-ari ni naru*	have
iku	*o-koshi ni naru*	go	*taberu*	*o-tabe ni naru*	eat
	o-ide ni naru		*kiru*	*o-meshi ni naru*	wear
matsu	*o-machi ni naru*	wait	*kuru*	*o-koshi ni naru*	come
yobu	*o-yobi ni naru*	call		*o-ide ni naru*	

b. *Okada-san* *ga* *[kita/irasshatta].*
NOM [come.PAST/come.HON.PAST]
'Ms. Okada has arrived.'

Irassharu corresponds to 'come', 'go', or 'be/exist/stay'. *Meshiagaru* is used for 'drink', 'eat', and 'smoke (a cigarette)' – that is, 'intake' in general.

B. ***O-V ni naru***: This formation adds the honorific prefix *o-* to the verb adverbial form followed by the particle *ni* and the verb *naru* 'become'. This is the most productive process from which to derive subject honorifics. Some combine formations A and B; that is, this process is applied to a different, honorific verb stem (see Table 20.5).[4]

(5) a. *Okada-san* *wa* *niku* *o* *[tabe-nai/o-tabe ni nar-anai].*
TOP meat ACC [eat-NEG.NPST/eat.HON-NEG.NPST]
'Ms. Okada does not eat meat.'

[4] There are idiosyncrasies in the usage of formation B. For *iu* 'say', *o-ii ni naru* is possible, but *ossharu* (formation A) is by far more common. For *nomu* 'drink', both *meshiagaru* (A) and *o-nomi ni naru* (B) are common, but for *taberu* 'eat', *o-tabe ni naru* (B) is less common than *meshiagaru*. For *iku* 'go', *o-iki ni naru* (B) is possible, although much less common than *o-ide ni naru/o-koshi ni naru* (A + B). By contrast, for *kuru* 'come', **o-ki ni naru* (B) does not exist. For *kiru* 'wear', *o-ki ni naru* is possible, but *o-meshi ni naru* (A + B) is more common. **O-mi ni naru* 'see' and **o-i ni naru* 'be/stay' do not exist.

Table 20.6 Go-*VN* ni naru.

Regular	Honorific	Gloss	Regular	Honorific	Gloss
annai suru	*go-annai ni naru*	guide	*kibō suru*	*go-kibō ni naru*	hope
hōmon suru	*go-hōmon ni naru*	visit	*shusseki suru*	*go-shusseki ni naru*	attend
kenkyū suru	*go-kenkyū ni naru*	research	*taizai suru*	*go-taizai ni naru*	stay

b. *Okada-san* *wa* *kuruma* *ga* *[aru/o-ari ni naru].*
TOP car NOM [exist.NPST/exist.HON.NPST]
'Ms. Okada has a car.'

Euphemism is also frequently employed. Instead of *o-kai ni naru* 'buy', *o-motome ni naru* 'wish' may be preferred and considered more respectful. *O-ne ni naru* 'sleep' is rare; *o-yasumi ni naru* 'rest' is used instead. **O-shini ni naru* 'die' does not exist; *o-nakunari ni naru* 'disappear' is used instead; *o-kakure ni naru* 'hide' for 'die' is now obsolete.

C. ***Go*-VN *ni naru***: VN stands for a verbal noun (see Subsection 5.2.1). Table 20.6 provides examples.

(6) *Okada-san* *wa* *kaigi* *ni* *[shusseki shita/go-shusseki ni natta].*
TOP meeting to [attend.NPST/attend.HON.NPST]
'Ms. Okada attended the meeting.'

When a VN does not take the honorific prefix *go-*, this formation does not apply.[5] Some VNs can take *go-* but nonetheless cannot form *go-*VN *ni naru*, e.g. *go-doryoku* 'endeavor', *go-junbi* 'preparation', *go-kon'yaku* 'marriage engagement', *go-renraku* 'contact', *go-ryokō* 'travel', *go-seikō* 'success', *go-shippai* 'failure', *go-shūshoku* 'obtain employment'.

D. ***O*-V *nasaru***: *Nasaru* is the honorific verb corresponding to *suru* 'do'. Although all *o*-V *ni naru* forms have the *o*-V *nasaru* counterpart, *o*-V *nasaru* sounds archaic and less polite than *o*-V *ni naru*. This less polite nuance is due to agentivity (see Section 7.5). As a general rule, the less agentive, the more polite: for example. *naru* 'become' is less agentive than *nasaru* 'do'.

[5] As a rule, native Japanese words take the honorific prefix *o-*, whereas Sino-Japanese words take the honorific prefix *go-*. However, some Sino-Japanese words, typically those referring to domestic items and activities, take *o-*, e.g. *o-genkan* 'entrance', *o-genki* 'healthy', *o-kagen* 'health condition', *o-keshō* '(cosmetic) makeup', *o-ryōri* 'cooking', *o-sanpo* 'a walk', *o-sentaku* 'laundry', *o-shōgatsu* 'the first month of the year', *o-shokuji* 'eating' o-*sōji* 'cleaning'.

Table 20.7 Go-*VN* nasaru.

Regular	Honorific	Gloss	Regular	Honorific	Gloss
doryoku suru	*go-doryoku nasaru*	make an effort	*ryokō suru*	*go-ryokō nasaru*	travel
junbi suru	*go-junbi nasaru*	prepare	*seikō suru*	*go-seikō nasaru*	succeed
kon'yaku suru	*go-kon'yaku nasaru*	engage	*shippai suru*	*go-shippai nasaru*	fail

Table 20.8 *VN* nasaru.

Regular	Honorific	Gloss	Regular	Honorific	Gloss
meiwaku suru	*meiwaku nasaru*	be annoyed, bothered, troubled	*unten suru*	*unten nasaru*	drive
konran suru	*konran nasaru*	get confused	*dokusho suru*	*dokusho nasaru*	read a book

Table 20.9 O-*V* asobasu/go-*VN* asobasu.

Regular	Honorific	Gloss	Regular	Honorific	Gloss
homeru	*o-home asobasu*	praise	*kuru*	*o-koshi asobasu*	come
mukaeru	*o-mukae asobasu*	greet	*hōmon suru*	*go-hōmon asobasu*	visit
miru	*go-ran asobasu*	see	*taizai suru*	*go-taizai asobasu*	stay

(7) *Shōgai-nenkin o [kangaeru/o-kangae nasaru] nara, go-sōdan kudasai.*
disability-pension ACC [think.NPST/think.HON.NPST] if consult please
'If you are considering (applying for) a disability pension, please consult us.'

E. ***Go*-VN *nasaru***: Unlike *go*-VN *ni naru*, *go*-VN *nasaru* is highly productive; most VNs can derive subject honorifics through this process. Unlike *o*-V *nasaru* (formation D), *go*-VN *nasaru* does not possess archaic overtones (see Table 20.7).

F. **VN *nasaru***: This formation has no restriction on it; it can derive a subject honorific from any VN verb (Table 20.8). It is considered less polite than formation E.

G. ***O*-V *asobasu/Go*-VN *asobasu***: These forms are extremely polite and somewhat archaic, but still in use in highly formal situations (Table 20.9).

H. **V-*(r)are-ru***: Another way to form subject-honorifics is to add the honorific suffix *-(r)are* to the stem of the verb (Table 20.10). This is a productive process, but less frequent than the *o*-V *ni naru* (formation B) because, in part, the resulting form of this process is identical to the passive form (Chapter 12), which can cause confusion.

Table 20.10 *V*-(r)are-ru.

Regular	Honorific	Gloss	Regular	Honorific	Gloss
iu	*iw-areru*	say	*yameru*	*yame-rareru*	quit
iku	*ik-areru*	go	*iru*	*i-rareru*	stay
kasu	*kas-areru*	lend	*miru*	*mi-rareru*	see
matsu	*mat-areru*	wait	*kuru*	*ko-rareru*	come
yomu	*yom-areru*	read	*suru*	*s-areru*	do

(8) *Okada-san wa shigoto o [yameta/yamerareta].*
NOM job ACC [quit.PAST/quit.HON.PAST]
'Ms. Okada quit her job.'

20.3.2 *Combination of verb honorifics*

Although the bestowing of excessive honor is normally rejected by many speakers, subject honorifics can be combined to express even higher degrees of politeness. Not all combinations are possible, and the order of combination is highly restricted. While inter-speaker variations are naturally expected, Table 20.11, using the verb *nomu* 'drink', provides my assessment of the degrees of politeness possible in discourse (formations C, E, and F are limited to VNs and are not shown).

20.3.3 *Adjectives*

When an adjective describes a person to be honored, his/her in-group members (see Subsection 13.2.1), or his/her possessions, an honorific form of the adjective can be employed. The general rule is to add the honorific prefix *o-* to native Japanese adjectives, and the honorific prefix *go-* to Sino-Japanese adjectives (even though many of them take *o-*). Table 20.12 provides examples.

(9) a. *Okada-san wa [yasashii/o-yasashii].*
TOP [kind.NPST/kind.HON.NPST]
'Ms. Okada is kind.'
b. *Okada-san wa [yūfuku da/go-yūfuku da].*
TOP [affluent.NPST/affluent.HON COP.NPST]
'Ms. Okada is affluent.'

20.3.4 *Nouns*

When a noun refers to the respected person, his/her in-group members, or his/her possessions, an honorific form of the noun can be used (see Table 20.13).

Table 20.11 *Combination of verb honorifics.*

	A	B	C	D	E	F	G	H	Combined
Highest	+						+	+	*o-meshiagari asobas-areru*
↑	+						+		*o-meshiagari asobasu*
							+		*o-nomi asobasu*
	+	+						+	*o-meshiagari ni nar-areru*
	+	+							*o-meshiagari ni naru*
	+			+					*o-meshiagari nasaru* (archaic)
	+							+	*meshiagar-areru* ≈ *o-nomi ni nar-areru*
		+						+	*o-nomi ni nar-areru* ≈ *meshiagar-areru*
	+								*meshiagaru* ≈ *o-nomi ni naru*
		+							*o-nomi ni naru* ≈ *meshiagaru*
				+					*o-nomi nasaru* (archaic)
↓								+	*nom-areru*
Lowest									*nomu*

Table 20.12 *Honorific form of* i*-adjectives.*

I-adjectives			*Na*-adjectives		
Regular	Honorific	Gloss	Regular	Honorific	Gloss
takai	*o-takai*	expensive	*kenkō da*	*go-kenkō da*	healthy
utsukushii	*o-utsukushii*	beautiful	*kirei da*	*o-kirei da*	beautiful
wakai	*o-wakai*	young	*tassha da*	*o-tassha da*	hale
yasashii	*o-yasashii*	kind	*yūfuku da*	*go-yūfuku da*	affluent

Table 20.13 *Honorific form of nouns.*

Regular	Honorific	Gloss	Regular	Honorific	Gloss
dare	*donata*	who	*musume*	*o-jō-san*	daughter
kaisha	*kisha*	company	*namae*	*o-namae*	name
otto	*go-shujin*	husband	*aisha* (SJ)	*go-aisha*	favorite car
tsuma	*okusan*	wife	*chosho* (SJ)	*go-chosho*	authored book
kao	*o-kao*	face	*jibun* (SJ)	*go-jibun*	self
kodomo	*o-ko-san*	child	*jūsho* (SJ)	*go-jūsho*	address

(10) a. *Okada-san no o-jō-san wa bengoshi da.*
GEN daughter TOP lawyer COP.NPST
'Ms. Okada's daughter is a lawyer.'

b. *Okada-san wa go-jibun de kono hon o o-kaki ni natta.*
TOP self by this book ACC write.HON.PAST
'Ms. Okada wrote this book by herself.'

20.4 Humilifics

The honorific expressions described above exalt the subject referents; therefore, they are called **SUBJECT HONORIFICS**. It is also possible to show respect to a non-subject referent by demoting the subject referent. This type of expression is referred to by the term **HUMILIFICS**, **HUMBLE FORMS**, or **NON-SUBJECT HONORIFICS**. Because it is the shortest, *humilifics* is utilized by this book. Subject honorifics do not necessarily demote non-subject referents, but humilifics necessarily demote the subject referent. Therefore, humilifics are used mostly when the subject refers to the speaker him/herself or to a member of the speaker's in-group.

20.4.1 Verbs

A. **Humilific verbs**: Although there is only a handful of verbs of this type, they occur frequently in conversation. *Ukagau* is the humilific of both *iku* 'go' and *kiku* 'hear/listen'; *zonjiru/zonzuru* is the humilific for both *omou* 'think' and *shiru* 'know'. Other examples are provided in Table 20.14. In (11), the honored person is Ms. Okada, who is referred to by the dative NP (see Section 7.2) in (11a), but by the accusative NP in (11b).

(11) a. *Watashi* *wa* *ashita* *Okada-san* *ni* *o-me ni kakaru.*
I TOP tomorrow DAT meet.HUM.NPST
'I'll meet with Ms. Okada tomorrow.'

b. *Watashi* *wa* *Okada-san* *o* *zonji-te* *imasu.*
TOP ACC know.HUM-TE exist.POL.NPST
'I know Ms. Okada.'

B. ***O*-V *suru***: *O*-V (adverbial) plus *suru* is highly productive (see Table 20.15).

(12) *Watashi* *wa* *Okada-san* *kara* *hon* *o* *o-karishita.*
I TOP from book ACC borrow.HUM.PAST
'I borrowed a book from Ms. Okada.'

Table 20.14 *Humilific verbs.*

Regular	Humilific	Gloss	Regular	Humilific	Gloss
au	*o-me ni kakaru*	meet	*kiku*	*ukagau*	hear
iu/yuu	*mōshi-ageru*	say		*haichō suru*	listen
omou	*zonjiru*	think	*shiru*	*zonjiru*	know
morau	*itadaku*	receive	*yomu*	*haidoku suru*	read
	chōdai suru		*ageru*	*sashi-ageru*	give
iku	*ukagau*	go	*miru*	*haiken suru*	see

Table 20.15 O-*V* suru.

Regular	Honorific	Gloss	Regular	Honorific	Gloss
au	*o-ai suru*	meet	*yobu*	*o-yobi suru*	call
kaku	*o-kaki suru*	write	*tsureru*	*o-tsure suru*	take
kasu	*o-kashi suru*	lend	*kariru*	*o-kari suru*	borrow

Table 20.16 Go-*VN* suru.

Regular	Honorific	Gloss	Regular	Honorific	Gloss
annai suru	*go-annai suru*	guide	*kyōryoku suru*	*go-kyōryoku suru*	cooperate
hōkoku suru	*go-hōkoku suru*	report	*sōkin suru*	*go-sōkin suru*	send money
hōmon suru	*go-hōmon suru*	visit	*suisen suru*	*go-suisen suru*	recommend

Table 20.17 *Humilific form of nouns.*

Regular	Humilific	Gloss	Regular	Honorific	Gloss
an	*gu-an*	idea	*kaisha*	*heisha, shōsha*	company
chichioya	*chichi*	father	*musuko*	*gu-soku*	son (obsolete)
chosho	*set-cho*	authored book	*ocha*	*so-cha*	tea
hahaoya	*haha*	mother	*okurimono*	*so-shina*	gift
jitaku	*set-taku*	home	*tsuma*	*gu-sai*	wife (obsolete)

C. ***Go*-VN *suru***: With verbs containing a Sino-Japanese verbal noun, prefixing *go-* plus *suru* makes the verb humilific productive (see Table 20.16).

(13) *Watashi wa Okada-san o kenkyūjo ni go-annai shita.*
I TOP ACC research.center to guide.HUM.PAST
'I guided Ms. Okada to the research center.'

20.4.2 Nouns

Nouns also have humilific forms that are used almost exclusively in written language. Although not productive, humilific prefixes include *gu-* 'stupid', *setsu-* 'unskillfulness' (in Table 20.17 it is realized as *set-* due to a euphonic change), and *so-* 'inferior'.

(14) *O-chikaku* *ni* *okoshi* *no* *setsu* *wa,* *zehi*
near.HON to come.HON GEN occasion TOP by.all.means
set-taku *ni* *mo* *o-tachiyori* *kudasai.*
house.HUM to also stop.by.HON please
'When you come to this neighborhood, please stop by my house.'

20.5 Humilifics as addressee honorifics

Humilific expressions show respect to a non-subject referent by demoting the subject referent. However, four humilific verbs – *itasu* 'do', *mairu* 'go/come', *mōsu* 'say', and *oru* 'be/stay' – simultaneously show respect to the addressee as well. Therefore, in modern Japanese, they must be combined with the addressee honorific *masu* when occurring in a main clause. (In classical Japanese, they could occur without *masu* anywhere.) In subordinate or embedded clauses, they can occur without *masu* as in (15c).

(15) a. *Watashi* *ga* *itashi-masu.*
I NOM do.HUM-POL.NPST
'I'll do (it).'
b. *Watashi* *wa* *3-ji* *ni* *mairi-mashita.*
I TOP 3-o'clock at go.HUM-POL.PAST
'I went (there) at 3 o'clock.'
c. *Musume* *ga* *mōsu* *ni* *wa,* *hannin* *wa* *tsukamatta* *sō desu.*
daughter NOM say in TOP culprit TOP be.arrested I.hear
'According to what my daughter says, the culprit has been arrested.'

Humilifics are prohibited when the honored target referent is someone who is considered inappropriate to show respect to linguistically, e.g. the speaker's brother as in (16a); however, these four special humilific verbs can apply to such a person as in (16b) (Bunkachō 2007: 19).

(16) a. *Ashita* *[sensei/#otōto]* *no* *tokoro* *ni* *ukagai-masu.*
tomorrow [teacher/brother] GEN place to go.HUM-POL.NPST
'Tomorrow I'll go to (my) [teacher's/#brother's] house.'
b. *Ashita* *[sensei/otōto]* *no* *tokoro* *ni* *mairi-masu.*
tomorrow [teacher/brother] GEN place to go.HUM-POL.NPST
'Tomorrow I'll go to (my) [teacher's/brother's] house.'

This difference is due to the fact that *ukagau* in (16a) is a pure humilific, which necessarily exalts a non-subject referent, whereas *mairu* in (16b) is humilific *qua* addressee honorific. Moreover, these special humilifics can be used with non-human subjects.

(17) a. *Ma mo naku* *densha* *ga* *mairi-masu.*
soon train NOM come.HUM-POL.NPST
'A train will arrive soon.'
b. *Asoko* *ni* *inu* *ga* *ori-masu.*
over.there at dog NOM exist.HUM-POL.NPST
'There is a dog over there.'

20.6 Beautification

The honorific prefix *o-* can be used to show one's linguistic refinement, not only to show respect to the addressee or to the referent. This use of *o-* is called **BEAUTIFICATION**, which is different from the use of *o-* in referent honorifics (see Subsection 20.3.4). Some examples are provided in Table 20.18.

(18) a.	*Koko*	*ni*	*[Okada-san/#watashi]*	*no*	*o-namae*	*o*	*kaki-mashita.*
	here	at		GEN	name.HON	ACC	write-POL.PAST

'I've written [Ms. Okada's/#my] name here.'

b.	*Kore*	*wa*	*[Okada-san/watashi]*	*no*	*o-cha*	*desu*	*ka?*
	this	TOP		GEN	tea	COP.POL.NPST	INT

'Is this [Ms. Okada's/my] tea?'

In (18a), because *o-namae* 'name' is a referent honorific, it cannot be used for the speaker him/herself. By contrast, *o-cha* 'tea' in (18b) is a beautified noun, so it can be used when it belongs to oneself. Beautification is more frequently used by women than by men, and some beautified nouns are almost exclusively used by women or by workers in service industries, e.g. *o-bīru* 'beer', *o-daidokoro* 'kitchen', *o-hana* 'flower', *o-kaimono* 'shopping', *o-kōcha* 'black tea', *o-kusuri* 'a medicine', *o-seki* 'seat', *o-tabako* 'cigarette', *o-toire* 'rest room', *o-tomodachi* 'friend'.

20.7 Honorifics as an indication of refinement

Referent honorifics (HON) can be used independently of addressee honorifics (POL). For example, (19a) is in the polite style with a referent honorific [+HON, +POL]; (19b) is also in the polite style but without a referent honorific [−HON, +POL]; (19c) is in the plain style with a referent honorific [+HON, −POL]; (19d) is in the plain style without a referent honorific [−HON, −POL].[6]

(19) a.	*Tanaka-san*	*ga*	*irasshai-mashita.*	[+HON, +POL]	[polite style]
		NOM	come.HON-PAST.POL		

'Ms. Tanaka has arrived.'

b.	*Tanaka-san*	*ga*	*ki-mashita.*	[−HON, +POL]	[polite style]
		NOM	come-PAST.POL		
c.	*Tanaka-san*	*ga*	*irasshat-ta.*	[+HON, −POL]	[plain style]
		NOM	come.HON-PAST		
d.	*Tanaka-san*	*ga*	*ki-ta.*	[−HON, −POL]	[plain style]
		NOM	come-PAST		

[6] It is not the case that the polite style consists merely of an addition of an addressee honorific to the plain style as the examples in (19) might suggest. These two styles are governed by different discourse principles, and what can be acceptably articulated varies, depending on the style (Suzuki 1997). For example, one can say *Kore ageru* 'I'll give this to you' in the plain style, but expressing the same idea in the polite style, *Kore agemasu*, is customarily unacceptable because *ageru* is closer to the meaning of 'donate, bestow, make a present of' than 'to give' in English, i.e. someone who is well off gives/donates something to someone less fortunate (see Section 13.4). Its use, therefore, is inappropriate in polite conversation.

Table 20.18 *Beautified nouns.*

Plain	Honorific	Gloss	Regular	Honorific	Gloss
cha	*o-cha*	tea	*mizu*	*o-mizu*	water
kane	*o-kane*	money	*sake*	*o-sake*	alcohol
kome	*o-kome*	rice	*tera*	*o-tera*	temple

Today, linguistic politeness is considered a political behavior. In eighteenth- and nineteenth-century Western society, however, linguistic politeness was not correlated with a consideration for or deference shown toward other individuals (Watts 1992). *Politeness* meant *prudence*, inextricably linked to social class and sociopolitical power. Politeness was considered a manifestation of a high degree of mental cultivation, elegant refinement, polished manners, and good taste. It was used to enhance one's own social standing and to signal membership in a particular social class (Sell 1992).

This older sense of politeness must be acknowledged when considering honorifics in contemporary Japanese. For example, in (20), the addressee and the person referred to by the covert subject of the honorific verb *irassharu* 'come' are identical, yet the speaker uses only a referent honorific without an addressee honorific.

(20) *Ashita* *irassharu?*
tomorrow come.HON.NPST
'Will (you) come tomorrow?'

This seemingly inconsistent combination referring to the same individual is commonly associated with so-called women's language (Chapter 28). It indicates the affective stance of the speaker: she considers the addressee psychologically close, so no addressee honorific is used, but she nevertheless prefers to apply a referent honorific to display her linguistic refinement.[7]

[7] The opposite combination, *Ashita kimasu?*, i.e. with an addressee honorific but not with a referent honorific, does not have the same implication.

21 Politeness and honorifics II

21.1 Introduction

This chapter continues the discussion of the relationship between politeness and honorifics. It begins by introducing Brown and Levinson's highly influential politeness theory as well as the main objections to it, and then addresses three problems surrounding the theory when applied to the Japanese honorific system. At that point, I propose some modifications to enhance its analytical framework in addition to an alternative conceptualization of politeness.

Brown and Levinson (1978/1987) contend that speakers choose to manifest politeness to minimize the risk of incurring a **FACE-THREATENING ACT** (FTA). They posit two types of face as universal notions: negative and positive. **NEGATIVE FACE** is defined as "the want of every 'competent adult member' that his actions be unimpeded by others," and **POSITIVE FACE** as "the want of every member that his wants be desirable to at least some others" (p. 62). Orders and requests, for instance, are inherently intrusive and, therefore, they potentially threaten the addressee's negative face, whereas disapproval and criticism are unfavorable reactions to the addressee's ideas or deeds and, consequently, are likely to threaten the addressee's positive face.

Brown and Levinson propose five politeness strategies: (i) not to do an FTA; (ii) to go off the record (i.e. giving only a hint); (iii) to use negative politeness ($\approx$ showing deference); (iv) to use positive politeness ($\approx$ appealing to intimacy, friendliness, and/or camaraderie); and (v) to do an FTA without redressive action (i.e. to say straightforwardly what one wants to accomplish). Based upon the social distance between speaker and addressee, the relative power difference between them, and the rank of imposition intrinsic to the FTA itself in a particular culture, the speaker chooses one of these options according to his/her calculation of the seriousness of the FTA. The riskier the FTA, the lower the number of the politeness strategy the speaker tends to employ (see Figure 21.1).

To illustrate how their theory works, consider a situation in which you want a pay raise. If you think that requesting it could possibly result in dismissal, you might refrain from pursuing what may well be a risky act. In other words,

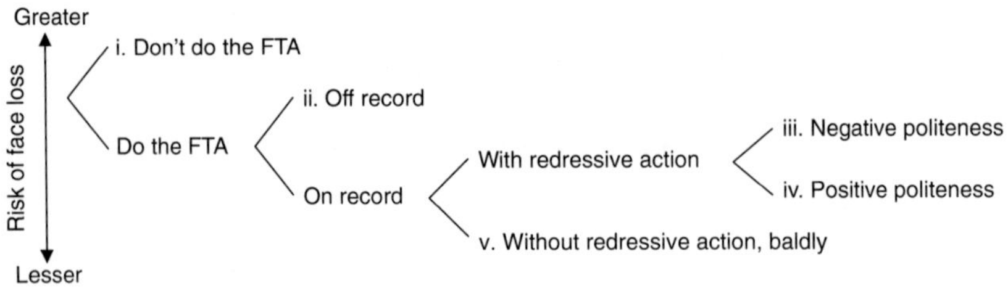

Figure 21.1. Strategies for doing FTAs.

you select Strategy (i), not to do an FTA. However, if you decide to take this path, you are unlikely to have your wish met. Other examples in Japanese are provided in (1).

(1) ii. Off-the-record strategy [intention: pay-raise request]
Sumimasen ga, watashi wa koko 3-nen shōkyū ga
sorry but I TOP this 3-years pay.raise NOM
nain desu ga
not COP.POL.NPST but
'I'm sorry, but I haven't received a pay rise in three years.'

iii. Utilize negative politeness
Anō konna koto o iu no wa totemo kokoro-gurushii
well this.kind thing ACC say NMLZ TOP very heart-painful
no desu ga, kyūryō o sukoshi age-te
NMLZ COP.POL.NPST but wage ACC a.little raise-TE
itadake-masen deshō ka?
receive-not.POL COP.POL.CNJ INT
'I'm awfully sorry to say this, but may I have a small pay rise?'

iv. Utilize positive politeness
Nē shachō, motto ganbaru kara, kyūryō chotto age-te yo.
hey boss more make.effort because wage a.little raise-TE SFP
'Uh, Chief, I'll make more of an effort, so raise my salary, please.'

v. Do an FTA without redressive action
Oi, kyūryō age-ro yo.
hey wage raise-IMP SFP
'Hey, raise my salary.'

In (1ii), the speaker does not assert that s/he wants a pay rise, but merely implies it by giving a reason, viz. not having received any raise in three years. Because the utterance does not carry the illocutionary force of request (see Section 19.1), the addressee can take it at face value and respond *I'm sorry to hear that* and do nothing. That is, the speaker might end up with failing to obtain a pay rise. On the other hand, if the situation turns tense, the speaker can defuse it by indicating that a pay rise was not exactly what s/he intended to convey. In (1iii), the speaker explicitly requests a pay rise, but softens (redresses) it by acknowledging the addressee's negative face, i.e. the want of his/her action unimpeded by others. (1iv) is also an explicit request, but emphatically acknowledges the addressee's positive face. In a small company, for instance, where the owner and employees are working closely together like a family, emphasizing this closeness *qua* openness can mitigate the degree of face threat. (1v) exhibits such openness one step farther. If the speaker is helping his/her friend's business prosper, this utterance might be appropriate and effective.

Brown and Levinson's approach is extremely insightful for investigating nebulous politeness phenomena in the world's languages, and, consequently, it has influenced virtually all research on politeness and related topics since its publication. The inclusion of positive politeness is particularly noteworthy because in ordinary language, politeness is conceived of as the opposite of intimacy, friendliness, or camaraderie. However, when politeness is interpreted as consideration for the addressee's face wants, the latter should also be included in human polite behaviors.

21.2 Objections to Brown and Levinson's theory

The inadequacy of Brown and Levinson's theory in accounting for Japanese politeness phenomena has for decades instigated intense debate. Ide (1982, 1989), for example, forthrightly criticizes their theory for dealing exclusively with politeness as a strategic move to minimize the impact of an FTA while totally neglecting what she claims are socially obligatory linguistic choices. She contends that the purpose in using honorifics is not exclusively to save face, because honorifics occur even when no FTA is involved. Consider, for example, (2), the content of which is unlikely to be face threatening; nevertheless, the addressee honorific is utilized:

(2) *Chikyū* *wa* *marui* *desu.*
earth TOP round COP.POL.NPST
'The earth is round.'

Ide uses the term **VOLITION** to refer to the strategically motivated practice of politeness and **DISCERNMENT** (**WAKIMAE**) for polite behavior that conforms to the culturally prescribed norm, which is "independent of the speaker's rational intention" (Ide 1989: 242). For her, volition-based politeness serves to save face, in accordance with Brown and Levinson, but discernment-based politeness is like a grammatical requirement, forming a socio-pragmatic concordance system. Therefore, Ide argues, Brown and Levinson's model, which deals only with one aspect of the politeness phenomena, is incomplete. She further argues that volition-based politeness prevails in Western societies while discernment does so in Japanese society.

To test this claim experimentally, Ide *et al.* (1992) investigated Japanese and American notions of politeness, asking their Japanese and American participants to associate ten adjectives with the most appropriate scene from fourteen interactional situations. The results suggested that the Americans tended to equate *polite* with *friendly* whereas the Japanese did not because they judged *teineina* (usually translated as 'polite') and *shitashigena* 'friendly' as categorically distinct. Ide *et al.* offer these findings as evidence supporting their claim that notions of politeness differ in American and Japanese cultures.

21.3 Counter-arguments to Ide's theory

Fukada and Asato (2004) effectively refute Ide's idea of discernment-based politeness as equivalent to grammatical concordance by demonstrating that discernment is not obligatory in the same sense that a grammatical feature such as concordance is. In a depiction of a person's dishonorable act, they show that the use of honorifics is inappropriate even when the person is in a position customarily deserving of honorifics, and offer, as evidence, the following sentence:

(3) ??*Sensei* *ga* *dōkyūsei* *o* *gōkan* *nasatta*
Teacher NOM classmate ACC assault do.HON.PAST
'My teacher assaulted [honorific] my classmate.'

Fukada and Asato further argue that Brown and Levinson's model can adequately account for Japanese politeness phenomena if one acknowledges that Japan is principally a vertical as well as hierarchical society.[1] That is, power and distance in Brown and Levinson's weightiness formula for measuring the seriousness of an FTA receive markedly high values, and thus the overall significance of an FTA is inevitably elevated regardless of the severity of imposition intrinsic to the FTA itself. This is why, they assert, honorifics are used even in non-FTA utterances. For this and other reasons, Fukada and Asato argue that Brown and Levinson's theory is superior to Ide's, and, consequently, there is no need to posit a separate politeness category such as discernment.

Another problem with Ide's dual category account is pointed out by Eelen (2001), who argues that Ide, like most other researchers in the field, assumes impoliteness to be the lack of politeness. Consequently, if an ability to use honorifics were like grammatical competence, impoliteness would have no place in Japanese society. That is, if one failed to use honorifics properly, it should then be taken as an indication of socio-pragmatic incompetence, rather than as deliberate impoliteness, which, of course, is not always the case.

[1] Japanese society is often characterized as *hierarchical*. This involves vertical stratification by an institution or group of institutions, rather than horizontal stratification by class or caste; each group is vertically organized based on the relationships between paternalistic superiors and their subordinates (Nakane 1970).

21.4 Honorifics and politeness

Many aspects of Ide's objection to Brown and Levinson's conceptualization of linguistic politeness as a universal notion appear refutable. Nevertheless, it is worth considering a further investigation of honorific language as fossilized and grammaticized politeness in relation to Brown and Levinson's modern, open-ended politeness strategies.

As explained in Section 20.1, the Japanese honorific system consists of two orthogonal dimensions: addressee honorifics (polite style vis-à-vis plain style) and referent honorifics. While Ide essentially equates Japanese linguistic politeness with the polite style, many researchers have pointed out that the polite style cannot always be equated with polite intention of the speaker towards the addressee; see, for example, Ikuta (1983), Maynard (1991), Okamoto (1997), Pizziconi (2003), and Cook (2006). Honorifics can sometimes also be interpreted as unfriendly, standoffish, haughty, or rejecting. Nevertheless, it is crucial to note that, in Japanese, *deference cannot be expressed without employing the polite style*. For example, *Dare da* 'Who are you?' (plain style) cannot convey the speaker's intention of deference in any circumstance. This fact would indirectly support Ide's (1991: 64) contention that "[f]or the Japanese people, linguistic politeness is mainly a matter of conforming to social conventions for a choice of linguistic forms," although the reality is far more complex than she suggests.

Ikuta (1983: 37) proposes that the basic meaning of the polite style involves neither *politeness* nor *formality*, but rather *distance* that may be social or attitudinal.[2] However, analyzing the polite style as directly motivated by distancing is unsatisfactory for the following reason. Addressee honorifics in Japanese are normally employed when the speaker considers the addressee psychologically distant and/or the speaker wishes to show deference to the addressee.[3] As a result, addressees are dichotomized linguistically into (i) distant and exalted (i.e. shown deference to), and (ii) intimate and not exalted. (Other factors are also involved in the selection of the speech style, e.g. the mode of communication and the degree of formality of the speech situation.) For (i), the norm is the use of the polite style; for (ii), it is the plain style. In situation (B) in Table 21.1, where the speaker considers the addressee psychologically distant but exaltation superfluous, the plain style is normally used, and the speech may sound vulgar or impolite, as in *Dare da* 'Who are you?'

[2] Ikuta also posits the notion of cohesional (or textual) distance, an indication of coherence and the hierarchical positioning of utterances in discourse. Although insightful, this part of her analysis is not directly relevant to the present discussion, and will therefore not be discussed further.

[3] Usami (1995: 31) reports that in her conversation data of nine Japanese speakers unfamiliar with each other, 93.9% of the utterances are in the polite style.

Table 21.1 *Dichotomy of addressees.*

Addressee	Intimate	Distant
Exalted	(A)	(i) Polite style
Not exalted	(ii) Plain style	(B) Plain style

and *Hairu na* 'Don't enter!' (The situation labeled (A) is problematic and will be discussed in Section 21.6.)

As Table 21.1 shows, the notion of distance can be expressed by either the polite or plain style. Therefore, Ikuta's claim that the basic function of addressee honorifics is simply to indicate the speaker's conception of distance is not adequate to explain their use.

21.5 Problems with Brown and Levinson's theory

21.5.1 Combining positive and negative politeness

Japanese honorifics, and possibly honorifics in most languages, conflate notions of distance and deference. They are used when addressing an unfamiliar person based on psychological distance, or in the case of an addressee of a higher social ranking to show deference. While the exhibition of deference is undoubtedly relevant to the central meaning of politeness, distancing is not inherently a polite behavior. Distancing can nevertheless be combined with deference to effectively enhance the speaker's politeness.

When interpreted as a reflection of polite intent, distancing (avoidance of intrusion into the addressee's space) can properly be categorized as a negative politeness strategy. However, giving deference is problematic. Brown and Levinson generally associate deference with negative politeness, but they also acknowledge that it satisfies an addressee's positive want to be treated as superior. In fact, when honorifics are not utilized as the addressee anticipates, it is the addressee's positive face that is damaged. If distancing indicates negative politeness but showing deference indicates positive politeness, then the use of honorific language necessarily mixes both strategies, thus rendering Brown and Levinson's theory inadequate in accounting for honorifics.

21.5.2 One strategy per FTA

In relation to the above, a second problem that arises with Brown and Levinson's theory involves the split between positive and negative politeness along a single dimension and on a per-FTA basis. Recall their ranking of the politeness strategies: (i) not to do an FTA; (ii) to go off the record; (iii) to use negative politeness; (iv) to use positive politeness; and (v) to do an FTA without redressive action. According to them, the riskier the FTA, the lower the strategy the speaker tends to select.

However, when honorifics are available in the language, positive and negative politeness strategies are frequently, even routinely, implemented in tandem. For example, the **PRE-SEQUENCES**[4] of making a request in the following utterances demonstrate the use of positive politeness in form and negative politeness in content, as in (4), and the reverse, as in (5).

(4) *Aki-chan, itsumo itsumo tanon-de bakkari de gomen ne. Demo*
always request-TE only sorry SFP but
kōyū kotot-te Aki-chan igai, chotto tanomenain da
this.kind.of thing-QUOT other-than a.little cannot.request COP
yonē. Sorede, . . .
SFP so
'Aki, I'm so sorry to ask you for favors all the time, but there's no one else. So . . .'

(5) *Kondo no kōshō wa, nankō ga yosoku sarerun*
this.time GEN negotiation TOP difficulty NOM can.be.anticipated
desu yo-ne. Sokode, yūben de, katsu, kado ga tatanai kata
COP SFP then eloquent and inoffensive person
to naru to, yahari Kōriyama-san de wa nai ka to . . .
if as-expected COP.TE TOP not INT QUOT
'We anticipate problems with our next negotiation. So, we need someone who will not offend while being effective. So, as you know, it ought to be Koriyama-san . . .'

In the first sentence in (4), the use of the plain form as well as the hypocoristic (i.e. a term of endearment) suffix *-chan* indicate the speaker's desire to display positive politeness (here, intimacy). By contrast, the semantic content indicates negative politeness, viz. apologizing for intrusion. In (5), the use of verbal honorifics and *kata* 'person' (an honorific variation) indicate negative politeness (i.e. deference), but the content aims at positive politeness, viz. praising Koriyama's tactfulness.

Mixing positive and negative politeness strategies is quite normal in Japanese. This fact raises a serious question regarding the fundamental conceptualization of Brown and Levinson's positive and negative politeness strategies, i.e. regarding positive and negative politeness as mutually exclusive concepts. This appears to be unjustifiable because there is no intrinsic reason for a speaker to appeal to only one facet of the addressee's face wants.

Brown and Levinson themselves acknowledge this problem, aware that their strategies can be mixed in discourse, providing as examples positive politeness markers embedded within negative politeness strategies as well as indirect requests or going off-the-record in positive politeness utterances

[4] A pre-sequence is a sequence of verbal exchanges preliminary to the main speech act (Chapter 19) aimed at obtaining the addressee's cooperation, e.g. *May I ask you a question?* before actually questioning.

(p. 17). Their defense consists of pointing out that a segment of talk might contain FTAs with different levels of intrinsic imposition (abbreviated as R), which, in turn, motivate multiple strategies. They also caution that hint-like utterances might actually be on the record if there is no ambiguity or vagueness of their interpretation in particular contexts. Further, they argue as follows:

> [O]ne possible source of confusion here is this: when describing positive politeness . . . we included the use of "markers" of social closeness, like intimate address forms; and when describing negative politeness . . . we included the use of "markers" of deference like honorifics. Now, although address forms and honorifics may . . . be FTA-sensitive- . . . on the whole such elements are tied relatively directly to the social relationship between speaker and addressee. The consequence of such direct "markers" of social relationship is that they may occur with an FTA of any R-value, and thus equally with markers of positive and negative politeness; if shifts are permissible at all, we should merely expect a shift towards a more "formal" address form than normally used . . . when R-values increase between the same interlocutors. Thus, certain aspects of, for example, positive politeness like "intimate" address forms may happily occur in off-record usages motivated by high R factors. What we did not expect, and have not found, is that there might be a shift to more "intimate" address forms with an increase in R (p. 18).

Brown and Levinson insist that the speaker must select one and only one strategy per FTA from their ranked strategies. They assert that in order to refute their one-dimensional and mutually exclusive ranking of strategies, one needs to show that an opposing ranking is possible.

> Despite the various deviations from our expected hierarchy that have emerged from some of these experimental tests, no one (to our knowledge) has come up with clear evidence of a counter-ranking: where (for example) positive politeness is used for greater FTAs, negative politeness for smaller ones, or where off record is used for smaller FTAs (or to lower-status Hs [hearers]) than negative or positive politeness (p. 20).

Genuine counter-examples do in fact exist.

(6) [A response to the survey question on how to call one's mother][5]

Ima	*demo*	*sō*	*desu*	*keredo,*	*"okāsan"*	*desu.*	*Okane*
now	even	same	COP.POL.NPST	but	mother	COP.POL.NPST	money
o	*nedaru*	*toki*	*dake,*	*"X-chan"*	*to*	*yobi-masu.*	
ACC	beg	when	only		QUOT	call-POL.NPST	

'I still call her *okāsan* ('mother'). But when I ask her for money, I call her *X-chan*.'

For the sake of this discussion, let us assume that the respondent in (6) is a male and his mother's name is Michiko. He usually (i.e. for FTAs with a lower R) addresses his mother as *okāsan*, but when he asks her for money

5 http://matsuri.site.ne.jp/taro/taro106.htm.

(a higher R), he calls her *Michiko-chan*, which is a less formal and a more intimate address form than *okāsan*. It is significant that this positively marked address term with *-chan* – rather than a negatively marked (i.e. distancing) address term, e.g. *-sama*, which is also possible as Brown and Levinson predict – can be used here when a higher R is involved. I argue that Brown and Levinson's one-dimensional and mutually exclusive ranking of strategies is untenable because there is no *a priori* reason to assume one strategy per FTA.

21.5.3 Risk avoidance as the sole motivation for politeness

Because politeness is a complex phenomenon, positing minimization of the risk of an FTA as the sole reason for striving to be polite appears to be an oversimplification. As a language user, I may apply a politeness strategy driven by affection, particularly when I select a positive-politeness strategy as occurs in (7).

(7) [To a person who recently lost her spouse]

Hontō ni	*o-tsurai*	*koto*	*de gozaimashita*	*nē.*	*Demo,*	*dōzo*	*o-ki*
really	difficult.HON	think	COP.POL.PAST	SFP	but	please	spirit

o	*shikkari*	*o-mochi ni nat-te,*	*ganbatte kudasaimase.*
ACC	firmly	have.HON-TE	be.persistent.HON.POL

'It must be really difficult (for you), but please keep your spirits up.'

When someone makes a statement like this, s/he is likely overwhelmed by a devastating situation and is trying to express his/her sympathy towards and for the addressee. Minimizing the potential risk of the FTA would be the least concern in such a situation.

21.6 Reconciling Brown and Levinson's theory and Japanese politeness

I have pointed out that Brown and Levinson's theory encounters three problems when applied to Japanese politeness phenomena. First, identifying the use of honorifics categorically with negative politeness is untenable because honorifics typically indicate both distance and deference. While distancing can properly be considered a negative politeness strategy, showing deference satisfies the addressee's positive face want. Second, dichotomizing positive and negative politeness as mutually exclusive concepts is unjustifiable because there is no inherent reason for the speaker to appeal to only one facet of the addressee's face wants. Third, positing minimization of the impact of an FTA as the sole motivation for politeness is simplistic as well as counter-intuitive; positive politeness can naturally be triggered by affection. The following subsections consider three approaches that appear to be useful in reconciling these problems.

21.6.1 *Robin Lakoff's theory*

Robin Lakoff's (1973, 1990) theory of politeness regards polite behavior as attempts to make the addressee feel good. She posits three rules for accomplishing this goal: (a) don't impose, remain aloof (distance); (b) give options (deference); (c) make the addressee feel good by being friendly (camaraderie). Her theory captures the insight that while distance and camaraderie are mutually contradictory by nature, distance and deference are not, nor are deference and camaraderie.

In this framework, the use of honorifics can be regarded as triggered by either the distance rule or by the deference rule. Therefore, utterance (4) above can be analyzed in such a way that its form signals the speaker's observation of the camaraderie rule, whereas its content signals the deference rule. In (5), the form signals the deference rule, and the content signals the camaraderie rule.

In this way, the dichotomy of mutually exclusive positive and negative politeness strategies, which cannot satisfactorily accommodate honorifics, can be avoided. In adopting Lakoff's theory, however, the term *camaraderie* needs to be extended to *intimacy*, for the former strongly evokes the notion of rapport among friends. Recall that *politeness* and *friendliness* are well correlated in American culture, but the Japanese concepts *teineina* and *shitashigena* are distinct and frequently contradictory (Section 21:2). The term *intimacy*, on the other hand, does not have to be limited to rapport among equals. Developing Lakoff's idea further may lead to a meaningful cross-cultural comparison that Brown and Levinson's theory fails to facilitate.

21.6.2 *Honorifics as a different politeness mode*

Can honorifics be considered as a different politeness mode, that is, one that is neutral with respect to Brown and Levinson's open-ended negative and positive politeness strategies? If so, honorifics can be employed independently of positive or negative politeness strategies. Brown and Levinson allude to this possibility in the quotation in Subsection 21.5.2 above, where they assert that honorifics are associated more directly and tied more strongly to the social relationship of interlocutors, and, therefore, are more stable and less sensitive to R values.

This remedy is superficially identical with Ide's proposal of separating volition-based and discernment-based politeness. However, their psychological underpinnings are quite different. Ide considers that these two types of politeness are triggered by different motivations: volition politeness is used strategically to minimize the impact of an FTA while discernment politeness is used to show one's willingness to conform to the culturally prescribed norm. By contrast, Brown and Levinson would argue that both are motivated by the same principle, viz. the speaker's desire to minimize the risk of an FTA. These two are certainly legitimate arguments and merit further scrutiny.

21.6.3 Modifying Brown and Levinson's theory

I contend that Brown and Levinson's claim regarding negative and positive face is universally valid. However, attributing all senses of politeness to a single motivation, i.e. minimizing the risk of an FTA, is unwarranted parsimony.

Furthermore, allowing one and only one strategy per FTA from their ranking is an unreasonable restriction. All competent language users have both negative and positive faces. However, we are also aware that being totally free of impediment from other people hinders attainment of positive face. Therefore, people somehow balance these competing wants. Given this, it is more natural to assume that speakers consider both types of addressees' desires together. Consequently, if there are linguistic resources available to perform negative *and* positive politeness simultaneously, it is logical to combine the two.

I hypothesize that at the beginning of a conversation, the speaker considers heuristically the addressee's as well as his/her own positive and negative face wants and the degree to which such wants should be attended based on affection towards the addressee, the speaker's own desire regarding how to present him/herself, what the social norm for the particular situation is, and the potential risk of the FTA, if any. Such decision-making concerning overall politeness can be fairly stable for the length of the conversation, or the speaker can modify it during the conversation.

The speaker next needs to determine how to express his/her decision about the desirable degree of linguistic politeness, during which Brown and Levinson's positive and negative politeness strategies become relevant. Here, the speaker's linguistic sophistication as well as social and regional standards undoubtedly come into play. While the speaker may have various concerns, s/he must plan his/her utterance to manifest some of them while hiding others.

The situation represented in (7) is close to the maximum in both negative and positive politeness.

(8)
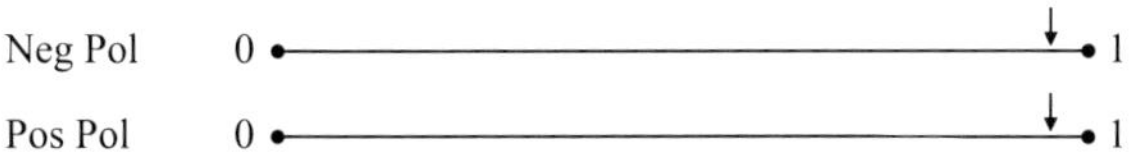

On the other hand, if one is indifferent to politeness, positive politeness will be at a minimum, although negative politeness might vary, attributable mainly to the speaker's self-image. Some persons do not mind being boorish, e.g. (9a), while others prefer to maintain a certain level of linguistic politeness in order to represent themselves as refined persons and/or because they may have found that in social intercourse civility is frequently more effective, as illustrated in (9b).

(9) a. *Urusai!* *Dete ike!*
noisy get.out.IMP
'Shut up! Get out!'

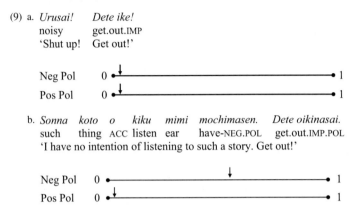

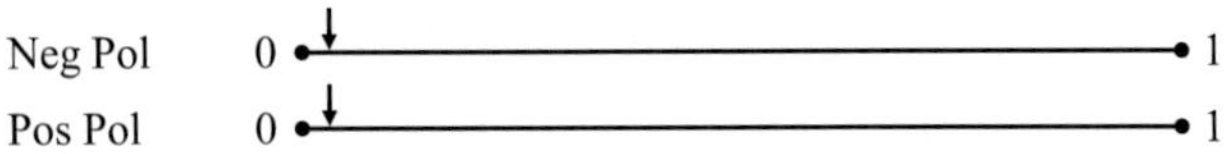

b. *Sonna koto o kiku mimi mochimasen. Dete oikinasai.*
such thing ACC listen ear have-NEG.POL get.out.IMP.POL
'I have no intention of listening to such a story. Get out!'

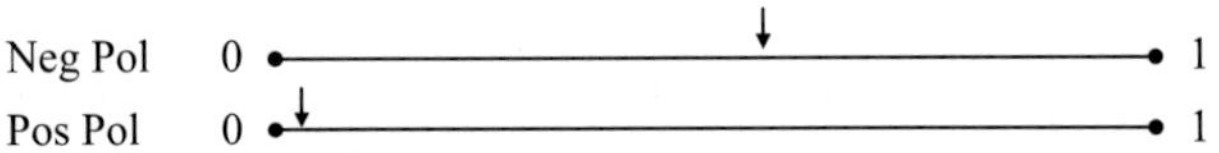

Regarding the relationship of honorifics to the use of their politeness strategies, Brown and Levinson point out that in Tamil (a language spoken in southern India and northeastern Sri Lanka), some direct requests of low R-value coming from subordinates to superordinates may occur if such requests are mitigated with appropriate honorifics. This might suggest that in some languages, politeness might be carried more by honorifics and less by matters of open-ended politeness strategies. However, Brown and Levinson conclude that this inference is not generally correct; they concur that there is not "a certain quantity of politeness to be conveyed by one channel (the grammaticized honorifics) or another (strategic language use) – politeness is usually redundantly expressed in both" (p. 25). What I propose is very different from what Brown and Levinson describe: that is, negative and positive politeness strategies should be considered separately, and can be used simultaneously, contrary to Brown and Levinson's strategy ranking.

These three approaches are not necessarily incompatible with each other. They may provide valid accounts for some aspects of politeness, while being inadequate for others. A highly complex phenomenon, linguistic politeness can naturally be expected to reflect different kinds of motivation, and its linguistic realizations can, therefore, vary considerably.

To conclude this chapter, I have pointed out that, as it stands, Brown and Levinson's universal theory of politeness cannot satisfactorily account for Japanese politeness phenomena, which heavily incorporate and depend upon the use of honorifics. I consider Ide's objections to their theory to be significant, but I do not agree that politeness has two separate components of volition and discernment. Rather, what needs reevaluation in Brown and Levinson's theory are the concepts of negative and positive strategies. They contend that negative and positive politeness are mutually exclusive, and that the speaker must select one, and only one, strategy for each FTA. However, because these strategies take into account the two types of face that people constantly maintain, they must not be ranked linearly and exclusively. I claim that, whenever resources are available, the speaker is sufficiently rational to make simultaneous use of both strategies. Furthermore, Japanese honorifics have grammaticized negative politeness (distancing) and positive politeness (showing deference) simultaneously. This fact supports my contention that these two strategies are not mutually exclusive.

22 Speech style shift

22.1 Introduction

Selection between the plain and polite speech styles not only *reflects* interlocutors' social relationships but also *constructs* them. Thus, linguistic interaction style is dynamic vis-à-vis the shifting and evolving of the interlocutors' relationships. For example, it is commonly observed that interlocutors who are unfamiliar with each other begin their conversation with the polite style, and, as they become familiar, switch to the plain style. Conversely, familiar interlocutors habitually use the plain style, but when the conversational topic becomes grave (e.g. a serious disputes, a death), they may switch to the polite style.

Although speech styles can shift back and forth even during a single span of conversation, such shifts are by no means arbitrarily made. In Japanese, a style shift is normally initiated by the superior interlocutor (Matsumura and Chinami 1998),[1] and when an interlocutor of a lower rank initiates a shift instead, different strategies are required (Neustupný 1982). This chapter introduces several previously proposed analyses of speech style shift, and is followed by my analysis of one of its most prominent functions, viz. simultaneous expression of deference and intimacy towards the addressee.

22.2 Affective distance

Ikuta (1983) points out that previously proposed analyses, which claim the polite style to be an indication of politeness or formality, are inadequate because they cannot account for speech style shifts in a conversation in which the social and situational conditions remain constant. Instead, she characterizes the basic function of the polite style metaphorically to be distancing (see Section 21.4): speech styles are selected to express whether the speaker considers the addressee close (plain style) or distant (polite style). She

[1] Interlocutors' relative statuses are normally determined in Japanese culture by their prescribed social roles and/or age.

contends that the dominant speech style is determined by the interlocutors' social relationship at the start of their conversation. As the conversation unfolds, style shifts will take place, reflecting the speaker's empathy with the addressee at that particular moment of speaking. She makes the generalization that empathy is expected when the speaker shows strong agreement, positively evaluates a preceding statement made by the addressee, or is admiring the addressee. For example, in the following conversation between two female interlocutors, the polite style is utilized in the first two utterances, but the third is in the plain style when K complements J's statement.[2]

(1) K: *Sono oheya wa koshitsu ni natte irun desu ka?*
that room TOP private.room made.as COP.POL.NPST INT
'Is that apartment designed for a single person?'
J: *Ē, rokujō to yojōhan to sanrūmu ga taihen hiroin desu no.*
yes 6-mat and 4.5-mat and sunroom NOM very spacious COP.POL.NPST SFP
'Yes, there is a six-mat (tatami) room, a four-and-a-half mat room, and a sunroom, which is very spacious.'
→ K: *Mā, zuibun ii no ne.* [plain style]
oh really good NMLZ SFP
'Oh, that's very nice.'

On the other hand, Ikuta contends, empathy is avoided (i.e. distancing is preferred) when the topic is a very private or sensitive matter. The utterances preceding (2) were in the plain style, for the interlocutors had become relaxed and frank. Then, K switched back to the polite style, using *Shitsurei desu kedo* 'Excuse me, but'.

(2) K: *Shitsurei desu kedo* [polite style], *Jō-san wa zutto dokushin de irassharu no?*[3] [plain style]
impolite COP.POL.NPST but TOP always single COP.HON.NPST SFP
'Excuse me, but have you always been single?'
J: *Īe, ano ne, nido oyome ni itta no.* [plain style]
no INTJ twice married SFP
'No, I have been married twice.'
K: *Ara, sō nan desu ka?* [polite style]
INTJ so COP.POL.NPST INT
'Oh, is that so.'

Ikuta explains that asking a person about highly personal topics such as her marital history is a delicate matter, so K employs the polite style as the ritual

[2] This conversation is between Tetsuko KUROYANAGI, a well-known female TV interviewer and her guest Natsuko JŌ, a professional writer in her seventies, older than Kuroyanagi.
[3] *De irassharu no?* in (2) exhibits the [+HON, −POL] strategy for the same individual, discussed in Section 20:7.

required before embarking on such a question. The rest of the utterance by K is in the plain style, which could have also been in the polite style: i.e. *zutto dokushin de irassharun desu ka?* 'Have you always been single?' Ikuta believes that maintaining the polite style (i.e. distancing) throughout this utterance would have made J more reluctant to speak without reserve, and that emphasizing closeness works better in this case.

While Ikuta's work is a significant contribution to our understanding of the speech style shift, some inaccuracies are readily observable. Contrary to Ikuta's claim, positive remarks in the plain style are not always appropriate when the speaker wants to show deference toward the addressee. For example, use of the addressee-oriented particle *yo* (see Section 23.3) is not acceptable in (3a), whereas its non-use in (3b) is. Ikuta's analysis is unable to account for this difference; this topic will be discussed further in Section 22:6.

(3) a. *Wā, tottemo niau yo.*
wow very suit SFP
'Wow, that suits (you) very well!'
b. *Wā, tottemo niau!*

22.3 Social roles

Analyzing the conversations of elementary school third graders, Okamoto (1997) reports that the use of the polite style is indicative of a speaker's *social identity*, the statements made in this style being representative of one's role as either a teacher or a student. The use of the plain style, on the other hand, conveys the meaning that statements are those of a private person, and do not reflect one's prescribed social role. In (4), the students were instructed to underline in their textbooks passages that explain why a girl from Tōkyō and her classmates in a rural school started fighting as well as those that explain the girl's feelings at that time. The teacher then speaks as follows:

(4) *Hai, dewa, empitsu oite kudasāi. Sorede, mada kakete nakutemo,*
ok then pencil please.put.down and yet if.not.finished.writing
tochū de ki ga tsuitara ne, happyō sureba iin desu kara
midway if.notice INTJ presentation if.do ok COP.POL.NPST because
ne. Ii desu ka?
SFP ok COP.POL.NPST INT
'Well, then, please put down your pencils. And if you haven't finished underlining, that's okay. If you notice (something), you can say it at that point. Okay?'
Hai, jā, mazu ne, sen o hippatta tokoro kara happyō shite
ok then first INTJ line ACC drew place from present
moraimāsu. Hai, jā, sen hippatta hito, te o agete kudasāi.
receive ok then line drew person hand ACC please.raise
'Well, first, please recite from the places you underlined. Ok, those of you who have underlined something, please raise your hands.'
→ [After wiping her perspiration] *Atsusa ni makezu ni gambarō ne.*
heat DAT not.being.defeated be.persistent SFP
'Let's not let the heat get (the better of) us!'

Hai, *jā,* *Miya Yutaka-san,* *onegai shimāsu.*
ok then please.do
'All right, MIYA Yutaka-san, please (tell us your results).'

In (4), the teacher's utterances are all in the polite style, except for the marked sentence, which should be taken as her personal and friendly encouragement, rather than as a routine classroom direction.

In (5), Yoshie IKUMA (Y), a female student, misreads the word *tori-musubu* 'to act as a go-between' as *musubu* 'to tie'. This error is corrected by a male classmate, Kazuhiro (K). The marked line in the teacher's utterance (T) employs a plain style to convey the fact that her utterance is intended only for Kazuhiro, not for the entire class.

(5) Y: *Hai,* *watashi* *wa* *"musunde kureta no desu"* *to iu* *tokoro* *ni* *sen*
ok I TOP "they tied it" QUOT place at line
o *hikimashita.*
ACC drew.POL
'Okay, I underlined "they tied it."'
T: *"Musunde kureta"* *no* *to-,* *tokoro* *desu* *ka?*
"they tied it" GEN place COP.POL.NPST INT
'You underlined "they tied it"?'
Y: *Hai.*
'Yes.'
K: [In background] *Tori-musubu,* *tori-musubu.*
go-between
'To act as a go-between, go-between.'
→ T: *N,* *chotto,* *n?* *Kazuhiro-kun,* *mō* *ichido* *it-te* *agete,* *ima*
um a.little um more once say-TE give-TE now
itta *tokoro.*
said place
'Um, well, Kazuhiro-kun, tell (Ikuma-san) again what you just said.'
K: *Ikuma-san* *ga* *itta* *koto* *wa,* *tabun* *"tori-musubu"* *no* *koto*
NOM said thing TOP probably "go-between" GEN thing
de *wa* *ari-masen* *ka?*
COP.TE TOP is-not.POL INT
'Didn't you mean "to act as a go-between," Ikuma-san?'
Y: *Hai,* *sō* *dēsu.*
yes so COP.POL.NPST
'Yes, that's right.'

Cook (2008) came to a similar conclusion to Okamoto concerning the social function of language by analyzing speech style shifts used by parents when speaking to their children. Consider, for example, the interaction in (6) among a father (F), a mother (M), and a two-year-old girl (C), with a slightly modified description derived from Cook (2008: 54).

(6) C: [Picks up a noodle from her bowl with her left hand and holds it up toward F.]
F: *Tōsan* *iranai.* [Turns away his hand.]
father need.not
'I don't want it.'

C: [Brings her left hand toward M.]
M: [Pretends to take a bite of the noodle.]
C: [Quickly puts the noodle in M's mouth, then takes it out and holds it out to F again.]

→ F: *Naaaa. Ippen kuchi ni ireta mono iri-masen.*
once mouth in put.in thing need-POL.NEG.NPST
'I don't want something that has already been in someone else's mouth.'

Cook contends that the use of the polite form here indicates a self-presentational stance, displaying one's positive social role to other individuals (i.e. *shisei o tadasu* 'to hold oneself up' or *kichin to suru* 'to do something neatly') (p. 46). By implication, such usage is extended to and highlighted in out-group contexts, where polite behavior is expected. By contrast, in the in-group context (e.g. within the family), a display of the self-presentational stance foregrounds a speaker's social identity in relation to group responsibilities (pp. 47–48). Therefore, parents tend to switch from the plain to the polite form when teaching children, doing household chores, and cooking and serving food in their children's presence. As part of the socialization process, parents use the polite style to show children how and when to present one's various social identities (p. 62).

22.4 Domains of information

Suzuki (1997) points out that the boundary between the speaker's and the addressee's domains of information (see Section 24.3) is clearly drawn in polite styles. As such, the speaker normally avoids invading the addressee's domain. In the plain style, by contrast, there is no clear boundary; the interlocutors value camaraderie more than deference. In (7), where an interlocutor of lower status (L) expresses appreciation to one of higher status (H) for the present H gave to L, the arrowed utterances shift from the polite to the plain speech style.

(7) L: *Kono aida wa dōmo arigatō gozaimashita.*
the.other.day TOP very thank.you.POL
'Thank you very much for (the present you gave me) the other day.'
→ *Are sugoku kirei.* [plain style]
that very pretty
'They were very pretty.'
H: *Sō deshō?*
so COP.CNJ
'Weren't they?'
[snip]
→ L: *Motto ippai hoshii nā.* [plain style]
more want SFP
'I want more of them.'
H: *Sora yokat-ta.* [plain style]
that good.PAST
'That's good.'

L: *Jibun de kaitain desu kedo, futsū ni uttemasu ka?*
self by want.to.buy COP.POL but always sell.POL INT
'I want to buy some more myself. Are they always on sale?'
H: *Shōzan ni aru kedo.* [plain style]
at exist but
'Shozan sells them.'

Suzuki points out that when a plain style is used by L, the statement is about something in L's domain of information (L thinks the item is pretty; L wants more of the item). When a statement is made regarding H's domain (e.g. expressing gratitude, question, request), L employs only the polite style. By contrast, H uses the plain style more freely.

22.5 Awareness of the addressee

Maynard (1991: 577–78) observes that the use of the plain style in casual conversations marks the speaker's "low awareness of the addressee" as a separate and potentially opposing entity. Conversely, high awareness plays an important role in the production and comprehension of the Japanese language, which requires speakers to select different linguistic expressions more forcefully than do speakers of European languages.

She asserts that the plain style is likely to be employed when the speaker (i) exclaims or suddenly recalls something; (ii) vividly expresses events scene-internally as if the speaker were right there; (iii) expresses internal thought self-reflexively, including soliloquies (or monologues); (iv) jointly creates utterances with the addressee, i.e. the ownership of the utterance is shared; (v) presents background information; or (vi) is in an intimate relationship with the addressee, expressing familiarity and closeness. I consider (i) to be a subtype of (iii), which was exemplified by (3b).

(3) b. *Wā, tottemo niau!*
wow very Suit
'Wow, that suits (you) very well!'

The sentence in (8) exemplifies (ii): a secretary reports in the polite style to the district public prosecutor why Harue, a neighbor of a crime suspect, is unfriendly toward the suspect. The description of the suspect's life style in the plain style adds vividness and credibility to the account (p. 563).

(8) *Tabun, Harue ni shitemireba, jibun to dōnenpai no onna ga hitori de*
perhaps for self as same.age GEN woman NOM alone
→ *shareta uchi ni sun-de, akanuketa minari de tsūkin shite iru.* [plain style]
stylish house in live-TE fashionable clothes in is.commuting
'Perhaps for Harue, (it was upsetting to see that) a woman about the same age as herself lives in a stylish house and goes to work wearing fashionable clothes.'
... *Sō yū hade na kurashi ga netamashikatta to yū koto*
such showy life NOM was.jealous QUOT say fact

ja-nai-n *deshō* *ka?* [polite style]
COP-NEG-NMLZ COP.CNJ INT
'Isn't it that Harue was jealous of such a showy life style?'

An example of (iv) is provided in (9), in which A and B jointly create an utterance (p. 559).

(9) A: *Ashita* *wa* *jikken* *repōto* *ga*
tomorrow TOP experiment report NOM
'Tomorrow, an experiment report'
B: *Aru.* [plain style]
there.is
'There is.'
A: *Un* *aru.* [plain style]
yes there.is
'There is.'

An illustrative example of (v) is given in (10), in which the sentence in the plain style provides the reason why the speaker does not value personal advising (p. 555).

(10) *Watashi* *wa* *higoro* *kara* *minoue* *sōdan* *no* *inchikisei* *ni*
I TOP always from personal advising GEN phoniness at
wa *gō o niyashite imasu.* [polite style]
TOP am.irritated
'I have always been quite irritated by the phoniness of personal affair advisors.'
→ *Aite* *to* *yohodo* *fukaku* *tsukiat-te* *minai koto ni wa,*
partner with considerably deep associate-TE unless
shinmina *kotae* *nado* *dekiru mono de wa nai.* [plain style]
thoughtful advice such cannot.do
'One cannot give thoughtful advice unless one is well-acquainted with and has known the advisee for quite some time.'
Okashii *de wa arimasen ka?* [polite style]
strange is.it.not
'Isn't it strange?'

Maynard argues that the polite style is likely to be employed when the speaker (a) expresses a thought that directly addresses the speech partner with expressions appropriate in terms of sociolinguistic variables, and (b) communicates essential information addressed directly to the listener. In short, the more the speaker is aware of the addressee as a separate entity, the more elaborate the discourse markers become, one of which is the use of *desu/masu*. Her generalization is, for the most part, valid. However, speakers of Japanese also apply the plain style when they are quite aware of the addressee – a topic which is explored in the next section.

22.6 The use of soliloquy to express intimacy and deference simultaneously

As was discussed in Section 21.4, the Japanese honorific system linguistically dichotomizes addressees, effectively putting them in two categories: (i) distant

Table 22.1 *Dichotomy of addressees.*

Addressee	Intimate	Distant
Exalted	(A)	(i) Polite style
Not exalted	(ii) Plain style	(B) Plain style

and exalted, as expressed by the polite style, and (ii) intimate and not exalted, as expressed by the plain style, as shown in Table 22.1.

In situation (B), wherein the speaker considers the addressee to be psychologically distant but is not concerned about sounding impolite or even vulgar, the plain style is used. A serious problem occurs in situation (A) when the speaker wishes to convey intimacy and deference simultaneously, because these two affective stances are incompatible in the Japanese honorific system. In fact, this is quite possibly a universal problem because, as seen in Brown and Levinson's (1978/1987) analysis of addressing terms, politeness is defined as the opposite of intimacy. The use of non-intimate expressions is, therefore, considered polite when addressing another person.

However, intimacy and deference are *not inherently incompatible*, and there are indeed times when speakers wish to articulate both affective stances simultaneously in speaking to an addressee. This need can be accomplished only by the application of deft, highly elaborated linguistic skills on the part of fluent and eloquent Japanese speakers who make use of subtle, non-conventional language cues and strategies,[4] among which the most prominent is **SOLILOQUY**, an utterance of one's thoughts without addressing another individual.[5]

As discussed in Chapters 20 and 21, a one-to-one correspondence does not exist between the use of honorifics and the speaker's polite attitude; that is, honorifics do not guarantee deference. They might be used merely to display the speaker's linguistic refinement or to imply his/her attitude of unfriendliness, standoffishness, haughtiness, or rejection. Nevertheless, it must be recognized that a unidirectional link does exist. While the polite style does not

[4] In many American graduate schools, students address professors by their first names, and vice versa. In Japan, this practice is unthinkable. Therefore, if a professor in the US is Japanese, students from Japan find themselves in a dilemma. They cannot address me, for example, as *Yoko*, which would clearly indicate their incompetence as mature speakers of Japanese. However, calling me *Hasegawa-sensei* 'Teacher Hasegawa', as happens in Japan, sounds stiff and obedient, and it would be considered a rather peculiar behavior in many American academic institutions. Therefore, many of my students address me as *Yoko-sensei* in an attempt to express both deference *and* intimacy. The use of the given name followed by *sensei* is not novel, but in Japan, it is generally restricted to addressing kindergarten teachers or teachers of arts and crafts or music.

[5] See Hasegawa (2010) for the use of soliloquy in linguistic communication.

necessarily indicate deference, *deference cannot be expressed without the use of the polite style*. Therefore, switching to the plain style in normal dialogic discourse necessarily disclaims deference. Faced with this dilemma, speakers temporarily disengage with the on-going dialogic discourse and switch to the soliloquy mode.

Native Japanese speakers are categorically aware of the soliloquy mode of discourse, but native English speakers normally are not. For example, when asked whether such a phrase as *I see* is dialogical or soliloquial, English speakers appear puzzled, and their answers vary considerably. This difference is due to the soliloquy mode of discourse having been, to some extent, incorporated in Japanese grammar, but not in English. In English, there is not much formal and structural difference when a sentence is used for oneself, e.g. for thinking, and when it is used to address another. By contrast, as Maynard (1991: 576) also emphasizes, the Japanese language makes this distinction more prominently.[6]

Is it possible, then, that the soliloquy mode plays a more significant role in Japanese than it does in English, even though it certainly has significance in both languages? For example, consider this scenario: a customer is in a check-out line, and a clerk is ringing up purchases. The clerk announces the total amount, and the customer notices and points out that the clerk rang up one item twice. The clerk (who is just completing an eight-hour shift) shakes his head slightly and without making eye contact with the customer says *I need to go home*, and then faces the customer and says *I'm sorry*. In this case, almost everyone would recognize *I need to go home* as soliloquy. Its significance here is to inveigle the customer into acknowledging the speaker's hard work without the speaker forthrightly complaining, which would be inappropriate and risky. This episode demonstrates that a speaker can use soliloquy rhetorically in order to be overheard: soliloquy is used for *showing* one's thoughts, not *telling* them. This strategy requires adroit *mental* acrobatics, making a switch from the dialogue to the soliloquy mode.

When Japanese speakers verbalize without expecting any reaction from hearers, they employ certain forms and avoid certain others. Such soliloquial utterances do not contain addressee-oriented elements: (i) certain SFPs (e.g. *yo/ze* 'I'm telling you'), (ii) directives (e.g. commands, requests, questions), (iii) vocative (calling) expressions (e.g. *oi* 'hey'), (iv) responses (e.g. *hai* 'yes', *iie* 'no'), (v) interactional adverbial phrases of various sorts (e.g. *sumimasen ga* 'excuse me, but', *koko dake no hanashi dakedo* 'it's between you and me'),

[6] Zwicky (2005) reports that the omission of *it be* in the following construction sounds like self reflection, e.g. *(It's) odd that Mary never showed up*; *(It's) too bad (that) she had to leave town so soon*; *(It's) amazing that he didn't spot the error*. Soliloquy in English may have various subtle cues yet to be discovered.

(vi) hearsay expressions (e.g. *sō da*/*-tte* 'I hear'), and (vii) addressee honorifics (e.g. *desu*/*masu*). As a positive indicator, soliloquy frequently involves exclamatory interjections (e.g. *wā, mā, hē, hūn*) and exclamatory SFPs (e.g. *nā, kana, ya*). Therefore, when a speaker uses or avoids certain of these forms, the hearer tends to interpret the utterance as soliloquy.[7] For example, such utterances as shown in (11) are usually recognized as soliloquy by most native speakers of Japanese.

(11) a. *A, sō nan da.*
oh so COP.NPST
'Oh, I see.'
b. *Honto darō ka.*
true COP.CONJ INT
'I wonder if it's true.'
c. *Naruhodo ne.*
reasonable SFP
'That makes sense.'

The distinction between the presence of addressee-oriented elements and the lack thereof explains why in (3), *Wā, tottemo niau yo* 'That suits you well (with the addressee-oriented particle *yo*)' is not acceptable, but *Wā, tottemo niau* (without *yo*) is, as discussed in Section 22.2. The following are typical examples of soliloquial utterances embedded in dialogic discourse, all made by female speakers of higher (H) and lower (L) status.

(12) H: *Honto ni ēgo de wa kurō shimasu.*
really English at TOP am.troubled.POL
'English is sure a pain in the neck!'
L: *Ē, honto desu kā?*
INTJ true COP.NPST.POL INT
'Oh, really?'
H: *Honto, honto.*
true true
'That's true.'
→ L: *Hē, sensē demo sō nan dā.* [plain style]
teacher also same COP.NPST
'Hmm, even teachers have trouble with it.'

(13) L: *Kore, saikin kekkō hayatterun desu.*
this recently fairly fashionable COP.POL.NPST
'These [a pair of gloves] are kind of popular nowadays.'
H: *Ara, kawaii. Dōmo arigatō gozaimasu.*
INTJ cute very thank.you.POL
'Oh, they're cute. Thank you very much.'

7 The TV serial drama *Kodoku no gurume* 'the solitary gourmet' consists mostly of soliloquies with occasional dialogues. Simply listening to the protagonist's voice, native speakers of Japanese can clearly distinguish which parts are soliloquies and which parts are not.

L:	*Ōkisa,*	*daijobu*	*desu*	*ka?*
	size	all-right	COP.NPST.POL	INT
	'Is the size right?'			
H:	*Chōdo*	*mitai.*		
	just	it.seems		
	'It looks just right.'			
→ L:	*Ā,*	*yokat-ta.*	[plain style]	
	INTJ	good-PAST		
	'Oh, good.'			

Insertion of soliloquy into a conversation can mitigate the psychological distancing that necessarily accompanies the polite style because it is tacitly assumed that showing one's inner thoughts does not occur unless one considers the hearer trustworthy. This switch between the dialogue and soliloquy modes occurs at a higher level of discourse organization and should, therefore, be recognized separately from the speech-style proper as exemplified in (4–6).

23 Sentence-final particles

23.1 Introduction

Sentence-final particles (SFPs) are those short elements that occur at the end of an utterance; some also occur utterance-medially as **interjective particles**. SFPs reflect the illocutionary force of the utterance (see Section 19.1) as well as the speaker's attitude towards the utterance and/or the interlocutor(s). SFPs occur frequently in Japanese conversation. Maynard (1997: 88) reports that in her 60-minute conversation data, SFPs occurred in about 40 percent of utterances. The ones most commonly used are: *ne* (364 times, 42.2% of SFPs), *sa* (148, 17.2%), *no* (138, 16.0%), *yo* (128, 14.8%), and *na* (49, 5.7%).

Beyond their conversational use, SFPs are routinely employed in soliloquy, wherein no addressee is involved. My recent collection of soliloquy data contains 3,042 utterances, of which 2,050 were made by 16 female speakers and 992 by 8 male speakers (Hasegawa 2010).[1] Of these, 48.8 percent (1,483 utterances) end in an SFP, which is close to Maynard's percentage. Thus, it is evident that SFPs are deeply seated in the act of speaking whether the utterance is used for communication with others or for thinking (i.e. soliloquy). The frequency of SFPs in my soliloquy data is summarized in Table 23.1.

23.2 Common sentence-final particles

The most common SFPs are explained below. *Ne* and *yo*, which have received the most attention in the linguistics literature, will be discussed separately in Section 23.3.

23.2.1 Ka

If accompanied by a falling intonation (↓), *ka* is used (i) when the speaker is doubtful or uncertain as exemplified in (1a), (ii) when a decision is about to be or has just been made e.g. (1b), or (iii) when newly acquired

[1] In this study, soliloquy data were collected experimentally from 24 native speakers of Japanese, who spoke for 10–15 minutes while alone in an isolated room.

Table 23.1 *Usage of SFPs by gender.*

	Female speakers	Number of occurrences (percentage)	Male speakers	Number of occurrences (percentage)
1	*ka-na*	275 (32.3%)	*ka-na*	150 (23.8%)
2	*ne*	195 (22.9%)	*na*	138 (21.9%)
3	*na*	152 (17.8%)	*ne*	122 (19.3%)
4	*ka*	95 (11.2%)	*yo-ne*	86 (13.6%)
5	*yo-ne*	41 (4.8%)	*ka*	81 (12.8%)
6	*ke*	25 (2.9%)	*yo-na*	18 (2.9%)
7	*wa*	19 (2.2%)	*ka-ne, ke*	7 (1.1%)
8	*kashira, yo-na*	9 (1.1%)	*wa, ya*	4 (0.6%)
9	*ya*	8, 0.9%)	*sa (yo*	3, 0.5%)
10	*no*	7 (0.8%)	*no*	2 (0.3%)

information is not totally incorporated into the speaker's conceptual world e.g. (1c). With a rising intonation (↑), *ka* converts the utterance into a question as in (1d). More to the point, the rising intonation itself solicits the addressee's response, with *ka* indicating that the response should be to supply an answer. Although, strictly speaking, *ka* itself does not form a question, this book nonetheless labels it the *interrogative particle* (INT).

(1) a. *Kare wa sansei suru darō ka*↓.
he TOP agree COP.CNJ INT
'Will he agree, I wonder.'

b. *Koko de taberu ka*↓.
here at eat INT
'I'll eat here.'

c. *A, sō desu ka*↓.
oh SO COP INT
'Oh, I see/Is that so?'

d. *Sono hon wa omoshiroi desu ka*↑.
that book TOP interesting COP INT
'Is that book interesting?'

23.2.2 Kashira

Kashira expresses uncertainty or curiosity, and, like some SFPs, conveys gender information; in the case of *kashira*, it is femininity. Men never use this SFP unless they wish to identify their gender as female, and today's women no longer use it frequently. (Gendered language is discussed in Chapter 28.)

(2) a. *Hontō ni sō kashira.*[2]
really so SFP
'I'm not sure if it's true.'

b. *Kono hoteru wa eki kara tōi kashira.*
this hotel TOP station from far SFP
'Is this hotel far from the station, I wonder.'

c. *Kimura-san wa mō uchi ni kaette iru kashira.*
TOP already home to return exist SFP
'Has Kimura-san come home yet, I wonder.'

23.2.3 Ke

Ke, realized as *-kke*, indicates that the speaker should remember the content of an utterance, but s/he is unsure about it. Formally, *-kke*↓ is not a question, but when an interlocutor hears it, s/he feels obliged to clarify the matter or to say that s/he does not know the answer.

(3) a. *Ashita shiken da-kke*↓.
tomorrow quiz COP-SFP
'There's a quiz tomorrow, I wonder.'
'Are we going to have a quiz tomorrow?'

b. *Mō kono hanashi shimashita-kke*↓.
already this story did.POL-SFP
'I wonder if I've already told you this.'
'Have I already told you this?'

Many native speakers of Japanese are reluctant to add *ke* to an *i*-adjective or a verb *ru*-form; instead, the nominalized construction (Chapter 15) *n da-kke* is preferred:

(4) a. *Kyōto wa ima goro [??atsui/atsui n da]-kke*↓.
TOP now [hot-SFP]
'I wonder if Kyoto is hot this time of the year.'
'Is Kyoto hot now?'

b. *Ano hito osake [??nomu/nomu n da]-kke*↓.
that person alcohol [drink-SFP]
'I wonder if s/he drinks.'
'Does s/he drink?'

When spoken with a rising intonation, *ke* is clearly understood to involve a question addressed to an interlocutor.

(5) A: *Konaida kashita hon, dō datta?*
the.other.day lent book how COP-PAST
'How was the book (I) lent (you) the other day?'

[2] The copula must be omitted before *kashira*, e.g. **sō da kashira*; however, when the copula is in the polite form, it can be used as a politeness indicator, e.g. *sō desu kashira*.

B: *E,* *karita-kke*↑.
oh borrowed-SFP
'Oh, (did I) borrow (a book)?'

23.2.4 Na

Na has three functions. As discussed in Section 6.4, it forms an affirmative command when following a verb adverbial form as in (6a) or a negative command when following a verb conclusive form as in (6b).

(6) a. *Kaeri* *na*↑.
return SFP
'Go home!'
b. *Kaeru* *na*↓.[3]
return SFP
'Don't go home!'

The second function is exclamatory, as in (7a), which is used by both males and females, and is often combined with another SFP as in (7b). An exclamation is when a person expresses emotion in the form of an utterance without addressing any particular interlocutor.

(7) a. *Tanoshii* *na*↑.
happy SFP
'It's a lot of fun!'
b. *Honto* *ka* *na*↑.
true INT SFP
'Is it true, I wonder.'

The third function of *na*, as exemplified in (8a), is as a masculine variation of *ne*. This third use of *na* can also appear as an interjectional particle, as happens in (8b), this particular instance demonstrating that the final vowels of SFPs can be elongated without changing their function.

(8) a. *Ii* *tenki* *da* *na*↑.
good weather COP SFP
'It's a fine day, isn't it?'
b. *Ano* *nā* *karita* *kane* *nā* *mō* *sukoshi* *nā* *matte* *kunnai?*
well SFP borrowed money SFP more longer SFP wait give.not
'Well, won't you wait a little longer for the money I borrowed from you?'

Whether or not an insertion of an SFP is possible at a certain position in a sentence determines unit constituency. For example, *na* cannot occur after *karita*, *mō*, or *matte* in (8b).

[3] In this phrase, the accent falls on /ka/, *káeru*, and the subsequent syllables are pronounced with a sustained low pitch contour.

b′. *Ano nā karita (*nā) kane nā mō (*nā) sukoshi nā matte (*nā) kunnai?*

This indicates that *ano*, *karita kane*, and *mō sukoshi* are phrase units whereas *karita*, *mō*, and *matte* are dependent elements that cannot by themselves form a phrase.

23.2.5 No

No is a nominalizer, which derives an NP from a clause, much like English *that* as in *That everyone knows my mistake is embarrassing*. (See Section 15.2 for a detailed discussion.) It frequently occurs in utterance-final position to add various nuances, typically softening the locution when addressing an interlocutor. It is, therefore, considered mildly feminine even though male speakers also use this particle.

(9) a. *Atama ga itai no↓.*
head NOM painful SFP
'I have a headache.'

b. *Ashita Tōkyō ni kaeru no↓.*
tomorrow to return SFP
'I'll go back to Tokyo tomorrow.'

c. *Mō tabe-nai no↑.*
any.more eat-not SFP
'Won't you eat any more?'

23.2.6 Sa

Sa intensifies an entire utterance, as in (10a), creating a very casual, possibly even vulgar, impression.

(10) a. *Sonna koto tokku ni shitteru sa.*
such matter already know SFP
'I already know that.'

Sa is used more frequently as an interjective particle to solicit the addressee's attention, as in (10b), but its overuse, like that of any SFP, is considered unsophisticated and irritating, much like overuse of *you know* in English.

b. *Watashi wa sā tomodachi ni sā kuruma o sā kariru.*
I TOP SFP friend from SFP car ACC SFP borrow
'I'll borrow a car from a friend.'

23.2.7 Wa

A feminine particle which by itself is no longer widely in use, *wa* stresses an entire utterance when spoken with rising intonation. Its co-occurrence with a polite form, as in (11b), sounds especially old-fashioned. However, its combinations with *ne* and *yo*, i.e. *wa-ne* and *wa-yo*, are still commonly observed. *Wa*↓ is gender-neutral or mildly masculine, e.g. (11c), and used more commonly in Kansai (Kyoto–Osaka area) dialects.

(11) a. *Watashi wa ik-anai wa*↑.
I TOP go-not SFP
'I won't go.'
b. *Watashi mo issho ni ikimasu wa*↑.
I also together go.POL SFP
'I'll go with you.'
c. *Kore wa uremasen wa*↓.
this TOP cannot.sell.POL SFP
'This won't sell.'

23.2.8 Ya

Ya also emphasizes an utterance, and its use is considered somewhat childish. It occurs only with a falling intonation and is highly limited in distribution. When appearing after an *i*-adjective, as in (12a), or the negative form *-(a)nai* of a verb, as in (12b), it is gender-neutral and normally expresses a negative or gloomy state of mind.

(12) a. *Kore, takai ya.*
this expensive SFP
'This is expensive.'
b. *Konna koto wakannai ya.*
this matter not.understand SFP
'I don't understand this kind of thing.'

When occurring after a verb volitional form, as in (13a), or a verb imperative form, in (13b), *ya* is a masculine particle attempting to convince an addressee who is otherwise unlikely to perform an action requested of him/her.

(13) a. *Takamine-san mo yobō ya.*
also invite.VOL SFP
'Let's invite Takamine-san too.'
b. *Hayaku shitaku shiro ya.*
quickly preparation do.IMP SFP
'Get ready quickly!'

23.2.9 Ze

Categorized as a masculine particle, *ze* forcefully accentuates an utterance. (*Ze*↓ is more forceful than *ze*↑.) It presupposes the presence of an addressee, and therefore does not occur in soliloquy.

(14) a. *Kono eiga naka-naka omoshiroi ze*↑.
this movie quite interesting SFP
'This movie is quite interesting.'

b. *Ano* *mise* *de* *nomō* *ze*↓.
that bar at drink.VOL SFP
'Let's have a drink at that bar.'

23.2.10 Zo

Marking strong determination as exemplified in (15a), *zo* occurs in both male and female soliloquies. In conversation, however, it is considered a masculine particle as shown in (15b).

(15) a. *Ganbaru* *zo!*
try.hard SFP
'I'll try hard/keep going!'
'I won't give up!'

b. *Uso* *o* *tsuku* *to* *okoru* *zo!*
lie ACC tell if get.angry SFP
'[Lit.] I'll get angry if you tell me a lie!'
'I won't tolerate lying!'

23.3 *Ne* and *yo* in conversation

Ne and *yo* occur routinely in Japanese conversation. As reported in Section 23.1, in Maynard's (1997: 88) 60-minute conversation data, *ne* and *yo* occurred 364 and 128 times, respectively, at an approximate ratio of 3:1. *Ne* is generally understood to indicate the speaker's assumption that s/he and the addressee have the same status regarding knowledge of, or belief about, the piece of information being conveyed, whereas *yo* is selected when different cognitive statuses are assumed. Uyeno (1971: 96), for example, contends that in (16), *ne* is used when the speaker assumes the addressee, like him/herself, is aware of the information, whereas *yo* is used when the speaker expects the addressee to be unaware of it.

(16) *Sonna* *koto* *wa* *atarimae* *da* *ne/yo.*
such thing TOP matter.of.course COP SFP
'That goes without saying.'

The functions of *ne* include requesting confirmation and seeking or showing agreement. These usages, taken from Ohso (1986: 91), are exemplified in (17)–(18).

(17) A: [Requesting confirmation]
Kyō *wa* *kinyōbi* *desu* *ne.*
today TOP Friday COP SFP
'Today is Friday, isn't it?'

B: *Ē,* *sō* *desu.*
yes so COP
'Yes, that's right.'

(18) A: [Seeking agreement]
Kyō wa kinyōbi desu ne.
today TOP Friday COP SFP
'Today is Friday, isn't it?'
B: [Showing agreement]
Sō desu ne. Yatto isshūkan owarimashita ne.
so COP SFP finally a.week ended SFP
'Yes. Finally, the week is over.'

However, as Kato (2001: 33–34) points out, this analysis cannot account for the use of *ne* in (19) nor for the use of *yo* in (20).

(19) A: *Jūbun ja nai desu ka.*
enough not COP INT
'It's enough, wouldn't you say?'
B: *Watashi to shite wa, mitome-raremasen ne.*
for.me TOP agree-cannot.POL SFP
'I can't agree with you.'

(20) [The interlocutors are seeing the rain together.]
Yoku furu ne/yo.
often fall SFP
'It's raining again.'

In (19), B's opinion is clearly not shared by A. In (20), while *ne* occurs with a rising pitch contour, *yo* cannot be with a rising pitch. On the other hand, when *yo* is spoken with a falling pitch, this utterance sounds to me like soliloquy. This issue will be examined in the next section.

Izuhara (2003) compares *ne*, *yo*, and *yo-ne*. She argues that they are all used to persuade the addressee to adopt the same cognitive state as that of the speaker. However, these particles differ with respect to how they are supposed to accomplish this goal. According to Izuhara, *yo* is used to change the addressee's cognition by asserting the speaker's own thought, e.g. (21); *yo–ne* is used to achieve the same goal by confirming whether or not the speaker's cognitive stance is shared by the addressee, e.g. (22); *ne* is used to do so by requesting agreement without necessarily asserting the speaker's own epistemic stance, e.g. (23).

(21) T: *A sōnan desu ka.* (Izuhara 2003: 6)
oh so COP INT
'Oh, is that so?'
K: *Sō yo.*
so SFP
'Yes, it is.'

(22) T: *Ikebe-san wa rikugun nandesu yo-ne.* (p.9)
TOP army COP.POL SFP
'Mr. Ikebe, you were in the army, weren't you?'

I: *Ē, boku wa rikugun no shichōtai, ima no yusōbutai da.*
yes I TOP army GEN transport.corps now GEN transport-corps COP
'Yes, I was in an army transport-corps called *shichōtai*, now called *yusōbutai*.'

(23) T: *Koshiji-san wa meshiagaru no mo osuki ne.* (p.10)
TOP eat NMLZ also like SFP
'Ms. Koshiji, you like to eat too, don't you?'
K: *Daisuki.*
like-very-much
'Yes, very much so.'

Because all of these particles request some modification in the addressee's cognition, Izuhara contends they may sometimes convey an obtrusive tone. Because of this fact, many speakers avoid using these particles when speaking to their supervisors as in (24):

(24) a. *Denwa desu kedo/yo.*
telephone COP but/SFP
'You have a phone call.'
b. *Ashita irasshaimasu ka/ne.*
tomorrow come.HON INT/SFP
'Will you come tomorrow?'

Cook (1990, 1992) contends that *ne* is not limited to solicitation of agreement on informational content, and that it frequently signals an *affective common ground* between speaker and addressee, requiring the addressee's cooperation. As such, *ne* is often used when the speaker must convey negative, unwelcome information as shown in (25):

(25) *Oshokuji no toki ni mama shikar-itaku-nai kedo nē. Hitoshi no*
meal GEN time mother scold-want-not but SFP GEN
sono tabekata ni wa mō mama yurus-enai.
that way.of.eating at TOP no.more mother forgive-cannot
'I don't want to scold you at dinner time. But I can't tolerate any more the way in which you [Hitoshi] eat.'

Katagiri (1995, 2007) asserts that *ne* and *yo* contribute to *the coordination of dialogue* by indicating the speaker's state of acceptance/nonacceptance regarding the information expressed by the utterance. *Yo* is used to present the information as already accepted by the speaker, whereas *ne* indicates that the information has not yet been thoroughly accepted. According to Katagiri, the addressee can subsequently use such input to determine for him/herself the acceptability of the speaker's utterances and the need for collaboration between the two:

Dialogues can be considered as communication through an unreliable channel. What a speaker says may not be heard by a hearer. Even if it is heard, it may not be understood. And even if it is understood, it still may not be accepted. In order to ensure that the dialogue proceeds successfully, dialogue participants have to collaborate with each other to assist and assure the establishment of mutual beliefs, and to secure common grounds, between them (2007: 1316).

23.4 *Ne* and *yo* in soliloquy

As mentioned in Section 23.1, it is likely that *ne* occurs in soliloquy as frequently as it does in conversation, while *yo* is extremely rare (Hasegawa 2010: 61). Therefore, the communication-based characterizations of *ne* as presented in the previous section are all inadequate to account for the whole range of the functions of *ne*.

23.4.1 Ne

Takubo and Kinsui (1997; Kinsui and Takubo 1998) consider that *ne* is primarily a monitoring device for the speaker's sake, rather than a communicative device, a recourse to an addressee's assumed knowledge of a given topic. Comparing the act of speaking with the operations of a computer, they contend that speaking involves registering, searching, computing, and inferring on the database, i.e. the speaker's permanent memory. In their theory, *ne*'s essential function is to mark *matching of information* between two sources. For example, suppose that the speaker tries to confirm that the addressee is John Smith. S/he would say:

(26) *Anata* *wa* *Jon Sumisu-san* *desu* *ne.*
you TOP COP SFP
'You are Mr. John Smith, aren't you?'

The two sources for matching may be opinions of two different persons or different data points within a single person, e.g. old and new information. *Ne* signals that the speaker is in the process of verification by matching, or self-confirmation.

For another example, in conversation (27), Speaker B first looks at his watch and finds that the little hand is pointing to "7" so concludes that the watch is accurate as regards timekeeping (Takubo and Kinsui 1997: 752). Lacking *ne*, utterance (27) would merely indicate that the time is seven o'clock, without implying any type of computation or confirmation on the part of the speaker.

(27) A: *Nan-ji* *desu* *ka?*
what-time COP INT
'What time is it?'
B: [Looking at her watch]
Ē to, *shichi-ji* *desu* *ne.*
well 7-o'clock COP SFP
'It's seven o'clock.'

If it is unlikely matching between two sources is involved, the use of *ne* will sound anomalous, as in (28).

(28) *#Watashi no namae wa Tanaka desu ne.*
I GEN name TOP COP SFP
'My name is Tanaka.'

This idea of matching seems to apply to most occurrences of *ne* in my soliloquy data. *Ne* occurs frequently with (i) such discourse adverbials as *yappari* 'as expected, of course', *sasuga* 'as might be expected', *igai to* 'contrary to expectation', *sō ie-ba* 'speaking of that', *naruhodo* 'reasonably, that explains why something is in such a state', *jissai* 'actually'; (ii) a conditional clause; and (iii) other kinds of comparison, such as *mukashi* 'old days'. These expressions indicate that the speaker has compared the current situation with a piece of information in his/her permanent memory.

23.4.2 Yo

Unlike *ne*, *yo* is extremely rare in soliloquy. It occurred only four times by itself and once as *ka-yo* in my experimental data. During one subject's recording, his cell phone rang, and after hanging up, he said the following with a falling intonation on *yo*.

(29) *Machigai denwa ka-yo. Kimu -tte dare da yo.*
wrong telephone SFP QUOT who COP SFP
'Wrong number? Who's Kim?'

Inoue (1997) distinguishes *yo*↑ (with a rising intonation) and *yo*↓ (with a falling *or level* intonation), contending that *yo*↓ forces both the speaker and the addressee to re-evaluate the conversational and other relevant contexts in such a way that the conveyed information must be recognized as true. He illustrates this idea with the following examples in (30), where the implicit messages are derived by the speaker's reconfirmation and reassessment of the relevance of each piece of information in relation to the particular context.

(30) a. *Ano hito, mada anna koto itteru yo*↓.
that person still such thing is.saying SFP
'That guy still says such things.'
[Message expected to be conveyed:]
Komatta mon da.
troublesome thing COP
'It's troublesome.'

b. *Otoko wa tsurai yo*↓.
man TOP hardship SFP
'A man's life is tough!'
[Message expected to be conveyed:]
Mā, shikata ga nai nā.
well cannot.help SFP
'Well, it's useless to complain since there is nothing to be done about it.'

Regarding *yo*↑, Inoue explains that not only does it force the interlocutors to reconfirm the situation with the information deemed to be valid, but it also obligates the addressee to consider his/her future act(s) accordingly.

(31) A: *Inoue-san kara no fakusu todoitemasu ka?*
from GEN fax has.arrived INT
'Has a fax from Inoue-san come yet?'
B: *Todoitemasu yo*↑.
has-arrived SFP
'Yes, it has.'
[Message expected to be conveyed:]
Dō saremasu ka?
how do.HON INT
'What are you going to do about it?'

This explanation accounts nicely for the situation represented in (32). With *yo*↓, the speaker conveys an opinion such as "so I don't want to go there," whereas with *yo*↑, the speaker asks whether the addressee still wants to go there.

(32) *Kushiro wa samui yo.*
TOP cold SFP
'It's cold in Kushiro.'

Only *yo*↓ can occur in soliloquy. This fact supports Inoue's analysis, wherein *yo*↓ need not involve an addressee while *yo*↑ necessarily does.[4]

23.5 Acquisition of sentence-final particles

Children acquire their first group of SFPs – *yo*, *no*, and *ne* in that order – between one and a half and two years of age, around the time that they start to produce two-word utterances (Okubo 1967: 84). Reporting that many early instances of *ne* follow partial repetition of adult utterances, Clancy (1986: 429) conjectures, "Such repetitions may serve as a kind of prototypical case of shared information, with mother and child repeating and agreeing with each other's utterances." *Ne* can also occur with information which is not available to the addressee; in this case, the child seeks to secure the addressee's acceptance of the information or speech act. "*Ne* is often used with requests, apologies, and in imparting information which the listener may not be pleased to hear, in an attempt to convey a sense of fellow-feeling, reduce any negative impact, and gain the listener's compliance" (p.29), a typical example being *Gomen ne* 'I'm sorry'. This supports Cook's (1990, 1992) analysis of *ne*

[4] The only exception to this generalization that comes to mind is *mate yo*↑ 'wait!', which can occur in soliloquy. Interestingly, *mate yo*↓ seems to require the presence of an addressee.

as creating and confirming an affective common ground between the speaker and the addressee.

Watamaki (1997) hypothesizes that if establishing social relationships is the primary function of *ne*, autistic children will not be able to use it as shrewdly as non-handicapped (NH) children do. Autistic children are generally believed to be unable to learn effective communication skills to interact smoothly with others because they lack the ability to attribute different mental states to themselves and to others, and to use such differentiation to infer others' intentions as well as to predict their future actions. Furthermore, autistic children rarely speak about cognitive mental states, e.g. thinking and believing, and they do not understand the source of such mental states. NH children, on the other hand, start talking about them at around two and a half years (Tager-Flusberg 1992). Another significant difference is that autistic children do not express requests for joint attention, e.g. *Look!*, whereas NH children begin to do so at about nine months of age.

Watamaki compares one-hour speech samples of a six-year-old autistic boy with no learning disability and a five-year-old developmentally challenged (DC) boy. The occurrences of SFPs in their speech are tabulated in Table 23.2 (the interpretations of the particles are by Watamaki). The data for the NH child are derived from Okubo (1967) when her female subject was between one and a half and two years of age and between two years and one month and three years.

The autistic child rarely used interactional particles and never used *ne*. Given that *ne* is the most commonly used particle among NH adult speakers

Table 23.2 *Acquisition of SFPs.*

	Autistic	DC	NH	NH
Age (years)	6	5	1;6–2;0	2;1–3;0
Utterances	580	530	809	1,934
yo (intimacy)	3	29	65	186
ne (sympathy)	0	25	44	292
no (neutral)	0	2	111	343
kana (suggestion)	0	20	1	1
na (exclamatory)	0	7	0	6
mon (regret, discontent)	0	4	7	23
kara (determination)	0	1	8	54
-tte (quotation)	0	2	16	22
zo (emphasis)	0	3	1	1
no (question)	32	0	0	0
-te (request)	6	18	65	113
ka (doubt)	3	4	2	21
TOTAL	44	115	320	1,062

(Kokuritsu Kokugo Kenkyūjo 1955: 118; Maynard 1997: 88), its total absence in this autistic subject's speech is quite noticeable, yet not totally unexpected. Another noteworthy fact is that, with the NH child, *ne* and *yo* occur almost equally in frequency during a very early period, but then, like in adult speech, the use of *ne* surpasses *yo*.

24 Modality and evidentiality

24.1 Modality

A useful way to analyze sentences is to parse them into the content (≈ factual) part and the part that expresses the speaker's attitude toward the content. For example, in (1a), the content is the speaker's attendance at the meeting, and *I must* expresses the speaker's attitude, namely, a feeling of obligation to perform this action. In (1b), *Joan attended the meeting* is the content, and *I think* expresses the speaker's attitude of wanting to assert this statement without absolute certainty.

(1) a. *I must attend the meeting.*
b. *I think Joan attended the meeting.*

The aspect of a speaker's utterance that expresses his/her attitude is referred to as **MODALITY**, which in Western scholarship is traditionally divided into **DEONTIC MODALITY** and **EPISTEMIC MODALITY**.[1]

24.1.1 Deontic modality

The term *deontic* is derived from the Greek word *deon* that means 'what is binding'; deontic modality, therefore, concerns obligation and permission. Obligation in Japanese is typically expressed by double negation "it cannot go without doing ~" – e.g. *nakereba naranai, nakereba ikenai, nakute wa naranai, nakute wa ikenai, nai wake ni wa ikanai. Nakereba naranai* is considered more formal than other expressions and frequently used in legal documents.

[1] In Japanese linguistics (e.g. Moriyama 1989; Nitta 1989; Iwasaki 2002), a more common division of modality is between the speaker's attitude toward the content, i.e. epistemic, and that toward his/her way of communication with the addressee. The latter is a broader category than deontic modality, including concerns about desire, speech acts (Chapter 19), sentence-final particles (Chapter 23), etc. This different conceptualization of modality is due in part to the significant characteristics of the Japanese language, which grammatically encodes many communicative intentions and functions.

(2) The Constitution of Japan, Article 66
Naikaku-sōri-daijin sonota no kokumu-daijin wa, bunmin de
prime-minister other GEN minister.of.state TOP civilian COP
nakereba naranai.
must
'The Prime Minister and other Ministers of State must be civilians.'

By contrast, when obligation is decided by one's own will, the use of *nakereba ikenai* or *nakute wa naranai/ikenai* is fairly common though *nakereba naranai* can also be used.

(3) *Motto yasai o tabe nakereba ikenai/nakute wa [naranai/ikenai].*
more vegetable ACC eat must
'(I) must eat more vegetables.'

Rather than using double negation, *beki da* 'ought to ~' can be used to express obligation affirmatively:

(4) *Sore wa chokusetsu honnin ni hanasu beki da.*
that TOP directly person to tell ought COP.NPST
'(You) ought to tell it directly to the person.'

Permission is normally expressed using the *te*-form followed by *(mo) ii* 'it is (also) good/acceptable to do ~'.

(5) *Kyō wa hayaku kaet-te (mo) ii.*
today TOP early return-TE (also) good.NPST
'(You) can go home early today.'

Prohibition is expressed using the *te*-form followed by *wa ikenai* or *wa naranai*.

(6) The Constitution of Japan, Article 19
Shisō oyobi ryōshin no jiyū wa, kore o okashi-te wa naranai.
thought and conscience GEN freedom TOP this ACC violate-TE must.not
'Freedom of thought and conscience shall not be violated.'

24.1.2 Epistemic modality

The term *epistemic* is derived from the Greek word *episteme* meaning 'knowledge'. Epistemic modality concerns the truth, falsity, or various degrees of probability of the content. There are many ways to express epistemic modality, and in Japanese, when the speaker is certain about the validity of the content, the following expressions are typically employed.

(7) a. Simple declarative sentence with or without an epistemic adverb
Buchō wa (tashikani) kaigi ni shusseki [shita/shinakatta].
manager TOP (certainly) meeting to attendance [did/did.not]
'(It is certain that) the manager [attended/did not attend] the meeting.'

b. *Ni chigai nai* 'discrepancy does not exist'
Buchō wa kaigi ni shusseki shita ni chigai nai.
manager TOP meeting to attended in discrepancy not.exist
'There is no doubt the manager attended the meeting.'

Epistemic adverbs include *zettai ni* 'absolutely', *kanarazu* 'without a doubt/without fail', *kitto* 'surely', *tabun* 'probably', *osoraku* 'maybe', and *moshika shite/hyotto shite* 'possibly/maybe'. When the speaker is uncertain about the reliability of information, the following expressions are commonly added to the tensed predicate.[2]

(8) a. *Hazu da* 'be bound to'
Buchō wa kaigi ni shusseki shita hazu da.
manager TOP meeting to attended bound.to COP.NPST
'The manager [must/was supposed to] have attended the meeting.'

b. *Omou* 'I think'
Buchō wa kaigi ni shusseki shita to omou.
manager TOP meeting to attended QUOT I.think
'I think the manager attended the meeting.'

c. *Darō/Deshō*, the conjectural form of the copula
Buchō wa kaigi ni shusseki shita darō/deshō.
manager TOP meeting to attended COP.CNJ
'It's likely the manager attended the meeting.'

d. *Ka mo shirenai* 'it cannot be known whether or not ~'
Buchō wa kaigi ni shusseki shita ka mo shirenai.
manager TOP meeting to attended INT also can.not.know
'The manager might have attended the meeting.'

e. *(Yōna) ki ga suru* 'I feel that ~'
Buchō wa kaigi ni shusseki shita (yōna) ki ga suru.
manager TOP meeting to attended (that) feel NOM do
'I feel (that) the manager may have attended the meeting.'

24.2 Evidentiality

Epistemic modality expressions signify the speaker's judgment regarding the truth, falsity, or probability of the content without clarifying the basis upon which the judgment is made. On the other hand, the speaker's epistemic stance can also be expressed by mentioning evidence. This type of epistemic modality is referred to as **EVIDENTIALITY**. The most common evidential expressions in Japanese are *sō da*, *-tte*, *yō da*, *mitai da*, and *rashii*.

24.2.1 Sō da

Sō da is used to convey two types of evidentiality differentiated by the conjugation form of the preceding predicate. When attached to the adverbial form of a verb (see Section 6.1) or to the stem of an *i*- or

[2] See Moriyama (1995) for details of these epistemic modality expressions.

na-adjective,[3] it indicates that some circumstance makes the speaker determine that the event in question is likely to happen in the future (in the case of a dynamic verb) as in (9a), or that some state of affairs is likely to exist (in the case of an adjective or a stative verb) as in (9b–9c). This use of *sō da* does not occur with a nominal predicate (i.e. a noun + the copula), e.g. **isha sō da* 'looks like a physician'.

(9) a. *Fukyō na node, kaisha wa shain o kaiko shi-sō da.*
depression because company TOP employee ACC dismissal do-EVID
'Because of the economic depression, the company seems about to dismiss some of its employees.'

b. *Kono ryōri wa oishi-sō da.* [*i*-adjective]
this dish TOP delicious-EVID
'This dish looks delicious.'

c. *Kono eiga wa kōshō-sō da.*[4] [*na*-adjective]
this movie TOP high.brow-EVID
'This movie seems high-brow to me.'

The speaker of (9a) anticipates dismissal of employees based on the bad economy. Even when the basis for such conjecture is not explicit, e.g. (9b–9c), the presence of *sō da* strongly implies that the speaker can provide evidence if solicited.

When *sō da* follows a tensed predicate, it indicates that the content is hearsay as exemplified in (10).

(10) a. *Mata gakuhi ga neage sareru sō da.*
again tuition NOM increase do.PASS.NPST EVID
'I hear that tuition will be raised again.'

b. *Sono eiga wa tsumaranakatta sō da.* [*i*-adjective]
that movie TOP boring.PAST EVID
'I hear the movie was boring.'

c. *Kono jinja wa yūmei da sō da.* [*na*-adjective]
this shrine TOP famous COP.NPST EVID
'I hear this shrine is famous.'

d. *Hannin wa miseinen datta sō da.* [noun + copula]
culprit TOP minor COP.PAST EVID
'I hear the culprit was a minor.'

24.2.2 -Tte

In casual speech, hearsay information is frequently marked with *-tte*, a variation of the quotative particle *to* (see Section 15.3).

(11) *Daigaku tōkyoku wa gakuhi o neage suru [to/-tte] itta.*
university administration TOP tuition ACC increase do QUOT said
'The university administration said that (they) would increase the tuition.'

[3] *Sō da* must be added to the irregular forms of the adjectives *ii* 'good' and *nai* 'non-existent' resulting in *yosa-sō da* and *nasa-sō da*, respectively, not **i-sō da* and **na-sō da*.

[4] Many *na*-adjectives do not co-occur with *sō da*, e.g. *futō* 'unjust', *haruka* 'far', *yūmei* 'famous'.

Although *-tte* is derived from *to*, it can also function in casual speech as a SFP, whereas *to* cannot serve as such.

(12) *Daigaku tōkyoku wa gakuhi o neage suru [#to/-tte].*
university administration TOP tuition ACC increase do [SFP]
'The university administration said that (they) would increase the tuition.'

Furthermore, Mushin (2001) points out that in quotative sentences, the quoted speaker can be identical with the reporting speaker, as in (13); however, when used as an SFP, the quoted speaker and the reported speaker must be distinct, as in (14). That is, *-tte* must be considered as a genuine hearsay marker.

(13) *Watashi wa okāsan ni daigaku o yameru [to/-tte] itta.*
I TOP mother to university ACC quit [QUOT] said
'I said to (my) mom that (I)'d quit university.'

(14) *[#Watashi/Otōto] wa daigaku o yameru [#to/-tte].*
[I/my.brother] TOP university ACC quit [QUOT]
'I heard that [#I/(my) brother] would quit university.'

24.2.3 Yō da/mitai da

Like the conjectural *sō da*, *yō da*, and *mitai da* denote that the speaker has some evidence for asserting the content. *Yō da* and *mitai da* are interchangeable, the latter being more colloquial than the former.

(15) a. *Hōan wa kaketsu sareta [yō da/mitai da].*
bill TOP approval do.PASS.PAST [EVID]
'It seems that the bill was approved.'

b. *Shiken wa muzukashikatta [yō da/mitai da].* [*i*-adjective]
examination TOP difficult.PAST [EVID]
'Apparently, the examination was difficult.'

When a *na*-adjective or a nominal predicate refers to a past situation, the copula *datta* is employed as in the case of the hearsay *sō da*. However, irregularities occur when it refers to a non-past situation. With a *na*-adjective, *yō da* requires the attributive form of the copula, *na*, while *mitai da* attaches directly to the stem of the *na*-adjective as in (15c). With a nominal predicate, e.g. (15d), *yō da* requires the attributive form of the copula, *no*, and *mitai da* attaches directly to the noun.

c. *Kotoshi no tenkō wa ijō [na yō da/mitai da].* [*na*-adjective]
this.year GEN weather TOP abnormal [COP EVID/EVID]
'The weather this year seems abnormal.'

d. *Ashita wa ame [no yō da/mitai da].* [noun + copula]
tomorrow TOP rain [COP EVID/EVID]
'It seems like there may be rain tomorrow.'

The major difference between the conjectural *sō da* on the one hand and *yō/mitai da* on the other is that the latter can accompany predicates in the past tense while the former, which attaches to the tenseless adverbial form, cannot. That is, the conjectural *sō da* can provide an indication only about a present or future situation. Another difference is that *sō da* is used to express more intuitive inferences, whereas *yō/mitai da* elicits more logical ones. For example, in (9b), the speaker thinks that the meal is delicious by merely seeing it, whereas if *yō/mitai da* is used instead, the speaker's inference will likely be based on circumstantial evidence, e.g. observing many people ordering it.

24.2.4 Rashii

Rashii, which was introduced in Section 6.7 as a suffix that derives an adjective from a noun, can function as an evidential auxiliary when following a tensed predicate, and is often interchangeable with *yō/mitai da* as in (16).

(16)	*Kotoshi*	*no*	*kaze*	*wa,*	*onaka*	*ga*	*itaku naru*	*[rashii/yō da/mitai da].*
	this.year	GEN	flu	TOP	stomach	NOM	hurt	[EVID]

'It seems that this year's flu can cause abdominal pain.'

To demonstrate differences among these evidentials, Moriyama (1989: 68–69) proposes a co-occurrence test involving the use of *omou ni* 'in my opinion'.

(17)	a.	*Omou ni,*	*rainen*	*atari*	*kyōkō*	*ga*	*ki-sō da.*
		in.my.opinion	next.year	around	financial.crisis	NOM	come-EVID

'In my opinion, a financial crisis is likely to occur sometime next year.'

b. *Omou ni, rainen atari kyōkō ga kuru [yō/mitai da].*

c. *#Omou ni, rainen atari kyōkō ga kuru sō da.*

The conjectural *sō da* in (17a) and *yō/mitai da* in (17b) can co-occur naturally with *omou ni*, which indicates that these evidentials are compatible when expressing inference. By clear contrast, the hearsay *sō da* in (17c) does not accommodate *omou ni* because these two expressions are semantically contradictory.

d. *??Omou ni, rainen atari kyōkō ga kuru rashii.*

The lower acceptability of (17d) demands more scrutiny. Miyake (1995: 188) contends that evidentials are used under two circumstances: (i) when the inference is made prior to the speech time, and (ii) when it is made on site. In the former, *rashii* suggests that the basis for making the inference is hearsay, although, unlike the genuine hearsay marker *sō da*, the content itself is not hearsay. Therefore, it cannot co-occur with *omou ni* as in (17d). When an inference is made on site and at the speech time, the evidence implied by *rashii* is not restricted to hearsay. For example, in (18), the speaker has just witnessed the lights being off and made the inference accordingly. In this situation, *rashii* can co-occur with *omou ni*.

(18) *Denki ga kiete iru. Omou ni, mada kaette inai rashii.*
light NOM is.off in.my.opinion yet return.not EVID
'The lights are off. In my opinion, (she) has not come home yet.'

Another difference between *yō/mitai da* and *rashii* is that the former can be used simply for softening an assertion, whereas the latter cannot be used for such a purpose. For example, when one witnesses his/her friend having gained weight, (19a) is acceptable, but (19b) is not.

(19) a. *Sukoshi futotta [yō/mitai da] ne.*
a.little have.gained.weight [EVID] SFP
'It looks like you have gained a little weight.'
b. *#Sukoshi futotta rashii ne.*

24.2.5 *Other types of evidential expressions*

In English, one can use the same word to describe the mental states (psychological, emotional, sensation, etc.) of both oneself and of other persons.

(20) a. *[I'm/Alice is] cold.*
b. *[I want/Alice wants] coffee.*
c. *[I want/Alice wants] to watch TV.*
d. *[I think/Alice thinks] Bill is smart.*

However, these predicates are interpreted differently. When I say *I want coffee*, I know I want coffee, and I am entitled to say so because I am the owner of that desire. By contrast, when I say *Alice wants coffee*, I am reporting my inference or conveying hearsay information.

In Japanese, one needs to use different phrases when talking about another person's mental state. Such phrases, e.g. the b-sentences below, are categorized as evidentials.[5] Those expressions that take only first-person subjects are called **PSYCH-PREDICATES**.[6]

(21) a. *Watashi wa samui.*
I TOP cold.NPST
'I'm cold.'
b. *Arisu wa samu-gatte iru.*
TOP cold-EVID
'Alice shows signs of feeling cold.'

(22) a. *Watashi wa kōhī ga hoshii.*
I TOP coffee NOM want
'I want (some) coffee.'

[5] See Aoki (1986) and Hasegawa and Hirose (2005) for further discussion.

[6] This restriction on the possible subject is not due to any grammatical constraints, but, rather, to a common understanding about the accessibility of information, i.e. the impossibility of perceiving other persons' mental states. In fiction, psych-predicates can take a third-person subject, as the author is the omniscient creator and therefore has direct access to characters' mental states. Banfield (1982) refers to such sentences as **UNSPEAKABLE SENTENCES**.

b.	*Arisu*	*wa*	*kōhī*	*o*	*hoshi-gatte iru.*[7]
		TOP	coffee	ACC	want-EVID

'Alice shows signs of wanting coffee.'

(23) a.	*Watashi*	*wa*	*terebi*	*[ga/o]*	*mi-tai.*[8]
	I	TOP	TV	[NOM/ACC]	watch-want

'I want to watch TV.'

b.	*Arisu*	*wa*	*terebi*	*o*	*mi-ta-gatte iru.*
		TOP	coffee	ACC	watch-want-EVID

'Alice shows signs of wanting to watch TV.'

(24) a.	*Watashi*	*wa*	*Biru*	*wa*	*atama*	*ga*	*ii*	*to*	*omou.*
	I	TOP		TOP	head	NOM	good	QUOT	think

'I think Bill is smart.'

b.	*Arisu*	*wa*	*Biru*	*wa*	*atama*	*ga*	*ii*	*to*	*omotte iru.*
		TOP		TOP	head	NOM	good	QUOT	is.thinking

'Alice thinks [Lit. is thinking] that Bill is smart.'

When a psych-predicate is used with a third-person subject, e.g. (21b, 22b, 23b), the use of the auxiliary *-gatte iru* is obligatory. With *omou*, a third-person subject requires *-te iru* as in (24b). This construction usually expresses the present progressive aspect. Nakau (1994: 51) explains that, as a modality expression, *omou* refers to the speech time. Of all the mental attitudes that manifest themselves simultaneously with the time of speech, it is only his/her own mental state that is accessible to the speaker. Therefore, the use of *omou* with a third-person subject results in anomaly. *Omotte iru*, on the other hand, is an expression for the continuous present and can be used to describe a mental activity of a third-person as well as the speaker him/herself.

24.3 Information territory

In conversations in Japanese, non-native speakers might respond in a grammatical, yet anomalous way as demonstrated in (25B).

(25) A:	*Ii*	*otenki*	*desu*	*ne.*
	good	weather	COP.NPST	SFP

'It's a fine day, isn't it?'

B:	*#Hai,*	*sō*	*desu.*
	yes	so	COP.NPST

'Yes, it is.'

In English, this exchange is natural, but in Japanese, speaker B must utilize the SFP *ne* to echo speaker A's use of the same particle (Chapter 23). In order to

[7] While *hoshii* is an *i*-adjective whose conceptual object is marked by the nominative *ga*, *hoshigaru* is a *u*-verb and its direct object is marked by the accusative *o* (see Section 7.6).

[8] The fluctuation between *ga* and *o* marking is discussed in Section 7.7.

discuss the oddity of (25B) and related phenomena, this section introduces Kamio's (1994, 1995) idea of information territory.

24.3.1 The theory of territory of information

Kamio posits two conceptual categories involving information, including how that information is used linguistically: the speaker's and the addressee's **TERRITORY OF INFORMATION**. A piece of information is said to fall into one's own territory if one of the following contingencies applies:

(26) a. the information is obtained through one's internal direct experience (e.g. pain, emotions, beliefs);
b. the information falls into one's professional or other areas of expertise;
c. the information is obtained by direct experience through the five senses;
d. the information is about persons, objects, events, and facts close to oneself, e.g. the birthday of one's self or one's spouse.

Consider this situation derived from Kamio (1995: 241–42): John, the president of a company, and Tom, his business associate, are talking in John's office. Susan, John's secretary, informs John, *You have a meeting at three*. When three o'clock approaches, John can say, *I have a meeting at three*. However, it would sound odd for Tom to say, *You have a meeting at three*. Instead, he is likely to say, *I guess/believe/understand you have a meeting at three*. Both John and Tom have obtained the information at the same time from the same source, but because it is about John's schedule, i.e. in John's information territory, Tom needs to employ a hedged, indirect statement. As demonstrated by this example, Kamio contends, the concept of information territory is relevant in language use, and the Japanese language is particularly sensitive to it.

In Japanese, information in one's own territory is expressed directly without any evidential expressions, while information outside one's territory must be expressed indirectly with an evidential expression or the conjectural *darō/deshō*. The former constitute **DIRECT FORMS**, the latter **INDIRECT FORMS**.

Consider another situation derived from Kamio (1994: 72–73): Taro is ill, and his friend, Noboru, visits him. If Noboru sees Taro lying in bed, he can say (27a), which is in a direct form. However, if Noboru cannot see Taro and is told by Taro's mother that Taro is ill, (27a) is inappropriate. Instead, an indirect form as in (27b) must be employed.

(27) a. *Tarō wa byōki desu.*
TOP ill COP.POL.NPST
'Taro is ill.'
b. *Tarō wa byōki [da-tte/rashii].*
TOP ill [COP-SFP/EVID]
'(I hear/It seems) Taro is ill.'

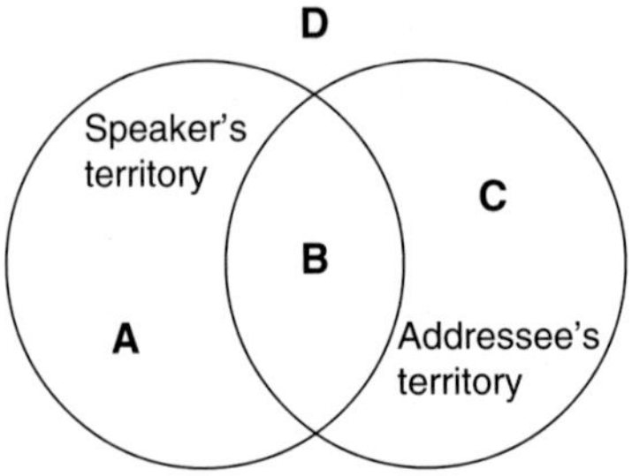

Figure 24.1. Territories of information.

By contrast, if Taro's father, who lives separately from his family, obtains the same information from Taro's mother by telephone and tells it to his colleague, (27a) is appropriate, even though, like Noboru, he did not see Taro in bed. In fact, an indirect form like (27b) gives the impression that the father is indifferent to his son's welfare. This is because the son's health situation falls within the father's territory of information.

24.3.2 Four cases of information

Kamio recognizes four distinct cases of information within his theory. The four cases are represented in Figure 24.1, and Kamio extrapolates upon each case.[9] In case A, a given piece of information falls within the speaker's territory but not within the addressee's. In this case, a direct form must be selected. As seen in the a-sentences in (21–24), the most salient examples of this are reports of how one feels. English also requires a direct form in this case; the use of an indirect form results in the anomaly illustrated in (28).

(28) a. *I have a headache.*
  b. #*I seem to have a headache.*

In case B, a piece of information falls within the speaker's as well as the addressee's territory as exemplified in (25). In this case, Japanese requires the use of a direct form accompanied by the SFP *ne*.[10] Another example of case B is provided in (29).

[9] Kamio posits two additional cases. However, they are based on psychological distance between a given piece of information and the speaker or the addressee, a concept that is not readily compatible with the spatial metaphor of territory. Therefore, they are not included in this chapter. See Kamio (1994) for these additional cases.

[10] This characterization of *ne* is made from a different perspective, but it does not contradict essentially with the explanations provided in Subsection 23.4.1.

(29) *Kimi,* *sukoshi* *yaseta* *ne.*
you a.little lost.weight SFP
'You've lost a little weight, haven't you?'

Although the information here concerns the addressee's personal appearance, and thus falls inherently within the addressee's territory, it is also in the speaker's territory because he has obtained it by observation, i.e. via direct external experience. In English, cases A and B are not distinguished, direct forms utilized for both:

(30) a. *It's a beautiful day.*
b. *You've lost some weight.*

Information in case C is in the addressee's territory but not in that of the speaker. This situation requires an evidential expression followed by *ne*. Neither the direct form, with or without *ne* (31b), nor the indirect form without *ne* (31c) sounds natural in this case.

(31) a. *Anata* *wa* *kibun* *ga* *warui* *mitai desu* *ne.*
you TOP feeling NOM bad EVID SFP
'You look like you're sick.'
b. #*Anata wa kibun ga warui desu (ne).*
c. #*Anata wa kibun ga warui mitai desu.*

Case C in English requires an indirect form:

(32) a. *I hear your German is excellent.*
b. *You seem worried.*
c. #*You feel dizzy.*

Case D refers to the situation in which a piece of information belongs in neither the speaker's nor the addressee's territory. In such a case, indirect forms of various sorts are used without *ne*.

(33) a. *Ano* *eiga* *wa* *omoshiroi* *[sō da/mitai da]* *yo.*
that movie TOP interesting [EVID/EVID] SFP
'[I hear/It looks like] that movie is interesting.'
b. *Ashita* *wa* *hareru* *darō.*
tomorrow TOP get.fair COP.CNJ
'I'm supposing the weather will be fine tomorrow.'

Like in case C, indirect forms are utilized in case D in English.

(34) a. *I hear summer in Alaska is beautiful.*
b. *This computer seems to have broken down.*

24.3.3 Obligatory vs. optional ne

Unlike cases B and C, in which the use of *ne* is obligatory, many cases exist where the use of *ne* is optional. For example, (35) and (36B) are instances of case A, and (37) is in case D. Optional *ne* functions to soften the locution and, therefore, expresses politeness.

(35) *Chotto* *yūbinkyoku* *e* *itte kimasu* *ne.*
a.little post.office to go SFP
'I'm going to the post office for a little while.'

(36) A: *Kore* *ikura* *desu* *ka?*
this how.much COP INT
'How much is this?'
B: *500* *en* *desu* *ne.*
yen COP SFP
'(It's) 500 yen.'

(37) *Ashita* *wa* *hareru* *deshō* *ne.*
tomorrow TOP get.fair COP.CNJ SFP
'I'm supposing the weather will be fine tomorrow.'

24.3.4 Hearsay

Information gained by hearsay is treated differently in Japanese and in English. In Japanese, it is not considered to belong to the speaker's territory,[11] whereas in English it is, if the information source is deemed reliable. Consider this situation, derived from Kamio (1995: 243): Jack, a friend of the Clark family, phones Jane Clark and says that he will visit them soon. Then Jane's mother asks her

(38) M: *What did Jack say?*
J: *He's coming to visit us soon.*

Jane can respond with a direct form as in (34J), but such an exchange is unacceptable in Japanese, where the use of a hearsay marker is obligatory.

(39) J: *Kondo* *asobi* *ni* *kuru-tte.*
soon play for come-QUOT
'I hear (he) will visit (us) soon.'

Because of this difference in expressing hearsay information in the two languages, native speakers of English frequently forget to employ hearsay markers when speaking Japanese (Kamada 2000: 169–70), thereby creating the impression that they are aggressively assertive when in all probability this is not the case.

[11] Hearsay information is generally treated as falling outside one's territory until it has been thoroughly processed and absorbed into one's body of knowledge. This process involves the integration of a given piece of information with various relevant linguistic and non-linguistic data already acquired.

25 Backchanneling

25.1 Introduction

The roles of speaker and listener constantly alternate in typical conversation. Person A is the speaker in a given moment, with B as the listener; then B takes his/her turn to speak, while A becomes the listener. Goffman (1974: 136) characterizes this state of affairs as follows.

> Talk is socially organized, not merely in terms of who speaks to whom in what language, but as a little system of mutually ratified and ritually governed face-to-face action, a social encounter. Once a state of talk has been ratified, cues must be available for requesting the floor and giving it up, for informing the speaker as to the stability of the focus of attention he is receiving. Intimate collaboration must be sustained to ensure that one turn at talking neither overlaps the previous one too much, nor wants for inoffensive conversational supply, for someone's turn must always and exclusively be in progress.

In both English-speaking societies and Japan, possibly worldwide, the conversational norm consists of one person speaking at a time, with the speaker changing in an orderly manner. If someone starts speaking while you are talking, you are likely to be offended. By contrast, if a speaker ends his/her utterance and a dead silence follows, it might be embarrassing to those present as most people feel a need to avoid silences during conversations. These tacit rules of conversation are studied in linguistics and other academic disciplines in terms of taking the **FLOOR** (i.e. the right to speak in interaction) or **TURN-TAKING.** For such investigation, Sacks *et al.* (1974) developed an analytical framework, **CONVERSATION ANALYSIS**, which has been widely used for describing the orderliness and sequential patterns of verbal interaction.

One of the fundamental concepts in conversation analysis is the **TURN CONSTRUCTIONAL UNIT**, which is a stretch of speech determined grammatically (phrase, clause, sentence), pragmatically (question, request, etc.), and/or intonationally (falling pitch, pause, etc.).[1] A turn constructional unit allows a

[1] For a detailed discussion concerning the definition of turn constructional unit, see Ford and Thompson (1996).

listener to project how an utterance will be completed, enabling the listener to plan how to react to it well in advance. This ability to forecast makes possible the split-second precision of speaker-role change that is observed frequently in conversation. The end of a turn constructional unit is called a **TRANSITION RELEVANCE PLACE**, a place at which a transition to another speaker might occur naturally.

It is well known that a participant who assumes the role of listener occasionally produces short phrases to acknowledge that the current speaker's turn is in progress. Such short utterances, which do not claim the floor, are termed **AIZUCHI** 'backchannel', and certain non-verbal behaviors such as responsive laughter and head movement (e.g. nodding), among other expressive gestures, are backchannels notifying the speaker that s/he still holds the floor.

Examine the following 30-second segment of a conversation derived from an Internet talk show with four participants: a host (H: Hakase SUIDOBASHI) and three guests (M: Tetsuya MIYAZAKI, S: Shinji MIYADAI, T: Hideto TOMABECHI).[2] The equals sign (=) indicates **LATCHING**, i.e. no interval between the end of the prior utterance and start of the next; brackets indicate regions of overlap; the arrows mark *aizuchi*.

(1) Talk Show Part 1, from 2:25 (2 minutes 25 seconds) to 2:55

1 H: *ano kankēsē to ieba ne, kono ofutari wa M2*
well relationship speaking.of SFP this two.HON TOP
'speaking about the relationship between these two, they are known as *M2*'[3]

→ 2 T: = *un*
'ok'

→ 3 M: = *hai hai*
'yes, yes'

4 H: *e konbi o kunde ne*
eh pair ACC form SFP
'they've formed a duo'

→ 5 T: = *un*
'yeah'

6 H: *shakaijihyō o zutto yattemashi [ta Saizō de ne*
social.commentary ACC long.time did in SFP
'commenting in *Saizo* magazine on social issues'

→ 7 T: *[un*
'yeah'

8 H: *dē koko de mata fukkatsu shite itadaite desune*[4]
and here at again revival do receive SFP
'and this talk show program revived it, and'

[2] This video is available at the book's website: http://hasegawa.berkeley.edu/Cambridge/introduction.php.

[3] *M2* is coined after the initial *M* of Miyadai and Miyazaki.

[4] *Desune* is the polite version of the interjection *ne*. In this case, *desu* is not the predicate 'be'. Thus, **fukkatsu shite itadaite desu* (without *ne*) is unacceptable.

9 M: *hai*
'yes'

10 H: *ē ikani ē ronkyaku to shite sugoi ka-tte iu no o misete*
how critic as excellent CMPL ACC show
itadakimashita keredomo
received though
'we've appreciated how extraordinary they are as commentators'

11 *soshite Tomabechi-san wā ofutari to menshiki -tte iu ka ne*
and TOP two with acquaintance like SFP

12 T: = *kekkō*
'occasionally'

13 H: *Miyadai-san to no men [shiki wa?*
with GEN acquaintance TOP
'how about with Mr. Miyadai?'

14 M: *[iya watashi wa kono 3-nin ga*
no I TOP this 3-people NOM
kō sorotta -tte hajimete
this.way gather CMPL first.time
'well, for me, it's the first time to see these three together'

→ 15 H: *a sō desu ka*
oh so COP INT
'oh, really?'

16 S: = *iya iya sonna koto nai desho?*
no no such thing NEG COP.CNJ
'no, I don't think so'

17 *datte Saizō de*
because in
'because we met for *Saizo*'

18 T: = *M3 yatte*
doing
'for the article entitled *M3*'

→ 19 M: *a sō ka*
'oh, that's right'

20 S: = *M3 de*
'for *M3*'

→ 21 M: *are M3 ka*
that INT
'that's right, *M3*'

Up to line 13, H (the host) takes the floor, and T and M support his turn by backchanneling in lines 2, 3, 5, 7, and 9. In line 12, T anticipates H's question and starts to answer it. H completes his question in line 13. M then takes the floor in line 14, answering the question, and H acknowledges this new speakership in line 15. In lines 16–17, S takes the floor and objects to M's response. Then, T completes M's statement in line 18. This kind of utterance is called a **CO-CONSTRUCTION**, or **COLLABORATIVE FINISH**. In line 19, M realizes that his previous answer was deficient while S continues his utterance in line 20. M repeats his correction in line 21. Whether or not to categorize lines 15, 19 and 21 as backchannels depends upon researchers' perspectives (see Section 25.3 below).

Researchers recognize that Japanese speakers constantly and consistently supply *aizuchi* in conversation, and some even consider a high rate of *aizuchi* to characterize Japanese conversation style as a whole. Nevertheless, the frequency of use of *aizuchi* varies considerably from person to person. This chapter discusses some findings on backchannel behavior among Japanese, English, and, to a lesser extent, Chinese speakers.

25.2 Frequencies of backchannels in Japanese and American English

Comparing forty videotaped three-minute segments of dyadic conversations in Japanese and American English, Maynard (1990) reports the following regarding the Japanese conversations:[5]

a. The frequency of backchannels across 20 Japanese pairs totaled 871.
b. Of the 871 cases, 703 occurred in the immediate neighborhood of pauses or breaks in tempo made by the primary speaker. (Pauses normally occur at the major clausal and sentential junctures, e.g. at the juncture of a subordinate clause.)
c. 70.5 percent of the backchannels were brief expressions, e.g. *un* 'uh-huh', *honto* 'really', and *sō* 'I see'.
d. Head movement accompanied these backchannels 62.9 percent of the time.
e. Head movement alone without verbal expressions accounted for 18.8 percent.
f. Backchannels consisting of laughter occurred 10.7 percent of the time.

Maynard also recognizes that pauses are frequently accompanied by such linguistic devices as SFPs (p. 406). Note that in (1), the SFP *ne* occurs at the end of lines 4, 6, and 8, and that each time a backchannel is supplied by a listener. *Ne* also occurs in line 11, but this time, a response (attempting to take the floor) follows, rather than a backchannel. In Maynard's data, SFPs occurred in 40.8 percent of all the cases when a backchannel was supplied. Auxiliary verbal endings (e.g. *deshō?* 'isn't it right?' and *ja-nai?* 'isn't it?') functioned similarly to SFPs, and 51 percent of backchannels occurred at a major grammatical juncture (p. 406).

Another characteristic reported by Maynard is that Japanese speakers frequently perform a vertical head movement at or near the final syllable of an utterance. Of all the backchannels in her data, 38.1 percent occurred in the context of speaker head movement (pp. 406–07). Regarding the American conversations (p. 408):

[5] Maynard's data consist of same-sex conversations: ten each of Japanese male pairs, Japanese female pairs, American male pairs, and American female pairs. In each conversation, the initial two-minutes were discarded, and the following three-minute segments were used as data.

a. The overall frequency of backchannels across 20 American pairs totaled 428.
b. Of the 428 cases, 373 occurred at or near a pause.
c. The American pairs produced far fewer back channels than did the Japanese pairs (871 instances).
d. Like the Japanese pairs, the most frequently occurring were such brief expressions as *uh-huh, yeah,* and *right,* totaling 50.2 percent of all backchannels.
e. Head movement accompanied backchannels 50.7 percent of the time, less frequently than in the Japanese data (62.9 percent).
f. Head movement without verbal expressions occurred in 35 percent of backchannels, more frequently than in the Japanese data (18.8 percent).
g. Laughter backchannels occurred 14.7 percent of the time, somewhat more frequently than in the Japanese data (10.7 percent).
h. 82.8 percent of backchannels occurred at a point of grammatical completion (clause or sentence). Thus, the grammatical completion point is the single most salient context for backchanneling in English.

25.3 Timing of backchannels

Clancy *et al.* (1996) examine audiotaped face-to-face conversations of pairs of friends in three languages: Japanese (9 conversations, totaling 23 minutes), English (8 conversations, 44 minutes), and Chinese (8 conversations, 23 minutes). Some pairs are of the same sex while others are of the opposite sex. Clancy *et al.* contend that non-primary speakers' utterances to support the on-going speaker's floor, which they refer to collectively as **REACTIVE TOKENS** (RTs), should be divided into several categories.

a. Backchannel: a non-lexical vocalic form: e.g. *un, hē* (Japanese); *hm, uh huh* (English); *ūm, aī* (Chinese).
b. **REACTIVE EXPRESSION**: a lexical word or phrase: e.g. *hai* 'yes', *hontō* 'really', *a sō ka* 'I see' (Japanese); *oh really, yeah, exactly* (English); *dui* 'right', *jiushi a* 'indeed' (Chinese).
c. Collaborative finish (i.e. co-construction): a non-primary speaker finishes the previous speaker's utterance.
d. **REPETITION**: a non-primary speaker repeats the primary speaker's utterance.
e. **RESUMPTIVE OPENER**: a non-lexical element that is used at a turn-initial point; it would be a backchannel were it not followed by floor-taking.

A collaborative finish is observed in (1) at line 18. (2) is an example of repetition, (d), derived from the *Talk Show* Part 1 video, from 1:11 to 1:23. In this segment, each guest holds in front of him a poster summarizing his professional accomplishments. T holds a large panel that obstructs his face, about which M comments:

(2) 1 M: *nan ja sore wa* ((laughter))
what COP that TOP
'what's that?'
2: *kao ga mien yan kē* ((laughter))
face NOM can't.see SFP
'your face is hidden'
3 T: ((laughter))
4 H: *datte kore futsū ni hon ni aru*
but this normally book in exist
5: *ano chosha shōkai kondake nagain desu yo*
well author introduction this-much long COP SFP
'but his self-introduction that appears in each of his books is this long'
6 T: *dokomo kezuru tokoro ga nakatta no*
no-place omit place NOM did-not-exist SFP
'nothing could be omitted'
→ 7 M: *dokomo kezuru tokoro ga nakatta no*
'nothing could be omitted'

Resumptive openers, (e), are exemplified by the *Talk Show* video Part 2, from 1:30 to 1:44.[6]

(3) 1 S: *masu media nanka ni*
mass media like DAT
2 H: *= un*
3 S: *= shakai ga kansatsu dekiru shikaku ga aru to*
society NOM can.observe capacity NOM exist QUOT
omotteru jiten de ōmachigai de
think point at big-mistake COP.and
'we are mistaken if we think that mass media are capable of observing society'
4 H: *= un*
5 S: *= masu media jishin ga*
self NOM
6 H: *= un*
7 S: *= kansatsu sareru beki shakai genshō dakara ne*
be.observed ought.to society phenomenon because SFP
'the mass media themselves are a social phenomenon that ought to be observed'
8 H: *= un un*
9 S: *= dakara shakai no byōri o masu media ga*
so society GEN pathology ACC NOM
10: *= [kaisetsu suru nante omottara machigai*
explain CMPL if-think mistake
'so, it's wrong to think that they can explain social problems'
11 M: *[a sō sō sō sō*
12 S: *= [masu media ga saidai no byōri desu kara ne*
NOM greatest pathology COP because SFP
'because mass media are the largest social problem'

[6] This video is available at the book's website: http://hasegawa.berkeley.edu/Cambridge/introduction.php.

13 M: [*sō sō sō sō*
→ 14: *sō sō sō* [*sore* *wa* *tadashiku-[te*
that TOP correct-TE
'that's correct, and'
15 S: [*un* [*un*

In line 14, M starts with an *aizuchi* (*sō sō sō*) and then commences speaking in turn. Clancy *et al.* consider this type of utterance a resumptive opener.

Clancy *et al.* compare and contrast RTs in the three languages, presenting these findings:

a. Japanese and English speakers used RTs more frequently than did Chinese speakers. The RT frequencies in these languages were 39.5 percent (Japanese), 37.3 percent (English), and 10 percent (Chinese).
b. In Japanese, 68 percent of all RTs were backchannels, 17 percent reactive expressions, and 12.5 percent resumptive openers.
c. In English, 37.9 percent were backchannels, 34.2 percent reactive expressions, and 10.4 percent resumptive openers.
d. In Chinese, 47.2 percent were backchannels, 31.1 percent reactive expressions, and 14.5 percent resumptive openers.

In order to obtain average frequencies of RTs, they divided the number of RTs by all speaker changes regardless of turn shifting. For example, in (1), there are 19 speaker changes (counting line 1 as a change), of which 9 are RTs, according to Clancy *et al.*'s definition. Thus, the RT frequency rate is (9/19 =) 47.4 percent. Regarding the placement of RTs, they find the following.

a. In Chinese, nearly all RTs occurred at a transition relevance place (TRP).
b. In English, RTs occurring at a TRP ranged from 30 percent to 66.7 percent differing from pair to pair.
c. In Japanese, RTs occurred at a TRP ranging from 12.1 percent to 50 percent.
d. The occurrences of RTs at grammatical (vis-à-vis intonational) completion points were 88 percent in Chinese, 78 percent in English, and 36.6 percent in Japanese.

It can be concluded that when supplying a RT, Chinese speakers are inclined to wait for the end of a grammatical clause, English speakers are a little less likely to do so, and Japanese speakers are least constrained by grammatical completion (see line 7 in (1) and lines 11, 13, and 15 in (3)).

Clancy *et al.* consider that the very high frequency of backchannels (68%) and the relatively low frequency of reactive expressions (17%) in the Japanese data are due to their positioning. Unlike backchannels, reactive expressions are lexical and thus contribute meaningful content. Therefore, they require syntactic and semantic processing on the part of the primary speaker, who is being engaged in formulating and producing his/her utterance. If RTs are to be provided while the primary speaker's turn is in progress, non-lexical backchannels, which place the least cognitive burden on the speaker, are deemed more appropriate.

Sending a backchannel is a more significant behavior of non-primary speakership in Japanese than in English or Chinese. However, if all RTs are taken into consideration, while Chinese speakers do so infrequently, Japanese and English speakers supply them with equal frequency. This contradicts Maynard's (1990) study, in which backchannels occur twice as frequently in Japanese conversations (871 times) as in American English ones (428 times).[7] Clancy *et al.* do not satisfactorily account for this discrepancy. Nevertheless, they explain how the anecdotal claim that Japanese use RTs much more frequently than do Americans comes about: Americans place 78 percent of RTs at grammatical completion points while Japanese speakers are much less likely to wait for a completion point (36.6%). Regardless of relative frequency, unexpected placement of RTs by Japanese interlocutors could lead Americans to feel that Japanese use RTs much more than anticipated. Listen to the Talk Show video Part 2 and judge for yourself.

Interpretation of the use of RTs differs from culture to culture. The use of RTs is not a dominant feature of Chinese conversation as is made clear by the strikingly low frequency of use in comparison with Japanese and English. When Chinese speakers react, they wait until a grammatical completion point, and their RTs are more likely lexical, i.e. reactive expressions rather than backchannels. Furthermore, when a listener says something, his/her intention is more likely to be to claim and gain the floor. Chinese interactional style favors participants not infringing the others' turn(s): backchanneling without waiting for a grammatical completion point is seen as presumptuous, intrusive, and impolite (Clancy *et al.* 1996: 382).

Japanese turn-management strategy can be characterized as a highly conventionalized, affect-laden interactional style. Non-primary speakers are expected to show concern for the primary speaker's sense of security in holding the floor by providing RTs during the primary speaker's turn. Failing to supply RTs may be interpreted as being uncooperative and lacking empathy (p. 381).

The Chinese and Japanese turn-management styles parallel the competing politeness strategies discussed in Chapter 21. The Chinese style can be said to focus on negative politeness (respecting the interlocutor's desire to be

[7] Maynard defines backchanneling as "occurrence of listener behavior where an interlocutor, who assumes primarily a listener's role, sends brief messages and signs during the other interlocutor's speaking turn" (p. 402). Her examples include Clancy *et al.*'s backchannels and reactive expressions.

unimpeded by others), whereas the Japanese style appeals to positive politeness (responding to the interlocutor's wish to be desirable and appreciated).

American turn-management style can be characterized as occupying a position between Chinese and Japanese. The relative high frequency of RTs suggests a strongly interactional style resembling Japanese. However, Americans do not usually supply RTs until a point of grammatical completion. If the listener does not wait, a RT might be interpreted as being dismissive and rude (*Yeah, yeah, I already know what you mean*) (p. 381).

> [Americans] tend to find Japanese RTs disruptive and even annoying, but the Mandarin paucity of RTs somewhat unnerving, leaving them wondering what the listener is thinking ... American non-primary speakers are more actively involved than their Mandarin counterparts, but are nevertheless expected to refrain from infringing on the primary speaker's on-going task of formulating propositions (Clancy *et al.* 1996: 383).

25.4 The co-construction puzzle

To recapitulate, the Japanese people prefer a cooperative conversation style. Mizutani (1984) contends that this tendency induces a high rate of RTs, including co-construction. However, Ono and Yoshida (1996) argue that, compared with English, co-constructions are rare in Japanese conversations, and they report only 20 instances in their 100 minutes of data. They attribute this rarity to a sociocultural norm: according to Ono and Yoshida, the Japanese in general consider it impolite to finish another person's sentence or to provide additional information on behalf of the primary speaker (p. 120). By contrast, adding information is a common type of co-construction in English as shown in (4)

(4) D: *I don't have any time for basketball*
G: *because you're working twelve hours* (Ono and Yoshida 1996: 121)

They believe the constraint on the territory of information (see Section 24.3) is operational in this regard: if a piece of information falls into the primary speaker's territory, non-primary speakers must refrain from expressing it.

Countering Ono and Yoshida, Hayashi and Mori (1998) claim that co-construction is not necessarily rare in Japanese; they report 65 occurrences in their 360 minutes of data. Regarding the territory constraint, Hayashi and Mori assert that Japanese interlocutors do infer others' inner thoughts and express them as co-constructions. They further contend that conversation is a dynamic social phenomenon, and that the boundaries of private territories of information are fluid: one's territory can become public and shared through interactive processes (p.90).

Suzuki and Usami (2006) compared in a more systematic way how the frequencies of co-construction vary in Japanese and in English. They analyzed 320 minutes of face-to-face, mostly dyadic, conversation data of all-female participants. Four types of interlocutors were engaged in these conversations: (i) Japanese non-acquaintances (30 conversations, 90 minutes), (ii) Japanese friends or family members (5 conversations, 130 minutes), (iii) English-speaking non-acquaintances (8 conversations, 24 minutes), and (iv) English-speaking friends or family members (3 conversations, 76 minutes). Suzuki and Usami calculated co-construction frequencies by two methods: frequency per minute and frequency per speaker-change. Co-construction occurrences are summarized below.

Data category	Co-construction	Data duration	Perminute
(i) Japanese non-acquaintances	62 times	90 minutes	0.69 times[8]
(ii) Japanese friends/family	47 times	130 minutes	0.36 times
(iii) English non-acquaintances	6 times	24 minutes	0.25 times
(iv) English friends/family	12 times	76 minutes	0.16 times

Contrary to Ono and Yoshida's claim, Suzuki and Usami found that Japanese speakers produced more co-constructions than did English speakers. The percentages of co-construction with respect to the total number of speaker changes are as follows:

Data category	Co-construction	Speaker changes	Percentage
(i) Japanese non-acquaintances	62 times	3,510	1.8
(ii) Japanese friends/family	47 times	3,474	1.4
(iii) English non-acquaintances	6 times	588	1.0
(iv) English friends/family	12 times	620	1.9

Regardless of relative frequencies, co-construction does not often occur in Japanese or English.

Suzuki and Usami then analyzed their data in terms of the territory of information. They divided the co-constructions according to whether the described event or state of affairs belonged to (a) the primary speaker's territory, (b) the second speaker's territory, or (c) neutral or non-judged territory. They excluded the friends/family data from this analysis because it is often difficult to determine the territory to which a given piece of information belongs, as friends and family members naturally share many of the same experiences.

Data category	Total	Primary sp	Second sp	Neither
(i) Japanese non-acquaintances	62	30	14	18

[8] This means that co-constructions occurred 69 times in 100 minutes of data.

According to Suzuki and Usami, nearly half of the co-constructions are concerned with information in the primary speaker's territory, suggesting that Japanese speakers do not refrain from talking about matters which are in others' information territories as Hayashi and Mori (1998) argue.

Suzuki and Usami's data support Mizutani's (1984) contention that co-construction occurs more frequently in Japanese than in English. However, Suzuki and Usami do not believe their results support Mizutani's more general claim, because the frequent use of co-construction does not necessarily indicate a more collaborative and cooperative attitude on the part of the non-primary speaker. They conclude that a linguistic form (i.e. co-construction in this case) and the speaker's actual intention do not necessarily coincide. Speakers can convey their intentions through various linguistic means, and not all occurrences of co-construction found in their data can be judged as either collaborative or cooperative in nature (p. 271). Their Japanese data show that co-construction occurred more frequently when interlocutors were not acquainted than when they were. They explain this by pointing out that non-acquaintances in their data always commence conversations with self-introduction and an exchange of such information as their names, occupations, and places of residence. In other words, most of the initial utterances are about information belonging to the primary speaker's territory. By reducing the social and psychological distances between them, speakers try to get to know each other. Extending this idea, Suzuki and Usami hypothesize that co-construction is a means of displaying positive politeness toward the interlocutor.

> The fact that there is less amount of shared information between non-acquaintances may even enhance the effect of such a display of politeness. The second speaker can show that she and the first speaker share the same values and ways of thinking, or in other words "stand on the same ground", by displaying that she can predict and complete the first speaker's sentence even without access to the particular information included in it (p.273).

Summing up, all of these studies by Japanese researchers portray somewhat different pictures of the phenomenon of co-construction among Japanese speakers. All of their claims seem valid with respect to the corresponding data sets, and it is understandable that very different results may be generated by distinct sets of data and corresponding analysis. What conclusion, then, can be drawn from their work? Is it possible to generalize, let alone make a cross-linguistic comparison with English regarding the general frequency of co-construction among Japanese speakers? Perhaps not – Hayashi and Mori (1998) point out the need for caution when making cross-linguistic comparisons of frequencies of interactional phenomena because the bases for such comparisons are not well established.

This is a profoundly difficult and intriguing issue. I have selected as data for this chapter a talk show by Hakase SUIDOBASHI (Examples 1, 2, and 3) because many of his videos are posted on YouTube, and in them speakers can be heard making abundant use of RTs. YouTube allows viewers to leave comments concerning videos, and some, apparently native speakers of Japanese, have commented that Suidobashi's *aizuchi* are too numerous to the point of being annoying. These comments indicate that not all Japanese people share the same linguistic norms surrounding the use of *aizuchi*.

26 Demonstratives

26.1 Introduction

Demonstratives constitute a class of words whose primary function is to locate a referent entity relative to the speaker and/or to the addressee. Demonstratives can be used by themselves, e.g. *I bought this* (called **pronominal**, behaving as a pronoun), or in combination with nouns, e.g. *I bought this laptop* (called **adnominal**, *ad* = 'to' + *nominal* = 'noun').

Conventional Japanese grammars describe demonstratives in the language as encoding a three-way distinction, referred to as the *ko-* (**proximal** = near), *so-* (**medial**), and *a-* (**distal**) series (see Table 26.1).

Pre-Modern Japanese had an additional *ka-* (distal) series. As described by Aston (1904), at the turn of the century (c. 1900) *ka-* was used in written language, and *a-* in spoken discourse. Prior to his time, Aston contends, the difference consisted of "*kare* being applied to the less remote, and *are* to the more remote, of persons or objects not conceived of as immediately present before the speaker or the person addressed. *Kare* would therefore correspond to the Latin *iste*, and *are* to *ille*" (pp. 59–60).

Haruma wage (a Dutch–Japanese dictionary compiled in the eighteenth century) included *kare* as a translation of the masculine third-person singular pronoun, whereas its feminine counterpart was translated with a compound word consisting of *kare* 彼 and *onna* 女 'woman' (Yanabu 1982: 197).[1] 彼女 was pronounced as *kano onna* 'that woman' until the late nineteenth century when it changed to the present-day pronunciation, *kanojo* 'she'.

When both speaker and addressee are physically facing in the same direction, the *ko*-series is selected for entities located close to them; the *so*-series for those at some distance from them; and the *a*-series for those even farther away. For example, when directing a taxi driver to a destination, one would say (1a) if the taxi is already right at the corner, (1b) when the taxi has not yet reached the corner, and (1c) if the corner in question is still at a considerable distance.

[1] In his 1890 novel, *Maihime* (*The Dancing Girl*), Mori Ogai (1862–1922) employed *kare* to refer to a female protagonist.

Table 26.1 *Japanese demonstratives.*

	Proximal	Medial	Distal
Modern Japanese			
Pronominal	*kore* 'this'	*sore* 'that'	*are* 'that over there'
Adnominal	*kono* 'this'	*sono* 'that'	*ano* 'that over there'
Thing/Person (Vulgar)	*koitsu* 'this one'	*soitsu* 'that one'	*aitsu* 'that one over there'
Place	*koko* 'here'	*soko* 'there'	*asoko* 'over there' *ako* (Kansai dialect)
Direction	*kotchi* 'this way/side'	*sotchi* 'that way/side'	*atchi* 'that way/side'
Direction/Person (Polite)	*kochira* 'this way/ side, this person'	*sochira* 'that way/ side, that person'	*achira* 'that way/side, that person over there'
Type/Kind	*konna* 'this kind of'	*sonna* 'that kind of'	*anna* 'that kind of'
State/Manner	*kō* 'in this way'	*sō* 'in that way'	*ā* 'in that way'
Pre-Modern Japanese			
Pronominal	*ko*, *kore* 'this'	*so*, *sore* 'that'	*ka*, *kare*, *a*, *are* 'that over there'
Adnominal	*kono* 'this'	*sono* 'that'	*kano*, *ano* 'that over there'
Place	*ko*, *koko* 'here'	*so*, *soko* 'there'	*ka*, *kashiko*, *a*, *ashiko*, *asoko* 'over there'
Direction	*ko*, *konata*, *kochi* 'this way/side'	*so*, *sonata*, *sochi* 'that way/side'	*ka*, *kanata*, *a*, *anata*, *achi* 'that way/side'

This characterization of the *ko-so-a* demonstratives is called the **DISTANCE MODEL**.

(1) a. *Kono* *kado* *o* *magatte* *kudasai.*
this corner ACC turning please.do
'Please turn at this corner.'
b. *Sono* *kado o magatte kudasai.*
that
'Please turn at that corner further down the block.'
c. *Ano* *kado o magatte kudasai.*
that
'Please turn at that corner much further down there.'

Contrastively, when the speaker and the addressee are facing each other, the *ko*-series is used to refer to entities near the speaker; the *so*-series to entities near the addressee; and the *a*-series to those at a distance from both. This characterization is called the **TERRITORY MODEL**. As the term *territory* suggests, the notion of control is also relevant here. Suppose that a mother is washing her son's back.

(2) S: *Okāsan,* *itai* *yo.*
mother painful SFP
'Mom, that hurts!'

M: *Doko* *ga?*
where NOM
'Where?'
S: *#Koko/Soko/#Asoko* *da* *yo.*
here/there/there COP.NPST SFP
'There/#Here.'

In this case, the location referred to by the demonstrative in the son's utterance is a part of his body. Therefore, he is at least as close to the location as is the addressee, and yet only *so-* is appropriate because the son does not have control over his mother's scrubbing – that is, his back is perceived to be within her territory. Interestingly, English and Japanese demonstratives behave identically in this regard.

The utility of the Distance and Territory Models according to the alignment and orientation of the speaker and the addressee has been widely recognized. However, these models have been challenged by Mikami (1970/1992), who claims that *ko-so-a* do not form a *triplet*, but, rather, a **DOUBLE BINARY**: i.e. *ko-* vs. *so-* on the one hand, and *ko-* vs. *a-* on the other. He explains that the fundamental opposition in communicative, face-to-face situations consists of the speaker and the addressee, who divide the metaphorically conceived space into two sub-spaces. This opposition is represented by *ko-* (the speaker's territory) and *so-* (the addressee's territory). This much is identical with the Territory Model. What differs is the total absence in this part of Mikami's framework of the concept of *a-*. On the other hand, when the speaker and the addressee face in the same direction, whether physically or metaphorically, they perceive themselves together in opposition to others. In this conceptualization, the joint territory of the speaker and addressee is expressed by *ko-*, and that of the others by *a-*. Therefore, in Mikami's theory, *ko-* and *so-* oppose each other as do *ko-* and *a-*, but there is no opposition between *so-* and *a-*. He claims further that the oppositions between *ko-* and *so-* and between *ko-* and *a-* differ in nature, and thus these three demonstratives never oppose each other in the same interactional context.

Mikami's argument is supported by evidence from lexicalization (word) patterns and fixed phrases. That is, there are phrases combining *a-* and *ko-* as well as *so-* and *ko-*, but never *so-* and *a-*.

(3) *a-* + *ko-* *are-kore* 'this and that', *areka-koreka* 'this or that', *achira-kochira* 'here and there', *atchi-kotchi* 'here and there'
so- + *ko-* *soko-koko* 'here and there', *sonna-konna de* 'because of this and that', *sore to kore to wa hanashi ga chigau* 'this and that are different stories', *sō-kō suru uchi ni* 'while doing this and that'
a- + *so-* none

The total lack of combinations of *a-* and *so-* is striking, lending credence to Mikami's double-binary theory. Nevertheless, I continue to believe that in the situation directing a taxi driver, the opposition between *a-* and *so-* is psychologically real. For example, the driver might respond by asking while pointing, *Soko desu ka, asoko desu ka?* 'Do you mean there, or over there?' In such a case, the selection is systematic: the closer one is invariably referred to with *so-*, and the farther one with *a-*. The Distance Model thus seems justifiable. Why, then, is there the lack of lexical patterns with *so-* and *a-*? It remains a mystery.

26.2 Deixis and anaphora

When a demonstrative is used to point to an entity present in the speech situation, it is called a **DEICTIC**, and this pointing characteristic or function is called **DEIXIS**. Typically, a deictic expression is used to refer to something visible or audible during the utterance, as exemplified in (1). Deixis can also be temporal (e.g. *now*, *then*) or personal (e.g. *I*, *you*). Unlike "normal" words (e.g. *cat*, *pen*, *sun*), the meaning of a deictic expression is relative to the speech situation. For example, *I* designates you, the reader, when you are speaking, whereas it designates Joan when Joan is speaking.

The location of the speaker in time and space normally establishes the **DEICTIC CENTER** (or **ORIGO**) and thereby governs the interpretation of deictics. Consider, for example, the deictic verbs *come* and *go*. The typical interpretation of an utterance like *Joan came to the park* is that the speaker was present at the park or the park in the speaker's territory. By contrast, *Joan went to the park* normally implies that the speaker was not present at the park. Rather, the speaker was at some other place (i.e. deictic center) from which the event of going to the park is described.

Another typical use of demonstratives is called **ANAPHORA**, commonly defined as the relationship between two linguistic expressions co-occurring and co-referencing within a single discourse. For example, in (4), *she* refers backward to *the manager*, and these two expressions co-reference the person identified as the manager.

(4) I walked right in and talked with the manager. She virtually hired me on the spot.

The phenomenon of anaphora consists of two entities, e.g. *the manager* and *she* in (4). The semantically and referentially autonomous expression (*the manager*) is called the **ANTECEDENT**, whereas the dependent expression (*she*) is called the **ANAPHOR**. Anaphora is characteristically interpretable solely on the basis of the linguistic context, without recourse to the knowledge of the speech situation (e.g. who the speaker is, when and where the utterance is made). When the autonomous expression follows the dependent one – e.g. *Near her, Joan found a snake* – the co-reference relationship is called **CATAPHORA**.

26.3 Anaphoric use of Japanese demonstratives

Kuno (1973: 282–90) makes the generalization that *ko-* is used only deictically, but that *so-* and *a-* can be used either deictically or anaphorically. For deixis, Kuno subscribes to the Territory Model. That is, *ko-* covers the speaker's territory, *so-* covers the addressee's territory, and *a-* covers that which lies outside either territory. For anaphora, he considers that *so-* is selected either (i) when the speaker does not know the referent well (i.e. the speaker has only *indirect knowledge*), or (ii) when the speaker does know the referent well (i.e. s/he has *direct knowledge*), but s/he nevertheless assumes that the addressee does not: the situation in (5a). By contrast, *a-* is selected when the speaker believes that both s/he and the addressee know the referent well or have a shared experience with the referent: the situation in (5b).

(5) a.

Kinō	*Yamada*	*to iu*	*hito*	*ni*	*aimashita.*	*Sono (#Ano)*	*hito,*
yesterday		as.named	person	DAT	met	that	person
michi	*ni*	*mayotte*	*komatte ita*	*node,*	*tasukete*	*agemashita.*	
way	DAT	lost	was.in.trouble	because	helping	gave	

'Yesterday, I met a man named Yamada. He [that person] had lost his way and was having difficulty, so I helped him.'

b.

Kinō Yamada-san ni aimashita. Ano (#Sono) hito	*itsumo*	*genki*	*desu*	*ne.*
	always	healthy	COP	SFP

'Yesterday, I met Mr. Yamada. He [that person] is always in great spirits.'

The phrase *to iu hito* 'a person named' in (5a) signals that the speaker believes that the addressee does not know Yamada. In such a case, the use of *sono* is appropriate, but *ano* is not. In (5b), on the other hand, the absence of *to iu hito* indicates that the speaker assumes that the addressee has direct knowledge of Yamada. In this case, *ano* is appropriate, but *sono* is anomalous.

Kuroda (1979/1992) examined the use of Japanese demonstratives in soliloquial utterances and found cases that counter-exemplify Kuno's generalizations. He questions (i) whether the deictic and anaphoric uses are fundamentally distinct, and (ii) whether language use should always be accounted for in terms of communication, in which the presence of an addressee is always presumed. Those who subscribe to a communicative explanation, Kuroda cautions, need be aware that some characteristics of language use are likely *derived from the communicative setting itself*, rather than from the properties of the expressions under consideration.

In order to examine demonstratives in soliloquy, Kuroda eliminates the addressee from Kuno's characterization. Then, when used anaphorically, *a-* should be acceptable when the speaker knows the referent well, as in (6a), and *so-* when s/he does not, as in (6b).

(6) a.

Kyō	*Yamada-san*	*ni*	*atta*	*kedo,*	*ano*	*hito*	*to*	*atta*	*no*
today		DAT	met	but	that	person	with	met	NMLZ

wa *ittai* *nannen buri* *no* *koto* *darō.*
TOP what.on.earth how.many.years GEN event I.wonder
'I ran into Yamada-san today. I wonder how many years it's been since the last time I saw him [that person].'

b. *Yamada-san* *wa* *Tanaka-sensei* *toka iu* *hito* *no* *koto* *bakari*
TOP called person GEN matter only
hanashite ita *keredo,* *sono* *hito* *wa* *sonnani* *erai* *hito*
was.talking but that person TOP that.much great person
nano *darō ka.*
COP I.wonder
'Yamada-san was talking about a professor called Tanaka, but I wonder if she [that person] is really so great.'

Regarding deictic usage, the elimination of the addressee from Kuno's description (i.e. the Territory Model) predicts that *ko-* should be used for a nearby entity, and *a-* for a distant entity, with *so-* being unusable. Kuroda, however, claims that *so-* can be used deictically in soliloquy, imagining a scenario in which someone has been informed that he has a stomach ulcer. He considers this and says (7a). On the other hand, one morning he may feel an unusual sensation in his stomach and say (7b).

(7) a. *Sore* *wa* *donna* *iro* *o* *shite iru* *no* *darō ka.*
that TOP what color ACC is NMLZ I.wonder
'I wonder what color it [that] is.'

b. *Ittai* *kore* *wa* *itsu* *made* *tsuzuku* *no* *darō.*
what.on.earth this TOP when until continue NMLZ I.wonder
'I wonder how long this will last.'

Kuroda declares that deictic and anaphoric usages of *so-* and *a-* are both determined by the speaker's familiarity with the referent. He then re-labels Kuno's direct knowledge as **EXPERIENTIAL KNOWLEDGE**, and Kuno's indirect knowledge as **CONCEPTUAL KNOWLEDGE**. If one knows an entity experientially, s/he is able to describe it theoretically in an infinite number of ways. For example, I can describe my mother in terms of her age, appearance, health, interests, skills, etc. By contrast, information about an entity obtained by some indirect means, e.g. via hearsay or inference, is inevitably conceptual, or linguistic; i.e. it is information conveyed by some communicative means. For example, if someone says to me *My high school friend Alice called me yesterday*, I learn that a person named Alice, probably a female, who attended the same high school as the speaker, telephoned the speaker the day before the utterance. However, I learn nothing more.

Kuroda argues that *a-* is used if one's knowledge about the referent is experiential, whereas *so-* is used when it is conceptual. To support this analysis, he provides examples including the phrase *X no koto da kara* 'considering the nature of X', which implies that the speaker knows X in an experiential sense. In this situation, the referent can therefore naturally co-occur with *a-*, but it would be anomalous when occurring with *so-* as happens in (8b).

(8) a. *Yamada-san o matte iru no desu. Ano/Sono hito wa kitto*
ACC am.waiting that person TOP surely
okurete kuru deshō.
late come will
'I'm waiting for Yamada. I'm sure he [that person] will be late.'

b. *Yamada-san o matte iru no desu. Ano/#Sono hito no koto da kara,*
considering.one's.nature
kitto okurete kuru deshō.
surely late come will
'I'm waiting for Yamada. Considering his habits, I'm sure he [that person] will be late.'

Kuroda then presents the following counter-example to Kuno's analysis.

(9) *Boku wa Ōsaka de Yamada Taro to iu sensei ni osowattan da*
I TOP in called teacher DAT learned.from
kedo, kimi mo ano sensei ni tsuku to ii yo.
but you too that teacher DAT study.under if good SFP
'I studied in Osaka with a professor named Taro Yamada. You should study with him [that professor], too.'

Like (5a), the use of *to iu sensei* 'professor named' in (9) signals that the speaker assumes the addressee's lack of knowledge of the professor; therefore, according to Kuno, *sono*, but not *ano*, must be used. However, in (9), it is perfectly natural to use *ano* as it conveys the fact that the speaker knows Professor Yamada very well.

26.4 *Ko-so-a* in soliloquy

Kuroda's (1979/1992) use of soliloquy is insightful, but his data are based solely on introspection and so the conclusions lack strong empirical confirmation. I engaged in a study to follow up on his claims, examining my own, experimentally obtained soliloquy data: 428 *ko*-words, 151 *so*-words, and 237 *a*-words (Hasegawa 2010).[2]

26.4.1 Ko-

Of 428 *ko*-words in the soliloquy data, all but two were clearly deictic.

[2] The soliloquy data examined here were collected from 24 native speakers of Japanese. Each was asked to speak aloud his or her thoughts for 10–15 minutes while alone in an isolated room. They were instructed not to speak to an imaginary person or object, but, rather, to verbalize forthrightly whatever came into consciousness.

(10) [Looking at the desk chair in the office]
A, kono isu chō-raku sō.
oh this chair super-comfortable look.like
'Oh, this chair looks super-comfortable.'

The two problematic *ko-* cases are exemplified in (11).

(11) *Mā, ārudeko no ii no ga attara, hoshii kedo, mā,*
well Art.Deco GEN good one NOM if.exist want but well
kore wa kinagani yarō.
this TOP without-haste will-do
'Well, if there's a good one in the Art Deco style, I want it, but I think I'll spend more time on this [shopping].'

Kuno (1973: 288) contends that when *ko-* appears to be anaphoric, it is actually "indicating something as if it were visible to both the speaker and the hearer at the time of the conversation, and thus it imparts vividness to the conversation." The speaker of (11) had been shopping for an ottoman (footstool) and was browsing a catalog while recording her speech. *Kore* in this utterance refers to the abstract concept of shopping, which is not visibly present in the speech situation. Therefore, it is not an obvious case of deixis. Nevertheless, *kore* refers to "the activity I'm engaged in *now*," namely furniture shopping. Because the deictic concept *now* is involved, it is appropriately categorized as deixis.[3]

26.4.2 So-

Regarding the *so*-series, all 151 instances in my experiment are clearly anaphoric. Although Kuroda's stomach ulcer episode in (7a) illustrates that deictic *so-* is logically possible, such usage seems to be extremely rare. The total absence of deictic *so-* suggests that the Distance Model (proximal *ko-*, medial *so-*, distal *a-*) does not operate in soliloquy. All of the soliloquy recorded in my experiment took place in a small room, and several participants mentioned the scroll hanging on the wall a few feet from where they were seated. Some used *ko-* to refer to it, while others used *a-* as in (12).

(12) *Ano kakejiku wa dare ga kaita no kanā.*
that scroll TOP who NOM wrote NMLZ SFP
'I wonder who drew that scroll.'

[3] In written Japanese, there is a rhetorical construction in which *ko-* is used anaphorically: e.g. *Shisō oyobi ryōshin no jiyū wa, kore o okashi-te wa naranai* 'Freedom of thought and conscience shall not be violated' (the Constitution of Japan, Article 19; see Section 24.1.1). In this construction, the antecedent is typically designated by the topic marker *wa* (see Section 8.1), and repeating the entity with anaphoric *kore* generates an emphatic tone. This style was borrowed from Chinese in ancient times.

My data support the Territory Model: *so-* refers to an addressee's territory, but, because no addressee is involved in soliloquy, *so-* is irrelevant. The data also support Mikami's (1970/1992) Double-Binary Model; i.e. only a two-way opposition exists in deixis, in this case *ko-* vs. *a-*. What is puzzling is why the Distance Model is operative when an addressee is present.

The anaphoric use of *so-* in soliloquy will be considered next. Absent an addressee, it is assumed that a speaker of soliloquy uses *so-* when s/he does not know the referent well, and *a-* when s/he does. Alternatively, in terms of Kuroda's characterization, *so-* is used when the speaker knows of the referent merely conceptually, and *a-* when s/he knows the referent experientially. In some cases, the use of anaphoric *so-* appears to support Kuno's and Kuroda's analyses, e.g. (13), but the majority of uses do not, the case in (14).

(13)

Sankanbi	*ja nakute,*	*bunkasai*	*ja nakute, ā,*	*namae*	*wasureta.*	*Ēto,*	
observation-day	is.not	open.house	is.not	name	forgot	well	
oyako	*nantoka.*	*Ē,*	*nande*	*sonna*	*kotoba*	*wasurerun*	*yaro.*
parent.child	something		why	that	word	forget	I.wonder
6-nenkan	*mainen*	*atta*	*noni.*				
6-years	every.year	existed	though				

'Not a [parents'] observation day, not an open house, oh, I forgot what we called it [a school event]. Hmm, parent–child, parent–child something. How could I forget such [that kind of] a word? We had one every year for 6 years ...'

(14)

Sō da,	*pasokon*		*ga*	*kowarechatta*	*kara,*	*sono* *shūri*
well	personal.computer		NOM	has.broken.down	because	that repair
mo,	*moshi*	*dekitara,*	*shitai shi.*			
also	if	possible	want.to.do			

'Oh yeah, my computer has broken down, so, if at all possible, I want to repair it [that] too.'

In (13), it can easily be inferred that the speaker does not know the referent well. However, in (14) the speaker has a very clear idea of the referent of *so-*, the speaker's own computer. This example demonstrates that, contrary to Kuno and to Kuroda, *so-* can be used to refer to a familiar entity.

26.4.3 A-

The *a*-series occurred 237 times in the data, and, as shown in (15), it often accompanies an antecedent (underlined). It can therefore be considered anaphoric.

(15) [Wondering which car her in-laws would buy]

Okāsan	*rekusasu*	*ki ni itteru*	*yō datta*	*kedo,*	*demo*	*are*	*wa*
mother	Lexus	like	it.seemed	but	but	that	TOP
okkii	*kuruma*	*da*	*shi*	*nē.*			
big	car	COP	and	SFP			

'Mother seems to like the Lexus, but it's a big car.'

However, *a-* also occurs frequently without any antecedent:

(16) a. *Ā, kyō mo hare. Ashita mo hare hen kana. Ashita*
today also fine tomorrow also fine not SFP tomorrow
haretara, ano sandaru hako.
if.fine that sandals will.wear
'Well, it's beautiful today too. Tomorrow too, I hope, and if it is, I'll wear those sandals.'

b. [Looking at the cooking section of a magazine]
Kore, are da. Zenmai da.
this that COP flowering.fern COP
'This is it [that]. A flowering fern.'

Although the referents are not visibly present in the speech situation in (16), both *ano* and *are* seem to be deictic. While the speakers were soliloquizing, certain entities apparently emerged in their consciousness, and they referred to them deictically with *a-*. It is not likely that these entities were linguistic (i.e. actual words or phrases); more likely, they were mental imagery, i.e. a quasi-perceptual experience. The speakers were referring respectively to their minds' images of sandals and a flowering fern. To elaborate, (16b) is equivalent to an "X is Y" type equation, wherein "X" refers to a photo in a magazine which is identified by the visually deictic *kore*, and "Y" non-visually by the deictic *are*. That is, upon seeing the photo, the speaker remembered the name of the entity, *zenmai* 'flowering fern', and named it.

A question arises as to whether (15) and (16) are so clearly separable into anaphoric (15) and deictic (16) usages. Considering the speakers' minds, both examples seem to function in the same way, regardless of whether the entities having been introduced linguistically prior to the use of *a-*. Because sorting the occurrences of *a-* in soliloquy into deictic and anaphoric categories according to the mere presence or absence of an antecedent is cognitively arbitrary, I analyze both of them straightforwardly as deictic. I also conjecture that even in conversation, *a-* is always deictic, pointing to a speaker's mental construct.

Like Kuroda, I contend that the variant effects of *so-* and *a-*, as in (5), repeated here as (17), can only be accounted for in terms of the act of communication.

(17) a. *Kinō Yamada to iu hito ni aimashita. Sono (#Ano) hito,*
yesterday as.named person DAT met that person
michi ni mayotte komatte ita node, tasukete agemashita.
way DAT lost was.in.trouble because helping gave
'Yesterday, I met a man named Yamada. He [that person] had lost his way and was having difficulty, so I helped him.'

b. *Kinō Yamada-san ni aimashita. Ano (#Sono) hito itsumo genki desu ne.*
always healthy COP SFP
'Yesterday, I met Mr. Yamada. He [that person] is always in great spirits.'

In this regard, Kinsui and Takubo (1992) consider that the anomaly of *ano* in (17a) is attributable not to the speaker's assumption of the addressee's lack of knowledge of Yamada, but, rather, to its *asocial* nature. Kinsui and Takubo contend (though I disagree with this part) that the *ano* in (17a) is anaphoric, indicating à la Kuroda that the speaker's knowledge of the referent is experiential. If the addressee is unlikely to know the referent, they continue, to suggest one's knowledge as experiential is not only useless, but also alienating.

This line of reasoning can be adapted to suggest that *ano* in (17a) is deictically pointing to a mental construct. However, unless the addressee has the same construct in mind, its use is ill-suited to the communicative situation. Bringing the same entity into the addressee's consciousness can be accomplished by a prior mention (an antecedent in anaphora), pointing to its presence in the speech situation (deixis), or by some other means. However, I contend that the selection of *a-* is not directly controlled by such means.

26.4.4 Chafe's model of consciousness

Recall that in Kuno's view, *ko-* is always deictic even when the referent is invisible. If indeed both *ko-* and *a-* are invariably deictic, then what is the difference between the two? Chafe's (1994) model of consciousness is helpful in accounting for this difference. Chafe defines consciousness as "an active focusing on a small part of the conscious being's self-centered model of the surrounding world" (p.28). While one is able to arouse such grand experiential totalities as one's father or one's years as an undergraduate student, no one can be conscious of their entire internal composition all at once. That is, one can focus one's attention on only a particular image or action of one's father, or on a particular person, place, or event within one's undergraduate days (p.28). Most of consciousness consists of the flow of experiences, perceptions, and actions, concomitant with co-occurring emotions, opinions, attitudes, desires, and decisions (p.31).

Chafe perceives consciousness to be like vision, constantly in motion, that people are able to focus their conscious attention on only a very limited amount of information at one time. Like foveal (i.e. sharp, central) vision, there is focal consciousness, and like peripheral vision, there is peripheral consciousness, providing a context for that which is focused upon – i.e. what draws our attention. A vast amount of information lies beyond peripheral consciousness, which is unattended to at any given moment. Information in the focal, peripheral, or unconscious state is referred to respectively as *active*, *semiactive*, or *inactive* (p.53).[4]

[4] Active and inactive information can be considered to correspond to short-term and long-term memory respectively (Atkinson and Shiffrin 1968), but Chafe (1994: 53) prefers not to use these terms because of the implication that memory is a *place*. He argues that relevant phenomena can be better captured in terms of activation, not by considering something to be *in* memory or to be retrieved *from* memory.

Now recall Kuroda's (1979/1992) contention that *a-* is used if one's knowledge of the referent is experiential, whereas *so-* is used when it is conceptual, i.e. obtained via some means of communication. Having analyzed my soliloquy data, it appears to me that how information was obtained about a subject is immaterial. I have constructed example (18) to illustrate this point.

(18)	*Ano/#Kono*	*hito*	*dare*	*nan*	*darō,*	*kinō*	*Okada-san*	*ga*
	that/this	person	who	COP	I.wonder	yesterday		NOM
	hanashiteta		*hito.*					
	was.talking.about		person					

'Who is that person? The one that Okada was talking about yesterday?'

In (18), the speaker wonders about the identity of the person that Okada had mentioned the day before. Here, the speaker does not personally know the referent, with his/her knowledge being obtained only linguistically (i.e. conceptually in terms of words or phrases) from Okada. Therefore, according to Kuroda, *a-* should be impossible. Nevertheless, the use of *a-* in (18) sounds quite plausible. I hypothesize that *a-* can be used deictically to refer to an entity if it is in one's peripheral consciousness and thus in a semiactive state. Exactly what mental construct *ano* deictically points to in this case is unclear. If I place myself in this situation, the mental imagery of the conversation with Okada is likely to come to my mind, but not the image of the person in question. Because the speaker of (18) does not know the person, that person him/herself cannot be totally activated in consciousness, and is therefore referred to by *ano*, suggesting that, in relation to the speaker, this unknown person exists "at some distance" metaphorically speaking.

Furthermore, the use of *ko-* in (18) would sound unnatural. I therefore hypothesize that *ko-* is used to refer deictically to an entity only if the speaker has focused his/her attention on that entity, and thus is in an active state at the moment of speech. Example (19) is another constructed utterance. Here, both *kore* and *are* can be used. Intuitively, the task that the speaker remembers is more clearly recognized when *kore*, rather than *are*, is selected.

(19)	*Ashita*	*nani*	*shinakucha ikenain*	*dakke.*	*A,*	*sō da,*	*gijiroku*	*da.*
	tomorrow	what	I.have.to.do	I.wonder	oh	I.see	minutes	COP
	Kore/Are	*mo*	*jikan*	*kakaru*	*nā.*			
	this/that	also	time	take	SFP			

'What do I have to do tomorrow? Oh, yeah, the minutes. It'll take time.'

The hypothesis that *a-* is used to refer to an entity in a semiactive state provides a clue to understanding the bewildering functions of *a-*. Although *a-* can be used to refer to something located in the distance, it is also frequently used for an entity with which the speaker is familiar, based on experiential knowledge, as argued by Kuno (1973) and Kuroda (1979/1992). Anecdotally, it is said that with the maturation of marriage, a couple tends to employ more *a-* as in example (20).

(20) *Are* *motte kite.*
bring.please
'Bring it [that] to me, please.'

A husband would say (20) to his wife, *are* being understood to refer to a newspaper if reading a newspaper is part of the husband's routine at the breakfast table. Likewise, a wife might say the same to her husband at the dinner table, and the husband immediately understands what she wants.

The association of familiarity/experiential knowledge with *ko-* (proximal) is intuitive, because familiar things are metaphorically close to one's self. By contrast, the construal of familiarity with distal *a-* is perplexing. We may be able to better understand the connection between *a-* and familiarity if we consider the referent of *a-* to be distal in the sense that it is in peripheral consciousness, but, at the same time, familiar because it is included in one's model of the surrounding world – i.e. in one's permanent memory – and therefore can be focused upon at will.[5]

[5] For further discussion of this topic, see Hasegawa (2012).

27 Represented speech

27.1 Introduction

When communicating, we frequently quote what other people have said. Such utterances are commonly characterized in terms of a dichotomy between **DIRECT** and **INDIRECT SPEECH**. It is frequently said that in direct speech, original expressions are faithfully reproduced in both form and content, whereas in indirect speech, reporters only commit themselves to the accurate rendering of the content. Nevertheless, in reality, one can rarely remember the exact wording of even one's own utterances, let alone those of others, unless there is some special quality that renders the form of the utterance memorable. Direct speech is normally spontaneous, with perhaps some rhetorical effects in mind, created by the reporter at speech time rather than a verbatim rendition of the original speech (Tannen 1989).

In English, the complementizer *that* is used in indirect speech, but not in direct speech as exemplified in (1). On the other hand, in written language, a comma and quotation marks are normally obligatory for direct speech, but prohibited for indirect speech.

(1) a. *She said, "A little simplification would be the first step toward rational living."*
b. *She said that a little simplification would be the first step toward rational living.*

Furthermore, the tense and personal pronouns used in the original utterance must be adjusted in indirect speech as in (2b).

(2) a. *Midori said, "I'm invited to the ceremony."*
b. *Midori said that she was/had been invited to the ceremony.*

Speech acts (Chapter 19) are often indicated separately from the content of the quotation by such speech act verbs as *apologize*, *ask*, *complain*, *congratulate*, *demand*, *insult*, *permit*, *prohibit*, *promise*, *request*, *suggest*, *warn*, etc. as in (3b) and (4b).

(3) a. *Midori said, "Who else is invited?"*
b. *Midori asked who else was invited.*

(4) a. *Midori said, "Don't use a cell phone in the room!"*
b. *Midori* <u>*demanded*</u> *no one use a cell phone in the room.*

Direct speech permits expressive elements that do not carry significant informational content, as in (5a), but such elements are prohibited in indirect speech, as in (5b).

(5) a. *Midori said, "Wow/Hello/Ouch."*
b. **Midori said that wow/hello/ouch.*

Moreover, direct-quotation clauses can be grammatically incomplete as in (6a), but indirect-quotation clauses must be complete as in (6b).

(6) a. *Midori said, "I want to go, but . . ."*
b. **Midori said that she wanted to go but . . .*

In Japanese, direct speech and indirect speech are not formally distinguishable. In both, the quotative particle *to* (or its colloquial variant *-tte*) marks a quoted clause (see Section 15.3), and quotation marks are not consistently employed.[1] As demonstrated in (7b), Japanese does not require tense agreement between the main and the quoted clause; the tense of the original utterance is retained. Occurrences of polite expressions, e.g. *masu* in (7a), in quoted speech will be discussed shortly.

(7) a.	*Midori*	*wa*	*"Biru*	*wa*	*manekarete imasen"*	*to*	*itta.*	[direct]
		TOP		TOP	is.not.invited.POL	QUOT	said	
	'Midori said, "Bill is not invited."'							
b.	*Midori*	*wa*	*Biru*	*wa*	*manekarete inai*	*to*	*itta.*	[indirect]
		TOP		TOP	is.not.invited	QUOT	said	
	'Midori said that Bill was [Lit. is] not invited.'							

27.2 Deixis in represented speech

In Section 26.2, we discussed the concept of deixis as expressed in *this/that, here/there, now/then, I/you,* and *come/go.* The spatiotemporal location of the speaker when the utterance is made routinely establishes the deictic center, which governs the interpretation of deictic expressions. In direct speech, there are two deictic centers and two types of addressee: one for the original speech situation, and the other for the reporting situation. By contrast, in indirect speech, the deictic center is limited to the reporting situation (see Figure 27.1). Therefore, the presence or absence of two deictic centers and two types of addressee dictates the distinction between direct vs. indirect speech (Coulmas 1985).

In (7) above, the original speech is quoted in two ways: with the polite form *masu* in direct speech, and with the plain form in indirect speech. Politeness in

[1] Japanese quotation marks are 「 (opening) and 」 (closing).

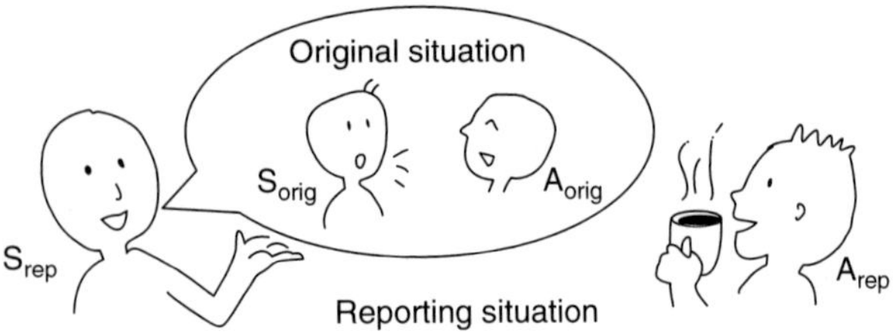

Figure 27.1. Two speech situations.

the original utterance indicates an attitude of the original speaker (S_{orig}) towards the original addressee (A_{orig}). It is, therefore, irrelevant in the case of indirect speech, which can communicate only the content, not the attitude, of the original utterance. Any politeness expressions in indirect speech encode the attitude of the reporter (S_{rep}) towards his/her addressee (A_{rep}). If S_{rep} wishes to convey S_{orig}'s polite attitude, s/he needs to describe it, for example, with *teinei ni itta* 'said politely'.

Other types of expressions tied to the original speech situation which must be adjusted in indirect speech include (i) demonstratives, (ii) SFPs (except the interrogative *ka*), and (iii) first- and second-person pronouns. The following pairs of direct and indirect speech demonstrate these types of adjustments.

(8) a.	*Shigeru*	*wa*	*"<u>Kono</u>*	*sakana*	*wa*	*oishii*	*<u>ne</u>"*	*to*	*itta.*
		TOP	this	fish	TOP	delicious	SFP	QUOT	said

'Shigeru said, "This fish is delicious, isn't it?"'

b.	*Shigeru*	*wa*	*<u>sono</u>*	*sakana*	*wa*	*oishii*	*to*	*itta.*
		TOP	that	fish	TOP	delicious	QUOT	said

'Shigeru said that the fish was [Lit. is] delicious.'

(9) a.	*Shigeru*	*wa*	*"<u>Kono</u>*	*sakana*	*wa*	*oishii*	*<u>desu</u>*	*ka"*	*to*	*itta.*
		TOP	this	fish	TOP	delicious	COP.POL	INT	QUOT	said

'Shigeru said, "Is this fish delicious?"'

b.	*Shigeru*	*wa*	*<u>sono</u>*	*sakana*	*wa*	*oishii*	*ka*	*to*	*kiita.*
		TOP	that	fish	TOP	delicious	INT	QUOT	asked

'Shigeru asked whether the fish was [Lit. is] delicious.'

As in English, *kono* 'this' in S_{orig}'s utterance needs to shift to *sono* 'that' or some other expression in indirect speech. The SFP *ne* in (8a) that is used by S_{orig} to solicit A_{orig}'s agreement plays no role in the reporting utterance, and therefore does not appear in (8b). However, the SFP *ka* in (9) concerns the S_{orig}'s mental state, i.e. one involving uncertainty, and has nothing to do with A_{orig}, so it must be retained in an indirect quote as in (9b).

First- and second-person pronouns are clearly bound to the original speech situation; therefore, they too must be adjusted in indirect speech.

(10) a.

Midori	*wa*	*watashi*	*ni*	*"Anata*	*wa*	*omoiyari ga nai"*	*to*	*itta.*
	TOP	I	to	you	TOP	inconsiderate	QUOT	said

'Midori told me, "You're inconsiderate."'

b.

Midori	*wa*	*(watashi*	*ni)*	*watashi*	*wa*	*omoiyari ga nai*	*to*	*itta.*
	TOP	(I	to)	I	TOP	inconsiderate	QUOT	said

'Midori said that I'm inconsiderate.'

(11) a.

Midori	*wa*	*"Watashi*	*wa*	*shiranai"*	*to*	*itta.*
	TOP	I	TOP	not.know	QUOT	said

'Midori said, "I don't know it."'

b.

Midori	*wa*	*jibun/kanojo*	*wa*	*shiranai*	*to*	*itta.*
	TOP	self/she	TOP	not.know	QUOT	said

'Midori said that self/she did not know it.'

In (10), S_{rep} is A_{orig}, so *anata* 'you' designates S_{rep}; therefore, in (10b), *anata* must be changed to *watashi* 'I'. If (11a) is uttered rather than written – i.e. the quotation marks are invisible to aid interpretation – it is ambiguous between direct- and indirect-speech interpretations, i.e. *watashi* may refer to Midori or S_{rep}. If, on the other hand, the polite form *shirimasen* 'do not know' is used instead of the plain *shiranai*, the utterance would normally be interpreted as direct speech, and, therefore, *watashi* would refer to Midori. In (11b), while the use of *kanojo* 'she' is possible, as is the case of English, the **REFLEXIVE PRONOUN**, *jibun* 'self', is more commonly selected when the pronoun refers to the speaker. This use of *jibun* in indirect speech is called **LOGOPHORIC**: the logophoric expression designates the person whose utterance or thought is being represented. While *kanojo* in (11b) can refer to a female person other than Midori, *jibun* is not ambiguous, uniquely pointing to Midori.[2]

27.3 Omission of verbs of saying/thinking

The quoting particle *to* is so strongly tied to a verb of saying or thinking that it can stand by itself and imply the presence of such a verb.

(12) a.

Midori	*wa*	*bakabakashii*	*to*	*tachiagatta.*
	TOP	ridiculous	QUOT	stood.up

'Midori stood up, (saying) "(that's) ridiculous."'

b.

Midori	*wa*	*shinjirarenai*	*to*	*watashi*	*o*	*mitsumeta.*
	TOP	cannot.believe	QUOT	I	ACC	gazed

'Midori gazed at me, (thinking that what I had just said) was unbelievable.'

c.

Midori	*wa*	*"kaette*	*kudasai"*	*to*	*doa*	*o*	*shimeta.*
	TOP	go.home	please	QUOT	door	ACC	closed

'Midori said "Please go home" and shut the door.'

Obviously, *tachiagaru* 'stand up', *mitsumeru* 'gaze', and *shimeru* 'close' do not take a quoted clause; therefore, hearers read in a verb of saying or thinking to complete the utterances semantically.

[2] See Hirose (1995) for further discussion regarding *jibun*.

27.4 Blended speech

In English, interrogative and imperative constructions cannot appear in indirect speech.

(13) a. **Joan said that could she take a day off on Monday?*
b. **Joan said that shred this report!*

By contrast, Japanese permits the following types of quotation.

(14) a.

Midori	*wa*	*jibun*	*o*	*shiranai*	*no*	*ka*	*to*	*itta.*
	TOP	self	ACC	not.know	NMLZ	INT	QUOT	said

'[Lit.] Midori said that don't you know me.'
'Midori asked if (I) didn't know her.'

b.

Midori	*wa*	*jibun*	*ni*	*denwa*	*shite*	*kure*	*to*	*itta.*
	TOP	self	to	telephone	do	give.IMP	QUOT	said

'[Lit.] Midori said that telephone me.'
'Midori told me to call her.'

The use of *jibun*, rather than *watashi*, to refer to Midori herself in (14) indicates that the quoted clauses are in indirect speech because Midori is unlikely to use *jibun* to refer to herself in actual speech. Nevertheless, the underlined part is interrogative in (14a) and imperative in (14b). Kuno (1988) calls such quotations **BLENDED SPEECH**, a mixture of indirect and **QUASI-DIRECT SPEECH**. In (15), because the second parts of the sentences are not verbatim quoted speech, they are considered quasi-direct.

(15) a. *Midori wa* *jibun o* (INDIRECT) *shiranai no ka* (QUASI-DIRECT) *to itta.*
b. *Midori wa* *jibun ni* (INDIRECT) *denwa shite kure* (QUASI-DIRECT) *to itta.*

The reported speech in (15) is considered quasi-direct because it may differ from the actual utterances. For instance, Midori's utterances are more likely to be something like (16).

(16) a.

Watashi	*o*	*shiranai*	*no*	*desu*	*ka.*
I	ACC	know.not	NMLZ	COP.POL	INT

b.

Watashi	*ni*	*denwa*	*shite*	*kudasai.*
	to	telephone	do	give.POL.IMP

However, in blended speech, polite expressions (i.e. those that can occur in the real direct quotations) are prohibited as in (17); plain forms must instead be utilized.

(17) a. #*Midori wa* *jibun o* (INDIRECT) *shiranai no desu ka* (DIRECT) *to itta.*
b. #*Midori wa* *jibun ni* (INDIRECT) *denwa shite kudasai* (DIRECT) *to itta.*[3]

[3] This utterance is possible if *jibun* is used contrastively. That is, *Please call ME, not someone else.*

Blended speech permits peculiar usage of donatory verbs (e.g. *ageru/kureru* 'give', *morau* 'receive'). As discussed in Chapter 13, donatory verbs have strict constraints in their distribution; the b-sentences below, for example, are ungrammatical.

(18) a.	*Boku*	*ga*	*Hanako*	*ni*	*okane*	*o*	*yatta.*
	I	NOM		to	money	ACC	gave

'I gave money to Hanako.'

b. **Hanako ga boku ni okane o yatta.*
'Hanako gave money to me.'

(19) a.	*Hanako*	*ga*	*boku*	*ni*	*okane*	*o*	*kureta*
		NOM	I	to	money	ACC	gave

'Hanako gave money to me.'

b. **Boku ga Hanako ni okane o kureta.*[4]
'I gave money to Hanako.'

The sentences in (18) testify to the fact that *yaru* cannot be used when the recipient is the speaker, whereas those in (19) demonstrate that *kureru* is incompatible in situations in which the speaker gives to a third person. Nevertheless, when a donatory event is reported, violation of these rules becomes acceptable, as happens in (20).

(20) a.	*Hanako*	*wa*	*boku*	*ni*	*okane*	*o*	*yatta*	*to*	*iifurashite iru.*
		TOP	I	to	money	ACC	gave	QUOT	is.spreading

'Hanako is telling everybody that she gave me money.'

b.	*Hanako*	*wa*	*boku*	*ga*	*kanojo*	*ni*	*okane*	*o*	*kureta*	*to*	*itte iru.*
		TOP	I	NOM	she	to	money	ACC	gave	QUOT	is.saying

'Hanako says that I gave money to her.'

Boku ni okane o yatta, which is ungrammatical in (18b), is grammatical in (20a). Likewise, *boku ga Hanako ni okane o kureta* is ungrammatical in (19b), but grammatical in (20b). According to Kuno, the sentences in (20) are examples of blended discourse with *boku ni/ga* in indirect speech, with the remainder in quasi-direct speech.

27.5 Free indirect speech

FREE INDIRECT SPEECH is typically used to refer to a literary technique in third-person narrative for representing a character's consciousness. In English, it combines the person and tense of indirect speech (e.g. *she would arrive, thought John*) with expressions appropriate to direct speech (e.g. *here, tomorrow*): *She would arrive here tomorrow, thought John*. This form allows a third-person narrative to incorporate a first-person point of view as exemplified in (21), the opening passage of Virginia Woolf's *Mrs. Dalloway*.

[4] This use of *kureru* is possible in some dialects.

(21) (a) *Mrs. Dalloway said she would buy the flowers herself.* (b) *For Lucy had her work cut out for her.* (c) *The doors would be taken off their hinges;* (d) *Rumpelmayer's men were coming.* (e) *And then, thought Clarissa Dalloway, what a morning – fresh as if issued to children on a beach.*

The novel begins with indirect speech, (21a), followed by free indirect speech. The verb tenses and colloquial usages of (21b–21d) indicate normal narrative flow, but the contents are direct representations of Mrs. Dalloway's thoughts, not those of the narrator. The beginning of (21e) is again in the form of indirect speech, supplying the main-clause predicate, *thought Clarissa Dalloway*, but *what a morning* is an exclamatory utterance inappropriate in indirect speech: **She thought (that) what a morning*.

In Japanese fiction, a character's consciousness is represented by the exclusive use of private expressions (vis-à-vis public expressions) normally in the non-past tense. **PUBLIC EXPRESSION** corresponds to the communicative function of language; **PRIVATE EXPRESSION** corresponds to the non-communicative, thought-expressing function of language (Hirose 1995). Public expression in Japanese frequently, but not always, includes interactional, or addressee-oriented, elements. These include: (i) directives (e.g. commands, requests, questions, warnings); (ii) certain SFPs (e.g. *ze* 'I tell you'); (iii) **VOCATIVES** (e.g. *oi* 'hey'); (iv) responses (e.g. *hai* 'yes', *iie* 'no'); (v) interactive expressions of various kinds (e.g. *sumimasen ga* 'excuse me, but', *koko dake no hanashi dakedo* 'it's between you and me'); (vi) polite forms (e.g. *desu/masu*), and (vii) hearsay expressions (e.g. *sō da* 'I hear that'). The lack of such elements, however, does not guarantee that the utterance is private.

The public/private distinction surfaces when different verbs are used to describe a person's thought or speech. While verbs of saying can accompany a quoted clause in both public expression (i.e. direct speech) and private expression (i.e. indirect speech), verbs of thinking permit only private expression.

(22) a.

Tarō	*wa*	*ame*	*da*	*to*	*omotte iru.*
	TOP	rain	COP	QUOT	thinks

'Taro thinks it's raining.'

b.

**Tarō*	*wa,*	*ame*	*da*	*ne*	*to*	*omotte iru.*
	TOP	rain	COP	SFP	QUOT	thinks

'Taro thinks "It's raining, you know."'

c.

**Tarō*	*wa,*	*ame*	*desu*	*to*	*omotte iru.*
	TOP	rain	COP.POL	QUOT	thinks

'Taro thinks politely "It's raining."'

d.

**Tarō*	*wa,*	*ame*	*da*	*sō da*	*to*	*omotte iru.*
	top	rain	COP	EVID	QUOT	thinks

'Taro thinks "I hear it's raining."'

In (23), quoted from KAWABATA Yasunari's *Yama no oto* 'The Sound of the Mountain', the narrative shifts from the *ta*-form to the *ru*-form.

(23) *"Oshi da." to Shingo wa tsubuyaita. Gyā! to itta semi*
mute COP QUOT TOP muttered QUOT said cicada
to wa chigau
from is.different
'"(This cicada) is mute," Shingo muttered. It was [Lit. is] different from the one that sang loudly.'

The *ta*-form in the first sentence (*tsubuyaita*) indicates that it is the narrator's voice, with a direct quotation of Shingo's utterance, whereas the *ru*-form in the second sentence (*chigau*) indicates that it is in free indirect speech, a direct representation of Shingo's thought. If the *ta*-form *chigatta* 'was different' had been employed, the sentence would no longer be in free indirect speech, but would be a description of the situation as an objective fact from the narrator's viewpoint.

Free indirect speech can also occur in first-person narrative, where the first-person pronoun refers to the person as either the narrator or the protagonist. The following is the opening sentence of KODA Aya's *Nagareru* 'Flowing' accompanied by Alan Tansman's (1993: 13) translation.

(24) *Kono uchi ni chigai-nai ga, doko kara haitte ii ka*
this house must.be but where from enter good INT
katteguchi ga nakatta.
kitchen.door NOM not.existed
'This was [Lit. is] certainly the house, but there was no kitchen door. Where was the entrance?'

The demonstrative *this* is selected in the translation based on the protagonist's perspective – i.e. the house is in front of the protagonist – but *was* is the narrator's past tense. Similarly, the interrogative form of the second sentence in translation reflects the protagonist's thought, but, again, the tense is anterior to the narrative time.

As another example of first-person narrative, (25) is derived from NATSUME Soseki's *Sanshirō*.

(25) *"Odeni narimasen ka" to kiku to sensei wa sukoshi*
come.out.not INT QUOT ask when professor TOP a.little
warai nagara, mugon no mama kubi o yoko ni futta.
smile while without.a.word neck ACC side to shook
Kodomo no yōna shosa o suru.
child GEN like gesture ACC do
'When (I) asked "Would you like to come out?" Professor smiled a little and shook his head side to side without saying a word, like a child does ([Lit.] He does a childish gesture).'

The first sentence in the past tense is part of narration, but the second is Sanshirō's inner thought about the professor's gesture. Only the shift of tense marker signals this rhetorical move.

27.6 Self-quotation

We quote not only other people's speech, but also our own speech, to qualify and emphasize our speech acts so as to ensure their efficacy. In the following conversation derived from Maynard (1996: 222), the teacher (T) springs a pop quiz on students, one of whom is Nonohara (N), the comic book's female hero. The teacher's utterance marked by "→" is a self-quote, emphasizing his prior speech.

(26) T: *Nonohara!!*
N: *Giku.* (surprised)
'Oops.'
T: *Misenasai!! Ima Kobayashi ga tsukue no ue ni oite itta kamikire o.*
show.IMP now NOM desk's.top on left paper ACC
'Show it to me! The piece of paper that Kobayashi left on (your) desk just now.'
N: *A ... Ano ...*
'Uhh ... Well ...'
→ T: *Misenasai to itte irun da!!*
show.IMP QUOT saying COP
'Show it to me, I say!'

Another use of self-quotation is to mock or parody one's own speech (Maynard 1996: 221). In this exchange, also derived from a comic, Hoshina (H) and Sari (S) are beginning to fall in love.

(27) H: *Kedo omae no me de wakaru.*
but you GEN eye with understand
'But I understand (you) by (looking into) your eyes.'
S: *Kā.* (embarrassed)
'Ohh ...'
→ H: *Nān chatte na.*
such say SFP
'Umm, just kidding.'

Having spoken quite intimately to Sari, Hoshina feels embarrassed and vulnerable. In order to circumvent possible rejection, he parodies his own speech act by self-quotation, *nān chatte na*, a colloquial, blunt male version of *nante itte shimatte ne* '[Lit.] I've ended up saying so; I shouldn't be saying this.' Another example of this type from Maynard (1996: 221) is provided in (28).

(28) *Ūn daigaku tte yappari kono kurai hirokunakucha ne to ka itte.*
uhh university QUOT after.all this much must.be.large SFP QUOT INT SAY
'Well, universities should after all be as large as this, you know ... just kidding.'

When the speaker of (28) and her friend are visiting a university campus, she compares the university's facilities with their own. Aware that their conversation is being recorded, the speaker feels it necessary to assuage her serious tone by means of self-parody using *to ka itte* '[Lit.] saying something like', which is, in effect, similar to the English qualifiers *just kidding* or *just saying* (delivered in a light, mocking tone).

The third function of speech-act qualification by self-quotation is mitigation, i.e. weakening the impact of a statement. *Omou* 'think' is frequently used for this purpose:

(29) a. *Gorikai* *itadaki-tai* *mono* *da* *to* *omoimasu.*
understanding.HON receive-want thing COP QUOT think.POL
'[Lit.] I think I hope you will understand it.'
b. *Gorikai* *itadaki-tai* *mono* *desu.*
'I hope you will understand it.'

(29a) is theoretically ambiguous, offering two possible interpretations of the utterance: it can be understood as a report/description of the speaker's thought, or as a qualified speech act. With the past tense *omoimashita* 'thought' is used instead, only the first interpretation is available; however, in the non-past tense, the second interpretation is more likely intended. With respect to the qualified speech-act interpretation, (29a) and (29b) deliver identical meaning. The effect of *omou* in (29a) is to soften the force of the assertion and create the impression that the speaker is not brash, tactless, or domineering. Such usage, however, can be judged negatively as too indirect or manipulative.

Self-quotation involves placing one's own speech or thought within a larger frame of saying. Or, in Kamada's (1988) account, self-quotation introduces one situation of talk into another situation. By so doing, one can objectify the quoted content and separate it from the speech act, which can then be qualified. Maynard (1996: 208–09) contends that when speakers take on character roles, they can make use of self-quotation, among other purposes, to expand their range of expression and to enhance the dramatic effects of their speech acts.

Speakers assume different character roles as they interact according to a context which the speakers themselves help create. When assuming the voice of a character, the speakers are capable of echoing multiple voices manipulated through . . . quotation strategies . . . what motivates the speaker to self-quote is a desire to manipulate a broader range of expressiveness in interaction. More concretely, self-quotation facilitates discourse functions such as dramatization and distancing. Self-quotation also serves to qualify speech acts as it mitigates, parodies, and/or emphasizes the act of "saying" itself.

Presenting part of a message as quotation enables the speaker to provide information that would otherwise be unavailable. For example, (30a) and (30b) convey the same message, but the underlined part of (30b) is a direct quotation of the speaker's inner speech with the emphatic SFP *zo*, and revealing it makes the utterance more vivid while conveying closeness and intimacy to the addressee (see Section 22.6).

(30) a. *Kono keiyaku wa kiken desu.*
this contract TOP risky COP.POL
'This contract is risky.'

b. *Kono keiyaku wa kiken da zo to omoimasu.*
this contract TOP risky COP SFP QUOT think.POL
'I think this contract is risky.'

Here is my favorite example that demonstrates how self-quotation enables a speaker's two roles – one for thinking, the other for communicating.

(31) *Temēra namen-na yo to mōshiage-tai.*
you not.take.lightly.IMP SFP QUOT say.HUM-want
'I'd like to say, "Listen, you pig, you'd better take me seriously, or else!"'

Suppose that (31) is uttered by a professor addressing his/her students in classroom. *Temēra* is a vulgar second-person plural pronoun, and *namen-na yo* '(I tell you) don't take me lightly' is a crude, unrefined command, both of which are inappropriate in the given situation. However, when they are embedded as a direct quote that includes *mōshiageru*, the humble form of 'say', (31) becomes utterable. The vulgar part exists within the professor's inner speech, which cannot and should not be controlled or controllable.

28 Gendered language

28.1 Introduction

While all languages probably lead their male and female speakers into somewhat different patterns of talk, Japanese is particularly well-known for conspicuously differentiated **GENDERED LANGUAGE/SPEECH**.[1] Beginning in the late 1970s, gendered language, particularly so-called **WOMEN'S LANGUAGE**, has attracted considerable attention from researchers. An increasing number have concluded that the alleged characteristics of Japanese gendered language are not necessarily grounded in empirical observations of the way Japanese men and women actually speak. Rather, it may be that these characteristics are firmly rooted in **LANGUAGE IDEOLOGY**, defined as "any sets of beliefs about language, articulated by the users as a rationalization or justification of perceived language structure and use" (Silverstein 1976: 193). This chapter will explore Japanese gendered language both as a reflection of linguistic ideology and as a phenomenon present in its day-to-day use.

When used in combination with an elaborate honorific system (see Chapters 20–21), Japanese gendered language makes possible depictions of multi-party conversations without overt identification of each speaker. Japanologist Edward Seidensticker (1989: 145), who translated numerous Japanese novels including *Genji monogatari* ['The Tale of Genji]', noted that if the following conversation were made by four interlocutors – Maude, George, Aunt Margaret, and Uncle John – it would be impossible to record it in English without labeling who said each line:

(1) a. *"You didn't!"*
    b. *"Oh, yes, I did."*

[1] The terms *sex* and *gender* are used to refer to related, but distinct, concepts. *Sex* is a biological and binary categorization based mainly on reproductive potential. (However, Blackless *et al.* (2000) estimates that approximately 1 percent of new-born babies have neither standard male nor female bodies.) *Gender* is a social construct that is learned and performed by members of a society. Unlike sex, gender is not a binary category; one's appearance and actions can be perceived as more masculine or more feminine than those of other individuals. A man, for example, can utilize female speech if he wishes to identify his gender as female, or vice versa.

c. *"But why?"*
d. *"Can't you guess?"*
e. *"Because I loved her."*
f. *"You should have told me."*

This conversation would have to be written in English along the lines of (2).

(2) a. *"You didn't!" exclaimed Maude.*
b. *"Oh, yes, I did," said George.*
c. *"But why?" wondered Aunt Margaret.*
d. *"Can't you guess?" said Uncle John.*
e. *"Because I loved her," responded George.*
f. *"You should have told me," declared Aunt Margaret.*

In Japanese, on the other hand, adroit selections of gendered language and honorific expressions make this conversation comprehensible without overt reference to any of the interlocutors. Interpreting this conversation to be about an extramarital affair on the part of George, who is Maude's husband, I would translate it as follows.

(3) a.

Nanimo	*nakattat-te*	*it-te*	*yo.*
nothing	happened-QUOT	say-TE	SFP

'Tell me nothing has happened.'

b.

Jibun	*o*	*osaeru*	*koto*	*ga*	*dekinakattanda.*
self	ACC	control	NMLZ	NOM	could.not

'I couldn't control myself.'

c.

Demo	*dōshite*	*desu*	*no?*
but	why	COP	SFP

'But why?'

d.

Omaesan	*ni wa*	*wakar-an*	*no*	*kane?*
you	for	understand-not	NMLZ	SFP

'You don't understand?'

e.

Soko	*made*	*ano*	*hito*	*o*	*suki ni*	*natteshimattanda.*
that	much	that	person	ACC	like	have.become

'I fell so in love with her.'

f.

Semete	*watakushi*	*ni wa*	*itte-kudasaru*	*beki*	*deshita*	*wa-ne.*
at.least	I	to	tell-give.HON	ought.to	was.POL	SFP

'You should have at least told me.'

In (3a), the *te*-form of the verb followed by the SFP (SFP) *yo* occurs mainly in casual female speech; its male counterpart is *itte kure yo*, where *kure* is the imperative form of *kureru* 'give'.[2] In (3b), *deki-nakat-ta-n-da* – the past tense of *deki-nai* 'cannot do' followed by the abbreviated form of the nominalizer *no* combined with the abrupt ending with the copula *da* – is normally judged as

[2] *Kureru* is a *ru*-verb, so the imperative form derived by regular rules is *kure-ro*, like *tabe-ro* 'Eat!'. However, the irregular *kure* is more commonly used as its imperative form.

male-speech style; the female counterpart is *deki-nakat-ta-no (yo)*. In (3c), *desu no* – the addressee honorific version of the copula and the SFP *no* – implies that the speaker is a female who speaks gracefully or standoffishly. In (3d), the use of *omae-san* 'you', *wakar-an*, a negative form of *wakaru* 'understand', and the combination of the SFPs *ka* and *ne* point to an elderly male speaker. In (3e), *shimat-ta-n-da* is in the same construction as in (3b). Regarding (3f), the use of *watakushi* in casual conversation is considered female speech; the use of the referent honorific *kudasaru* 'give' determines the speaker to be a reserved or aloof woman. This utterance also contains the addressee honorific *deshita*, which in casual conversation is more likely to be used by female speakers. Finally, the combination of SFPs *wa* and *ne* is stereotypical female speech.

28.2 Formal characteristics of Japanese gendered speech

Gendered expressions are scattered throughout Japanese speech. As discussed in Section 20.6, the beautifier prefix *o-* (e.g. *o-hana* 'flower') is more frequently used by female speakers than by male speakers, and when the addressee and the referent are identical, as explained in Section 20.7, the use of a referent honorific without an addressee honorific (e.g. *Ashita irassharu?* 'Will you come tomorrow?') is found exclusively in female speech.[3] Other areas in which gender differences are prominent include the selection of (i) personal pronouns, (ii) interjections, (iii) SFPs, (iv) directives (e.g. commands, requests, questions), (v) gendered vocabulary, (vi) vowel coalescence in pronunciation, (vii) presence or absence of the copula, and (viii) other miscellaneous expressions. In the following descriptions of these areas, "M" stands for masculine, "N" for neutral, and "F" for feminine expressions.

(4) a. First-person pronouns
M: *ore, boku, oira* (very casual), *washi* (obsolete)
N: *watashi* (formal), *watakushi* (very formal)
F: *atashi*

b. Second-person pronouns
M: *omae, kimi, kisama* (dramatic), *temē* (vulgar)
N: *anata, anta* (very casual), *otaku* ([Lit.] 'your house'), *sochira* ([Lit.] 'that side')

Watashi in (4a) is gender-neutral, while *atashi* is female speech. Note, however, that for male speakers, *watashi* is restricted to formal registers. In casual

[3] Honorifics are not gender specific. However, women tend to use honorifics more frequently than men.

conversations, males use *boku* and the cruder *ore*. For example, in the Tōkyō dialect, (5) is interpreted as a male utterance because of the use of the male first-person pronoun *ore*.[4]

(5) *Ore* *kaeru.*
I go.home
'I'm going home.'

(6) Interjections
M: *che!, oi, oya?, yō*
N: *ā, hā?, fūn, hē, hō, hora, uwā*
F: *ara, mā, sōnē*

(7) *Ara,* *omoshiroi.*
oh interesting
'Oh, it's interesting.'

(7) is understood as a female utterance due to the use of the exclamatory interjection *ara* (with a falling intonation).

(8) Sentence-final particles
M: *na, yo-na, zo, ze*
N: *ne, yo, yo-ne*
F: *kashira, no-ne, no-yo-ne, wa, wa-ne, wa-yo*

(9) M: *Ame* *ga* *furu* *zo/ze.*
rain NOM fall SFP
'It's going to rain.'
F: *Ame* *ga* *furu* *wa-yo.*

(10) M: *Atsui* *na.*
hot SFP
'It's hot, isn't it?'
F: *Atsui* *wa-ne.*

(11) Commands
M: *Kore* *kopī* *shiro* *(yo).*
this copy do.IMP SFP
'Copy this!'
N: *Kore* *kopī* *shi-nasai.*[5]
do-IMP

(12) Negative commands
M: *Kore* *kopī* *suru* *na* *(yo).*
this copy do NEG.IMP SFP
'Don't copy this!'

[4] During the Edo period (1603–1867), *ore* was used by both male and female commoners in Tokyo (then called *Edo*). However, women, especially those belonging to an upper class, began to avoid its use. As a consequence, it became a male first-person pronoun (Komatsu 1988: 94–95). In some of today's dialects, *ore* is still gender-neutral.

[5] *Nasai* is the imperative form of the honorific verb *nasaru* 'do'.

N: *Kore kopī shi-nai-de.*
do-NEG-TE

(13) Requests
M: *Kore kopī shi-te kure.*
this copy do-TE give.IMP
'Please copy this.'
F1: *Kore kopī shi-te ne.*
do-TE SFP
F2: *Kore kopī shi-te chōdai.*[6]
do-TE give.IMP

(14) Questions
M: *Shiai mi ni iku kai?*
game see for go INT
'Are you going to see the game?'
N: *Shiai mi ni iku?*

(15) Gendered vocabulary
M: *meshi* (for *gohan* 'meal'), *kuu* (for *taberu* 'eat'), *dekai* (for *ōkii* 'big')
F: *iyān* (for *iya* 'no'), *suteki* 'marvelous' (not exclusively in female speech, but men use it much less frequently)

(16) Vowel coalescence in pronunciation: *ai > ē*
M: *Mizu nomi-tē.* (< *nomi-tai*)
water drink-want.to
'I want to drink water.'
M: *Mendokusē nā.* (< *mendokusai*)
troublesome SFP
'It's troublesome.'

(17) The copula + a sentence-final particle
M: *Kore wa kumo da yo/ne/yo-ne.*
this TOP spider COP SFP
'This is a spider.'
F: *Kore wa kumo Ø yo/ne/yo-ne.*

Gendered language has been undergoing rapid and drastic change. For more than twenty-five years, I rarely had occasion to watch Japanese movies, television dramas, and theatrical productions. Recently, however, I have examined more than 200 random samples of contemporary cultural media, and found that while male speech has not undergone many changes, female speech has changed considerably. Most female characters are now portrayed as publicly using what was formally considered male speech, as in (17M), and do so much more frequently than their cohorts did two-plus decades ago.

Koto, which is generally used to refer to an abstract object – e.g. *ashita suru koto* 'things I (have to) do tomorrow' – also functions as a nominalizer (see Section 15.1). Like English *that* – as in *That we are not alone in the universe is*

[6] *Chōdai* is a colloquial version of *kudasai* 'give me'.

evident – *koto* can convert a clause into a noun. It is widely agreed that completing a sentence forthrightly might on occasion sound too assertive, so some female speakers prefer to end an utterance with *koto*.[7]

(18) F: *Hē* *omoshiroi* *koto.*
hmm interesting NMLZ
'Hmm, that's interesting!'

Due to specific male and female speech forms, if an utterance were transcribed and subjected to judgment with no further contextual information included, most native speakers of Japanese could determine the speaker's gender. If the form, however, were gender-neutral, this kind of determination would be impossible or simply random.

There are many variations and gradations of gendered-speech. Okamoto and Sato (1992) posit five categories: *strongly masculine* (e.g. 4M, 5, 8M, 9M, 11M, 12M, 13M,14M, 15M, 16), *moderately masculine* (10M, 17M), *neutral* (e.g. 4N, 6N, 8N, 11N, 12N, 14N), *moderately feminine* (13F1) and *strongly feminine* (e.g. 4F, 7, 8F, 9F, 10F, 13F2, 15F, 17F, 18). One way to interpret these categories is as follows: when moderately masculine forms are used by a female speaker or when moderately feminine forms are used by a male speaker, such utterances may not necessarily draw special attention from the hearer(s) with respect to gendered role-behavior. However, when strongly masculine or strongly feminine forms are used by members of the opposite sex, they will necessarily be considered marked language uses, and the hearers are likely to make inferences regarding the potential motivations of such marked selections, e.g. attempts at feminizing, joking, mimicking, ridiculing.

Regarding prescriptive categorizations of gendered speech, it is unreasonable to expect that native speakers of Japanese uniformly agree with all of them *in toto*. Nevertheless, such categorizations represent the intuition of many native speakers, and most native speakers agree with the classifications of most of the expressions cited above.

28.3 Role language

It is significant that when native speakers of Japanese read prescriptively gendered language, they frequently regard it as being an excerpt from a novel rather than a transcript of a real conversation. In other words, gendered language markers are more often literary conventions than reflections of real-life speech. Kinsui (2003)

[7] This feminine use of *koto* attaches to the copula, *i*-adjectives, or *na*-adjectives + *na*. When *koto* follows the conclusive form or the negative form of a verb in utterance-final position, it is understood as a command, e.g. *Enpitsu de kaku koto* 'Write with a pencil!', *Hairanai koto* 'Do not enter!'.

calls such social-identity markers **YAKUWARI-GO** 'role language', i.e. indicators of stereotyped, sometimes fictitious, speech styles useful for the depiction of a particular social role. The use of such language automatically identifies the character's relevant social role, allowing the writer to avoid lengthy characterization of each character in a novel. Even today's best-selling novelists occasionally produce ideologically constructed stereotyped language that is unheard of in modern-day Japanese life. Novelist SHIMIZU Yoshinori (2003: 34–36) perceptively asserts that if the writer depicts utterances of a supporting character (a non-protagonist) as if in transcribing a real, tape-recorded conversation, too much weight will be placed on that character and the story-line might be compromised. Therefore, if, for example, a male supervisor in a story asks his subordinate to carry out an assigned task, it is considered appropriate, indeed conventional, to write the dialogue in stereotyped language (e.g. *Kyōjū ni yatte oite kure tamae* 'Please complete this today'). The word *tamae*, to be explained shortly hereafter, is no longer routinely used. Nevertheless, this is acceptable, even preferable, because the reader will easily comprehend the conveyed information without paying special attention to the actual locution of the utterance.

One typical role language is **HAKASE-GO** 'doctor's language' ("doctor" as in a learned person, not a medical doctor), as is illustrated in the two sentences in (19) derived from the comic book series *Tetsuwan Atomu* 'Astro Boy'.

(19)	*Oya*	*ja*	*to?*	*Washi*	*wa*	*Atomu*	*no*	*oya-gawari*	*ni*
	parent	COP	QUOT	I	TOP		GEN	parent-surrogate	to
	nattoru		*wai.*						
	has.become		SFP						

'Parent? I've been Atomu's surrogate parent.'

The use of *ja* (a variation of the copula), *washi* (a first-person pronoun), *oru* for *iru* as in *natt-oru* (abbreviation of *natte-iru*) and *wai* (an SFP) invariably lead native Japanese speakers to identify these sentences as uttered by an elderly man. In such entertainment genres as *manga* 'comics', most wise, and thus elderly, men speak this way despite the fact that in real life elderly men do not speak in this manner.[8]

28.4 Origins and development of gendered language in Japanese

Gendered speech in the Japanese language originated in ancient times. Sei Shōnagon (ca. 966–1017), for instance, wrote in her celebrated collection of essays *Makura no sōshi* ['The Pillow Book'] that men's and women's

[8] A parallel might be drawn between role language and the so-called "royal *we*," e.g. *We are not amused* (= *I am not amused*), allegedly uttered by Queen Victoria. Although the royal *we* is obsolete, "it is very much alive in the 'royalese' of satirical journalism, parody and caricature, a crude symbol of royalty" (Wales 1996: 64).

language would sound different even when both conveyed an identical meaning.[9] However, scholars generally agree that in earlier historical periods gendered speech must have exhibited considerably fewer distinct formal traits than do their modern counterparts (Mashimo 1969). In those earlier periods, a woman expressed her femininity submissively: by not initiating a conversation, by not completing utterances, and by not clearly articulating her ideas, muttering to herself instead (Sato 2006: 110–11).

During the Muromachi period (1392–1568), distinctions between masculine and feminine speech became clearer. For instance, women used honorific markers – e.g. the verbal auxiliary *masu* – more frequently than men did (Mashimo 1969: 9–10). This period also witnessed the development of so-called **NYŌBŌ KOTOBA** 'court ladies' language', whose lexicon included many vocabulary items still used by modern women, and to a lesser extent by men: e.g. *himoji(i)* 'hungry', *oishi(i)* 'delicious', *o-furu* 'used article', *o-hada* 'skin', *o-hiya* 'cold water', *o-kazu* 'side dish', *o-miashi* 'legs', *o-shiru* 'soup', *o-tsumu* 'head'.

Although the tradition of differentiating men's and women's language has ancient roots, most of the stylistic characteristics of Japanese gendered language as we know them today emerged in the Meiji period (1868–1912) (Komatsu 1988; Inoue 2004, 2006; Nakamura 2006). In order to demonstrate this development, Komatsu (1988) compares the SFPs that appear in the dialogues of SHIKITEI Sanba's *Ukiyoburo* ['Floating-World Bathhouse'], published in 1809–13 during the Edo period (1603–1867) with those of NATSUME Soseki's *Sanshirō* (the male protagonist's first name), published in 1909 during the Meiji period (see Table 28.1). *Ukiyoburo* depicts conversations of diverse groups of people in terms of age, occupation, region, sex, and social class, whereas *Sanshirō*'s conversations are those of characters who are young intellectuals of both sexes. A subset of the data compiled by Komatsu is presented in Table 28.1, wherein "MW" indicates that the form was used by both men and women, "M" exclusively by men, and "W" exclusively by women. *Da* is the copula in its non-past form; "Ø" indicates absence of SFPs; "N" stands for a noun.

Table 28.1 clearly indicates that gender divergence became more prominent during the Meiji Era. That is, during Meiji many previously gender-neutral particles became gender-specific. For example, *zo* was used by both sexes in *Ukiyoburo*, as shown in (20a), which is uttered by the female bathhouse owner

[9] *Koto kotonaru mono. Hōshi no kotoba. Otoko onna no kotoba. Gesu no kotoba ni wa kanarazu moji amari shitari* (from the *Nōinbon* version of *Makura no sōshi*) 'Different ways of speaking. A priest's language. The speech of men and of women. The common people always tend to add extra syllables to their words' (translation by Ivan Morris, Sei Shonagon ca. 1000/1991).

Table 28.1 *Development of gendered SFPs.*

Sentence-final form	*Ukiyoburo* 1809–13	*Sanshirō* 1909	Sentence-final form	*Ukiyoburo* 1809–13	*Sanshirō* 1909
da Ø	MW	M	*~wa*	MW	W
da na	MW	M	N *ne*	MW	W
da ne	MW	M	N *yo*	MW	W
da yo	MW	M	*da te*	M	
da ze	MW	M	*da te ne*	M	
da zo	MW	M	*da e*	W	
~na	MW	M	*da no ya*	W	
~sa	MW	M	*da yo nē*	W	
~ya	MW	M	*da yo nō*	W	
~ze	MW	M	N *nē*		W
~zo	MW	M	*~na no*		W
da wa	MW	W	*~no ne*		W
~no	MW	W	*~wa ne*		W
~noyo	MW	W	*~wa yo*		W

to greet female customers, but this particle is used exclusively by men in *Sanshirō*. (Note that the honorific prefix *go-* in *go-genki* 'healthy' co-occurs with *zo* in (20a),[10] an unacceptable combination in today's Japanese because *zo* is characterized as a casual-to-vulgar masculine particle.) Conversely, *no-yo* is used exclusively by women in *Sanshirō*, but by both sexes in *Ukiyoburo*, as shown in (20b), where it is uttered by a man to his friends.

(20) a. *Itsumo* *go-genki* *de* *ii* *zo.*
always healthy.HON COP.TE good SFP
'Good to see you're well!'

b. *Katsu* *ga* *iu ni wa,* *kiden* *ga* *ii* *to* *iu* *no-yo.*
NOM in.saying you NOM good QUOT say SFP
'According to Katsu, you'd be suitable.'

Many researchers contend that present-day gendered language was invented during the Meiji period – that is, during Japan's early modernization. For example, by 1880, innovative features of the speech preferred by elitist, male secondary-school (similar to today's high school) students had begun to play a pivotal role in shaping modern gendered language. In (21), *kimi* 'you', *boku* 'I' and *tamae* 'give (imperative)' exemplify newly emerged **SHOSEI KOTOBA** 'schoolboys' language', which, to a great extent, shaped modern-day men's language (Tanaka 1988: 8).

[10] In Modern Japanese, the prefix *o-* is used, as in *o-genki*.

(21) a. *Kimi ga chakufuku shita ni chigainai.*
you NOM embezzle no.doubt
'You must have pocketed it.'

b. *Kore dake ga boku no inochi no tsuna da.*
this only NOM I GEN life GEN rope COP
'Only this is my lifeline.'

c. *Kakusazu dashi-tamae.*
not-hiding show-IMP
'Don't hide it. Show it to me!'

Even more influential than *shosei kotoba* was **JOGAKUSEI KOTOBA** 'schoolgirls' language' in the development of modern-day women's language. *Jogakusei* referred to the "girls and young women of the elite classes who attended the women's secondary schools that had been instituted as part of the early Meiji modernization project inspired by Western liberal Enlightenment thought" (Inoue 2006: 38). Because of the high frequency of the sentence-final expressions *te-yo* and *da-wa*, *jogakusei kotoba* was also called **TEYO-DAWA KOTOBA** (Tanaka 1988: 8), which the four expressions in (22) exemplify.

(22) a. *Yokutte yo.*
good SFP
'It's OK.'

b. *Ara iya da wa.*
oh disagreeable COP SFP
'Oh, I don't like it.'

c. *Iku koto yo.*
go NMLZ SFP
'I'll go.'

d. *Kuru kashira.*
come SFP
'I wonder if she will come.'

To conservative ears, schoolgirls' speech sounded cacophonous, shrill, and, consequently, it was widely criticized and characterized as vulgar by intellectuals and newspaper columnists. Nevertheless, by 1890, *teyo-dawa kotoba* had spread even to upper-class women, and by 1900 this new speech style had become well established as a more general and inclusive women's language (Komatsu 1988: 102–06). Because of its vibrancy, this language was quickly disseminated by its adoption in novels and magazines, and this wide circulation in print bestowed upon it prestige and authority (Inoue 2006: 126). By the 1930s, *teyo-dawa kotoba* had largely been accepted as the ideal female speech style, and upper-middle class women begun to put it into daily practice (p. 133).

28.5 Gendered language in soliloquy

Gendered language is selected by a speaker according to the public persona s/he wishes to present. Therefore, it is of interest to scrutinize how gendered language manifests itself in soliloquy, where no addressee or bystanders influence the speaker's selection of gendered expressions.

As mentioned in Section 23.1, I experimentally collected a total of 3,042 soliloquy utterances from 24 native speakers of Japanese (Hasegawa 2010), 2,050 utterances made by 16 female speakers (aged between 20 and 60), and 992 by 8 male speakers (7 in their 20s and one in his 40s). Of the 2,050 female utterances, only 76 (3.7%) involved women's language. Male speakers used gendered language slightly more frequently (67 times, or 6.8% of utterances).

However, both men and women used men's language; only first-person male pronouns were used exclusively by men. With one exception, all male participants consistently used *ore*, a pronoun that is more casual than *boku*. The subject who used *boku* never used *ore*. Masculine expressions were almost exclusively used by male participants (e.g. *meshi* 'meal') and vowel coalescence (e.g. *mendokusē* 'troublesome' < *mendokusai*), although some female participants occasionally used them. The SFP *yo-na* is not strongly masculine, but its distribution is nevertheless highly skewed towards men's language. By contrast, the distribution of *ka-ne* is less skewed, but is still more common among male speakers. Significantly, male participants never used women's language.

In the past, information such as the speaker's gender, geographical origin (identified as a regional dialect), and social class membership was considered to be the **EVOKED MEANING** of particular linguistic expressions. By contrast, in recent years, an increasing number of investigations of gendered language have suggested that certain linguistic expressions point to a multiplicity of sociocultural significances, including the spatiotemporal locus of the communicative situation (deixis, see Chapter 26) and speech acts (Chapter 19). This relationship between a linguistic expression and its context is referred to as **INDEXICALITY**, derived from the term *index*, a system in which one entity points to another, as, until recently, index cards in library card catalogs pointed to books located on shelves.

Ochs (1993, 1996) considers affective stances as **DIRECT INDEXES** (i.e. the pragmatic meaning of a linguistic expression) while gender and social relationships are **INDIRECT INDEXES**. In the course of her analysis, Ochs concludes that Japanese SFPs *ze* and *wa* directly index affective stances of coarse versus delicate intensity, respectively, and that these affective stances in turn indirectly index gender and gender images of masculinity and femininity. Therefore, women can utilize masculine forms not necessarily to express masculinity, but to express an affective stance of directness or assertiveness, heretofore restricted and attributed to men.

When applied to soliloquy, Ochs' analysis proves problematic. For example, contrary to Ochs' contention, there seems to be no flexibility in the choice of first-person pronouns, male speakers invariably using either *ore* or *boku*, and female speakers either *watashi* or *atashi*. In other words, these pronouns directly index speakers' gender identities.

Of related interest, Nakamura (2001) reports the same phenomenon in Japanese children's acquisition of what she calls *gender-appropriate language*. Observing twelve boys and twelve girls aged between three and six, Nakamura recognizes that when speaking with their mothers, boys tend to use gender-neutral or moderately masculine forms, but when speaking with same-sex peers, they use strongly masculine forms like *omae* 'you' and *dō surun da yo* 'what are you doing?' (p.18). By contrast, girls tend to use gender-neutral forms in both types of situations, with the occasional use of feminine forms (p.18).

According to Nakamura, as early as age three, Japanese children have already acquired an awareness of gendered language, and are corrected by peers more frequently than by their mothers when gender-inappropriate language is used. For example, a four-year-old girl was criticized by her peers when she said *umai nā!* 'this is delicious!' – using the masculine *umai* rather than the neutral *oishii* – which her female peers immediately rejected as inappropriate. Likewise, a three-year-old boy was frequently teased by his male peers for using the feminine SFP *wa*. "Peers often assure the observance of gender-stereotyped norms by teasing and taunting the child who fails to conform" (p. 34). Nakamura also recognizes some persistent gender-based linguistic differences, saying:

> we need to distinguish between the linguistic features most closely tied to the speaker's gender identity as male or female (i.e. linguistic features that are used all the time) and those that relate to specific role-situational constraints to be socially masculine or feminine (i.e. linguistic features that vary according to one's stance as influenced by contextual and situational constraints . . .). For example, even when girls are engaged in rough-and-tumble play in an aggressive manner, they do not use masculine first person pronouns such as *ore* and *boku,* although they might use masculine sentence-final particles such as *zo* and *ze*. This occurs because some gender-based linguistic forms seem to be linked more closely to the fixed gender identity of the speaker than others, and incorrect use of some linguistic forms is more marked than incorrect use of others (p. 37).

The second problem with Ochs' model of indexicality in language use is its inability to account for the asymmetry observed in the present soliloquy data. That is, while women might use masculine forms to emphasize such attributed masculine characteristics as coarseness, men do not use feminine forms to convey gentility. All feminine expressions were used exclusively by female participants, whereas all masculine expressions, except for the male first-person pronouns, were used by both sexes, with the frequency of women's usage varying considerably. Regarding this issue, Nakamura (2001: 20) reports virtually identical traits among young children when playing with boys' and girls' toys.

> Girls often were willing to play with many of the toys that boys typically play with (e.g. blocks), but it was difficult to get boys to play with toys associated with girls (e.g. tea sets). This tendency increased with age. Boys sometimes were willing to try girls' toys when playing with their mothers but refused to do so when playing with other boys.

She also notes that girls can be assertive and rough, using masculine linguistic forms, but boys normally do not use feminine forms with their same-sex peers (p.35).

Why does this pronounced asymmetry arise if men's and women's languages do not directly index gender or gender images of masculinity and femininity, but, rather, different yet gender-neutral affective stances? There must be some factors that motivate women and girls to use masculine expressions, but discourage men and boys from using feminine expressions. Before undertaking this inquiry, I will review two different, but well-accepted approaches to the study of gendered linguistic behavior.

The two commonly recognized approaches utilize either the **DOMINANCE FRAMEWORK** or the **DIFFERENCE FRAMEWORK** (Cameron 1998: 215–21). The former claims that male dominance in society is reflected in, as well as the major cause of, gendered language (e.g. Lakoff 1975; Fishman 1983; West and Zimmerman 1983, 1987). Dominance is not only attributed to individual males, but is also an institutional power granted to them collectively by society. Because of their lower status and the social pressures on them to "speak like a lady," many women tend to use more hedges, polite forms, etc. for conveying their unassertiveness and insecurities as well as trivializing their talk and accountability.

The difference framework (e.g. Maltz and Borker 1982; Tannen 1986, 1993) focuses more on linguistic "miscommunication" between the two sexes and concludes that dominance and power do not play a significant role in such "miscommunication." This approach perceives men and women as belonging to different subcultures and having different-but-equally valid rules of conversation acquired from same-sex social interactions throughout their adolescent years. Therefore, even when both men and women attempt to treat each other as equals, subcultural miscommunication can occur.

Uchida (1992: 558) strongly questions the validity of the anti-power-based difference framework, claiming that the most important difference is male dominance. In fact, male dominance exists and asserts itself regardless of what the individual intends to communicate. She argues that while the difference approach appeals to our desire to believe in the equality of men and women, social equality in principle and social equality in reality are two different matters wherein the former does not guarantee the latter.

We can now see a parallel between the difference framework and Ochs' double-tiered indexing approach to gendered language. Neither can account for the asymmetry in linguistic behavior of males and females. In soliloquy, where social pressure is minimal, female speakers use masculine forms for expressing whatever attributes such forms bear, whereas male speakers do not use feminine forms at all. Similarly, girls use masculine forms when they are assertive and strong, but boys normally do not use feminine forms when they are tender. In this regard, Uchida (1992: 560) makes this telling observation.

The observation of power structure can also be made when we look at the speech patterns acquired by girls and boys through same-sex interactions with peers. Girls' principles of cooperation, collaboration, equality, sharing and relating and showing empathy perfectly coincides with the "typical" female characteristics: nurturing, supportive, expressive, emotive, friendly, relationship-oriented, and other similar adjectives, which are also associated with "weakness" and "powerlessness." Boys' patterns, on the other hand, involve competing for and holding on to the floor, asserting, challenging, arguing, showing one's dominance and verbal aggressiveness, which are associated with "powerful" and "masculine" traits.

Postulating that certain expressions directly index tough intensity and power is reasonable, but associating delicate intensity and powerlessness appears quite arbitrary unless one acknowledges how *femininity* factors into these traits. I thus conclude that Japanese "women's language" directly indexes the feminine gender image, which is considered inferior to the masculine gender image in the social hierarchy. This is why males consciously or unconsciously fear and reject feminine gendered language. They shun it despite its association with gentility – a characteristic which is claimed to be esteemed by both men and women.

References

Adachi, Taro. 1995. Tekara to ato(de): Dekigoto no keikiteki setsuzoku. In *Nihongo ruigi hyōgen no bunpō II*, ed. Tatsuo Miyajima and Yoshio Nitta, 547–53. Tokyo: Kurosio.

Akatsuka, Noriko. 1985. Conditionals and the epistemic scale. *Language* 61: 625–39.

Alfonso, Anthony. 1971. On the "adversative" passive. *The Journal – Newsletter of the Association of Teachers of Japanese* 7 (1): 1–7. www.jstor.org/stable/488843.

Amanuma, Yasushi. 1988. Kokugo mondai no rekishi. In *Nihongo hyakka daijiten*, ed. Haruhiko Kindaichi, Oki Hayashi, and Takeshi Shibata, 1229–38. Tokyo: Taishūkan.

Aoki, Haruo. 1986. Evidentials in Japanese. In *Evidentiality: The Linguistic Coding of Epistemology*, ed. Wallace Chafe and Johanna Nichols, 223–38. Norwood, NJ: Ablex Pub. Corp.

Arisaka, Hideyo. 1957. Jōdai ni okeru sa-gyō no tōon. In *Kokugo on'inshi no kenkyū*, 145–59. Tokyo: Sanseidō.

Arita, Setsuko. 1993. Nihongo jōkenbun kenkyū no hensen. In *Nihongo no jōken hyōgen*, ed. Takashi Masuoka, 225–78. Tokyo: Kurosio.

2007. *Nihongo jōkenbun to jiseisetusei*. Tokyo: Kurosio.

Aston, William. 1904. *A Grammar of the Japanese Written Language*. www.archive.org/details/gram00marofjapanesastorich.

Atkinson, Richard, and Richard Shiffrin. 1968. Human memory: a proposed system and its control processes. In *The Psychology of Learning and Motivation*, ed. Kenneth Spence and Janet Spence, 89–195. New York: Academic Press.

Atsuji, Tetsuji. 1994. *Kanji no bunkashi*. Tokyo: NHK Publishing.

Austin, John. 1962. *How to Do Things with Words*. Cambridge, MA.: Harvard University Press.

Banfield, Ann. 1982. *Unspeakable Sentences: Narration and Representation in the Language of Fiction*. Boston: Routledge & Kegan Paul.

Barnlund, Dean, and Shoko Araki. 1985. Intercultural encounters: the management of compliments by Japanese and Americans. *Journal of Cross-Cultural Psychology* 16 (1): 9–26.

Baum, Robert. 1981. *Logic*. New York: Holt, Rinehart and Winston.

Beebe, Leslie, Tomoko Takahashi, and Robin Uliss-Weltz. 1990. Pragmatic transfer in ESL refusals. In *Developing Communicative Competence in a Second Language*, ed. Robin Scarcella, Elaine Andersen, and Stephen Krashen, 55–73. New York: Newbury House.

Brown, Penelope, and Stephen Levinson. 1978/1987. *Politeness: Some Universals in Language Usage*. Cambridge University Press.

Blackless, Melanie, Anthony Charuvastra, Amanda Derryck, Anne Fausto-Sterling, Karl Lauzanne, and Ellen Lee. 2000. How sexually dimorphic are we? Review and synthesis. *American Journal of Human Biology* 12: 151–66.

Blum-Kulka, Shoshana, and Elite Olshtain. 1984. Requests and apologies: a cross-cultural study of speech act realization patterns (CCSARP). *Applied Linguistics* 5 (3): 196–213.

Bybee, Joan. 1985. *Morphology: A Study of the Relation between Meaning and Form*. Amsterdam: John Benjamins.

Bunkachō. 2004. *Heisei 15 nendo kokugo ni kansuru yoronchōsa no kekka ni tsuite*. www.bunka.go.jp/1kokugo/15_yoron.html.

2007. *Keigo no shishin*. www.bunka.go.jp/bunkashingikai/soukai/pdf/keigo_tousin.pdf.

Cameron, Deborah. ed. 1998. *The Feminist Critique of Language: A Reader*. London: Routledge.

Chafe, Wallace. 1976. Givenness, contrastiveness, definiteness, subjects, topics, and point of view. In *Subject and Topic*, ed. Charles Li, 25–56. London and New York: Academic Press.

1994. *Discourse, Consciousness, and Time: The Flow and Displacement of Conscious Experience in Speaking and Writing*. University of Chicago Press.

Chomsky, Noam. 1973. Conditions on transformations. In *A Festschrift for Morris Halle*, ed. Stephen Anderson and Paul Kiparsky, 232–86. New York: Holt, Rinehart & Winston.

Clancy, Patricia. 1986. The Acquisition of Japanese. In *The Acquisition of Japanese*, ed. Patricia Clancy and Dan Slobin, 373–524. Hillsdale, NJ: Lawrence Erlbaum Associates.

Clancy, Patricia, Sandra Thompson, Ryoko Suzuki, and Hongyin Tao. 1996. The conversational use of reactive tokens in English, Japanese, and Mandarin. *Journal of Pragmatics* 26: 355–87.

Cohen, William. 1972. *To Walk in Seasons: An Introduction to Haiku*. Rutland, Vermont: Tuttle.

Comrie, Bernard. 1976. *Aspect*. Cambridge University Press.

Cook, Haruko. 1990. The sentence-final particle ne as a tool for cooperation in Japanese conversation. In *Japanese Korean Linguistics*, ed. Hajime Hoji, 29–44. Stanford: CSLI.

1992. Meanings of non-referential indexes: a case study of Japanese sentence-final particle *ne*. *Text* 12: 507–39.

2006. Japanese politeness as an interactional achievement: academic consultation sessions in Japanese universities. *Multilingua* 25: 269–91.

2008. *Socializing Identities Through Speech Style*. Bristol: Multilingual Matters.

Coulmas, Florian. 1985. Direct and indirect speech: general problems and problems of Japanese. *Journal of Pragmatics* 9: 41–63.

Daikuhara, Midori. 1986. A study of compliments from a cross-cultural perspective: Japanese vs. American English. *Penn Working Papers in Educational Linguistics* 2 (2): 103–34. www.gse.upenn.edu/wpel/archive/f1986.

Davidson, Donald. 1980. *Essays on Actions and Events*. Oxford University Press.

Donnellan, Keith. 1967. Reasons and causes. In *The Encyclopedia of Philosophy, Volume* 7, ed. Paul Edwards, 85–88. New York: Macmillan.

Eelen, Gino. 2001. *A Critique of Politeness Theories*. Manchester: St. Jerome Publishing.

Fillmore, Charles. 1990. Epistemic stance and grammatical form in English conditional sentences. *Papers from the Twenty-sixth Regional Meeting of the Chicago Linguistic Society*, 137–62.

Fishman, Pamela. 1983. Interaction: the work women do. In *Language, Gender, and Society*, ed. Barrie Thorne, Cheris Kramarae, and Nancy Henley, 89–101. Rowley, MA: Newbury House.

Fleischman, Suzanne. 1990. *Tense and Narrativity*. Austin: University of Texas Press.

Ford, Cecilia, and Sandra Thompson. 1996. Interactional units in conversation: syntactic, intonational, and pragmatic resources for the projection of turn completion. In *Interaction and Grammar*, ed. Elinor Ochs, Emanuel Schegloff, and Sandra Thompson, 134–84. Cambridge University Press.

Fry, Dennis. 1958. Experiments in the perception of stress. *Language and Speech* 1: 126–52.

Fujii, Seiko Yamaguchi. 1993. The use and learning of clause-linkage: case studies in Japanese and English conditionals. Ph.D. dissertation, University of California, Berkeley.

Fujii, Seiko. 2004. Lexically (un)filled constructional schemes and construction types: the case of Japanese modal conditional constructions. In *Construction Grammar in a Cross-Language Perspective*, ed. Mirjam Fried and Jan-Ola Östman, 121–56. Amsterdam: John Benjamins.

Fujisaki, Hiroya, and Miyoko Sugito. 1977. Onsei no butsuriteki seishitsu. In *Iwanami Kōza Nihongo 5: On'in*, 63–106. Tokyo: Iwanami.

Fujiwara, Yoichi. 1983. *Hōgengaku genron*. Tokyo: Sanseidō.

Fukada, Atsushi, and Noriko Asato. 2004. Universal politeness theory: application to the use of Japanese honorifics. *Journal of Pragmatics* 36: 1991–2002.

Funk, Wolf-Peter. 1985. On a semantic typology of conditional sentences. *Folia Linguistica* 19: 365–414.

Givón, Talmy. 1982. Tense–aspect-modality: the creole proto-type and beyond. In *Tense–Aspect: Between Semantics & Pragmatics*, ed. Paul Hopper, 115–63. Amsterdam: John Benjamins.

Goffman, Erving. 1974. The neglected situation. *American Anthropologist* 66 (6): 133–36.

Greenberg, Joseph. 1963. Some universals of grammar with particular reference to the order of meaningful elements. In *Universals of Language*, ed. Joseph Greenberg, 73–113. Cambridge, MA: MIT Press.

Grice, Paul. 1975. Logic and conversation. In *Speech Acts*, ed. Peter Cole and Jerry Morgan, 41–58. New York: Academic Press.

Haberman, Clyde. 1988. Some Japanese (one) urge plain speaking. In *The New York Times*. www.nytimes.com/1988/03/27/world/some-japanese-one-urge-plain-speaking.html?pagewanted=all&src=pm.

Habu, Junko. 2004. *Ancient Jomon of Japan*. Cambridge University Press.

Haegeman, Liliane, and Herman Wekker. 1984. The syntax and interpretation of futurate conditionals in English. *Journal of Linguistics* 20 (1): 45–55.

Hammer, Michael, and Satoshi Horai. 1995. Y chromosomal DNA variation and the peopling of Japan. *The American Journal of Human Genetics* 56: 951–62. www.ncbi.nlm.nih.gov/pmc/articles/PMC1801189/pdf/ajhg00030-0136.pdf.

Hanihara, Kazuro. 1991. Dual structure model for the population history of the Japanese. *Japan Review* 2: 1–33. shinku.nichibun.ac.jp/jpub/pdf/jr/IJ0201.pdf.

Hart, Herbert, and Anthony Honoré. 1959. *Causation in the Law*. Oxford: Clarendon.

Hasegawa, Yoko. 1988. Question pull: a diagnostic test for the complement/adjunct distinction in Japanese. *Proceedings of the 14th Annual Meeting of the Berkeley Linguistics Society*, 66–77. http://hasegawa.berkeley.edu/Papers/Hasegawa88.pdf.

1989. Questioning vs. identifying: a functional analysis of the [A candidate that which professor recommend was hired?] construction in Japanese. *Proceedings of the 15th Annual Meeting of the Berkeley Linguistics Society*, 138–49. http://hasegawa.berkeley.edu/Papers/Hasegawa89.pdf.

1992. On the ambiguity between the perfect and the resultative: evidence from V-*te ar-* constructions in Japanese. *Proceedings of the 18th Annual Meeting of the Berkeley Linguistics Society*, 88–99. http://hasegawa.berkeley.edu/Papers/PerfectResultative.pdf.

1995. Against marking accent locations in Japanese textbooks. *Japanese-Language Education Around the Globe* 5: 95–103. http://hasegawa.berkeley.edu/Accent/accent.html.

1996a. *A Study of Japanese Clause Linkage: The Connective TE in Japanese*. Stanford and Tokyo: CSLI; Kurosio.

1996b. The (nonvacuous) semantics of TE-linkage in Japanese. *Journal of Pragmatics* 25: 763–90. http://hasegawa.berkeley.edu/Papers/TE.pdf.

1999a. Pitch accent and vowel devoicing in Japanese. In *Proceedings of the 14th International Congress of Phonetic Sciences*, 523–26. http://hasegawa.berkeley.edu/Accent/0099.pdf.

1999b. Tense-aspect controversy revisited: the *-TA* and *-RU* forms in Japanese. In *Pragmatics in 1998: Selected Papers from the 6th International Pragmatics Conference*, ed. Jef Verschueren, 225–40. Antwerp: International Pragmatics Association. http://hasegawa.berkeley.edu/Papers/Hasegawa99.pdf.

2006. Embedded soliloquy and affective stances in Japanese. In *Emotive Communication in Japanese*, ed. Satoko Suzuki, 209–29. Amsterdam: John Benjamins. http://hasegawa.berkeley.edu/Papers/EmbeddedSoliloquy.pdf.

2010. *Soliloquy in Japanese and English*. Amsterdam: John Benjamins.

2011. *The Routledge Course in Japanese Translation*. London: Routledge.

2012. Deictic and anaphoric uses of the Japanese demonstratives, *ko-so-a*. *Journal of Japanese Linguistics* 28: 43–59. http://hasegawa.berkeley.edu/Papers/JJL28%20Hasegawa.pdf.

Hasegawa, Yoko, and Kazue Hata. 1992. Fundamental frequency as an acoustic cue to accent perception. *Language and Speech* 35: 87–98.

Hasegawa, Yoko, and Yukio Hirose. 2005. What the Japanese language tells us about the alleged Japanese relational self. *Australian Journal of Linguistics* 25: 219–51. http://hasegawa.berkeley.edu/Papers/Self.pdf.

Hasegawa, Yoko, Wakae Kambara, Noriko Komatsu, Yasuko Konno Baker, Kayo Nonaka, Chika Shibahara, Miwako Tomizuka, and Kimiaki Yamaguchi. 2005. *Elementary Japanese, Volume 1*. Boston: Tuttle.
Hasegawa, Yoko, Russell Lee-Goldman, Kyoko Hirose Ohara, Seiko Fujii, and Charles Fillmore. 2010. On expressing measurement and comparison in English and Japanese. In *Contrastive Studies in Construction Grammar*, ed. Hans Boas, 169–200. Amsterdam: John Benjamins. http://hasegawa.berkeley.edu/Papers/Comparison.pdf.
Hashimoto, Osamu. 1990. Hobun hyōshiki "no" "koto" no bunpu ni kakawaru imi kisoku. *Kokugogaku* 163: 101–12.
Hashimoto, Shinkichi. 1938. Kokugo on'in no hensen. *Kokugo to Kokubungaku* October: 3–40. www.aozora.gr.jp/cards/000061/files/377_46838.html.
1980. *Kodai kokugo no on'in ni tsuite – Hoka 2 hen*. Tokyo: Iwanami. www.aozora.gr.jp/cards/000061/files/510_46839.html.
Hattori, Shiro. 1951. Genshi nihongo no akusento. In *Kokugo akusento ronsō*, eds. Kishio Terakawa, Haruhiko Kindaichi, and Inagaki Masayuki, 45–65. Tokyo: Hōsei Daigaku Shuppankyoku.
1976. Jōdai Nihongo no boin-taikei to boin-chōwa. *Gekkan Gengo* 5 (6): 2–14.
Hayata, Teruhiro. 1999. *Onchō no taiporojī.* Tokyo: Taishūkan.
Hayatsu, Emiko, and Kyoungmi Ko. 2012. *Kōpasu ni motozuku nihongo shiekibun, tadōshibun no jittai.* Tokyo: Global COE Program, Tokyo University of Foreign Studies.
Hayashi, Makoto, and Junko Mori. 1998. Co-construction in Japanese revisited: we do "finish each other's sentences." In *Japanese/Korean Linguistics Volume 7*, ed. Noriko Akatsuka, Hajime Hoji, Shoichi Iwasaki, Sung-Ock Sohn, and Susan Strauss, 77–93. Stanford: CSLI.
Himeno, Tomoko. 1991. Irai to kanyū: Juekisha hyōgen no nichi-ei taishō o chūshin ni. *Japanese-language Education around the Globe* 1: 69–81. www.jpf.go.jp/j/japanese/survey/globe/01/06.pdf.
Hinds, John, and Wako Tawa. 1975. Conditions on conditionals in Japanese. *Papers in Japanese Linguistics* 4: 3–12.
Hino, Sukezumi. 1986. *Nihon no hōgengaku*. Tokyo: Tōkyōdō.
Hinton, Leanne, Johanna Nichols, and John Ohala. 1994. *Sound Symbolism*. Cambridge University Press.
Hirose, Yukio. 1995. Direct and indirect speech as quotations of public and private expression. *Lingua* 95: 223–38.
Hopper, Paul. 1979. Aspect and foregrounding in discourse. In *Syntax and Semantics, Volume 12, Discourse and Syntax*, ed. Talmy Givón, 213–41. New York: Academic Press.
Hopper, Paul, and Sandra Thompson. 1980. Transitivity in grammar and discourse. *Language* 56: 251–99.
Horn, Laurence. 1985. Metalinguistic negation and pragmatic ambiguity. *Language* 61: 121–74.
Hume, David. 1748. *An Enquiry Concerning Human Understanding*. www.gutenberg.org/ebooks/9662.
Ide, Sachiko. 1982. Japanese sociolinguistics: politeness and women's language. *Lingua* 57: 357–85.

1989. Formal forms and discernment: two neglected aspects of universals of linguistic politeness. *Multilingua* 8: 223–48.
1991. How and why do women speak more politely in Japanese? In *Aspects of Japanese Women's Language*, ed. Sachiko Ide and Naomi McGloin, 63–79. Tokyo: Kurosio.
Ide, Sachiko, Beverly Hill, Yukiko Carnes, Tsunao Ogino, and Akiko Kawasaki. 1992. The concept of politeness: an empirical study of American English and Japanese. In *Politeness in Language Studies in its History, Theory and Practice*, ed. Richard Watts, Sachiko Ide, and Konrad Ehlich, 281–97. Berlin: Mouton de Gruyter.
Ikawa-Smith, Fumiko. 1978. The history of early paleolithic research in Japan. In *Early Paleolithic in South & East Asia*, ed. Fumiko Ikawa-Smith, 247–86. The Hague: Mouton de Gruyter.
Ikuta, Shoko. 1983. Speech level shift and conversational strategy in Japanese discourse. *Language Sciences* 5: 37–53.
Inoue, Masaru. 1997. Moshi moshi, kippu o otosaremashita yo. *Gekkan Gengo* 26 (2): 62–67.
Inoue, Miyako. 2004. Gender, language, and modernity: toward an effective history of "Japanese women's language." In *Japanese Language, Gender, and Ideology*, ed. Shigeko Okamoto and Janet Smith, 315–30. Oxford University Press.
2006. *Vicarious Language: Gender and Linguistic Modernity in Japan*. Berkeley, CA: University of California Press.
Ishihara, Noriko, and Andrew Cohen. 2010. *Teaching and Learning Pragmatics: Where Language and Culture Meet*. Harlow, Essex: Longman.
Ito, Masamitsu. 2007. Zasshi ni mirareru gaikokugo to gairaigo. www.ninjal.ac.jp/products-k/event/forum/30/haihu_30.pdf.
Iwasaki, Shoichi. 2002. *Japanese*. Amsterdam: John Benjamins.
Iwasaki, Takashi. 1995. "Node" to "kara". In *Nihongo ruigihyōgen no bunpō II*, ed. Tatsuo Miyajima and Yoshio Nitta, 506–13. Tokyo: Kurosio.
Izuhara, Eiko. 2003. Shūjoshi "yo", "yone", "ne" saikō. *The Journal of Aichi Gakuin University* 51 (2): 1–15.
Izui, Hisanosuke. 1967. *Gengo no kōzō*. Tokyo: Kinokuniya.
Josephs, Lewis. 1972. Phenomena of tense and aspect in Japanese relative clauses. *Language* 48 (1): 109–33.
Kabashima, Tadao. 1977. Kanji kara rōmaji made: nihongo hyōki taikei no keisei. In *Nihongo no rekishi*, ed. Atsuyoshi Sakakura, 115–54. Tokyo: Taishūkan.
Kageyama, Taro. 1996. *Dōshi imiron: gengo to ninchi no setten*. Tokyo: Kurosio.
Kamada, Osamu. 1988. Nihongo no dentatsu hyōgen. *Nihongogaku* 7: 59–72.
2000. *Nihongo no in'yō*. Tokyo: Hituzi Syobō.
Kamei, Takashi, Tokihiko Oto, and Toshio Yamada. eds. 2007. *Nihongo no rekishi: atarashii kougo e no ayumi*. Tokyo: Heibonsha.
Kamio, Akio. 1994. The theory of territory of information: the case of Japanese. *Journal of Pragmatics* 21: 67–100.
1995. Territory of information in English and Japanese and psychological utterances. *Journal of Pragmatics* 24: 235–64.
Katagiri, Yasuhiro. 1995. Shūjoshi ni yoru taiwa chōsei. *Gekkan Gengo* 24: 38–45.
2007. Dialogue functions of Japanese sentence-final particles "yo" and "ne." *Journal of Pragmatics* 39: 1313–23.

Kato, Masanobu. 2009. On'in gaisetsu. In *Kōza Hōgengaku 1: Hōgen Gaisetsu*, 69–95. Tokyo: Tosho Kankōkai.

Kato, Shigehiro. 2001. Bunmatsu joshi "ne" "yo" no danwa kōsei kinō. *Toyama Daigaku Jinbun Gakubu Kiyō* 35: 31–48.

Kawamoto, Takao. 1980. *Nihongo no Genryū – Nantōgo Kigenron*. Tokyo: Kōdansha.

Kenkyūjo Kokuritsu Kokugo. 1955. *Danwago no Jittai*. Tokyo: Kokuritsu Kokugo Kenkyūjo.

1958. Gendaigo no goichōsa, Part II. www6.ninjal.ac.jp/siryokan_data/drep_siryokan/report_nijla/R0013.PDF.

1964. Gendai zasshi 90-shu no yōji yōgo, Part III. www6.ninjal.ac.jp/siryokan_data/drep_siryokan/report_nijla/R0025.PDF

Keshikawa, Ritsuji. 1983. Aichiken no hōgen. In *Kōza hōgengaku 6: Chūbu Chihō no Hōgen*, ed. Kiichi Iitoyo, Sukezumi Hino, and Ryoichi Sato, 207–41. Tokyo: Tosho Kankōkai.

Kibe, Nobuko. 1999. Hōgen onsei/akusento no genzai. In *Tenbō: Gendai no Hōgen*, ed. Shinji Sanada, 33–61. Tokyo: Hakuteisha.

Kindaichi, Haruhiko. 1950. Kokugo dōshi no ichi bunrui. *Gengo Kenkyū* 15: 48–63.

1953. On'in. In *Nihon Hōgengaku*, ed. Misao Tojo, 87–176. Tokyo: Yoshikawa Kōbunkan.

Kinsui, Satoshi. 1984. "Iru, aru, oru": sonzai hyōgen no rekishi to hōgen. *Eureka* 16 (12): 284–93.

1997. The influence of translation on the historical development of the Japanese passive construction. *Journal of Pragmatics* 28: 759–79.

2003. *Vācharu nihongo: Yakuwarigo no nazo*. Tokyo: Iwanami.

Kinsui, Satoshi, and Yukinori Takubo. 1992. Danwa kanri riron kara mita nihongo no shijishi. In *Shijishi*, ed. Satoshi Kinsui and Yukinori Takubo, 123–49. Tokyo: Hituzi Syobō.

1998. Danwa kanri riron ni motozuku "yo, ne, yone" no kenkyū. In *Onsei ni yoru Ningen to Kikai no Taiwa*, ed. Shuji Doshita *et al.*, 257–70. Tokyo: Ohmsha.

Kiparsky, Paul, and Carol Kiparsky. 1970. Fact. In *Progress in Linguistics: A Collection of Papers*, ed. Manfred Bierwisch and Karl Heidolph, 143–56. Hague: Mouton.

Klein, Wolfgang. 1992. The present perfect puzzle. *Language* 68: 525–52.

Kobayashi, Takashi. 1999. Hōgen goi/hyōgenhō no genzai. In *Tenbō: Gendai no Hōgen*, ed. Shinji Sanada, 62–80. Tokyo: Hakuteisha.

Kokugogakkai. 1980. *Kokugogaku Daijiten*. Tokyo: Tōkyōdō.

Komatsu, Hideo. 1981. *Nihongo no on'in*. Tokyo: Chūō Kōron.

1999/2001. *Nihongo wa Naze Henka suru ka*. Tokyo: Kasama Shoin.

2001. *Nihongo no Rekishi*. Tokyo: Kasama Shoin.

1988. Tōkyōgo ni okeru danjosa no keisei: Shūjoshi o chūshin to shite. *Kokugo to Kokubungaku* 65: 94–106.

Kotsinas, Ulla-Britt. 1989. Come, stay, finish: on the development of aspect markers in interlanguage and pidgin/creole languages. In *Proceedings of the Second Scandinavian Symposium on Aspectology*, ed, Lars-Gunner Larsson, 33–48. Stockholm: Almqvist & Wiksell International.

Kouchi, Makiko. 1983. *Geographic Variation in Modern Japanese Somatometric Data and Its Interpretation*. University of Tokyo Press.

Kubozono, Haruo. 2001. On the markedness of diphthongs. *Kobe Papers in Linguistics* 3: 60–73.
Kudo, Mayumi. 1985. *No, koto* no tsukaiwake to dōshi no shurui. *Kokubungaku Kaishaku to Kanshō* 50 (3): 45–52.
Kunihiro, Tetsuya. 1967. *Kōzōteki imiron – Nichi-ei Ryōgo Taishō Kenkyū*. Tokyo: Sanseidō.
Kuno, Susumu. 1973. *The Structure of the Japanese Language*. Cambridge, MA: MIT Press.
1988. Blended quasi-direct discourse in Japanese. In *Papers from the Second International Workshop on Japanese Syntax*, ed. William Poser, 75–102. Stanford, CA: CSLI.
Kuroda, S.-Y. 1972. The categorical and the thetic judgment: evidence from Japanese syntax. *Foundations of Language* 9: 153–85.
1979/1992. (Ko) so a ni tsuite. In *Shijishi*, ed. Satoshi Kinsui and Yukinori Takubo, 91–104. Tokyo: Hituzi Syobō.
Kurylowicz, Jerzy. 1964. *The Inflectional Categories of Indo-European*. Heidelberg: C. Winter.
Ladefoged, Peter. 1982. *A Course in Phonetics*. New York: Harcourt Brace Jovanovich.
Lakoff, Robin. 1973. The logic of politeness, or, minding your p's and q's. In *Papers from the Ninth Regional Meeting of the Chicago Linguistic Society*, 295–305.
1975. *Language and Woman's Place*. New York: Harper & Row.
1990. *Talking Power: The Politics of Language in Our Lives*. Glasgow: HarperCollins.
Lambrecht, Knud. 1994. *Information Structure and Sentence Form: Topic, Focus and the Mental Representations of Discourse Reference*. Cambridge University Press.
Langacker, Ronald. 1987. *Foundations of Cognitive Grammar, Volume 1, Theoretical Prerequisites*. Stanford University Press.
2008. *Cognitive Grammar: A Basic Introduction*. New York: Oxford University Press.
Lee, Nagiko. 1998. Hatsuwa kōi (speech act) ni arawareru gengo bunka – Nihongo bogowasha no tokuchō. *Ritsumeikan Keizaigaku* 46 (6): 778–92.
Leonard, Wesley. 2001. A comparative study of the English *while* with Japanese *nagara* & *aida ni*: an investigation of semantics, usage restrictions, and prominence. Unpublished MS. Berkeley, CA: University of California, Department of Linguistics.
Maeda, Naoko. 1995. Ba, to, tara, nara. In *Nihongo Ruigihyōgen no Bunpō II*, ed. Tatsuo Miyajima and Yoshio Nitta, 483–95. Tokyo: Kurosio.
Maltz, Daniel, and Ruth Borker. 1982. A cultural approach to male–female miscommunication. In *Language and Social Identity*, ed. John Gumperz, 196–216. New York: Cambridge University Press.
Martin, Samuel. 1962. *Essential Japanese – An Introduction to the Standard Colloquial Japanese*. Rutland, Vermont: Tuttle.
1975. *A Reference Grammar of Japanese*. New Haven and London: Yale University Press.
Mashimo, Saburo. 1969. *Fujingo no Kenkyū*. Tokyo: Tōkyōdō.
Maslov, Jurij. 1988. Resultative, perfect, and aspect. In *Typology of Resultative Constructions*, ed. Vladimir P. Nedjalkov, 63–85. Amsterdam: John Benjamins.

Masuoka, Takashi. 1991. *Modaritī no Bunpō*. Tokyo: Kurosio.
1993a. *Nihongo no Jōken Hyōgen*. Tokyo: Kurosio.
1993b. Nihongo no jōken hyōgen ni tsuite. In *Nihongo no Jōken Hyōgen*, ed. Takashi Masuoka, 1–20. Tokyo: Kurosio.
1997. *Fukubun*. Tokyo: Kurosio.
Matsumoto, Katsumi. 2003. Nihongo no keitō – ruikei chirironteki kōsatsu. In *Perspectives on the Origins of the Japanese Language*, ed. Toshiki Osada and Alexander Vovin, 41–129. Kyoto: International Research Center for Japanese Studies.
Matsumoto, Yoshiko. 1988. Grammar and semantics of adnominal clauses in Japanese. Ph.D. dissertation, University of California, Berkeley.
Matsumura, Yoshiko, and Kyoko Chinami. 1998. Nihongo danwa ni okeru sutairu kōtai no jittai to sono kōka. *Gengokagaku* 33: 109–18.
Maynard, Senko. 1987. Thematization as a staging device in Japanese narrative. In *Perspectives on Topicalization: The Case of Japanese Wa*, ed. John Hinds, Senko Maynard, and Shoichi Iwasaki, 57–82. Amsterdam: John Benjamins.
1990. Conversation management in contrast: listener response in Japanese and American English. *Journal of Pragmatics* 14: 392–412.
1991. Pragmatics of discourse modality: a case of *da* and *desu/masu* forms in Japanese. *Journal of Pragmatics* 15: 551–82.
1996. Multivoicedness in speech and thought representation: the case of self-quotation in Japanese. *Journal of Pragmatics* 25: 207–26.
1997. *Japanese Communication: Language and Thought in Context*. Honolulu: University of Hawai'i Press.
McGloin, Naomi Hanaoka. 1976. The speaker's attitude and the conditionals *to*, *tara*, and *ba*. *Papers in Japanese Linguistics*: 181–91.
1987. The role of *wa* in negation. In *Perspectives in Topicalization: The Case of Japanese 'Wa'*, ed. John Hinds, Senko Maynard, and Shoichi Iwasaki, 165–83. Amsterdam: John Benjamins.
Michaelis, Laura. 1993. Toward a grammar of aspect: the case of the English perfect constructions. Ph.D. dissertation, University of California, Berkeley.
Mikami, Akira. 1953. *Gendai gohō Josetsu*. Tokyo: Tōkō Shoin.
1970/1992. Kosoado-shō. In *Shijishi*, ed. Satoshi Kinsui and Yukinori Takubo, 35–37. Tokyo: Hituzi Syobō.
Miller, Roy. 1967. *The Japanese Language*. University of Chicago Press.
1971. *Japanese and the Other Altaic Languages*. University of Chicago Press.
1975. Do the Japanese know how to tell time? *The Journal of the Association of Teachers of Japanese* 10: 1–18.
Miura, Akira. 1974. The V-*u* form vs. the V-*ta* form. *Papers in Japanese Linguistics* 3: 95–121.
Miyajima, Tatsuo. 1971. *Koten Taishō Goihyō*. Tokyo: Kasama Shoin.
Miyake, Tomohiro. 1995. Rashii to yōda. In *Nihongo ruigi Hyōgen no Bunpō I: Tanbun-hen*, ed. Tatsuo Miyajima and Yoshio Nitta, 183–89. Tokyo: Kurosio.
Miyata, Koichi. 1927. Nihongo no akusentokan to akusento hyōkihō. *Onsei no Kenkyū* 1: 18–22.
Mizutani, Nobuko. 1984. Nihongo kyōiku to hanashikotoba no jittai: aizuchi no bunseki. In *Kindaichi Haruhiko hakase koki kinen Ronbunshū*, 261–79. Tokyo: Sanseidō.

Morita, Yoshiyuki. 1989. Goi. In *Nihongo Gaisetsu*, ed. Akihiko Kato, Keizo Saji, and Yoshiyuki Morita, 65–93. Tokyo: Ōfūsha.
1994. *Dōshi no Imironteki Bunpō Kenkyū*. Tokyo: Meiji Shoin.
Moriyama, Takuro. 1989. Ninshiki no mūdo to sono shūhen. In *Nihongo no Modaritī*, ed. Yoshio Nitta and Takashi Masuoka, 57–120. Tokyo: Kurosio.
1995. To omou, hazuda, ni chigai nai, darō, fukushi ~Ø. In *Nihongo ruigi Hyōgen no Bunpō I: Tanbun-hen*, ed. Tatsuo Miyajima and Yoshio Nitta, 171–82. Tokyo: Kurosio.
Murayama, Shichiro. 1974. Nantōgo kigensetu ni tsuite. *Gekkan Gengo* 3 (1): 11–18.
1988. *Nihongo no Kigen to Gogen*. Tokyo: San'ichi Shobō.
Mushin, Ilana. 2001. Japanese reportive evidentiality and the pragmatics of retelling. *Journal of Pragmatics* 33: 1361–90.
Nakamoto, Masachie. 1981. *Nihongo no genkei*. Tokyo: Rikitomi Shobō.
Nakamura, Keiko. 2001. Gender and language in Japanese preschool children. *Research on Language and Social Interaction* 34: 15–43.
Nakamura, Momoko. 2006. Gengo ideorogī to shite no "onna kotoba": meijiki "jogakusei kotoba" no seiritsu. In *Nihongo to Jendā*, ed. Mizue Sasaki, 121–38. Tokyo: Hituzi Syobō.
Nakane, Chie. 1970. *Japanese Society*. London: Weidenfeld & Nicolson.
Nakau, Minoru. 1994. *Ninchi Imiron no Genri*. Tokyo: Taishūkan.
Nedjalkov, Vladimir, and Sergey Je Jaxontov. 1988. The typology of resultative constructions. In *Typology of Resultative Constructions*, ed. Vladimir Nedjalkov, 3–62. Amsterdam: John Benjamins.
Neustupný, Jiri. 1982. *Gaikokujin to no Komyunikēshon*. Tokyo: Iwanami.
Nitta, Yoshio. 1989. Gendai nihongo-bun no modaritī no taikei to kōzō. In *Nihongo no Modaritī*, ed. Yoshio Nitta and Takashi Masuoka, 1–56. Tokyo: Kurosio.
Noda, Harumi. 1995. No to koto. In *Nihongo ruigi Hyōgen no Bunpō 2: Fukubun, Renbun-hen*, ed. Takuro Moriyama and Yoshio Nitta, 419–28. Tokyo: Kurosio.
1997. *No (da) no kinō*. Tokyo: Kurosio.
Nomura, Masaaki. 1988. Nihongo no kanji. In *Nihongo Hyakka Daijiten*, ed. Haruhiko Kindaichi, Oki Hayashi, and Takeshi Shibata, 329–45. Tokyo: Taishūkan.
Ochs Keenan, Elinor. 1976. The universality of conversational postulates. *Language in Society* 5: 67–80.
Ochs, Elinor. 1993. Indexing gender. In *Sex and Gender Hierarchies*, ed. Barbara Miller, 146–69. Cambridge University Press.
1996. Linguistic resources for socializing humanity. In *Rethinking Linguistic Relativity*, ed. John Gumperz and Stephen Levinson, 407–37. Cambridge University Press.
Ohala, John. 1994. The frequency code underlies the sound–symbolic use of voice pitch. In *Sound Symbolism*, ed. Leanne Hinton, Johanna Nichols, and John Ohala, 325–47. Cambridge University Press.
Ohara, Kyoko Hirose. 1996. A constructional approach to Japanese internally headed relativization. Ph.D. dissertation, University of California, Berkeley.
Ohso, Mieko. 1986. Goyō-bunseki I "kyō wa ii tenki desu ne." – "Hai, sō desu." *Nihongogaku* 5: 91–95.

Okamoto, Masataka. 2009. Gengo futsū no rettō kara tan'itsu gengo hatsugen e no kiseki. *Fukuoka kenritsu daigaku ningen shakai gakubu kiyō* 17 (2): 11–31. www.fukuoka-pu.ac.jp/kiyou/kiyo17_2/1702_okamoto.pdf.

Okamoto, Noriko. 1997. Kyōshitsu-danwa ni okeru buntai-shifuto no shihyōteki kinō: Teineitai to futsūtai no tsukaiwake. *Nihongogaku* 16: 39–51.

Okamoto, Shigeko. 1997. Social context, linguistic ideology, and indexical expressions in Japanese. *Journal of Pragmatics* 28: 795–817.

Okamoto, Shigeko, and Shie Sato. 1992. Less feminine speech among young Japanese females. In *Proceedings of the Second Women and Language Conference*, ed. Kira Hall, Mary Bucholtz, and Birch Moonwomon, 478–88. University of California, Berkeley.

Okubo, Ai. 1967. *Yōji gengo no hattatsu*. Tokyo: Tōkyōdō.

Okumura, Mitsuo. 1980. Rendaku. In *Kokugogaku Daijiten*, ed. Kokugo Gakkai, 925–26. Tokyo: Tōkyōdō.

Okutsu, Keiichiro. 1967. Jidōka, tadōka oyobi ryōkyokuka tenkei: Ji-ta dōshi no taiō. *Kokugogaku* 70: 46–66.

Omoto, Keiichi. 1978. Blood protein polymorphisms and the problem of genetic affinities of the Ainu. In *Evolutionary Models and Studies in Human Diversity*, ed. Robert Meier, Charlotte Otten. and Fathi Abdel-Hameed, 333–41. The Hague: Mouton Publishers.

Onishi, Takuichiro. 1993. Nihon no hōgen gaisetsu. In *Hōgen to nihongo kyōiku*, 1–83. Tokyo: Kokuritsu Kokugo Kenkyūjo.

Ono, Susumu. 1957. *Nihongo no kigen*. Tokyo: Iwanami.

1981. *Nihongo to Tamirugo*. Tokyo: Shinchōsha.

Ono, Tsuyoshi, and Eri Yoshida. 1996. A study of co-construction in Japanese: we don't finish each other's sentences. In *Japanese/Korean Linguistics, Volume 5*, ed. Noriko Akatsuka, Shoichi Iwasaki, and Susan Strauss, 115–29. Stanford, CA: CSLI.

Onoe, Keisuke. 1995. Grounding keishiki to shite no shita, shiteiru. Paper presented at *CLC Gengogaku Shūchū Kōgi*.

Osada, Natsuki. 1974. Nihongo hoppōkigensetsu – Arutaigaku no tachiba kara. *Gekkan Gengo* 3 (1): 2–10.

Osada, Toshiki. 2003. Nihongo tōkeiron wa naze hayaranakunatta no ka – Nihongo tōkeiron no genzai, kako, mirai. In *Perspectives on the Origins of the Japanese Language*, ed. Toshiki Osada and Alexander Vovin, 373–418. Kyoto: International Research Center for Japanese Studies.

Ota, Akira. 1972. Tense correlations in English and Japanese. In *Studies in Honor of Albert H. Marckwardt*, ed. James E. Alatis, 121–34. Washington, DC: Teachers of English to Speakers of Other Languages.

Pierrehumbert, Janet, and Mary Beckman. 1988. *Japanese Tone Structure*. Cambridge, MA: MIT Press.

Pizziconi, Barbara. 2003. Re-examining politeness, face and the Japanese language. *Journal of Pragmatics* 35: 1471–506.

Poser, William. 1985. The phonetics and phonology of tone and intonation in Japanese. Ph.D. dissertation, MIT.

Reichenbach, Hans. 1947. *Elements of Symbolic Logic*. New York: Macmillan.

Russell, Bartland. 1917. *Mysticism and Logic*. London: Allen and Unwin.

Sacks, Harvey, Emanuel Schegloff, and Gail Jefferson. 1974. A simplest systematics for the organization of turn-taking for conversation. *Language* 50 (4): 696–735.
Sampson, Geoffrey. 1985. *Writing Systems*. Stanford University Press.
Sanada, Shinji. 2002. *Hōgen no Nihon Chizu: Kotoba no tabi*. Tokyo: Kōdansha.
Sanders, Ted, José Sanders, and Eve Sweetser. 2009. Causality, cognition and communication: a mental space analysis of subjectivity in causal connectives. In *Causal Categories in Discourse and Cognition*, ed. Ted Sanders and Eve Sweetser, 19–59. Berlin, New York: Mouton de Gruyter.
Satake, Hideo. 1988. Hyōki kōdō to kisoku. In *Nihongo Hyakka Daijiten*, ed. Haruhiko Kindaichi, Oki Hayashi, and Takeshi Shibata, 310–19. Tokyo: Taishūkan.
Sato, Ryoichi. 1979. Hōgen no bunpu. In *Nihon no Hōgen Chizu*, ed. Munemasa Tokugawa, 3–52. Tokyo: Chūōkōronsha.
Sato, Sekiko. 2006. "Genji monogatari" to gendā: "Shukusei" o iwanu onnnagimi. In *Nihongo to Jendā*, ed. Mizue Sasaki, 109–20. Tokyo: Hituzi Syobō.
Sato, Takuzo. 2005. *Jidōshibun to Tadōshibun no Imiron*. Tokyo: Kasama Shoin.
Schiffrin, Deborah. 1981. Tense variation in narrative. *Language* 57: 45–62.
Seeley, Christopher. 2000. *A History of Writing in Japan*. Honolulu: University of Hawai'i Press.
Sei Shōnagon. ca. 1000/1991. *The Pillow Book of Sei Shonagon*. trans. by Ivan Morris. New York: Columbia University Press.
Seidensticker, Edward. 1989. On trying to translate Japanese. In *The Craft of Translation*, ed. John Biguenet and Rainer Schulte, 142–53. University of Chicago Press.
Seidensticker, Edward, and Kiyoshi Nasu. 1962. *Nohongo rashii Hyōgen kara eigo rashii Hyōgen e*. Tokyo: Baifūkan.
Sell, Roger. 1992. Literary texts and diachronic aspects of politeness. In *Politeness in Language: Studies in Its History, Theory, and Practice*, ed. Richard Watts, Sachiko Ide, and Konrad Ehlich, 109–29. Berlin: Mouton de Gruyter.
Shibata, Takeshi. 1958. *Nihon no Hōgen*. Tokyo: Iwanami.
Shibatani, Masayoshi. 1985. Passives and related constructions: a prototype analysis. *Language* 61: 821–48.
1990. *The Languages of Japan*. Cambridge University Press.
1994. An integrational approach to possessor raising, ethical datives, and adversative passives. *Proceedings of the 20th Annual Meeting of the Berkeley Linguistics Society*, 461–85.
Shibuya, Katsumi. 1999. Hōgen bunpō no genzai. In *Tenbō: Gendai no Hōgen*, ed. Shinji Sanada, 81–99. Tokyo: Hakuteisha.
Shimizu, Yoshinori. 2003. *Nihongo Hisshō Kōza*. Kodansha bunko. Tokyo: Kōdansha.
Shirakawa, Hiroyuki. 1995. Riyū o arawasanai "kara". In *Fukubun no Kenkyū I*, ed. Yoshio Nitta, 189–219. Tokyo: Kurosio.
Shōgaku Tosho. ed. 1981. *Kokugo Daijiten*. Tokyo: Shōgakkan.
Silverstein, Michael. 1976. Hierarchy of features and ergativity. In *Grammatical Categories in Australian Languages*, ed. Robert Dixon, 112–71. Canberra: Australian Institute of Aboriginal Studies.
Smith, Tomoko Yamashita. 2005. Affectedness constructions: how languages indicate positive and negative events. Ph.D. dissertation, University of California, Berkeley.

Soga, Matsuo. 1983. *Tense and Aspect in Modern Colloquial Japanese*. Vancouver, BC: University of British Columbia Press.
Sugito, Miyoko. 1969/1982. *Nihongo Akusento no Kenkyū*. Tokyo: Sanseidō.
1998. *Nihon rettō Kotoba no Tanken*. Tokyo: Fujitsū BSC.
Sunakawa, Yuriko. 2011. Hakereru, mirereru. In *Mondai na Nihongo: Sono 4*, ed. Yasuo Kitahara, 124–29. Tokyo: Taishūkan.
Suzuki, Kazuhiko. 1977. Bunpō no utsurikawari. In *Nihongo no Rekishi*, ed. Atsuyoshi Sakakura, 197–242. Tokyo: Taishūkan.
Suzuki, Mutsumi. 1997. Nihongo-kyōiku ni okeru teineitai-sekai to futsūtai-sekai. In *Shiten to Gengo-kōdō*, ed. Yukinori Takubo, 45–76. Tokyo: Kurosio.
Suzuki, Shigeyuki. 1965. *Gendai Nihongo no dōshi no tensu*. Tokyo: Kokuritsu Kokugo Kenkyūjo.
Suzuki, Takashi, and Mayumi Usami. 2006. Co-constructions in English and Japanese revisited: a quantitative approach to cross-linguistic comparison. In *Gengo Jōhōgaku Kenkyū Hōkoku 13: Shizen kaiwa Bunseki e no gengo Shakai Shinrigakuteki Apurōchi*, 263–76. Tokyo: Graduate School of Area and Culture Studies, Tokyo University of Foreign Studies.
Suzuki, Yoshikazu. 1993. *Nara* jōkenbun no imi. In *Nihongo no Jōken Hyōgen*, ed. Takashi Masuoka, 131–48. Tokyo: Kurosio.
Sweetser, Eve. 1990. *From Etymology to Pragmatics: Metaphorical and Cultural Aspects of Semantic Structure*. Cambridge University Press.
Tager-Flusberg, Helen. 1992. Autistic children's talk about psychological states: deficits in the early acquisition of a theory of mind. *Child Development* 63: 161–72.
Takeuchi, Toshio. 1982. *Tōkai no Kotoba Chizu*. Tokyo: Roppō Shuppansha.
Takubo, Yukinori, and Satoshi Kinsui. 1997. Discourse management in terms of mental spaces. *Journal of Pragmatics* 28: 741–58.
Tamamura, Fumio. 1975. Goiron kara mita keiyōshi. *Dōshisha Kokubungaku* 10 (2): 87–104.
Tanaka, Akio. 1988. Tōkyōgo no jidai kubun. *Kokugo to Kokubungaku* 65: 1–16.
Tannen, Deborah. 1986. *That's Not What I Meant! How Conversational Style Makes or Breaks Your Relations with Others*. New York: William Morrow.
1989. *Talking Voices: Repetition, Dialogue, and Imagery in Conversational Discourse*. Cambridge University Press.
ed. 1993. *Gender and Conversation Interaction*. Oxford University Press.
Tansman, Alan. 1993. *The Writings of Koda Aya: A Japanese Literary Daughter*. New Haven: Yale University Press.
Teramura, Hideo. 1982. *Nihongo no Shintakusu to imi. Volume* 1. Tokyo: Kurosio.
1984. *Nihongo no Shintakusu to imi. Volume* 2. Tokyo: Kurosio.
Tesnière, Lucien. 1959/1976. *Éléments de Syntaxe Structurale*. Paris: Klincksieck.
Tojo, Misao. 1953. Josetsu. In *Nihon Hōgengaku*, ed. Misao Tojo, 1–86. Tokyo: Yoshikawa Kōbunkan.
Tokashiki, Kyoko. 2006. Jidōshi shieki no joshi ni tsuite no ichi-kōsatsu. *Papers in Teaching Japanese as a Foreign Language, Kansai Gaidai University* 16: 47–60. http://opac.kansaigaidai.ac.jp/cgi-bin/retrieve/sr_bookview.cgi/U_CHARSET.UTF-8/DB00000210/Body/n16_06.pdf.
Tokugawa, Munemasa. 1979. Bunken kokugoshi to hōgen. In *Nihon no Hōgen Chizu*, ed. Munemasa Tokugawa, 141–200. Tokyo: Chūōkōronsha.

Tokunaga, Misato. 1986. Affective deixis in Japanese: a case study of directional verbs. Ph.D. dissertation, University of Michigan.

Tsujimura, Natsuko. 2007. *An Introduction to Japanese Linguistics*. 2nd edn. Cambridge, MA: Blackwell.

Tsukimoto, Masayuki. 1988. Heian jidai. In *Nihongo Hyakka Daijiten*, eds. Haruhiko Kindaichi, Oki Hayashi and Takeshi Shibata, 73–82. Tokyo: Taishūkan.

Tsukishima, Hiroshi. 1988. Nihongoshi no jidai kubun. In *Nihongo Hyakka Daijiten*, ed. Haruhiko Kindaichi, Oki Hayashi, and Takeshi Shibata, 59–65. Tokyo: Taishūkan.

Tsuzuku, Tsuneo. 1986. Bunpō gaisetsu. In *Kōza Hōgengaku 1: Hōgen Gaisetsu*, ed. Kiichi Iitoyo, Sukezumi Hino, and Ryoichi Sato, 117–48. Tokyo: Tosho Kankōkai.

Uchida, Aki. 1992. When "difference" is "dominance": a critique of the "anti-power-based" cultural approach to sex differences. *Language in Society* 21: 547–68.

Ueda, Kazutoshi. 1895. Hyōjungo ni tsukite. *Teikokubungaku* 1 (1): 14–23.

1898. *P on kō*. *Teikokubungaku* 4 (1): 41–46.

Ueda, Makoto. 1970/1982. *The Master Haiku Poet: Matsuo Bashō*. Tokyo: Kōdansha International.

Usami, Mayumi 1995. Danwa-reberu kara mita keigo shiyō: supīchi reberu shifuto seiki no jōken to kinō. *Gakuen* 662: 27–42.

Uyeno, Tazuko. 1971. A study of Japanese modality: a performance analysis of sentence particles. Ph.D. dissertation, University of Michigan.

Vance, Timothy. 1987. *An Introduction to Japanese Phonology*. State University of New York.

Wada, Akemi. 1994. *Kodai nihongo no Jodōshi no Kenkyū*. Tokyo: Kazama Shobō.

Wales, Katie. 1996. *Personal Pronouns in Present-Day English*. Cambridge University Press.

Watabe, Shintaro. 1995. *Kokugo kokuji no Konpon Mondai*. Osaka: Shinpū Shobō.

Watamaki, Toru. 1997. Jiheishōji ni okeru kyōkan kakutoku hyōgen joshi 'ne' no shiyō no ketsujo: jirei kenkyū. *Hattatsu Shōgai Kenkyū* 19: 146–57.

Watanabe, Minoru. 1997. *Nihongoshi Yōsetsu*. Tokyo: Iwanami.

Watts, Richard. 1992. Linguistic politeness and politic verbal behaviour: reconsidering claims for universality. In *Politeness in Language: Studies in Its History, Theory, and Practice*, ed. Richard Watts, Sachiko Ide, and Konrad Ehlich, 43–70. Berlin: Mouton de Gruyter.

West, Candace, and Don Zimmerman. 1983. Small insults: a study of interruptions in cross-sex conversations between unacquainted persons. In *Language, Gender, and Society*, ed. Barrie Thorne, Cheris Kramarae, and Nancy Henley, 103–17. Rowley, MA: Newbury House.

West, Candace, and Don Zimmerman. 1987. Doing gender. *Gender & Society* 1: 125–51.

Wetzel, Patricia. 1984. Uchi and soto ("in-group and out-group"): Social deixis in Japanese. Ph.D. dissertation, Cornell University.

Wierzbicka, Anna. 1979/1988. The Japanese "adversative" passive in a typological context (Are grammatical categories vague or multiply polysemous?). In *The Semantics of Grammar*, 257–92. Amsterdam: John Benjamins.

Wolfson, Nessa. 1979. The conversational historical present alternation. *Language* 55: 168–82.

Yamaguchi, Akiho. 1988. Kamakura, Muromachi jidai. In *Nihongo hyakka daijiten*, ed. Haruhiko Kindaichi, Oki Hayashi, and Takeshi Shibata, 83–92. Tokyo: Taishūkan.

Yamashita, Kiyo. 1995. keiyōshisei setsubiji -poi -rashii -kusai ni tsuite. *Kōza Nihongo Kyōiku* 30: 183–206. http://dspace.wul.waseda.ac.jp/dspace/handle/2065/3305.

Yanabu, Akira. 1982. *Hon'yakugo Seiritsu Jijō*. Tokyo: Iwanami.

Yanagita, Kunio. 1930. *Kagyūkō*. Tokyo: Tōkō Shoin.

Yasuda, Naomichi. 1988. Jōdai. In *Nihongo Hyakka Daijiten*, ed. Haruhiko Kindaichi, Oki Hayashi, and Takeshi Shibata, 65–73. Tokyo: Taishūkan.

Zwicky, Arnold. 2005. Language log: saying more with less. http://itre.cis.upenn.edu/~myl/languagelog/archives/001995.html.

Index

Made in United States
North Haven, CT
21 December 2025

85334335R00228